Vocabulary Quest

1101+ Essential Words to Succeed in English

Copyright © 2017 by Manda Education, LLC.

Manda Education
30 N. Gould St.
Suite 4001
Sheridan, WY 82801
USA

All Rights Reserved. No part of this publication may be reproduced, distributed, or transmitted in any form or by any means, including photocopying, recording, or other electronic or mechanical methods, without the prior written permission of the publisher, except in the case of brief quotations embodied in critical reviews and certain other noncommercial uses permitted by copyright law.

Editorial:
Justin Grosslight, head author and editor.

First Edition, 2016

ISBN: 978-0-9974232-2-8

10 9 8 7 6 5 4 3 2 1

Vocabulary Quest

1101+ Essential Words to Succeed in English

Justin Grosslight

Published by Manda Education, LLC

Preface

Becoming an expert in any language is hard work. Regardless of whether English is your mother tongue, more advanced reading and vocabulary skills often accrue slowly and only with a sustained commitment. Because of this, transitioning from communicating in popular English to becoming a consumer of scholarly and intellectual prose can be an arduous journey. While there is no supplement for reading erudite materials, building a vocabulary and an understanding of intellectual concepts is critical for language mastery.

In writing the *Vocabulary Quest*, I had in mind the myriad individuals who are fluent in conversational English but who want to take their writing skills and vocabulary to the next level. Many of today's students and professionals seek to build these skills, but find the task extraneous to their immediate needs, overly pedantic, or dreadfully time consuming. *Vocabulary Quest* aims to ease that process. Unlike other vocabulary books, many of which are merely extended lists, ours are replete with exercises; there are also lessons to help you understand the roots of words and intellectual terms. And the words are useful: they have been gleaned from statistical examination of dozens of SAT® and ACT® college entrance exams, which in turn excerpt their readings from a wide array of sophisticated prose materials.

These words in this book are suitable for either classroom study or independent preparation. Lessons should be done sequentially, noting that the most common words occur in the first 100 lessons. Lessons 101-220 contain somewhat less frequently used words, though they are still prevalent in intellectual and scholarly English. Do note, however, that the words in this book do not constitute an exhaustive vocabulary list necessary for success.

Writing these books has been an evolving process, and I have enjoyed receiving feedback as it develops. In particular, I would like to thank Vu Le, Antonio Madrid, Uyen Nguyen, and especially Yannick Lalonde for their contributions, sustained support, and constructive criticism. Several students – Helen Dang, Duc Doan, Julian Ho, Quoc Huynh, Phong Le, Alice Nguyen, Nguyen Nguyen, and Hannah Truong – have gladly provided input and frank suggestions as they used drafts of this book to prepare for their SAT® examinations. I also would like to thank Dr. Clive Keevil for allowing pilot versions of these lessons to be taught at the Australian International School (AIS) in Ho Chi Minh City. Last but not least, I would like to thank Grace Ho for her cover design upon the book's completion.

I hope that this book will be as immensely useful to you as it has been for the students who used it in its gestation period. With that said, good luck on your vocabulary endeavors!

Justin Grosslight

How to Use This Book

This book is intended to help build your vocabulary; it is a strategically organized catalogue of over 1,100 words that appear in intellectual and scholarly English, especially in college and university entrance examinations. It is not, however, intended to be your sole source of learning words. Ideally, this book should be used in tandem with reading other scholarly and intellectual materials to help nurture your vocabulary growth.

Often to fully understand a word and its meaning(s), it is helpful to see a word used in context many times. To reinforce this idea, the exercises contained in this book often require dictionary use. By looking up words in a dictionary, you can read samples of their uses in various settings and then apply what you have learned to the exercises in this text. Doing so will provide an active approach to building an extensive vocabulary. This book's exercises also use a consistent intellectual vocabulary to complement the focal words of each lesson. Learning these words should further enhance your verbal skills.

At a stable pace, one should be able to absorb approximately fifty words, or ten lessons, per week. We have provided review quizzes after every ten lessons to help facilitate your study. One can study more words, of course, but diminishing returns may occur if more than twenty lessons are absorbed each week. Ideally this book should be studied at a moderate pace consistently over a long duration, allowing for time to let words sink in slowly. There are also many reasons why someone should use this book: whether you want to build a more solid vocabulary, you want to prepare for an examination, or you simply hope to sound erudite, all are good reasons for using this text. Whatever your purpose of study, however, it is imperative that you never cease to explore new vocabularies.

Possessing a solid vocabulary can help you enter a strong academic program, can make you more attractive for a corporate job, and can make you sound more articulate and knowledgeable. I hope you enjoy your quest to broaden your vocabulary with this book.

TABLE OF CONTENTS

The Origins of English 2

Lesson 1 4
    Crossword Puzzle: Lessons 1-10 14
    Vocabulary Review: Lessons 1-10 15
    Introduction to Word Roots 16
    Word Roots: Unit 1 17
    Occupations and Careers I 19

Lesson 11 22
    Word Search: Lessons 11-20 32
    Vocabulary Review: Lessons 11-20 33
    Word Roots: Unit 2 34
    Occupations and Careers II 36

Lesson 21 38
    Crossword Puzzle: Lessons 21-30 48
    Vocabulary Review: Lessons 21-30 49
    Word Roots: Unit 3 50

Lesson 31 51
    Word Search: Lessons 31-40 61
    Vocabulary Review: Lessons 31-40 62
    Word Roots: Unit 4 63

Lesson 41 65
    Crossword Puzzle: Lessons 41-50 75
    Vocabulary Review: Lessons 41-50 76

Word Roots: Unit 5 77

Lesson 51 78
Word Search: Lessons 51-60 88
Vocabulary Review: Lessons 51-60 89
Word Roots: Unit 6 90

Lesson 61 92
Crossword Puzzle: Lessons 61-70.. 102
Vocabulary Review: Lessons 61-70 103
Word Roots: Unit 7 104

Lesson 71 105
Word Search: Lessons 71-80 115
Vocabulary Review: Lessons 71-80 116
Word Roots: Unit 8 117

Lesson 81 118
Crossword Puzzle: Lessons 81-90.. 128
Vocabulary Review: Lessons 81-90 129
Word Roots: Unit 9 130

Lesson 91 131
Word Search: Lessons 91-100 141
Vocabulary Review: Lessons 91-100 142
Word Roots: Unit 10 143

Lesson 101 144
Crossword Puzzle: Lessons 101-110.. 154
Vocabulary Review: Lessons 101-110 155
Word Roots: Unit 11 156

Lesson 111 157
Word Search: Lessons 111-120 167
Vocabulary Review: Lessons 111-120 168

Word Roots: Unit 12 169

Lesson 121 170
Crossword Puzzle: Lessons 121-130 180
Vocabulary Review: Lessons 121-130 181
Word Roots: Unit 13 182

Lesson 131 183
Word Search: Lessons 131-140 193
Vocabulary Review: Lessons 131-140 194
Word Roots: Unit 14 195

Lesson 141 196
Crossword Puzzle: Lessons 141-150 206
Vocabulary Review: Lessons 141-150 207
Word Roots: Unit 15 208

Lesson 151 209
Word Search: Lessons 151-160 219
Vocabulary Review: Lessons 151-160 220
Word Roots: Unit 16 221

Lesson 161 222
Crossword Puzzle: Lessons 161-170 232
Vocabulary Review: Lessons 161-170 233
Literary and Drama Terms 234

Lesson 171 236
Word Search: Lessons 171-180 246
Vocabulary Review: Lessons 171-180 247
A Crowd of "ISMs": A-L 248

Lesson 181 250
Crossword Puzzle: Lessons 181-190 260
Vocabulary Review: Lessons 181-190 261

A Crowd of "ISMs": M-Z 262

Lesson 191 .... **264**
　　Word Search: Lessons 191-200 274
　　Vocabulary Review: Lessons 191-200 275
　　Long Live Latin! 276
　　Idiomatic Expressions I 278

Lesson 201 .... **283**
　　Crossword Puzzle: Lessons 201-210 293
　　Vocabulary Review: Lessons 201-210 294
　　Idiomatic Expressions II 295

Lesson 211 .... **300**
　　Word Search: Lessons 211-220 301
　　Vocabulary Review: Lessons 211-220 311
　　Idiomatic Expressions III 312

Answer Key **316**

Glossary **358**

The Origins of English

English belongs to the family of Indo-European languages, which today comprise many languages spoken on the Earth. Most directly, the roots of English lay with Latin, the language of the Roman Empire that was spoken in the Mediterranean region two thousand years ago. From Latin emerged two families of European languages, Romance Languages and Germanic Languages. English is a Germanic language by structure and heritage, but also has borrowed much in style and vocabulary from French over the centuries (hence its proximity to French on the chart below). Many of the origins of English words stem from Latin, and still more come from Greek. The dashed line connecting Greek and Latin indicates that the languages had a cultural overlap, but that the former did not directly spawn the latter.

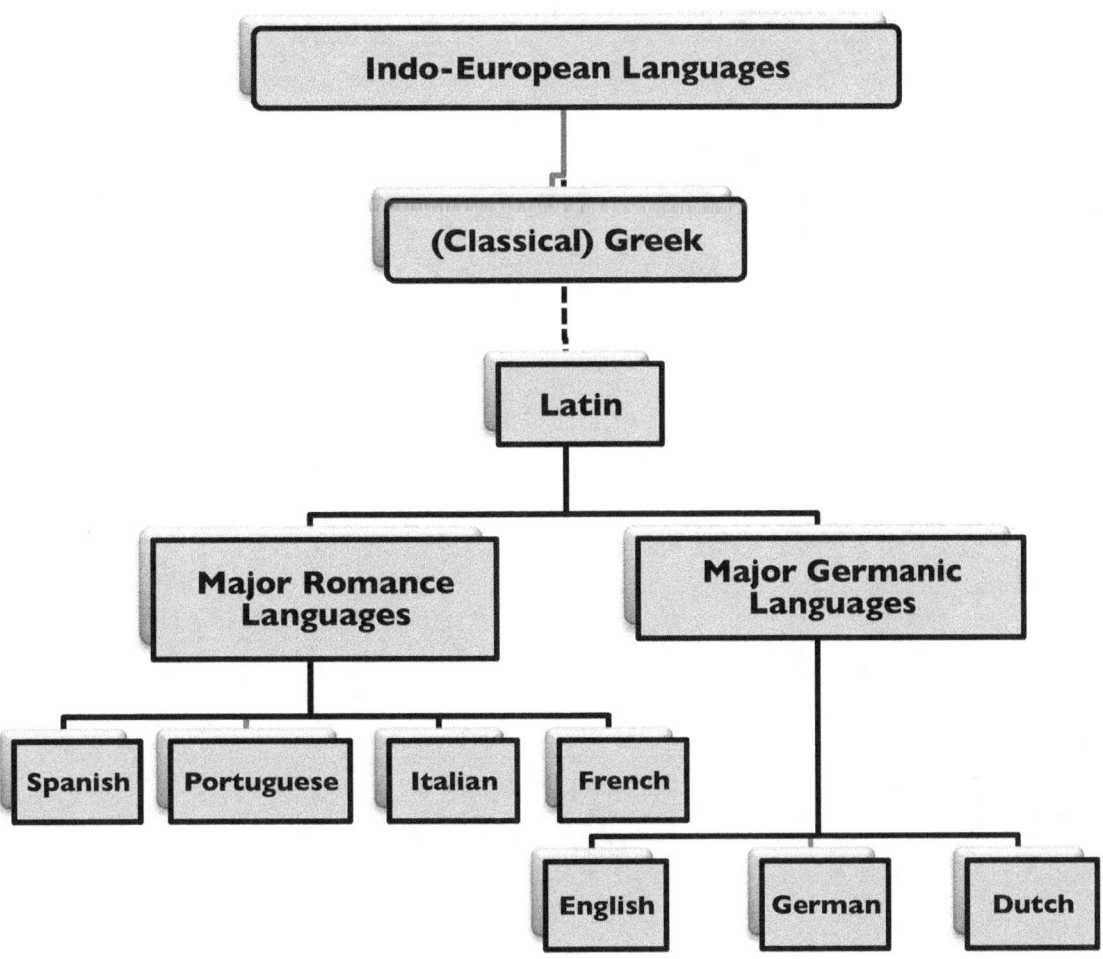

In future sections we will explore techniques on how to decipher words you do not know. Often the best way to do this is to have an understanding of the roots of a word. Nearly all of the roots for English words come from Greek and Latin. As English became more globalized from the early modern era to today, it spread beyond its original confines of England thus borrowing and assimilating words from other languages. According to the Global Language Monitor, the English language contains over one million words and that number is growing. Though many such words are outmoded, over 170,000 are in current use. Luckily, to sound intellectual or scholarly, you only need to know a subset of these words.

Lesson 1

COMING AROUND

NEW WORDS

pragmatic
praɡˈmatik

indignant
inˈdiɡnənt

astute
əˈst(y)oot

altruism
ˈaltroōˌizəm

prosaic
prōˈzāik

After recovering from a major accident, Jay, an **astute** and ambitious entrepreneur, gave up her job as a manager of a lucrative business. She now devotes her weekends giving free tuition to underperforming kids and helping various charities. Some people are **pragmatic** about her **altruism** and have remarked that Jay will not be able to maintain such **prosaic** lifestyle. However, Jay does not feel **indignant** with what other people say about her choices. She is contented with her current life.

Definitions: Try matching the words in the list with the appropriate definitions. If you are stuck, check the glossary in the back of the book or the passage at the top of the page.

1.	pragmatic	_____	a.	having keen judgment or insight
2.	indignant	_____	b.	dull and boring
3.	astute	_____	c.	practical; realistic
4.	altruism	_____	d.	annoyed by seemingly unfair treatment
5.	prosaic	_____	e.	disinterested or selfless concern for others

Sentences: Try to use the words above in a sentence below. Remember that a word ending may be changed or its figure of speech slightly altered.

6. Unlike Teena, who discussed theoretical ideas all day, Jake was _____ and attempted to earn money by starting a business.

7. Phong's teacher gave a lecture that was extremely _____: throughout the entire talk, Phong kept playing video games on his telephone.

8. It is _____ to spend your Saturday evenings helping the homeless.

9. Clive's judgment was so _____ that he was able to assess the teacher's personality after only two minutes of conversation.

10. After hearing that his girlfriend had sold his favorite video games, James sent her an _____ email.

4

Lesson 2

IT'S NOT ALWAYS WHAT IT SEEMS

Although Krystine was leading the **extravagant** lifestyle of a celebrity that many young girls dream of, she felt a lack of **autonomy** deep down. Everyone around her was calculating, and she had no true friends to confide in. Sometimes, she even got **cryptic** messages from strangers threatening to reveal her wrongdoings to the public. When Krystine was alone, she often had **reminiscence** of her past, a difficult and yet happy life. Krytine decided to express her emotions in her paintings, hoping that making art would be a **curative** endeavor against her desolation.

NEW WORDS

curative
ˈkyoorətiv

extravagant
ikˈstravəgənt

reminiscence
ˌreməˈnisəns

autonomy
ôˈtänəmē

cryptic
ˈkriptik

Definitions: Try matching the words in the list with the appropriate definitions. If you are stuck, check the glossary in the back of the book or the passage at the top of the page.

1. curative _____ a. mysterious, obscure
2. extravagant _____ b. able to remedy or heal something, typically disease
3. reminiscence _____ c. the right of self-government; freedom
4. autonomy _____ d. spending money excessively
5. cryptic _____ e. the act of recalling past events

Sentences: Try to use the words above in a sentence below. Remember that a word ending may be changed or its figure of speech slightly altered.

6. The archaeologist is trying to decipher the _____ messages written on the ancient stones that may reveal the history of a lost civilization.
7. Jane immediately fell into a personal _____ after having seen the picture of her old classmates.
8. Unlike her mother, who values a frugal lifestyle, Jane is extremely _____ in her spending.
9. Ginger extract has _____ properties that can assuage giddiness or motion sickness.
10. The new school rules, although effective, undermine the _____ of the students and staff.

NEW WORDS

fastidious
fasˈtidēəs

paramount
ˈparəˌmount

squander
ˈskwändər

appease
əˈpēz

clandestine
klanˈdestən, -ˌtīn, -ˌtēn, ˈklandəs-

Lesson 3

A FRUGAL HUSBAND

Keefe is particularly **fastidious** about financial matters: saving money is his **paramount** priority in life. He is very **clandestine** about divulging details of his monthly paycheck — especially to his wife who often asks Keefe how much he receives from his job. Keefe believes that by practicing frugality, he will not be forced to **squander** his money just to **appease** his wife's insatiable appetite for shoes.

Definitions: Try matching the words in the list with the appropriate definitions. If you are stuck, check the glossary in the back of the book or the passage at the top of the page.

1. fastidious _____ a. to waste (money, time, etc.)
2. paramount _____ b. to calm, quell, assuage
3. squander _____ c. very particular about details
4. appease _____ d. secretive
5. clandestine _____ e. of the greatest importance, supreme

Sentences: Try to use the words above in a sentence below. Remember that a word ending may be changed or its figure of speech slightly altered.

6. Often spies use _____ means to procure information from their enemies.

7. Leslie _____ his entire paycheck at the local casino in an hour only to return home depressed that he had no funds until his next paycheck arrived.

8. Nobody can please Teena, but at least Armand has the ability to _____ her.

9. Don't spend sleepless nights cramming for exams; sleep is still _____.

10. John's _____ nature will help him with his experiments in the analytical lab where precision is highly valued.

Lesson 4

A CULTURAL HYPOTHESIS?

Last year a team of archaeologists travelled to the Lower Nile in order to **excavate** the tomb of an ancient pharaoh. Once the tomb was unearthed, they deciphered writings indicating that people in the pharaoh's kingdom were **philanthropic** and helped build medical facilities for their poor. **Demographers** have since concluded that this population was extremely large and that many inhabitants likely **migrated** to Egypt from present day Israel. Further, scholars have concluded that the pharaoh was an **ingenuous** ruler who did not suspect that his own brother-in-law would poison him.

NEW WORDS

demography
diˈmägrəfē

excavate
ˈekskəˌvāt

ingenuous
inˈjenyooəs

migrate
ˈmīˌgrāt

philanthropic
ˌfilənˈTHräpik

Definitions: Try matching the words in the list with the appropriate definitions. If you are stuck, check the glossary in the back of the book or the passage at the top of the page.

1. demography _____ a. to move from one place to another
2. excavate _____ b. naïve, innocent
3. ingenuous _____ c. to dig out
4. migrate _____ d. caring for humanity
5. philanthropic _____ e. the study of populations, especially changes in populations (birth rate, death rate, income, disease rates)

Sentences: Try to use the words above in a sentence below. Remember that a word ending may be changed or its figure of speech slightly altered.

6. The newly discovered fossil bones are being _____ from the ground.
7. The _____ girl did not know that her boyfriend was dating her only for bragging rights and social advancement.
8. Born in the river, salmon _____ to the sea to gain their body mass before returning to the freshwater streams to spawn.
9. The Bill & Melinda Gates Foundation is one of the largest _____ organizations in the world.
10. A careful analysis of the _____ of Detroit will revel that, in the latter part of the twentieth century, the population declined sharply and became increasingly African-American.

Lesson 5

A SKEW OPINION

NEW WORDS

recant
riˈkant

soporific
ˌsäpəˈrifik

tyranny
ˈtirənē

garrulous
ˈgar(y)ələs

indict
inˈdīt

"If only this lecture hall were a law-court", Hien spoke quietly to herself, "I would **indict** my **garrulous** Biology professor for giving such a **soporific** lecture and his **tyranny** for forcing me to redo my 20-page research assignment." But after having seen other students being engaged in his lecture, Hien **recanted** her statements. Perhaps she had not put enough effort into her assignment to meet her professor's high expectations.

Definitions: Try matching the words in the list with the appropriate definitions. If you are stuck, check the glossary in the back of the book or the passage at the top of the page.

1. recant _____ a. inducing sleep
2. soporific _____ b. overly talkative
3. tyranny _____ c. to say one no longer holds a belief, especially a heretical one
4. garrulous _____ d. to accuse or charge someone with crime
5. indict _____ e. unreasonable use of authority

Sentences: Try to use the words above in a sentence below. Remember that a word ending may be changed or its figure of speech slightly altered.

6. Jake _____ his heretical theories after considering his friends' pragmatic feedback.
7. Many people prefer a democracy to a(n) _____ because a democracy often fosters autonomy and change.
8. The lecturer's monotone voice is really _____.
9. James is generally not a(n) _____ person but he can talk a lot when it comes to programming- his main interest.
10. The man was _____ on ten counts of animal cruelty.

8

Lesson 6

REDUCING FUND WILL CAUSE TROUBLE

The school's board of management **lamented** the decline of government funding for specialized schools. The managers had gathered signatures from their students and parents to **bolster** their proposal to request for increased funding. They clearly **articulated** their view that the decline in financial support would greatly undermine the students' learning. However, the government was **ambivalent** about the issue and advised the school to try to appease the parents who were giving **provocative** comments online while the proposal was being considered.

NEW WORDS

ambivalent
amˈbivələnt

lament
ləˈment

bolster
ˈbōlstər

articulate
ärˈtikyəlit (adj.); ärˈtikyəˌlāt (v.)

provocative
prəˈväkətiv

Definitions: Try matching the words in the list with the appropriate definitions. If you are stuck, check the glossary in the back of the book or the passage at the top of the page.

1. ambivalent _____ a. to grieve
2. lament _____ b. to support, strengthen
3. bolster _____ c. stimulating strong reactions
4. articulate _____ d. having mixed feelings about something
5. provocative _____ e. (adj.) written or spoken clearly and/or persuasively; (v.) to express oneself in speech or writing clearly and/or persuasively

Sentences: Try to use the words above in a sentence below. Remember that a word ending may be changed or its figure of speech slightly altered.

6. My mom _____ the lack of fresh vegetables at the supermarket.
7. Eliot holds _____ views on which computer model is superior because they both offer similar features.
8. The mutual visits of the two presidents are meant to _____ ties between the two countries.
9. Jean is able to _____ her views very well on the complex political issue.
10. The _____ remarks will only worsen the conflict.

Lesson 7

A BULLY AT SCHOOL

NEW WORDS

deride
diˈrīd

facetious
fəˈsēSHəs

retract
riˈtrakt

bane
bān

decry
diˈkrī

Georgia enjoyed attending school in Iowa until she met Thomas, the school bully. Thomas became the **bane** of Georgia's existence, as he was constantly **deriding** her by insulting her personality, stature, and habits. Unfortunately, when she demanded that Thomas **retract** his insults, Thomas retorted that his comments about her were just **facetious** remarks rather than anything serious. Georgia eventually went to her school principal and **decried** Thomas' behavior as abusive, at which point an investigation occurred and Thomas was expelled from school. Only with ardent intervention on Georgia's part was justice able to prevail.

Definitions: Try matching the words in the list with the appropriate definitions. If you are stuck, check the glossary in the back of the book or the passage at the top of the page.

1. deride _____ a. a cause of distress or destruction
2. facetious _____ b. to openly disapprove
3. retract _____ c. to ridicule
4. bane _____ d. to draw in; to withdraw or go back on (an undertaking or a promise)
5. decry _____ e. flippant; treating serious matters jokingly

Sentences: Try to use the words above in a sentence below. Remember that a word ending may be changed or its figure of speech slightly altered.

6. Vy's _____ remarks reflect her levity on the issue.
7. It seems discouraging, and also embarrassing, to _____ a published study that you put so much time and effort in.
8. Thu _____ everybody on her design team, thinking that his ideas were supreme.
9. It is embarrassing to be _____ a heretic by your community.
10. Sylvia's older brother was the _____ of her existence: all he ever did was cause her stress and heartache.

Lesson 8

DISAGREEMENT

Claire was a **fervent** proponent of an informal, down-to-earth teaching style while Luke was more **pedantic** in his approach. Due to their differences, they had a conflict when working on a joint project. While Claire **commiserated** over the project's failure and could not **subdue** her tendency to blame Luke for his poor work ethics, Luke insisted that Claire should not point fingers and **apportion** blame.

NEW WORDS

fervent
ˈfərvənt

pedantic
pəˈdantik

subdue
səbˈd(y)oo

apportion
əˈpôrSHən

commiserate
kəˈmizəˌrāt

Definitions: Try matching the words in the list with the appropriate definitions. If you are stuck, check the glossary in the back of the book or the passage at the top of the page.

1. fervent _____ a. to hold back, control
2. pedantic _____ b. to divide, distribute
3. subdue _____ c. energetic, passionate
4. apportion _____ d. to feel or express sympathy or pity
5. commiserate _____ e. showing unnecessary knowledge or excessive concerns for details

Sentences: Try to use the words above in a sentence below. Remember that a word ending may be changed or its figure of speech slightly altered.

6. Wayne is an old, _____ academic who likes to nit-pick the faults of his inexperienced interns.
7. Lucy is a(n) _____ advocate of animal rights.
8. Exercise alone is insufficient; you need to _____ your desire for food.
9. They cannot help but _____ over their failed project.
10. It is difficult to _____ responsibility among the team members; everyone should also know the jobs of one another.

Lesson 9

OUT OF CONTROL

NEW WORDS

denounce
di'nouns

exemplify
ig'zemplə,fī

innocuous
i'näkyooəs

miser
'mīzər

pilfer
'pilfər

Tarap had been unemployed for over a year, and that fact greatly devastated his outlook on life. He **denounced** his wealthy friends as hypocritical and **miserly** when they all refused to help him with his difficult financial situation. Tarap felt so desperate that he thought it would be **innocuous** to **pilfer** on the streets to get by. Tarap's situation **exemplifies** the harsh reality of soaring unemployment rates in many countries nowadays.

Definitions: Try matching the words in the list with the appropriate definitions. If you are stuck, check the glossary in the back of the book or the passage at the top of the page.

1. denounce _____ a. causing no harm
2. exemplify _____ b. to publicly condemn, criticize
3. innocuous _____ c. to serve as an ideal example of something
4. miser _____ d. to steal
5. pilfer _____ e. a frugal person who hoards money and refuses to spend

Sentences: Try to use the words above in a sentence below. Remember that a word ending may be changed or its figure of speech slightly altered.

6. Carbon doesn't _____ the best characteristics desired in a Lithium ion battery's anode material.
7. These seemingly _____ and trivial matters can build up to become a major threat one day.
8. To avoid conflict, we should not praise one religion and _____ the other.
9. Businesses sometimes _____ ideas, trade secrets and technological innovations from their rivals.
10. Because Patrick is such a(n) _____, he has saved enough money to buy a new house.

12

Lesson 10

"GOOD WINE NEEDS NO BUSH"

In business, when sales are **stagnant** for a sustained period of time, some people are not **resigned** to the prospect of declining profits and might submit to **inane** devices to boost sales without upholding business ethics. However, it is advisable that businesses still keep up their **rectitude** and **underscore** their business ethics even more when developing new strategies to promote growth. As an old adage goes, "good wine needs no bush."

NEW WORDS

rectitude
ˈrektəˌt(y)ood

stagnant
ˈstagnənt

underscore
ˈəndərˌskôr

resigned
riˈzīnd

inane
iˈnān

Definitions: Try matching the words in the list with the appropriate definitions. If you are stuck, check the glossary in the back of the book or the passage at the top of the page.

1. rectitude _____ a. silly; stupid
2. stagnant _____ b. to emphasize or underline something
3. underscore _____ c. 1. (of water) not flowing or lacking a current; 2. showing no activity, sluggish
4. resigned _____ d. morally correct behavior or thought; righteousness
5. inane _____ e. submissive; accepting one's unpleasant reality

Sentences: Try to use the words above in a sentence below. Remember that a word ending may be changed or its figure of speech slightly altered.

6. The government is pouring funds to lift the _____ economies.
7. New policies should_____ the use of clean energy to reduce pollution.
8. John is an exemplar of moral_____, always living by his values and ethics.
9. Because their parents need to save money, the kids are _____ to spending a Christmas without gifts.
10. The media is flooded with _____ ads that feature ghastly thin models as fixed ideals of beauty.

Crossword Puzzle
Lessons 1-10

ACROSS

3 annoyed by seemingly unfair treatment
5 to dig out
8 having mixed feelings about something
9 of the greatest importance, supreme
10 submissive; accepting one's unpleasant reality
11 showing unnecessary knowledge or excessive concerns for details
13 spending money excessively
16 a cause of distress or destruction
17 to accuse or charge someone with crime
18 naïve, innocent
19 energetic, passionate
20 flippant; treating serious matters jokingly

DOWN

1 the act of recalling past events
2 to emphasize or underline something
4 to steal
6 disinterested or selfless concern for others
7 secretive
12 to publicly condemn, criticize
14 (adj.) written or spoken clearly and/or persuasively; (v.) to express oneself in speech or writing clearly and/or persuasively
15 to say one no longer holds a belief, especially a heretical one

Vocabulary Review
Lessons 1-10

Directions: Match each word with its best approximate definition. Note that definitions are not necessarily repeated verbatim from the lesson exercises.

1. pragmatic _____
2. prosaic _____
3. autonomy _____
4. cryptic _____
5. fastidious _____
6. squander _____
7. demography _____
8. migrate _____
9. soporific _____
10. garrulous _____
11. lament _____
12. provocative _____
13. deride _____
14. bane _____
15. subdue _____
16. apportion _____
17. innocuous _____
18. miser _____
19. stagnant _____
20. inane _____

a. to waste something, especially money
b. mysterious, enigmatic
c. a source of harm or annoyance
d. the study of populations (often statistics on births, deaths, income and disease)
e. a person who hoards money and who spends as little as possible
f. silly; foolish
g. an expression of grief or sorrow; to mourn a loss or a death
h. showing no activity, dull, sluggish; (of water) having no flow or current
i. to ridicule; to show contempt
j. obsessed with details
k. to divide into pieces; to ration
l. to move from one region to another
m. sleep inducing
n. dull and boring
o. to overcome; to bring under control
p. practical
q. the right or condition of self-government; free from external control or pressures
r. talkative
s. trying to cause a strong reaction
t. harmless

Introduction to Word Roots

As we have seen, many of the origins of English come from (Classical) Greek and Latin. Though these languages are defunct today, English contains a number of words with roots whose derivatives stem from these languages.

Consider, for example the (Classical) Greek word φόβος, or phobos. Translated into English as "phobia" or "phobe," this word means "fear." While (Classical) Greek is no longer an active language, the root "phobia" persists in English language to describe an extreme irrational fear of something. Consider the following examples:

agora<u>phobia</u> (n.):	extreme irrational fear of large crowded places
arachn<u>ophobia</u> (n.):	extreme irrational fear of spiders
techn<u>ophobe</u> (n.):	a person who is afraid of or who dislikes technology
xen<u>ophobia</u> (n.):	extreme irrational fear of people from other countries

Just as was so with (Classical) Greek, English has words whose root derive from Latin. Consider, for example, the Latin word *placere*, meaning to please. Certain English words containing "plac" are related to the concept of pleasing someone or something:

<u>plac</u>ate (v.):	to make less angry or hostile
im<u>plac</u>able (adj.):	unable to be pleased or appeased (note that the root "im" means "not" and is taught in our first word root lesson)

Roots, therefore, can help us decipher potential meanings of words without knowing exactly what a word means. Note, however, that not every word has roots, nor does a word that contains letters that look like a root imply that the word is related to its root meaning. The word "<u>plac</u>ard" refers to a poster or sign used in public display, which has nothing to do with pleasing anyone. In this book, we provide you with a number of units to help you identify and practice identifying word roots.

Word Roots: Unit 1

ROOTS AND THEIR MEANINGS

In/il/im/ir:	not	chron:	time
ex/ej:	out	a:	without
re:	again	morph:	shape

Here are a few examples of some words that use the above roots:

intolerable:	not tolerable
illegal:	not legal
improper:	not proper
incapable:	not capable
irrational:	not rational
exit:	(place) to go out
eject:	to force or throw out
chronology:	telling a story where events are arranged in order of their occurrence
amorphous:	having no definite shape

Now try to fill in the table below by finding the appropriate root(s) and interpreting the meaning of each word:

Word	Root(s)	Guessed Meaning	Actual Meaning
inaccurate			
incapable			
illegitimate			
impolite			
inactive			
excrete			
chronicle			
morphology			
asexual			
atypical			
anachronism			

irreverent			
apolitical			
inexplicable			

Remember that not every group of letters forming a root implies that there is a root for a given word. Consider, for example, the word "apple." One may think that the "a" in apple means not, but the "a" is merely a letter. Also the word "real" has "re" in the beginning, but it has nothing to do with doing something again. Roots, therefore, are only tools to help *possibly* identify the meaning of a word if you are completely stuck.

Occupations and Careers I

As you learn more advanced English, you will be exposed to many papers that discuss what different scholars, intellectuals, or professionals do in their careers. Knowing what people in different careers do is helpful for understanding the gist of many pieces of writing. Furthermore, people in these careers are discussed frequently on school entrance examinations. The list of occupational roles below and in the next section is not exhaustive, but rather is an attempt to help define a number of specific and sophisticated occupations to which you may be exposed to or read about as an intellectual.

SCIENTIFIC JOBS

anatomist: one who practices anatomy, e.g. the body structures of humans and other living creatures, often through dissection to examine their innards

astronomer: one who practices astronomy, e.g. celestial objects, space, and the physical universe as a whole

biologist: one who practices biology, e.g. living organisms, their morphology, physiology, anatomy, behavior, and distribution

botanist: one who practices botany, e.g. plants, their physiology, structure, genetics, ecology, distribution, classification, and economic importance

chemist: one who practices chemistry, e.g. chemicals and their reactions

geneticist:	one who practices genetics, e.g. heredity and the variation of inherited characteristics through genes
geologist:	one who practices geology, e.g. Earth's physical structure and composition, its history, and forces that affect it
meteorologist:	one who practices meteorology, e.g. the study of the atmosphere and the weather
oceanographer:	one who practices oceanography, e.g. the physical and biological processes of the seas
paleontologist:	one who practices paleontology, e.g. the fossil elements of animals and plants
physicist:	one who practices physics, e.g. the study of the nature and properties of matter and energy
seismologist:	one who practices seismology, e.g., the science of earthquakes and related incidents
zoologist:	one who practices zoology, e.g. the behavior, structure, distribution, and classification of animals

MEDICAL OR MEDICALLY RELATED JOBS

anesthesiologist:	one who practices anesthesia, e.g. administering gases or drugs to make patients insensitive to pain before surgical operations
coroner:	an official who investigates deaths, especially violent or suspicious deaths

hygienist: specialist who promotes sanitary conditions to maintain good health

pharmacist: specialist who is professionally qualified to prepare and dispense drugs

surgeon: one who practices surgery, e.g. the treatment of the body through incision and manipulation

veterinarian: a doctor and surgeon for animals

NEW WORDS

nostalgia
nä'staljə, nə-

paradox
'parə‚däks

bombast
'bämbast

austere
ô'sti(ə)r

replicate
'repli‚kāt (v.); -kit (adj.; noun)

Lesson 11

HIGH SCHOOL REUNION

Filled with **nostalgia** about reuniting with her classmates, Muriel gaily attended her high school ten-year reunion. The situation seemed somewhat **paradoxical** to her, largely because she did not particularly enjoy her high school years. Having lived with her **austere** parents, she led a solitary adolescent life of intense scholarship while many of her classmates spoke with **bombast** about their boyfriends, homecoming dates, and football victories. Now, however, Muriel was famous and successful in her lucrative fashion design career. She knew that, with her accumulated successes, she would never be able to **replicate** the experience she had earlier in life.

Definitions: Try matching the words in the list with the appropriate definitions. If you are stuck, check the glossary in the back of the book or the passage at the top of the page.

1. nostalgia _____ a. severe or strict in manner or attitude; plain in style or appearance; having little luxury
2. paradox _____ b. two seemingly opposite but true things
3. bombast _____ c. (adj.) of the nature of a copy or repetition of a scientific trial or experiment; (n.) a close or exact copy of something; (v.) to reproduce an exact copy of something
4. austere _____ d. high-sounding language with little meaning
5. replicate _____ e. a longing for time past, especially childhood or home

Sentences: Try to use the words above in a sentence below. Remember that a word ending may be changed or its figure of speech slightly altered.

6. Paul was unable to _____ his science experiment before his classmates; they consequently questioned his results.
7. Whenever Sally passes by a Burger King she feels a sense of _____ about eating whoppers with her mother when she was four years old.
8. The politician spoke with much _____ about the new tax incentives in his district: most people thought his words were empty.
9. Truman gave up all his toys to live a(n) _____ life.
10. It was a(n) _____ that someone so ugly could be so kind.

22

Lesson 12

THE CHESS LEADER

Eddie **imperiously** assumed leadership over his chess club, causing many of the group participants to view his leadership with **scorn**. Though Eddie claimed to be an expert at chess, several members secretly knew that he **beguiled** them by talking like a skilled chess fanatic. In reality, however, Eddie was merely a **dilettante** at chess who proved unable to make his club members **deferential** to his commands.

NEW WORDS

dilettante
ˌdiliˈtänt, -ˈtäntē

imperious
imˈpi(ə)rēəs

scorn
skôrn

beguile
biˈgīl

deferential
ˌdefəˈrenCHəl

Definitions: Try matching the words in the list with the appropriate definitions. If you are stuck, check the glossary in the back of the book or the passage at the top of the page.

1. dilettante _____ a. an amateur
2. imperious _____ b. assuming power without justification; arrogant and domineering
3. scorn _____ c. to charm or enchant in a deceptive way
4. beguile _____ d. (n.) the feeling or belief that something or someone is worthless or despicable; (v.) 1. to feel contempt for; 2. to reject something in a contemptuous way
5. deferential _____ e. showing respect to those of authority or power or rank

Sentences: Try to use the words above in a sentence below. Remember that a word ending may be changed or its figure of speech slightly altered.

6. Minh's neighbor looked at her with _____ ever since she had been caught stealing candy bars from the local drug store.
7. In Japan, one is supposed to bow low to one's elders as a sign of _____ to one's elders.
8. Because of James' _____ attitude, he assumed control of the student government without any objections.
9. Many thieves try to _____ their victims before cheating them.
10. Mark is something of a(n) _____: he is a jack of all trades and a master of none.

Lesson 13

NEW WORDS

forbear
fərˈber, fôr-

pedestrian
pəˈdestrēən

subjective
səbˈjektiv

apprehensive
ˌapriˈhensiv

comprehensive
ˌkämpriˈhensiv

BAD ENGLISH TEACHER

Every year, the students at Washington High were **apprehensive** about taking English classes with Mrs. Smith. She was reputed to be very **subjective** in grading student papers, basing her marks not upon the intellectual merit of a work but rather upon how active the student was in class. Moreover, her lectures were **pedestrian** in nature, despite her having received **comprehensive** training on how to teach students effectively in class. Those unlucky students who took Mrs. Smith's class found it difficult to **forbear** constantly complaining about the quality of their instruction.

Definitions: Try matching the words in the list with the appropriate definitions. If you are stuck, check the glossary in the back of the book or the passage at the top of the page.

1. forbear _____ a. biased; non-objective; throwing one's emotions into things
2. pedestrian _____ b. (adj.) lacking zest and enthusiasm; dull; (n.) a person walking along a road
3. subjective _____ c. to refrain from doing something
4. apprehensive _____ d. thorough; covering all aspects
5. comprehensive _____ e. anxious; hesitant about something

Sentences: Try to use the words above in a sentence below. Remember that a word ending may be changed or its figure of speech slightly altered.

6. Final exams are usually _____ in nature, covering everything in the entire course.
7. Elena could not _____ watching her little brother go to the dance: she really wanted to see him and his date.
8. Momin is _____ about riding tall roller coasters: he has a terrible fear of heights.
9. Asking a girl to dinner and a movie is perceived my many as a rather _____ type of first date.
10. When Aunt Millie gave one of the triplets a far more expensive birthday present than the other two, she was accused of being _____.

24

Lesson 14

THE SLICK MAGICIAN

To call Schuyler **dexterous** would be an understatement. Despite his **insolent** attitude, nobody can deny that his magic performances are **pivotal**: each one is more incredible and revolutionary than the one that came before it. Schuyler has even found an **expedient** way of convincing people that he can fly while on stage. But when people call him a fraud or a showman, Schuyler insists that such titles are **misnomers**: he truly insists that he is making magic happen.

NEW WORDS

dexterous
ˈdekst(ə)rəs

expedient
ikˈspēdēənt

insolent
ˈinsələnt

misnomer
misˈnōmər

pivotal
ˈpivətl

Definitions: Try matching the words in the list with the appropriate definitions. If you are stuck, check the glossary in the back of the book or the passage at the top of the page.

1. dexterous _____ a. convenient or practical, though not necessarily proper or ethical
2. expedient _____ b. extremely decisive or important in affecting something or its outcome
3. insolent _____ c. arrogant and rude
4. misnomer _____ d. using the wrong name
5. pivotal _____ e. skillful, especially with the hands

Sentences: Try to use the words above in a sentence below. Remember that a word ending may be changed or its figure of speech slightly altered.

6. Deciding what type of career you want can be a(n) _____ decision: it is likely to affect your friends and values for life.
7. To call the Pacific Ocean "peaceful" would be a(n) _____: it is, in fact, hardly calm.
8. Jill was so _____ that her boyfriend didn't even notice her taking money from his wallet.
9. Sometimes it is more _____ to walk away from a project than to complete it, even if it is ethically wrong.
10. Unlike Martha, who was humble and obliging, Mark was _____.

Lesson 15

UYEN'S SINGAPORE DAYS

NEW WORDS

redolent
ˈredl-ənt

stipulate
ˈstēpyəˌlāt

unequivocal
ˌəniˈkwivəkəl

respite
ˈrespət, riˈspīt

immune
iˈmyoon

Back when she was in high school in Singapore, Uyen studied without any **respite** or vacation: it almost seemed that she was **immune** to the idea of taking breaks. In actuality, however, Singapore culture **stipulates** that, in order to be successful, one needs to work extremely hard. Pauses, therefore, are **unequivocally** frowned upon. Nowadays, Uyen is no longer in Singapore. Only when she has to pull all-nighters for her work projects does she experience feelings and memories that are **redolent** of her time in Singapore.

Definitions: Try matching the words in the list with the appropriate definitions. If you are stuck, check the glossary in the back of the book or the passage at the top of the page.

1.	redolent	_____	a.	leaving no doubt; unambiguous
2.	stipulate	_____	b.	strongly suggestive of something (usually referring to sense of smell)
3.	unequivocal	_____	c.	to demand or specify something, usually as part of an agreement
4.	respite	_____	d.	unable to be affected by something
5.	immune	_____	e.	a brief pause or rest

Sentences: Try to use the words above in a sentence below. Remember that a word ending may be changed or its figure of speech slightly altered.

6. Vaccinations for measles can help make someone _____ to the virus.

7. After nineteen hours of working straight, Juila begged for a brief _____ before finishing her twenty-hour shift.

8. Harvey _____ to his boss that he would only continue working if he got a three dollar raise and a free lunch every Friday.

9. The soup that my girlfriend makes is _____ of the days when my mother and I cooked together.

10. Fred _____ insisted that he did not steal popcorn from the theater.

26

Lesson 16

BORDER TENSIONS

Though the idea of a multiracial America may sound **aesthetically** pleasing, American citizens have heard numerous **anecdotes** about Mexican immigrants illegally crossing the border into the United States. Many come to the United States to escape **callous** treatment from their government in the hope of a better economic life. Still others think that the American economy is more **resilient** than the one back at home, easily stabilizing after hard times to offer them fresh jobs. Nevertheless, the United States has adopted strict standards for admitting Mexicans into the country, and it refuses to **conciliate**, despite many immigrant pleas for looser immigration laws.

NEW WORDS

aesthetic
esˈTHetik

anecdote
ˈanikˌdōt

conciliate
kənˈsilēˌāt

callous
ˈkaləs

resilient
riˈzilyənt

Definitions: Try matching the words in the list with the appropriate definitions. If you are stuck, check the glossary in the back of the book or the passage at the top of the page.

1. aesthetic _____ a. to stop someone from being angry or discontented; placate; pacify
2. anecdote _____ b. insensitive and a bit cruel
3. conciliate _____ c. a short story or tale to explain something
4. callous _____ d. able to recover easily after difficulty or trauma
5. resilient _____ e. considering or pertaining to art or beauty

Sentences: Try to use the words above in a sentence below. Remember that a word ending may be changed or its figure of speech slightly altered.

6. Often one is advised to begin personal essays with a(n) _____, as a personal story can help others best understand somebody.
7. It would be _____ to tell a person who was just hit by a motorbike to walk to the nearest doctor alone to seek help.
8. Many New Yorkers were very _____ after September 11, 2001. Even though their city had been attacked, they resumed work as quickly as possible.
9. Unlike Sam, who cannot appreciate sculpture at all, Melanie has a passion for things _____.
10. There was nothing Faisal could do to _____ his girlfriend after she caught him cheating on her.

NEW WORDS

diminutive
diˈminyətiv

impetuous
imˈpeCHooəs

serendipity
ˌserənˈdipitē

belie
biˈlī

castigate
ˈkastəˌgāt

Lesson 17

THE ECCENTRIC VALENTINE

Despite his **diminutive** stature and **impetuous** nature, many ladies seem attracted to John's strange behavior. Last week, for example, John hid himself in his girlfriend Susie's school locker making her Valentine's Day cards. Rather than **castigating** John for hiding in her personal space, Susie thanked him for keeping her locker safe, for she knew that his unusual behaviors always **belied** his genuine intentions. Perhaps it was **serendipity** that someone who behaved so strangely was so admired by his girlfriend: most girls would have thought John a creep!

Definitions: Try matching the words in the list with the appropriate definitions. If you are stuck, check the glossary in the back of the book or the passage at the top of the page.

1. diminutive _____ a. to lambaste; to criticize harshly
2. impetuous _____ b. small in stature; unusually small
3. serendipity _____ c. to fail to give a true impression of something; disguise or contradict
4. belie _____ d. happening randomly and with a positive effect
5. castigate _____ e. hasty or without thought

Sentences: Try to use the words above in a sentence below. Remember that a word ending may be changed or its figure of speech slightly altered.

6. It was complete _____ that, after losing his favorite teddy bear, Vu saw it sitting on the shelf at his favorite bookshop.
7. Helen's mother _____ her for staying out three hours past her curfew.
8. Often people who act _____ get themselves into trouble because they do not consider the consequences of their actions.
9. Because of Arthur's _____ frame, it was difficult for him to be a star on the school basketball team.
10. Geraldine's cruelty _____ her pretty smile and charming figure.

Lesson 18

AN EVIL SISTER

Nancy's older sister Tanya would do anything to get Nancy into trouble. Last spring, for example, Tanya decided to **forego** her spring vacation to Thailand so that she could attend Nancy's prom. Ruthlessly **penetrating** into a dance where she did not have tickets, Tanya showed no **compunction** about pushing around the security and students at the school dance. When she finally saw Nancy at the dance, Tanya grabbed a microphone and told students that her sister was a thief who was **apt** to steal money from their wallets. In the end, Tanya was unable to **substantiate** her claims with facts. She was ultimately removed from the dance and Nancy spent the rest of her night happily with her boyfriend.

NEW WORDS

forgo/forego
fôrˈgō

penetrate
ˈpeniˌtrāt

substantiate
səbˈstanCHēˌāt

apt
apt

compunction
kəmˈpəNG(k)SHən

Definitions: Try matching the words in the list with the appropriate definitions. If you are stuck, check the glossary in the back of the book or the passage at the top of the page.

1. forgo/forego _____ a. to go without; omit; decline to take
2. penetrate _____ b. to verify something
3. substantiate _____ c. 1. appropriate or suitable in circumstances; 2. having tendency to do something; 3. quick to learn
4. apt _____ d. to push through a barrier or boundary into something
5. compunction _____ e. feeling guilt or sorrow for poor behavior

Sentences: Try to use the words above in a sentence below. Remember that a word ending may be changed or its figure of speech slightly altered.

6. Vishnu felt no _____ about telling his sister she was mean after the latter kicked the family cat.
7. Air can _____ through a window with a screen, but a large bug likely cannot.
8. If you study diligently and for an extended time period, you are _____ to succeed on your college entrance exams.
9. The manager's testimony in court helped _____ the fact that Cedric was, indeed, guilty of stealing milk from the grocery store.
10. It is hard to _____ a trip to the museum because I enjoy art and history so much.

Lesson 19

NEW WORDS

dilatory
ˈdiləˌtôrē

fabricate
ˈfabrəˌkāt

instill
inˈstil

mitigate
ˈmitəˌgāt

plastic
ˈplastik

INTIMIDATING POLICE OFFICER

Officer Sandusky is reputed to be one of the most intimidating police officers in town. When he catches a speeding driver, he speaks to the traffic offender in such a way as to **instill** fear into his or her heart. Furthermore, the traffic offender can do nothing to **mitigate** Officer Sandusky's austere demeanor, for the officer is not a very **plastic** person. If he catches the traffic offender **fabricating** a story to defend his or her street behavior, Officer Sandusky often doubles the traffic fine. And always, he uses **dilatory** behavior to deliberately delay drivers from making any of their appointments on time.

Definitions: Try matching the words in the list with the appropriate definitions. If you are stuck, check the glossary in the back of the book or the passage at the top of the page.

1. dilatory _____ a. to make something up; to concoct
2. fabricate _____ b. to gradually establish something in a person's mind
3. instill _____ c. (adj.) 1. easily changeable; flexible; 2. fake; superficial; (n.) a synthetic material made from a range of polymers
4. mitigate _____ d. to make seem or feel less harsh or severe
5. plastic _____ e. delaying; trying to delay

Sentences: Try to use the words above in a sentence below. Remember that a word ending may be changed or its figure of speech slightly altered.

6. Most parents try to _____ a sense of responsibility in their children by making them do chores and homework.
7. Many companies like hiring people in their twenties and thirties because they are more _____ than older folks who are set in their ways.
8. Because of Sharon's _____ behavior, we missed the 5:00 movie.
9. When his parents asked him why he was late for dinner, Atisha _____ a story about getting stuck on the subway for two hours.
10. In order to _____ the pain of their breakup, Lydia told Phillip that she hoped that they could be really good friends forever.

Lesson 20

ARROGANT PROFESSOR

Perhaps out of **hubris**, Professor Park was **reluctant** to ever acknowledge that she was wrong. She **strenuously** defended her views, even if it was clear that the logic behind her reasoning was flawed. One day, however, she met Alec, an extremely bright and outspoken student. Alec tried his best to **refute** all of Professor Park's arguments until one day she admitted that she did not know what she was talking about. Admitting her lack of knowledge was an **unprecedented** act on behalf of Professor Park, who regularly mourned having to admit she was not perfect after this incident.

> **NEW WORDS**
>
> **refute**
> riˈfyoot
>
> **strenuous**
> ˈstrenyooəs
>
> **unprecedented**
> ˌənˈpresəˌdəntid
>
> **reluctant**
> riˈləktənt
>
> **hubris**
> ˈ(h)yoobris

Definitions: Try matching the words in the list with the appropriate definitions. If you are stuck, check the glossary in the back of the book or the passage at the top of the page.

1. refute _____ a. excessive self-confidence or pride
2. strenuous _____ b. to disprove or show something is false
3. unprecedented _____ c. never seen or done before
4. reluctant _____ d. showing hesitation or unwillingness
5. hubris _____ e. with excessive exertion, usually excessive physical exertion

Sentences: Try to use the words above in a sentence below. Remember that a word ending may be changed or its figure of speech slightly altered.

6. Training for a decathlon is _____: you need to work several different muscles in your body as well as your cardiovascular system.
7. Because of his _____, Aaron never could admit that he was a poor listener in his relationship with his last girlfriend.
8. In a(n) _____ move, the television network fired all of its employees at once and built a completely new newscast.
9. When Harold's teacher said he never turned in his research paper, Harold _____ the comment by handing her the paper with her comments written all over it.
10. Because Teresa is afraid of spiders, she is _____ to pet her cousin's pet tarantula.

Word Search
Lessons 11-20

```
N S U B J E C T I V E L Q L L
A T N E L O S N I E N U M M I
I Y L W J A W X S Y D Y L T Y
R Z T X P D N T O I R D X Q Z
T S Q I D E I C L D E N T D S
S U D Y P P N E C V A J L U Y
E O J I U I T E I D R R O P T
D R E L L T D T T E O U A N N
E E A T A A U N S R N T A P T
P T L N A N T I E E A T E S W
E X T I I G L O R R C T A W M
Y E D M U I I T R U E B E K T
Z D I P E G S T L Y M S A P T
R D Y N Q L E E I O V G R M X
R K T B G J R B B M R Y P T K
```

1. two seemingly opposite but true things
2. high-sounding language with little meaning
3. an amateur
4. to charm or enchant in a deceptive way
5. (adj.) lacking zest and enthusiasm; dull; (n.) a person walking along a road
6. biased; non-objective; throwing one's emotions into things
7. skillful, especially with the hands
8. arrogant and rude
9. to demand or specify something, usually as part of an agreement
10. unable to be affected by something
11. a short story or tale to explain something
12. able to recover easily after difficulty or trauma
13. small in stature; unusually small
14. happening randomly and with a positive effect
15. to push through a barrier or boundary into something
16. 1. appropriate or suitable in circumstances; 2. having tendency to do something; 3. quick to learn
17. delaying; trying to delay
18. to make seem or feel less harsh or severe
19. with excessive exertion, usually excessive physical exertion
20. showing hesitation or unwillingness

Vocabulary Review
Lessons 11-20

Directions: Match each word with its best approximate definition. Note that definitions are not necessarily repeated verbatim from the lesson exercises.

1.	nostalgia	_____	a.	a longing for time past
2.	austere	_____	b.	strongly suggestive of something
3.	imperious	_____	c.	arrogant, bossy
4.	deferential	_____	d.	severe or strict in attitude; stringent in engaging with worldly goods
5.	apprehensive	_____	e.	using a wrong name
6.	comprehensive	_____	f.	impulsive; hasty
7.	misnomer	_____	g.	to gradually establish something in a person's mind
8.	pivotal	_____	h.	unambiguous
9.	redolent	_____	i.	insensitive and a bit cruel
10.	unequivocal	_____	j.	to scold verbally
11.	aesthetic	_____	k.	pertaining to art or beauty
12.	callous	_____	l.	never done before
13.	impetuous	_____	m.	to concoct; to fake
14.	castigate	_____	n.	to establish by proof
15.	substantiate	_____	o.	extremely important
16.	compunction	_____	p.	anxious; hesitant about something
17.	fabricate	_____	q.	showing respect to higher authority
18.	instill	_____	r.	complete; including all or almost all elements of something
19.	unprecedented	_____	s.	excessive pride
20.	hubris	_____	t.	a feeling of guilt after doing something bad or unethical

Word Roots: Unit 2

ROOTS AND THEIR MEANINGS

ante:	before	pre:	before
loc/loq/log:	to speak	bi/di:	two
sci:	to know	bene:	good
sub:	under, less than	inter:	between, among

Here are a few examples of some words that use the above roots:

antedate: to date before something; to come before something else in time
loquacious: talkative
science: the study of how the world works (biologically, chemically, physically or otherwise); knowing about the world through these properties
predecease: to die before someone or something
subordinate: lower in rank or position; to work under someone
benefit: an advantage
bicycle: a pedal-powered vehicle with two wheels
interstate: existing or carried between states

Now try to fill in the table below by finding the appropriate root(s) and interpreting the meaning of each word:

Word	Root(s)	Guessed Meaning	Actual Meaning
antecedent			
subservient			
eloquent			
prescient			
beneficial			
predecessor			
dialogue			

interlocutor			
biweekly			
subway			
internecine			
benediction			
dichotomy			
submissive			
conscience			
predetermined			

Occupations and Careers II

This section continues the list of occupations and careers from the previous section. As before, we have broken them up by field.

SOCIAL SCIENCE RELATED JOBS

anthropologist: one who practices anthropology, e.g. the study of humankind, its culture, its development, or its evolution and ecology

cartographer: one who practices cartography, e.g. the practice of drawing maps

demographer: one who practices demography, e.g. the study of births, deaths, income, and other structural elements of human populations

psychiatrist: one who practices psychiatry, e.g. one with whom one can discuss personal, mental, and social problems; unlike a psychologist a psychiatrist can prescribe medication to help a patient

psychologist: one who practices psychology, e.g. the study of the mind and emotions that govern behavior in specific contexts; a therapist with whom one can discuss personal, mental, and social problems

sociologist: one who practices sociology, e.g. the study of social problems relative to the structure, development, and functioning of human society

JOBS IN THE LEGAL FIELD

bailiff: an official of the court who keeps order, looks after prisoners, executes writs, and carries out arrests

criminologist: one who practices criminology, e.g. the study of crime and criminals

magistrate: a civil officer or lay judge who administers the law for minor offenses or for screening of larger offenses

POLITICAL JOBS

governor: the elected head of a state in the United States; the title of the head of a colony in British colonies

mayor: someone elected head of a town, city, or other designated municipality

representative: (1) someone who serves in the United States House of Representatives; (2) a person (often legally) elected to speak on behalf of a group and imbued with legislative power

senator: someone who serves on the United States Senate

Lesson 21

BECOMING OUTSPOKEN

NEW WORDS

reticent
ˈretəsənt

circumspect
ˈsərkəmˌspekt

conventional
kənˈvenCHənl

condemn
kənˈdem

rhetoric
ˈretərik

Just a year ago, Indranil was known by his friends to be a **reticent** individual, who always was **circumspect** in examining details before taking a stand on an issue. Such behavior was indeed **conventional** for high school students in Farmbrook, a community that valued using good judgment and following social norms. But when Indranil's best friend Shri ran for class president, Indranil supported her thoroughly. He used persuasive **rhetoric** to coax his classmates into voting for her, and he vehemently **condemned** Shri's opponents. Because of Indranil's commitment, Shri became class president, and Indranil became known as a very vocal student.

Definitions: Try matching the word in the box with the appropriate definition. If you are stuck, check the glossary in the back of the book or the passage at the top of the page.

1. reticent _____ a. wary and unwilling to take risks
2. circumspect _____ b. not readily revealing thoughts, sparing of words
3. conventional _____ c. the art or use of persuasive writing to affect an audience
4. condemn _____ d. to express public disapproval of; censure
5. rhetoric _____ e. following typical social norms/conventions

Sentences: Try to use the words above in a sentence below. Remember that a word ending may be changed or its figure of speech slightly altered.

6. Unlike Minh, who was a very ineloquent writer, Tanya wrote with beautiful _____, always moving her audience.
7. The Roman Catholic Church _____ Galileo and sentenced him to house arrest because he defended his view that the Earth revolves about the sun.
8. It is _____ to wear black clothing to a funeral in the United States.
9. In contrast to Tim, who is very talkative, Mario is more _____: often he does not directly express his thoughts or ideas about things.
10. The detective was _____ in looking at all the evidence before accusing the woman of murder.

Lesson 22

ISRAEL-PALESTINE CONFLICT

Much to the **dismay** of many people, it appears that fighting between the Jewish state of Israel and its neighbor, the Muslim country Palestine, may never cease. In fact, fighting has been so intense that there has hardly been a single **serene** day along the border between these two nations in the past three decades. Because many of the Israelis and Palestenians find that their belief systems are **incongruent** with each other's, the result has been sustained **belligerence**. Sadly, it appears as though these issues will continue on in the foreseeable future; we can only hope that one day the need for conflicts between these two nations will be seen as **defunct**.

> ### NEW WORDS
>
> **dismay**
> disˈmā
>
> **incongruent**
> inˈkäNGgrooənt, ˌinkənˈgroo-
>
> **serene**
> səˈrēn
>
> **belligerent**
> bəˈlijərənt
>
> **defunct**
> diˈfəNGkt

Definitions: Try matching the words in the list with the appropriate definitions. If you are stuck, check the glossary in the back of the book or the passage at the top of the page.

1. dismay _____ a. calm and peaceful; soothing
2. incongruent _____ b. hostile; warlike; aggressive
3. serene _____ c. (n.) consternation and distress, often caused by something unexpected; (v.) to cause someone to feel consternation or distress
4. belligerent _____ d. no longer in use or functional
5. defunct _____ e. not compatible; does not fit together

Sentences: Try to use the words above in a sentence below. Remember that a word ending may be changed or its figure of speech slightly altered.

6. Many people would argue that in today's digital era, typewriters are now _____ objects.
7. My older sister finds sitting on the beach in the morning a(n) _____ experience: nothing can disturb her while she is there.
8. Shontel's quiet personality is _____ with her outspoken rhetoric. One would think such a shy girl would not be so caustic with a pen.
9. The _____ boy always threatened to beat up kids who opposed his ideas and judgments.
10. Much to Julia's _____, her boyfriend told her he was going to be ending their seemingly happy relationship.

Lesson 23

NEW WORDS

frivolous
ˈfrivələs

perfunctory
pərˈfəNGktərē

suppress
səˈpres

arcane
ärˈkān

conceal
kənˈsēl

A SORT OF DEPRESSING FAIRY TALE

Once upon a time in the town of Ishtar, there lived a poor boy named Yannick. One day, while playing hide and seek with his pet monkey, Yannick discovered a crack in the wall that **concealed** a hidden treasure map. As Yannick began to read the map, he noticed that its language and symbols were so **arcane** that only his linguistics professor could interpret it, and even then the professor only did so in a **perfunctory** manner. Yannick could hardly **suppress** his anger at the professor's hasty interpretation, and worried that others saw his attempt to find a lost treasure with a nearly indecipherable map as **frivolous**. In the end, sadly, Yannick got no treasure and threw away the useless map.

Definitions: Try matching the words in the list with the appropriate definitions. If you are stuck, check the glossary in the back of the book or the passage at the top of the page.

1. frivolous _____ a. understood by few; mysterious; secret
2. perfunctory _____ b. to hide or cover up something
3. suppress _____ c. done with minimum effort or reflection
4. arcane _____ d. to forcibly put an end to, inhibit, or quell
5. conceal _____ e. wasteful, not having serious purpose or value

Sentences: Try to use the words above in a sentence below. Remember that a word ending may be changed or its figure of speech slightly altered.

6. Thomas knew everything about the Battle of Tours in 732 A.D; his command of such _____ and uncommon knowledge was truly impressive.
7. In many Islamic countries, women often _____ their entire bodies by wrapping them in clothing.
8. Tony wrote his paper so _____ that its arguments made no sense and it was filled with grammatical flaws.
9. It would be _____ to bet and lose all of your life savings in one day on poker games.
10. In order to _____ criticisms of his draconian rule, the tyrant executed his political opponents.

Lesson 24

PLEASING MR. SACHS

Last week my sister found an **interloper** snooping through her papers at work. She was particularly angry because her desk drawer contains notes with **fertile** ideas about how to start her own business. Upon seeing the stranger rummaging through her writings, she began to scream so incessantly that nobody at work could **mollify** her. Eventually she calmed down and tried to speak **diplomatically** to the intruder so as to not offend the man. But the man dismissed her tactful words as mere **platitudes** before he left the office. Luckily everything turned out okay in the end for all parties.

NEW WORDS

diplomatic
ˌdipləˈmatik

fertile
ˈfərtl

interloper
ˈintərˌlōpər, ˌintərˈlōpər

mollify
ˈmäləˌfī

platitude
ˈplatiˌt(y)ood

Definitions: Try matching the words in the list with the appropriate definitions. If you are stuck, check the glossary in the back of the book or the passage at the top of the page.

1. diplomatic _____ a. an intruder or eavesdropper
2. fertile _____ b. to appease the anger or anxiety of someone
3. interloper _____ c. an overused remark that has lost meaning
4. mollify _____ d. having or showing the ability to deal with people in a sensitive way
5. platitude _____ e. capable of producing things, ideas, or offspring in an abundant way

Sentences: Try to use the words above in a sentence below. Remember that a word ending may be changed or its figure of speech slightly altered.

6. Fiona's mother could do nothing to _____ her after her older sister stole all of her money to go shopping.

7. Last week a(n) _____ snuck into my neighbor's home and stole a laptop; luckily the police apprehended him immediately.

8. Stuart is a master at being _____: he can criticize people easily without ever offending them in the least.

9. Most graduation speeches are filled with _____: each year a speaker says the same thing about students being tomorrow's future. Such comments no longer have import with the freshly minted graduates.

10. Universities are _____ places for developing and testing new ideas.

Lesson 25

AUNT MARY IS GROWING OLD

NEW WORDS

regressive
ri′gresiv

strident
′strīdnt

unstinting
ˌən′stintiNG

quarantine
′kwôrən̩tēn

harbinger
′härbənjər

For the past few years, I have watched my Aunt Mary decline mentally. Perhaps the first **harbingers** to the problem were when she no longer could recall where she left household items or what the names of her pets were. In time, she mentally grew more **regressive**, forgetting even basic things like her children's names, how to drive her car, and her home address. **Unstinting** family intervention has been the only way in which we can make sure that Aunt Mart will be okay. But to become involved, we have to speak **stridently** to her about what she needs to remember; even then, there is no surety that she will listen. Sadly, if Aunt Mary continues to deteriorate, she may need to be **quarantined** in a special facility for rehabilitation.

Definitions: Try matching the words in the list with the appropriate definitions. If you are stuck, check the glossary in the back of the book or the passage at the top of the page.

1. regressive _____ a. becoming less advanced; returning to a former state
2. strident _____ b. to isolate or seal off
3. unstinting _____ c. a sign that symbolizes or announces the approach or arrival of something
4. quarantine _____ d. given without restraint; unsparing
5. harbinger _____ e. loud and harsh; grating

Sentences: Try to use the words above in a sentence below. Remember that a word ending may be changed or its figure of speech slightly altered.

6. Oriana's singing was so _____ that all of the windows in her house broke as she belted out her tunes.
7. Because of its _____ commitment to gender equality, Main Street Company has always paid men and women equal wages for jobs.
8. Because Mona had a viral disease that was potent and lethal, she was _____ in a room for a week.
9. Sean, who was 35 years old, suddenly began acting like he was 12; his friends were appalled by his _____ manners.
10. In many seafaring cultures, a red-colored sky at night is a(n) _____ for a delight at sea the next day.

Lesson 26

FOOD CRITIC

Kevin is known to be one of the most preeminent food **connoisseurs** in the United States. Each week, he writes a **robust** article in the local newspaper about the best food he ate all week. Part of his fame is garnered from the **cynical** tone of his writing, which is anything but **diffident**. Many of his fans have formed **conjectures** that, because of his wit and candor, Kevin is the most impressive food critic they have ever met.

NEW WORDS

cynical
ˈsinikəl

connoisseur
ˌkänəˈsər, -ˈsoor

diffident
ˈdifidənt

conjecture
kənˈjekCHər

robust
rōˈbəst, ˈrōˌbəst

Definitions: Try matching the words in the list with the appropriate definitions. If you are stuck, check the glossary in the back of the book or the passage at the top of the page.

1. cynical _____ a. an expert at something (usually the arts or cuisine)
2. connoisseur _____ b. (n.) 1. an opinion or conclusion based on incomplete information; 2. an unproven math theorem; (v.) to form an opinion about something based on incomplete information
3. diffident _____ c. believing that humans are motivated only by self-interest; distrusting of human sincerity
4. conjecture _____ d. strong and healthy; flourishing
5. robust _____ e. shy because of a lack of self-confidence

Sentences: Try to use the words above in a sentence below. Remember that a word ending may be changed or its figure of speech slightly altered.

6. Samuel _____ that there are indeed an infinite number of prime numbers that differ by two.
7. The _____ girl lacked the courage to tell her aunt that she was cruel.
8. Barry is a remarkable food _____: each week he eloquently critiques a local restaurant in the city newspaper.
9. Sherry's friends chided her for being too _____: they asserted that she felt that they cared only about themselves and not others in the world.
10. The tree outside looks _____; its leaves are green and it is flourishing.

NEW WORDS

docile
ˈdäsəl

inscrutable
inˈskro͞otəbəl

steadfast
ˈstedˌfast

benevolent
bəˈnevələnt

detached
diˈtaCHt

Lesson 27

THE IDEAL BOYFRIEND?

Many girls insist that the perfect boyfriend for them must be **steadfast** and kind. Rather than throwing fits, he should discuss his opinions respectfully without being too **docile** or too much of a pushover. With a little luck, he will be articulate enough so as to not make his actions **inscrutable**. Generally, this type of demeanor is indicative of a **benevolent** soul who cares enough about society to be engaged, but who also is not too **detached** from life around him. This, in the eyes of some girls, is an ideal boyfriend.

Definitions: Try matching the words in the list with the appropriate definitions. If you are stuck, check the glossary in the back of the book or the passage at the top of the page.

1. docile _____ a. committed and unswerving
2. inscrutable _____ b. ready to accept instruction; submissive
3. steadfast _____ c. impossible to understand or interpret
4. benevolent _____ d. emotionally unengaged; without passion
5. detached _____ e. kind and caring; well-intentioned

Sentences: Try to use the words above in a sentence below. Remember that a word ending may be changed or its figure of speech slightly altered.

6. Many authoritarian rulers like a(n) _____ audience because they are submissive and easy to manipulate.
7. When judging a debate it is best to remain emotionally _____ and to not let personal bias stand in the way of one's judgments.
8. My uncle is a(n) _____ person who always takes me to baseball games and often treats me to dinner at my favorite restaurant.
9. Fred was _____ in his commitment to serve at the local soup kitchen: for an entire year he showed up every Tuesday night to serve the homeless.
10. Most people find my doctor's handwriting to be so _____ that they cannot even read his prescriptions.

Lesson 28

DIGITAL MUSIC CREATOR

Jonas was a **pioneer** in the field of digital music. Together with three workers, he was able to **synthesize** different types of music on a computer program. His goal was to make different, inconsonant musical genres **concord** with each other with the help of his digital **artifice**. Luckily, his attempts in creating a computer program were not **futile**; Jonas has made millions of dollars from the results of his success.

NEW WORDS

futile
ˈfyoŏtl, -ˌtīl

pioneer
ˌpīəˈnir

synthesize
ˈsinTHiˌsīz

artifice
ˈärtəfis

concord
ˈkäNGˌkôrd, ˈkän-

Definitions: Try matching the words in the list with the appropriate definitions. If you are stuck, check the glossary in the back of the book or the passage at the top of the page.

1. futile   _____   a. something designed to trick or deceive
2. pioneer   _____   b. agreement or harmony between people or groups
3. synthesize   _____   c. hopeless; fruitless
4. artifice   _____   d. (n.) 1. a person who is among the first to settle a new area; 2. a person who is among the first to research or develop a new field; (v.) to be among the first to develop or apply (a new method, technology, or activity)
5. concord   _____   e. to combine something into a coherent whole

Sentences: Try to use the words above in a sentence below. Remember that a word ending may be changed or its figure of speech slightly altered.

6. Most magicians are masters of _____: they are excellent at deceiving their audience through creating shrewd illusions.
7. The purpose of an integrated math curriculum is to _____ different branches of mathematics together in a single course.
8. Bill Gates was a(n) _____ in computer science: he was one of the first and most influential people to develop the field.
9. It would be _____ to expect to win the lottery three times in a row; nobody has ever accomplished such a feat.
10. Trying to make my results _____ with those of my professor seems difficult; our data is simply too incongruous to match up.

Lesson 29

NEW WORDS

(1) discreet; (2) discrete
disˈkrēt

finesse
fəˈnes

intrepid
inˈtrepid

momentous
mōˈmen(t)əs, mə-

poignant
ˈpoinyənt

WHY SUSIE BROKE UP

Though she has **poignant** memories of their time together, Susie broke up with her boyfriend Mark last week. In a **momentous** moment, she saw him kiss another girl in public without being the least bit **discreet** about his behavior. She felt sad and hurt, but was **intrepid** enough to confront him on the spot. She told him that he had to make a choice between two **discrete** options: he either could end their relationship immediately, or tell the new girl to go away forever. With little **finesse**, Mark immediately walked away from both women never to be seen or heard from again.

Definitions: Try matching the word in the box with the appropriate definition. If you are stuck, check the glossary in the back of the book or the passage at the top of the page.

1.	discreet _____	a.	fearless
2.	discrete _____	b.	of great or extreme importance; pivotal
3.	finesse _____	c.	evoking a sense of sadness or regret
4.	intrepid _____	d.	divided into separate, countable parts
5.	momentous _____	e.	done with subtlety or tact
6.	poignant _____	f.	(n.) refined or intricate delicacy; (v.) to do something in a subtle or delicate manner

Sentences: Try to use the words above in a sentence below. Remember that a word ending may be changed or its figure of speech slightly altered.

7. The day that astronauts from the America landed on the moon is considered by many to be a(n) _____ day in the history of space exploration.

8. The _____ hiker dared to scale the mountain even though he was advised not to do so alone.

9. Unlike with water, it is possible to cut a cake into many _____ pieces.

10. With much _____, Clara criticized her opponents without offending them.

11. Marcus was not _____ about his actions and was caught red handed on camera stealing money from the local bakery.

12. Many adults have _____ memories of their college days: they wish they could return back to school but they have family and career commitments to meet.

Lesson 30

A GOOD DISCIPLE

Many mentors enjoy taking on talented **protégés** during their career. Most would admit that the best qualities of such disciples are that they have an **unswerving** commitment to working long hours. Such dedication should be **reinforced** through producing measureable or discernable results. Under these conditions, chances of success are not **fortuitous**; rather, they are the result of sustained hard work. In sum, there is no **succinct** or easy way to achieve success.

NEW WORDS

reinforce
ˌrē-inˈfôrs

succinct
sə(k)ˈsiNG(k)t

unswerving
ˌənˈswərviNG

protégé
ˈprōtəˌZHā, ˌprōtəˈZHā

fortuitous
fôrˈtooətəs

Definitions: Try matching the words in the list with the appropriate definitions. If you are stuck, check the glossary in the back of the book or the passage at the top of the page.

1. reinforce _____ a. steadfast; completely committed
2. succinct _____ b. a sign of something good to come; good omen
3. unswerving _____ c. a disciple who is generally gifted
4. protégé _____ d. to strengthen or supplement something
5. fortuitous _____ e. brief and to the point

Sentences: Try to use the words above in a sentence below. Remember that a word ending may be changed or its figure of speech slightly altered.

6. Abra was _____ in her commitment to lose weight: nobody could stand in the way of her goal to become fit.

7. Unlike my old boss, who rambled on for hours during meetings, my new boss is very _____.

8. How _____ it was that Chicago, which is usually frozen and snowy when I visit in January, happened to be mild and sunny!

9. Teachers often assign homework to _____ lessons taught in class each day.

10. Every great teacher should have at least one _____ in his or her career; someone needs to follow in his or her footsteps.

47

Crossword Puzzle
Lessons 21-30

ACROSS

4 to hide or cover up something
10 calm and peaceful; soothing
11 not compatible; does not fit together
12 loud and harsh; grating
14 to strengthen or supplement something
16 capable of producing things, ideas, or offspring in an abundant way
17 (n.) 1. an opinion or conclusion based on incomplete information; 2. an unproven math theorem; (v.) to form an opinion about something based on incomplete information
18 committed and unswerving
19 not readily revealing thoughts, sparing of words

DOWN

1 given without restraint; unsparing
2 a sign of something good to come; good omen
3 evoking a sense of sadness or regret
5 agreement or harmony between people or groups
6 an overused remark that has lost meaning
7 strong and healthy; flourishing
8 emotionally unengaged; without passion
9 done with minimum effort or reflection
12 to combine something into a coherent whole
13 of great or extreme importance; pivotal
15 to express public disapproval of; censure

Vocabulary Review
Lessons 21-30

Directions: Match each word with its best approximate definition. Note that definitions are not necessarily repeated verbatim from the lesson exercises.

1.	conventional	_____	a.	kind and well-meaning
2.	rhetoric	_____	b.	based on accordance with norms or what is normally done or believed
3.	dismay	_____	c.	understood by few, mysterious
4.	belligerent	_____	d.	submissive; ready to accept control or instruction
5.	frivolous	_____	e.	to isolate, usually after having received an infectious disease
6.	arcane	_____	f.	intruder
7.	diplomatic	_____	g.	incapable of producing any useful result; hopeless
8.	interloper	_____	h.	a person who is among the first to explore a new area, either geographically or intellectually
9.	quarantine	_____	i.	the art of persuasive speaking or writing
10.	harbinger	_____	j.	a person who is guided and supported by an older, more experienced person
11.	connoisseur	_____	k.	brief and to the point
12.	diffident	_____	l.	fearless, adventurous
13.	docile	_____	m.	hostile and aggressive
14.	benevolent	_____	n.	individually separate and distinct
15.	futile	_____	o.	modest or shy because of lack of self-confidence
16.	pioneer	_____	p.	dealing with people in a sensitive, tactful, and effective way
17.	discrete	_____	q.	a person or thing that announces the signal or approach of another
18.	intrepid	_____	r.	an expert judge in matters of taste
19.	succinct	_____	s.	disappointment; causing distress or consternation
20.	protégé	_____	t.	lacking serious purpose or value

Word Roots: Unit 3

ROOTS AND THEIR MEANINGS

phil:	love of	**intra:**	within, inside
pot:	power, ability	**culp:**	blame
omni:	all, every	**anthr/andr:**	man, mankind

Here are a few examples of some words that use the above roots:

philosophy: the study of the nature of knowledge, reality, or existence
potent: having great power, influence, or effect
intramural: situated or taking place within the walls of a building or within a single educational institution or community
omniscient: knowing everything
culprit: a person who is responsible for a crime
anthropology: the study of humankind, its existence, its evolution, and its development

Now try to fill in the table below by finding the appropriate root(s) and interpreting the meaning of each word:

Word	Root(s)	Guessed Meaning	Actual Meaning
philanthropy			
omnipotent			
philology			
culpable			
anthropomorphic			
excrete			
android			
intravenous			
exculpate			
potentate			

Lesson 31

A SKEPTIC

Ms. K is a **skeptical** manager when it comes to the efficiency of individual effort. She **deliberately** arranges for frequent group meetings so that everyone in her team can discuss new ideas, provide constructive feedback and then reach a **consensus**. She draws on experiences from her previous managing position where she had many employees proposing **eccentric** ideas with **dubious** validity and none knew what their teammates were up to.

NEW WORDS

deliberate
di'libərit (noun); -ˌrāt (verb)

dubious
'd(y)oobēəs

eccentric
ik'sentrik

consensus
kən'sensəs

skeptical
'skeptikəl

Definitions: Try matching the words in the list with the appropriate definitions. If you are stuck, check the glossary in the back of the book or the passage at the top of the page.

1. deliberate _____ a. (describing a person and his or her behavior) unconventional, bizarre
2. dubious _____ b. a general agreement
3. eccentric _____ c. not easily convinced; showing distrust
4. consensus _____ d. done with careful planning and intention
5. skeptical _____ e. causing doubt

Sentences: Try to use the words above in a sentence below. Remember that a word ending may be changed or its figure of speech slightly altered.

6. The promise is quite _____- it sounds too good to be true.
7. The juxtaposition of many random objects in the painting is a(n) _____ arrangement to create a sense of dissonance.
8. The manager believes that her team would grow and unite through active participation in reaching a(n) _____, so as a leader she usually avoids making authoritative decisions.
9. Although he was trying his best to be agreeable to the group's proposal, one could read from his eyes that he was rather _____.
10. The _____ personality and creativity of the British designer Alexander McQueen was often reflected in his outlandish fashion designs.

Lesson 32

UNHAPPY MOTHER

NEW WORDS

duplicitous
d(y)oo'plisitəs

laud
lôd

supplant
sə'plant

brood
brood

didactic
dī'daktik

My difficult childhood has taught me the values of hard work, compassion and faith. When I tell my children about my past, I try to avoid being **didactic** and not make my lessons explicit. My life now is no longer difficult- it is different in a way that makes me feel uneasy. Although I often **laud** my children for their great career success and say I enjoy the material goods they provide, I am hiding from them the fact that I frequently **brood** over my past austere life which is now **supplanted** with only superficial wealth. I feel **duplicitous** and downright false.

Definitions: Try matching the words in the list with the appropriate definitions. If you are stuck, check the glossary in the back of the book or the passage at the top of the page.

1. duplicitous _____ a. to praise highly
2. laud _____ b. to supersede and replace
3. supplant _____ c. instructive, usually involving a moral lesson or ulterior motive
4. brood _____ d. double-dealing, deceptive
5. didactic _____ e. to think deeply about something, often something that makes one unhappy

Sentences: Try to use the words above in a sentence below. Remember that a word ending may be changed or its figure of speech slightly altered.

6. The outdated business model has been _____ by a more innovative and effective one.
7. Jane finds it difficult to find an honest friend because there are many _____ people around her.
8. A fast learner, Jay was _____ by the coach for having mastered the new routine quickly.
9. I prefer teachers who incorporate interactive exercises so as to limit their _____ lecturing.
10. Ray should stop _____ over his misfortunes and start looking out for new opportunities in life.

Lesson 33

MR. LIM

Mr. Lim is an extremely strict disciplinary master. All students are scared of him because he does not **condone** any act that violates school rules. Although it is **hackneyed** to say that a book should not be judged by its cover, the connection between Mr. Lim's **placid** expression when dealing with students and his personality is **tenuous**. He is indeed warm-hearted and has a strong **aspiration** to help his students build good characters.

NEW WORDS

hackneyed
ˈhaknēd

placid
ˈplasid

tenuous
ˈtenyoōəs

aspiration
ˌaspəˈrāSHən

condone
kənˈdōn

Definitions: Try matching the words in the list with the appropriate definitions. If you are stuck, check the glossary in the back of the book or the passage at the top of the page.

1. hackneyed _____ a. a great desire to achieve something
2. placid _____ b. trite because of having been overused; dull
3. tenuous _____ c. (of a person or animal) not easily upset or excited; calm, even-tempered
4. aspiration _____ d. to overlook, allow or forgive something
5. condone _____ e. unsubstantiated, weak and shaky; slim, fine

Sentences: Try to use the words above in a sentence below. Remember that a word ending may be changed or its figure of speech slightly altered.

6. An's _____ is to contribute his talents to the development of his country.
7. Tom generally writes good stories, but he tends to use _____ terms excessively, which make some paragraphs appear trite and dull.
8. After many years of thrilling adventures across the globe, he finally wishes to settle down for a more _____ life.
9. Acts of violence of any sort will not be _____.
10. He may sound persuasive in speech, but his arguments are _____ and unconvincing.

Lesson 34

NEW WORDS

disseminate
di'semə,nāt

flagging
flagiNG

ironic
ī'ränik

myopic
mī'äpik

precocious
pri'kōSHəs

UNDESIRABLE INCIDENT

Information on corrective measures should be **disseminated** across the company immediately in order to curb the employers' **flagging** enthusiasm about recent policies imposed by the board of management. It is **ironic** that such a youthful group of capable and **precocious** managers who allegedly possess corporate and interpersonal insights would make such **myopic** decisions in their new policies.

Definitions: Try matching the words in the list with the appropriate definitions. If you are stuck, check the glossary in the back of the book or the passage at the top of the page.

1.	disseminate	_____	a.	nearsighted, lacking intellectual insight
2.	flagging	_____	b.	to circulate, broadcast, spread widely
3.	ironic	_____	c.	to decrease in intensity, to weaken
4.	myopic	_____	d.	mature early in mental aptitude
5.	precocious	_____	e.	happening the opposite way to what is expected

Sentences: Try to use the words above in a sentence below. Remember that a word ending may be changed or its figure of speech slightly altered.

6. Essential documents will be _____ to all board members before the general meeting.

7. During the Ebola breakout, many people were so _____ attentive that they overlooked checking for other infectious diseases.

8. Lim's enthusiasm about developing new software was _____ after several failed attempts.

9. Einstein syndrome is a term coined for children with delayed speech but who may possess other extraordinary abilities such as _____ analytical thinking or memory.

10. It is _____ that famed artist Vincent van Gogh (1853-90) could only sell one painting during his lifetime but his artwork is now purchased at exorbitantly high prices.

Lesson 35

INDELIBLE MEMORIES

I can tell from the **sullen** look on Dad's face that he is again disturbed by his bitter memories. Dad had a **primitive** urge to help groups of less fortunate people and to establish his role within these groups. But there were individuals who made **vacuous** promises and took advantage of his trust and love. I have often consoled Dad by **reiterating** that there are still good eggs out there, but he was deeply hurt, in a way that I cannot **fathom**.

NEW WORDS

reiterate
rēˈitəˌrāt

sullen
ˈsələn

vacuous
ˈvakyəwəs

primitive
ˈprimətiv

fathom
ˈfaTHəm

Definitions: Try matching the words in the list with the appropriate definitions. If you are stuck, check the glossary in the back of the book or the passage at the top of the page.

1. reiterate _____ a. (n.) a unit of length equal to six feet, usually to measure depth; (v.) to figure out, comprehend
2. sullen _____ b. archaic, ancient, original and often crude
3. vacuous _____ c. to restate or redo something in order to emphasize
4. primitive _____ d. empty, devoid of substance
5. fathom _____ e. gloomy, moody, brooding

Sentences: Try to use the words above in a sentence below. Remember that a word ending may be changed or its figure of speech slightly altered.

6. Because my aunt is hard of hearing, I often have to _____ what I am saying until she comprehends my words.
7. A woman's mind is not easily _____; one cannot tell from her words what she really thinks.
8. To a morose man, even the brilliant blue sky appears _____.
9. Knowing of Quang's limited education, his friends usually forgive his _____ statements that are unsubstantiated by logical or scientific evidence.
10. The sculpture is still in a(n) _____ state; it needs refinement and development before a public showcase.

NEW WORDS

disparage
di'sparij

inevitable
in'evitəbəl

enigma
i'nigmə

dearth
dərTH

superfluous
soo'pərfləwəs

Lesson 36

WHY DO WE HAVE MASS?

Although Professor Peter Higgs successfully theorized the existence of Higgs particles to explain the origin of mass in the 1960s, Higgs particles still remained as an **enigma** and could not be experimentally confirmed due to a **dearth** of technological devices at that time. However, Professor Higgs and the scientists at CERN were not **disparaged**. After many years of countless experiments, Higgs particles were finally detected in 2012. **Inevitably**, Professor Higgs and his discovery which won the Nobel prize in Physics have garnered **superfluous** attention world-wide since.

Definitions: Try matching the words in the list with the appropriate definitions. If you are stuck, check the glossary in the back of the book or the passage at the top of the page.

1.	disparage	_____	a.	a mystery, a puzzling situation
2.	inevitable	_____	b.	to belittle, hurt the reputation of
3.	enigma	_____	c.	excessive and unnecessary
4.	dearth	_____	d.	unavoidable
5.	superfluous	_____	e.	a deficiency, a scarcity, a lack of

Sentences: Try to use the words above in a sentence below. Remember that a word ending may be changed or its figure of speech slightly altered.

6. If people pursue their goals with passion and determination, success is almost _____.

7. Don't be _____ by harsh competitions; perceive them as opportunities to help you become more resilient.

8. The term "intellectually disabled" used to be a(n) _____ to me; I could only understand the concept better after I had interacted with some patients at a voluntary welfare organization.

9. The message of the book would come off stronger if _____ passages were cut out.

10. There is a(n) _____ of reliable scientific evidence that consumption of certain foods can reduce cancer risks.

Lesson 37

WRITING CONCISELY IS NOT EASY

In John's essay about today's global economic shift, he presented an **eclectic** mix of viewpoints and thoughts which made his arguments appear fragmented and barely **lucid**. In some paragraphs, he argued favorably for the growing power of the East, but **cajoled** the readers into believing that the Western economies would not be overtaken in other paragraphs. After John's mother had proofread his essay, she was **vexed** by its ambiguity and thought it would be **disingenuous** of her to praise her son's work.

NEW WORDS

eclectic
iˈklektik

lucid
ˈloosid

vex
veks

cajole
kəˈjōl

disingenuous
ˌdisinˈjenyooəs

Definitions: Try matching the words in the list with the appropriate definitions. If you are stuck, check the glossary in the back of the book or the passage at the top of the page.

1. eclectic _____ a. clear, easy to understand
2. lucid _____ b. comprising of elements from diverse sources
3. vex _____ c. insincere, dishonest
4. cajole _____ d. to bother, frustrate, irritate
5. disingenuous _____ e. to coax, persuade someone to do something through flattery and pleasing words

Sentences: Try to use the words above in a sentence below. Remember that a word ending may be changed or its figure of speech slightly altered.

6. Trung has a(n) _____ taste for music: he listens to various genres such as classical, hard rock and country music.

7. Young girls should not let themselves be _____ by the mass media into being thin to feel that they are beautiful.

8. Respectable magazines like *The New Yorker* keep high journalism standards – a(n) _____ comprehension of English is essential for contributions.

9. Curating an art exhibition is difficult; the curator can get _____ by numerous minor details.

10. Daisy is a nice girl, but the fact that she keeps praising everyone she meets can make her appear a little _____.

Lesson 38

NEW WORDS

infatuated
in'faCHoo͟͞,āt

prodigy
'prädəjē

verbose
vər'bōs

augment
ôg'ment

contemptible
kən'tem(p)təbəl

PRESS ON, LINH!

Linh has been deeply **infatuated** with the languages ever since she was a child, and she aspires to become a writer and a linguist. Her friends do not believe that Linh will ever achieve her goals and some have even remarked that Linh is only a mediocre student whose writings are **verbose** and ineloquent. Linh finds those comments unhelpful and **contemptible** but she is not easily discouraged. Linh believes that even a **prodigy** needs to **augment** his or her skills and talent through consistent practice so she has been working with great determination to achieve her goals.

Definitions: Try matching the words in the list with the appropriate definitions. If you are stuck, check the glossary in the back of the book or the passage at the top of the page.

1.	infatuated	_____	a.	lengthy, using words excessively
2.	prodigy	_____	b.	to be motivated by a short-lived but intense fascination for someone or something
3.	verbose	_____	c.	deserving of scorn
4.	augment	_____	d.	a young person with exceptional talents, a child genius
5.	contemptible	_____	e.	to increase, add to something so that it becomes greater

Sentences: Try to use the words above in a sentence below. Remember that a word ending may be changed or its figure of speech slightly altered.

6. Maya has been unusually _____ with plays and movies ever since she was a little girl; she is now a talented actress.

7. Desiring wealth is by no means _____; violating laws and morality to obtain wealth, however, is.

8. José Martí was multilingual at a young age; people called him a child _____.

9. For writers of any level, being concise is always harder than being _____.

10. The second child may experience _____ pressure from his family and relatives to prove his capabilities, especially when his older brother or sister has achieved great success.

Lesson 39

IS IT TRUSTWORTHY?

Dietary supplements nowadays are so widely promoted in **flamboyant** advertisements that our minds are **predisposed** to believe in the benefits, however **nuanced**, of those extra pills. There is yet any reliable evidence either to **downplay** or to buttress the roles of the dietary supplements. But surely, even a **judicious** use of those pills cannot fix the effects of poor eating habits and an unhealthy lifestyle.

> **NEW WORDS**
>
> **downplay**
> ˈdounˌplā
>
> **flamboyant**
> flamˈboiənt
>
> **judicious**
> jooˈdiSHəs
>
> **nuance**
> ˈn(y)ooˌäns
>
> **predispose**
> ˌprēdiˈspōz

Definitions: Try matching the words in the list with the appropriate definitions. If you are stuck, check the glossary in the back of the book or the passage at the top of the page.

1. downplay _____   a.   showy and vivacious, extravagant
2. flamboyant _____   b.   done with caution and good judgment
3. judicious _____   c.   (n.) a subtle difference in meaning, shade, sound, or expression; (v.) to give subtle differences in meaning, shade, sound, or expression to something
4. nuance _____   d.   to make someone susceptible or liable to a specific attitude, action, or condition
5. predispose _____   e.   to make something seem less important than it actually is

Sentences: Try to use the words above in a sentence below. Remember that a word ending may be changed or its figure of speech slightly altered.

6. The church of San Zenone in North Italy demonstrates the beauty of Romanesque architecture – its simple interior is unblemished by anything _____.
7. By emphasizing much on the artwork's cultural context, are we risking _____ its inherent beauty and its sheer visual qualities?
8. Arthur is a composed and _____ man; he carefully considers all information before making a decision.
9. Professionals can help people _____ to eating disorders restructure their eating habits and build a healthier relationship with food.
10. The _____ in shade between Vermillion paint and Orange paint can be difficult to tell for people who are not painters.

Lesson 40

UNETHICAL BUSINESS

NEW WORDS

reprehensible
ˌrepriˈhensəbəl

surreptitious
ˌsərəpˈtiSHəs

vapid
ˈvapid

perplexed
pərˈplekst

extrapolate
ikˈstrapəˌlāt

The investigators have been **surreptitiously** collecting waste samples that company ABC has dumped into the environment. From those small samples, they have **extrapolated** a larger conclusion that the company has heavily polluted sources of drinking water. The residents living around the area were **perplexed** not only by the **reprehensible** acts of the company but also by its **vapid** responses when the public requested corrective measures to clean up the pollution.

Definitions: Try matching the words in the list with the appropriate definitions. If you are stuck, check the glossary in the back of the book or the passage at the top of the page.

1.	reprehensible	_____	a.	dull, lifeless, uninteresting
2.	surreptitious	_____	b.	deserving criticism, blameworthy
3.	vapid	_____	c.	to estimate a possibility beyond the existing values/situation with the assumption that the current trend will continue
4.	perplexed	_____	d.	secretive, furtive, underhanded
5.	extrapolate	_____	e.	greatly puzzled, bewildered

Sentences: Try to use the words above in a sentence below. Remember that a word ending may be changed or its figure of speech slightly altered.

6. It is _____ that many businesses only care about piling up money and disregard the safety and long-term health of customers.

7. Jane's _____ personal statement fails to reflect her true personality, as she is a bright, enthusiastic and bubbly girl.

8. Wong made a(n) _____ arrival at his hometown to avoid being recognized by his acquaintances.

9. The statistical data of Singapore's birth rates over the past five years are used to _____ a possible population value for the coming months.

10. For a moment, Tom was _____ by his parents' revelation: they adopted him after his biological mother had left him.

Word Search
Lessons 31-40

```
V V T D R Z C D Y N K M B T W B V M K M
D Q Q N R J G I R M L R N E N R T N W M
T X N D R K Q P T D D T T N M O L G B M
L Z B Q V D Y R T C W J M U T Q R R N D
J K R L D T J L L X E N E O Q D G L F M
Q Q J G T Z R R T N J L D U N P K A X P
D E T A U T A F N I B I C S D P T D R G
T R S M X W Q J Z A S N M E R H P E N X
Y N U P E L B I T P M E T N O C D P N N
Z Q R Q N J M I A M T P P M M I R P P G
J L R L R V V R R N I M D T S E D E W Q
D Q E D Y E A Z A S P R T P C L R R D D
N Y P D N G I L V M U X O O M P U O Z M
Q D T I E Z P T D T D S C N L P W C Q J
V L I J W P R Y E U E I N E I N V D I P
R R T N U W M Q B R O T X E P C Z N L D
N N I S B Q D I B U A E D L S J V A P K
T V O T T R O N S M D T A P N N C T D Y
Y Q U R Y U R B T Z L Y E B L I O G G T
Y B S K S X D L Q W M B B L D P Z C D J
```

1 causing doubt
2 a general agreement
3 to supersede and replace
4 to think deeply about something, often something that makes one unhappy
5 not easily disturbed, calm, even-tempered
6 unsubstantiated, weak and shaky; slim, fine
7 happening the opposite way to what is expected
8 mature early in mental aptitude
9 to restate or redo something in order to emphasize
10 (n.) a unit of length equal to six feet, usually to measure depth; (v.) to figure out, comprehend
11 to belittle, hurt the reputation of
12 unavoidable
13 comprising of elements from diverse sources
14 clear, easy to understand
15 to be motivated by a short-lived but intense fascination for someone or something
16 deserving of scorn
17 to make something seem less important than it actually is
18 to make someone susceptible or liable to a specific attitude, action, or condition
19 secretive, furtive, underhanded
20 greatly puzzled, bewildered

Vocabulary Review
Lessons 31-40

Directions: Match each word with its best approximate definition. Note that definitions are not necessarily repeated verbatim from the lesson exercises.

1. eccentric _____
2. skeptical _____
3. laud _____
4. didactic _____
5. hackneyed _____
6. aspiration _____
7. flag _____
8. myopic _____
9. sullen _____
10. vacuous _____
11. enigma _____
12. dearth _____
13. vex _____
14. disingenuous _____
15. prodigy _____
16. augment _____
17. flamboyant _____
18. nuance _____
19. reprehensible _____
20. vapid _____

a. a dream or hope
b. to expand or increase in size or value
c. unconventional, strange
d. a subtle difference (often in shade, expression, or sound)
e. to annoy
f. not genuine or sincere
g. mystery
h. showy; attracting attention by stylishness or exuberance
i. to praise; extol
j. flat; dull; boring
k. lacking significance through being overused
l. nearsighted; focused narrowly on something
m. not easily convinced; doubting
n. empty, lacking thought or intelligence
o. worthy of censure or punishment
p. sad; dejected
q. a child genius
r. a lack of something; not abundant
s. teaching through repeated instruction
t. lacking energy; torpid

Word Roots: Unit 4

ROOTS AND THEIR MEANINGS

super:	over, beyond	**post:**	after
terr:	earth	**bel(l):**	war
amb:	walk	**trans:**	across
mis/mit:	to send	**fid:**	trust, faith

Here are a few examples of some words that use the above roots:

<u>super</u>hero: a fictional icon who does good deeds and who possesses powers greater than what humans are capable of possessing

<u>terra</u>centric: a model or system of the universe in which the Earth is at the center rather than the sun.

<u>amb</u>le: to walk in a casual, relaxed, slow pace

<u>post</u>date: to assign a later date than the actual one to a document or event

<u>bell</u>icose: exhibiting aggression and willingness to fight

<u>trans</u>cend: to go beyond the range or limits of something

re<u>mit</u>: to send money in payment as form of a gift (one of many definitions of remit)

<u>fid</u>elity: faithfulness to a person, belief, or cause by showing signs of support and/or loyalty

Now try to fill in the table below by finding the appropriate root(s) and interpreting the meaning of each word:

Word	Root(s)	Guessed Meaning	Actual Meaning
intermittent			
amble			
transnational			
belligerent			
fiduciary			

transmit			
subterranean			
posterior			
rebellion			
supercede			
terrain			
superconductor			
infidelity			
terrarium			
ambulatory			
missive			
transit			

Lesson 41

REFLECTIONS BY A PHYSICS LOVER

Many people consider concepts like time dilation and length contractions to be **abstruse** concepts. But because I am **partisan** toward modern physics, the concepts are quite engrossing. Learning about relativity-related concepts such as these never makes me **melancholy**; in fact, I often wonder why people have **disdain** for those who like to share their passion for theoretical physics with others. I try to be polite to them, but often am subjected to their **flippant** remarks about how I am too focused on strange concepts to have a sense of what is important in the world. I could not disagree more.

NEW WORDS

partisan
ˈpärtəzən

melancholy
ˈmelənˌkälē

flippant
ˈflipənt

disdain
disˈdān

abstruse
abˈstroos

Definitions: Try matching the words in the list with the appropriate definitions. If you are stuck, check the glossary in the back of the book or the passage at the top of the page.

1. partisan _____   a. very sad, gloomy, sorrowful
2. melancholy _____   b. supporting one side, biased
3. flippant _____   c. understood by only a few, esoteric
4. disdain _____   d. not demonstrating a serious or respectful attitude
5. abstruse _____   e. contempt, scorn

Sentences: Try to use the words above in a sentence below. Remember that a word ending may be changed or its figure of speech slightly altered.

6. Mr. Boh is a(n) _____ art collector; his home gallery only displays artwork by Andy Warhol.

7. The _____ remarks of Dale's best friend insulted him immensely.

8. Everyone knows that Valerie loves her cat, Brownie, very much and that she has been very _____ since Brownie died last month.

9. To prepare for the next class discussion, the teacher has required the students to read a few science articles which are too _____ for high school level.

10. Tom cannot hide his _____ for people who use money as an easy way to get whatever they want.

Lesson 42

FALLING APART

NEW WORDS

egotism
ˈēgəˌtizəm

mendacity
menˈdasitē

vindicate
ˈvindəˌkāt

censure
ˈsenSHər

divisive
diˈvīsiv

Ariel and Anh used to be best friends, but their friendship deteriorated as a result of Anh's **egotism**. Although Ariel acknowledged the positive aspects of her friend and did not **censure** Anh's inflated sense of self-importance, she nevertheless thought that Anh regarded only herself as important – a **divisive** issue in their friendship. The fact that Anh often told **mendacious** stories about how splendid her life was without any regard to Ariel's feelings **vindicated** Ariel because it made her assessment feel like it stood on solid footing.

Definitions: Try matching the words in the list with the appropriate definitions. If you are stuck, check the glossary in the back of the book or the passage at the top of the page.

1. egotism _____ a. fabrication, deceitfulness
2. mendacity _____ b. contentious, causing disagreement
3. vindicate _____ c. arrogance, self-importance
4. censure _____ d. to clear of guilt or accusation using justification and proof
5. divisive _____ e. (n.) an expression of formal disapproval; (v.) to express severe disapproval of someone or something, often formally

Sentences: Try to use the words above in a sentence below. Remember that a word ending may be changed or its figure of speech slightly altered.

6. Phan is known for his _____; he tells different stories to different people.
7. The charges of the man were dismissed in court and thus he was _____.
8. A sense of _____ embodies Kylie: her sense of pride is greatly inflated.
9. *Fountain*, a work of Marcel Duchamp (1887-1968) featuring a porcelain urinal as a piece of art, was greatly _____ by many art critics in 1917.
10. I try to avoid potentially _____ topics when hanging out with Trung and Anh who often have strongly differing opinions.

Lesson 43

AN ANGRY SILENCE

Lee is unhappy with the **corrupt** practices of the current ruling officials in his district. They introduce many **prohibitive** rules that benefit mostly themselves. These same regulations appear **lackluster** to residents appealing for real change. Unfortunately, Lee cannot envision a more **auspicious** future for his country unless the corruption is eradicated. But Lee, like other powerless youths of his generation, is unable to voice himself. In remaining quiet, Lee and his generation are getting even more dissatisfied, and more **vindictive**.

NEW WORDS

lackluster
ˈlakˌləstər

prohibitive
prəˈhibitiv, prō-

vindictive
vinˈdiktiv

auspicious
ôˈspiSHəs

corrupt
kəˈrəpt

Definitions: Try matching the words in the list with the appropriate definitions. If you are stuck, check the glossary in the back of the book or the passage at the top of the page.

1. lackluster _____ a. 1. referring to a price or charge that is excessively high; 2. concerning a restrictive law or rule; 3. describing a condition that prevents one from doing something
2. prohibitive _____ b. bland, lacking in liveliness
3. vindictive _____ c. marked by immoral and dishonest behavior
4. auspicious _____ d. having or showing a strong desire for revenge
5. corrupt _____ e. promising, propitious

Sentences: Try to use the words above in a sentence below. Remember that a word ending may be changed or its figure of speech slightly altered.

6. Zev's _____ performance on his math test left his parents wondering if he needed extra help with his algebra.

7. Zoe is quite a(n) _____ person, so her friends avoid getting close to her.

8. It's difficult to buy a property in Singapore; the steep, high prices are _____.

9. In a country where _____ among the government officials is a norm, it's hard to ensure fairness and justice.

10. Looking at this year's fruitful harvest, the farmers hope to have another _____ year.

Lesson 44

IRONY

NEW WORDS

ecstasy
ˈekstəsē

foster
ˈfôstər, ˈfäs-

juxtapose
ˌjəkstəˈpōz, ˈjəkstəˌpōz

obfuscate
ˈäbfəˌskāt

pristine
ˈprisˌtēn, priˈstēn

Mary was in **ecstasy** when she received news that she was about to become a proud **foster** mother to an orphaned little boy. It was a stark **juxtaposition** to her tragic background: a girl abandoned on the streets when she was no more than a squalling infant. The lack of parental oversight and, indeed, of even the most basic necessities of life led to a less than **pristine** track record in her youth, as she struggled to survive on mere instinct and street-smarts. Thankfully, she managed to fight her way out of nameless poverty and bribe her way to **obfuscating** her dubious past, and was now on her way to saving another child from the same fate that befell her.

Definitions: Try matching the words in the list with the appropriate definitions. If you are stuck, check the glossary in the back of the book or the passage at the top of the page.

1. ecstasy _____ a. to place different things side-by-side, often to underscore contrast
2. foster _____ b. to befuddle, make unclear
3. juxtapose _____ c. overpowering feeling of happiness
4. obfuscate _____ d. pure, in an original state
5. pristine _____ e. (adj.) concerning someone that has family ties through being raised and not through birth; (v.) 1. to encourage the growth of; 2. to bring up a child that is not one's by birth

Sentences: Try to use the words above in a sentence below. Remember that a word ending may be changed or its figure of speech slightly altered.

6. Khang was in _____ upon receiving the news that he got into the university of his dreams.
7. In the painting, the _____ of the colors Blue and Red intensifies the contrast in hue.
8. The purpose of team-building games is to help _____ friendship among the participants.
9. The petty details and examples seem to _____ his main argument more than they clarify it.
10. The Belalong tropical forest of Brunei is fairly _____; there are even species of flora and fauna waiting to be discovered.

Lesson 45

KEEP CALM

"To be moderately confused" is an extreme **euphemism** to describe Bach's **vehemence** of anger caused by Mr. Tan, Bach's boss. Bach understands that Mr. Tan is only too eager to bring a **resurgence** to their company after the financial difficulty, but the tasks that Mr. Tan has given Bach are too **onerous** to be completed in a couple of days. Bach is trying his best to be **tactful** in negotiating the deadlines with Mr. Tan.

NEW WORDS

resurgence
riˈsərjəns

tactful
ˈtak(t)fəl

vehement
ˈvēəmənt

onerous
ˈōnərəs, ˈänərəs

euphemism
ˈyoofəˌmizəm

Definitions: Try matching the words in the list with the appropriate definitions. If you are stuck, check the glossary in the back of the book or the passage at the top of the page.

1. resurgence _____ a. strong, intense, forceful
2. tactful _____ b. revival, reappearance
3. vehement _____ c. taxing, requiring a great amount of effort
4. onerous _____ d. having consideration in dealing with others or with difficult situations
5. euphemism _____ e. mild expression to avoid being blunt when referring to something unpleasant

Sentences: Try to use the words above in a sentence below. Remember that a word ending may be changed or its figure of speech slightly altered.

6. Because Khanh is very _____ when dealing with her business partners, she has received a few good contracts.
7. In bad weather, the _____ waves seem like an angry monster waiting to gulf down the houses along the seashore.
8. It is a(n) _____ task to write an index for a book: it takes a long time to sort all key words and nearly as long to write it up.
9. Someone who says he is buying a "pre-loved vehicle" instead of a secondhand car is a fan of _____.
10. The company's _____ after having had a disastrous financial crisis is unexpected.

Lesson 46

A FILM PROJECT

NEW WORDS

candid
ˈkandid

meticulous
məˈtikyələs

indulgent
inˈdəljənt

elite
əˈlēt, āˈlēt

apologetic
əˌpäləˈjetik

When George was assigned a film project that explored the term 'discrepancy', he chose to document the daily lives of an **elite** businessman and of a modest farmer with a **candid** and upfront perspective. George hoped to contrast the frivolous and **indulgent** lifestyle of the rich with the struggle to make ends meet of the poor. He worked **meticulously** on his project so that he would not feel **apologetic** about not giving his best afterwards.

Definitions: Try matching the words in the list with the appropriate definitions. If you are stuck, check the glossary in the back of the book or the passage at the top of the page.

1. candid _____ a. 1. a select part of a group that is superior in ability; 2. a class of people having great societal influence because of their wealth
2. meticulous _____ b. tending to be lenient and permissive
3. indulgent _____ c. very careful and attentive to detail, painstaking
4. elite _____ d. forthright; frank; honest
5. apologetic _____ e. 1. regretfully excusing or acknowledging a failure or offense; 2. concerning a reasoned argument or writing in justification of something

Sentences: Try to use the words above in a sentence below. Remember that a word ending may be changed or its figure of speech slightly altered.

6. In most of his paintings, Johannes Vermeer _____ rendered even the smallest details such as the wooden texture of the furniture.
7. Tim is getting spoiled by his overly _____ parents; all his wishes, even unreasonable, are always met.
8. In 1994, Kevin Carter won the Pulitzer Prize for his _____ picture of a starving Sudanese child being stalked by a hungry vulture.
9. Eliz was born in a privileged _____ family and never knew of the struggles of the working class.
10. He felt very _____ after having broken his dad's favorite clock.

Lesson 47

ELAINE'S CHARACTER

Elaine has a **charismatic** personality. She is **eloquent** in speech, **effusive** in her expressions and natural in social situations. Elaine's friends find her really amiable and they can connect with her easily. But sometimes, Elaine can get very emotional and expose her **vulnerability** without restraint. The cause of her mood swings is often **nebulous**.

> **NEW WORDS**
>
> **eloquent**
> ˈeləkwənt
>
> **nebulous**
> ˈnebyələs
>
> **vulnerable**
> ˈvəln(ə)rəbəl
>
> **charisma**
> kəˈrizmə
>
> **effusive**
> iˈfyoosiv

Definitions: Try matching the words in the list with the appropriate definitions. If you are stuck, check the glossary in the back of the book or the passage at the top of the page.

1. eloquent _____ a. susceptible to emotional or physical damage
2. nebulous _____ b. personal charm or quality that enables a person to attract and influence other people
3. vulnerable _____ c. expressing emotions or enthusiasm in an unrestrained manner
4. charisma _____ d. fluent and persuasive in speech or writing
5. effusive _____ e. cloudy, hazy; ill-defined in terms of concept, idea, or shape

Sentences: Try to use the words above in a sentence below. Remember that a word ending may be changed or its figure of speech slightly altered.

6. I'm trying to write a fiction, but the storyline is still _____.
7. Not only is Sherily a terrific writer, she is also a(n) _____ speaker.
8. Reading Woo Jin's letter, I am very touched by her _____ thanks.
9. Daisy does not share her emotions and _____, so people who are not close to her think that she is rather cold.
10. As a candidate running for election of presidency of the student council, your talents and _____ will be evaluated by the school population.

Lesson 48

REFUSAL

NEW WORDS

lucrative
ˈlookrətiv

prudent
ˈproodnt

voracious
vəˈrāSHəs

aversion
əˈvərZHən

credulity
krəˈd(y)oolitē

Geneva reads **voraciously** about various topics in her free time and she is characterized by her massive knowledge, creativity and **prudence**. She was once asked to join a multinational advertisement company and the manager said that she could make a **lucrative** career out of her strengths. However, Geneva had a strong **aversion** to the way the ad company worked, manipulating people's **credulity** to sell products. She declined the offer without any hesitance.

Definitions: Try matching the words in the list with the appropriate definitions. If you are stuck, check the glossary in the back of the book or the passage at the top of the page.

1. lucrative _____ a. acting with care and showing sound judgment
2. prudent _____ b. very profitable, remunerative
3. voracious _____ c. strong dislike
4. aversion _____ d. having excessive craving and greediness for food or other things
5. credulity _____ e. willingness or readiness to believe something is true

Sentences: Try to use the words above in a sentence below. Remember that a word ending may be changed or its figure of speech slightly altered.

6. Many college students think that a career in the financial sector is _____ so they choose finance-related majors.
7. Yi Shuen is a(n) _____ reader and thus a hoarder of books.
8. Employees new to the company will be regularly evaluated based on _____ assessments of their performance.
9. Katie's adventurous stories stretch _____ but they are not that unbelievable.
10. I have an insurmountable _____ to spiders, especially their long hairy legs.

Lesson 49

MATTHEW BOURNE'S *SWAN LAKE*

One can say that Matthew Bourne is an **iconoclast** who refused to behave with **obsequious** deference to the norm in the ballet world: he asked male dancers to take the roles of the white swans in the ballet Swan Lake! It is indeed **edifying** to witness the masculine and yet beautiful movements of the male dancers. The **prodigious** success of Matthew Bourne's *Swan Lake* is a **laconic** answer to those who used to doubt Matthew's idea of introducing male swans.

NEW WORDS

edify
ˈedəˌfī

iconoclast
īˈkänəˌklast

laconic
ləˈkänik

obsequious
əbˈsēkwēəs

prodigious
prəˈdijəs

Definitions: Try matching the words in the list with the appropriate definitions. If you are stuck, check the glossary in the back of the book or the passage at the top of the page.

1. edify _____ a. to enlighten, help someone understand
2. iconoclast _____ b. using very few words, curt and concise
3. laconic _____ c. someone who attacks established principles, beliefs, ideas
4. obsequious _____ d. remarkably large in size, quantity or extent
5. prodigious _____ e. obedient to a servile degree

Sentences: Try to use the words above in a sentence below. Remember that a word ending may be changed or its figure of speech slightly altered.

6. Every year for Christmas Mai's family goes to Paris; Mai's decision to go to Malé instead this year was regarded as _____ by her family.

7. Reading the *New York Times* opinion page can be a(n) _____ experience.

8. Ziyi's speech is _____ but persuasive, so everyone in the room is completely swayed.

9. When Tue handed in a paper with 247 footnotes, it became clear that he put in a _____ amount of effort into his research.

10. While some dogs can be very _____, others are wild and disobedient.

NEW WORDS

resuscitate
riˈsəsəˌtāt

tangential
tanˈjenCHəl

veracity
vəˈrasətē

nomad
ˈnōˌmad

entrepreneur
ˌäntrəprəˈnoor, -ˈnər

Lesson 50

A BOLD DECISION

A **veracious** person who could not tell a lie, Xing Jing said frankly to her family that she had lost her interest in school and that a university degree was **tangential** to her life's main goal, which was to explore the world. After high school, she left her home to live the life of a **nomad**, moving constantly from one country to another, and she worked multiple jobs while travelling. Perhaps years of cultural immersion had **resuscitated** her interest in education, as she went back to a university to obtain a degree with a major in religious studies and a minor in **entrepreneurship**.

Definitions: Try matching the words in the list with the appropriate definitions. If you are stuck, check the glossary in the back of the book or the passage at the top of the page.

1. resuscitate _____ a. 1. conforming to facts, honesty; 2. habitual truthfulness
2. tangential _____ b. to revive, to regain consciousness
3. veracity _____ c. someone who starts and operates a business or businesses, assuming greater risk than normal in doing so
4. nomad _____ d. digressive, having little relevance to the issue
5. entrepreneur _____ e. someone who moves from place to place and has no permanent home

Sentences: Try to use the words above in a sentence below. Remember that a word ending may be changed or its figure of speech slightly altered.

6. Mary has the special gift of _____ even the dullest topic in her storytelling.
7. Ali's outstanding personal qualities, especially his _____, make him a stellar candidate for the leadership position.
8. Andy has the potential to become a(n) _____ in the future: he has many brilliant ideas and he's able to take calculated risks.
9. Although the campus is beautiful, it is _____ to the main reason that has influenced my decision to attend the school.
10. My grandfather used to lead the life of a(n) _____: he had lived in many places across Vietnam until he met his wife and settled down in Saigon.

Crossword Puzzle
Lessons 41-50

ACROSS

3 not demonstrating a serious or respectful attitude
7 remarkably large in size, quantity or extent
13 overpowering feeling of happiness
14 strong, intense, forceful
15 understood by only a few, esoteric
17 1. regretfully excusing or acknowledging a failure or offense; 2. a reasoned argument or writing in justification of something
18 digressive, having little relevance to the issue
19 personal charm or quality that enables a person to attract and influence other people
20 bland, lacking in liveliness

DOWN

1 taxing, requiring a great amount of effort
2 to clear of guilt or accusation using justification and proof
4 expressing emotions or enthusiasm in an unrestrained manner
5 to encourage the growth of
6 willingness or readiness to believe something is true
8 to revive, to regain consciousness
9 tending to be lenient and permissive to someone
10 promising, propitious
11 fabrication, deceitfulness
12 having excessive craving and greediness for food or other things
16 using very few words, curt and concise

Vocabulary Review
Lessons 41-50

Directions: Match each word with its best approximate definition. Note that definitions are not necessarily repeated verbatim from the lesson exercises.

1.	partisan	_____	a.	evil; cruel
2.	melancholy	_____	b.	forthright; frank; honest; direct
3.	censure	_____	c.	unadulterated; pure
4.	divisive	_____	d.	one who shuns, destroys, or rejects tradition
5.	vindictive	_____	e.	using words carefully so as not to offend
6.	corrupt	_____	f.	to express severe disapproval of
7.	juxtapose	_____	g.	wanderer; itinerant
8.	pristine	_____	h.	menial; servile; low
9.	resurgence	_____	i.	dishonest, often for money in return for favors
10.	tactful	_____	j.	a strong dislike for something
11.	candid	_____	k.	to place side by side
12.	meticulous	_____	l.	generating a lot of money
13.	eloquent	_____	m.	truthfulness
14.	nebulous	_____	n.	biased
15.	lucrative	_____	o.	using words beautifully
16.	aversion	_____	p.	something that causes disagreement or hostility between people
17.	iconoclast	_____	q.	unclear or hazy conception of something
18.	obsequious	_____	r.	revival or increase after period of little activity
19.	veracity	_____	s.	painstaking attention to detail
20.	nomad	_____	t.	sad; dejected

Word Roots: Unit 5

ROOTS AND THEIR MEANINGS

path:	feeling	cred:	believe
uni/mono:	one	circ/circum:	around
cog(n)	to know	ac/acr:	sharp, bitter

Here are a few examples of some words that use the above roots:

em<u>path</u>y:	the ability to understand and share the feelings of another
<u>uni</u>cycle:	a cycle with one wheel, often used by circus entertainers or acrobats
<u>mono</u>cle:	a single eyeglass that one wears
<u>cog</u>nitive:	related to thinking or the mind
in<u>cred</u>ible:	hard to believe; unbelievable
<u>circum</u>vent:	to find a way around an obstacle
<u>ac</u>erbic:	sharp and forthright; bitter or sour tasting

Now try to fill in the table below by finding the appropriate root(s) and interpreting the meaning of each word:

Word	Root(s)	Guessed Meaning	Actual Meaning
sociopath			
uniform (adj.)			
circumnavigate			
credibility			
acrid			
incredulous			
credulous			
acrimonious			
monochrome			
recognize			
incognito			
circumlocution			
circumspect			

Lesson 51

AN ORDINARY DAILY LIFE

NEW WORDS

convoluted
ˈkänvəˌlootid

mundane
ˌmənˈdān

intricate
ˈintrikit

erudite
ˈer(y)əˌdīt

assuage
əˈswāj

Born and having grown up in a post-apocalyptic world, Keith has always found the wasteland to be a **mundane** sight. Every morning he repeats his routine of studying **convoluted** scientific theories among scattered journal pages and degraded books. After some lunch, he preaches about the causes of the war and prays for salvation from the gods to **assuage** his suffering. In the evening, he examines the **intricate** artifacts left behind from the ancient, pre-apocalyptic civilization and tries to understand its unique designs in an attempt to comprehend it. He dreams of the day when his **erudite** knowledge becomes useful to Canterville.

Definitions: Try matching the words in the list with the appropriate definitions. If you are stuck, check the glossary in the back of the book or the passage at the top of the page.

1. convoluted　_____　a.　showing profound knowledge or learning
2. mundane　_____　b.　very complicated or detailed
3. intricate　_____　c.　to mitigate; to soothe
4. erudite　_____　d.　complicated
5. assuage　_____　e.　ordinary; prosaic

Sentences: Try to use the words above in a sentence below. Remember that a word ending may be changed or its figure of speech slightly altered.

6. The directions on the cake mix were so _____ that I was unsure if what I was baking would turn out to be edible.
7. Vu always comes up with _____ solutions to simple problems in life because he constantly worries about other people's perception of him.
8. Nora's family tried to _____ her after her boyfriend dumped her at the local pizzeria.
9. Often scientists engage in routine, _____ lab work for years in order to have one breakthrough discovery.
10. The room was full of _____ applicants, thus making it really difficult for the interviewer to locate the best candidate for the job.

Lesson 52

A SURPRISING STORY

Feeling **wistful** and nostalgic at the sight of his birthplace, Jim began to chronicle his rise to power. He not only worked hard to revolutionize teleportation, but he also admitted that it would have been impossible without some **chicanery**. He had to deceive investors about his short-term results and **endure** their inevitable wrath in order to gain enough funding to perfect the technology. Furthermore, he had to **elude** debt collectors by constantly flying around the world with his family. No one would ever think that his current **opulence** and success stemmed from years of shady and illegal activities.

NEW WORDS

elude
iˈlood

opulence
ˈäpyələns

wistful
ˈwistfəl

chicanery
SHiˈkānərē, CHi-

endure
enˈd(y)oor

Definitions: Try matching the words in the list with the appropriate definitions. If you are stuck, check the glossary in the back of the book or the passage at the top of the page.

1. elude _____ a. great wealth or luxuriousness
2. opulence _____ b. to avoid; to escape
3. wistful _____ c. deception; dishonesty
4. chicanery _____ d. showing a feeling of regretful longing
5. endure _____ e. to tolerate; to bear

Sentences: Try to use the words above in a sentence below. Remember that a word ending may be changed or its figure of speech slightly altered.

6. Uyen was able to _____ the dangerous alley where two gangs engaged in a territorial dispute by taking the long way home.
7. In India, there is a strikingly obvious contrast between the _____ homes of the wealthy and the shanties in the slums.
8. Having to move to a different country at the age of 14, Misha spent most of his first few months abroad engaged in _____ thinking of his homeland.
9. He resorted to the worst flattery and _____ to get promoted to the regional manager position.
10. In any environment, you have to be able to _____ hardship and injustice in order to succeed.

Lesson 53

A DEVIOUS MOVE

NEW WORDS

mediocre
ˌmēdēˈōkər

rebut
riˈbət

whimsical
ˈ(h)wimzikəl

awe
ô

cunning
ˈkəniNG

Despite Greg's myriad theories and extensive research concerning ancient life forms on Ganymede, scientists continued to **rebut** his findings, discarding them as unscientific. To extrapolate on the problem, his **whimsical** nature made it even more difficult for colleagues to take anything he says seriously. However, a recent event completely changed Greg's fate. During his trip to the University of Oregon, he had to **cunningly** gather a large group of biology students for a lecture by giving them free gift cards to Starbucks. The students came in expecting to endure two hours of **mediocrity** when Greg unveiled a new life form, claiming to have retrieved it from Ganymede. Everyone left the talk in **awe** and began to spread the news.

Definitions: Try matching the words in the list with the appropriate definitions. If you are stuck, check the glossary in the back of the book or the passage at the top of the page.

1. mediocre _____ a. amazement; astonishment
2. rebut _____ b. devious
3. whimsical _____ c. playful; comical
4. awe _____ d. to argue against; to deny
5. cunning _____ e. of merely moderate quality; not very good

Sentences: Try to use the words above in a sentence below. Remember that a word ending may be changed or its figure of speech slightly altered.

6. Unlike Phong, who spent days and nights in the library, Jessica exerted _____ efforts in preparation for the final exam (which ultimately led to her predictable failure).

7. Teenagers tend to _____ their parents' traditional, perhaps even obsolete, way of life.

8. Not only must a successful teacher have expertise in his or her subject, he or she must also have a(n) _____ nature in order to connect with students and keep them interested.

9. Minh Anh was left in _____ when her boyfriend told her he would not marry her for at least ten more years.

10. The _____ child was able to put the blame of his wrongdoings on the neighbor's daughter.

Lesson 54

A JUSTIFIED DECEPTION

For years, Min Ho has been repeatedly discouraged by his peers who have been telling him that his gaming dream is **ostensibly** childish and impractical. As if to further hinder his goal, Min Ho's failure to qualify for his first tournament in the face of great expectations by the gaming community led to a series of **languid** days spent lazing around in his dimly lit bedroom. As the manager of the team, Daniel decided to **embolden** Min Ho by providing him with a staged match in order to give him an **illusory** victory, hoping to reinvigorate his passion. The match ended with Min Ho's **profound** speech on following one's passion and overcoming adversities.

NEW WORDS

embolden
emˈbōldən

illusory
iˈloosərē, -zərē

languid
ˈlaNGgwid

ostensible
äˈstensəbəl, əˈsten-

profound
prəˈfound, prō-

Definitions: Try matching the words in the list with the appropriate definitions. If you are stuck, check the glossary in the back of the book or the passage at the top of the page.

1. embolden _____ a. to give courage or confidence to someone to do something or to behave in a certain way
2. illusory _____ b. deep; intellectual, thoughtful
3. languid _____ c. lazy; sluggish
4. ostensible _____ d. appearing to be true, but not necessarily so
5. profound _____ e. not real; imagined

Sentences: Try to use the words above in a sentence below. Remember that a word ending may be changed or its figure of speech slightly altered.

6. Trang needs to be _____ in her studies by someone because she is currently failing most of her classes.

7. In the past, Republicans adamantly believed that global warming is _____ and fallacious despite the copious amount of supporting data proving otherwise.

8. For students, summer is usually filled with _____ days of lazing around doing nothing in particular.

9. People were skeptical about Katie's _____ reason for skipping the field trip because she clearly expressed her preference to go to the upcoming municipal concert.

10. It took a(n) _____ act of courage for the politician to admit his wrongdoings and resign his position because he violated the law.

Lesson 55

NEW WORDS

retaliate
ri'talē͵āt

taunt
tônt

versatile
'vərsətl

negligent
'neglәjәnt

entrenched
en'trenCHt

POTENTIAL CAUSES FOR ANOTHER WORLD WAR

The supreme leader of North Korea has received numerous **taunts** from neighboring countries ever since they discovered secret weapons on North Korean soil. A growing Alliance of countries thus hopes to force North Korea into action so that they can justifiably **retaliate** and retrieve information on these weapons. Despite the Alliance's **negligent** attitude and **entrenched** belief of natural superiority, North Korea's display of **versatile** war tactics has surprised the world.

Definitions: Try matching the words in the list with the appropriate definitions. If you are stuck, check the glossary in the back of the book or the passage at the top of the page.

1. retaliate _____ a. (n.) a comment made to annoy, anger, or provoke someone; (v.) to provoke or challenge with insulting remarks; to tease
2. taunt _____ b. careless; sloppy
3. versatile _____ c. established firmly or solidly
4. negligent _____ d. to make an attack or assault in return for a similar attack
5. entrenched _____ e. adjustable; flexible

Sentences: Try to use the words above in a sentence below. Remember that a word ending may be changed or its figure of speech slightly altered.

6. Jason's endless _____ of Tim led to a fistfight that ended with both students being escorted to the police station.
7. Despite heavy fines and copious warning signs, Vietnamese adults continue to smoke inside children's hospitals: a(n) _____ attitude that is extremely detrimental to the well being of the young patients.
8. Ming Ho's _____ skillset allows him to become the prime candidate for many international firms.
9. Russia _____ against international sanctions by befriending with North Korea, a dictatorial country hated by almost everyone in the world.
10. Traditional cultural values are deeply _____ within an older generation, which can sometimes hinder social advancement.

Lesson 56

PARENTING MISTAKE

Recently graduated from David Douglas High School as valedictorian, Thuy's accomplishments are commonly **embellished** by her parents, which results in she having developed a natural sense of superiority. Her continuous display of arrogance **evokes** anger and irritation even from her best friends. As a childhood friend, Isabella tries to **invoke** Thuy's modesty by reminiscing about the time when Thuy first came to America. Unfortunately, after repeated failures, even Isabella begins to wish for Thuy's **naïve** arrogance to be shattered by her college experiences because they all know that, aside from her excessive daily studying, her creative thinking skill is very **banal**.

NEW WORDS

embellish
emˈbeliSH

naïve
nīˈēv

invoke
inˈvōk

evoke
iˈvōk

banal
ˈbānl, bəˈnal, -ˈnäl

Definitions: Try matching the words in the list with the appropriate definitions. If you are stuck, check the glossary in the back of the book or the passage at the top of the page.

1. embellish _____ a. innocent; sincere
2. naïve _____ b. to elicit; to consciously bring to mind
3. invoke _____ c. mundane; hackneyed
4. evoke _____ d. to cite or appeal to an authority or a thing for support or action in an argument
5. banal _____ e. to make something, a statement, or a story appear more attractive by adding extra details (often which are untrue)

Sentences: Try to use the words above in a sentence below. Remember that a word ending may be changed or its figure of speech slightly altered.

6. Jennifer _____ her car as soon as she got it, plastering the beautiful Maserati with Hello Kitty decals.

7. Having a(n) _____ nature makes it really difficult for Katelyn to become successful in the business world, a place filled with chicaneries and intense competition.

8. Johnson _____ the 1st Amendment – Freedom of Speech – in order to protect himself after burning the American flag in 1989.

9. President Obama's State of the Union speeches are meant to _____ a feeling of hope within the citizens.

10. Marketing is all about providing a cloak to dress up ill-conceived and _____ ideas as brilliant insight.

Lesson 57

NEW WORDS

empirical
em'pirikəl

ornate
ôr'nāt

adept
ə'dept

chronicle
'kränikəl

ephemeral
ə'fem(ə)rəl

AN UNEXPECTED DISCOVERY

An **empirical** formula for time travel was discovered in 1945 by the Nazis, who then attempted to create a time machine to test their findings. However, thanks to the Allies' timely intervention, Nazi happiness was **ephemeral** and their experiment never succeeded. 200 years later, during Allen's attempt to **chronicle** World War II in his doctoral thesis, he discovered a note detailing a mysterious gathering of **adept** and renowned scientists right after the fall of Berlin. Further investigation led him to discover the existence of the time machine 20 miles underneath what is now Berlin's **ornate** Louis Vuitton store. All the secrets of the world are about to be revealed.

Definitions: Try matching the words in the list with the appropriate definitions. If you are stuck, check the glossary in the back of the book or the passage at the top of the page.

1. empirical _____ a. (n.) 1. a factual written account of historical events in chronological order; 2. a writing that describes a series of events; (v.) to record events in a factual and detailed way
2. ornate _____ b. very skilled or proficient at something
3. adept _____ c. momentary, fleeting
4. chronicle _____ d. based on experimental trials of something rather than pure theory or logic
5. ephemeral _____ e. elegant, fancily decorated

Sentences: Try to use the words above in a sentence below. Remember that a word ending may be changed or its figure of speech slightly altered.

6. The beautiful birthday cake was replete with _____ designs made of chocolate chips, which amazed the ravenous Billy.
7. *The Theory of Everything* (2014) is a movie that _____ the story of Stephen Hawking – a renown physicist of the 20th and 21st centuries.
8. Christina is very _____ at badminton: she won the regional tournament just a few months ago.
9. Clive's _____ pleasure from his successful campaign was quickly replaced by his son's criminal conviction.
10. Despite the _____ evidence for the existence of global warming, opponents continue to deny the idea by declaring it a conspiracy.

Lesson 58

A SHOCKING DISCOVERY

Despite being **repudiated** when he first proposed proof of a flying machine, Logan braced for **backlash** from skeptics who questioned his **mercurial** research habits. Nevertheless, Logan continued to push forward with his research. He remembered that it was an extremely **daunting** task but he could not give up at that time. Ten years later, humanity finally understood the reason for his perseverance. Ever since he unveiled a contraption that allowed humans to fly, Logan has been receiving consistent **acclaim** for his work.

NEW WORDS

mercurial
mər͵kyoorēəl

repudiate
ri'pyoodē͵āt

acclaim
ə'klām

backlash
'bak͵laSH

daunting
'dôntiNG, 'dänt-

Definitions: Try matching the words in the list with the appropriate definitions. If you are stuck, check the glossary in the back of the book or the passage at the top of the page.

1. mercurial _____ a. to give approval, to laud
2. repudiate _____ b. a person subject to unpredictable changes of mood or mind
3. acclaim _____ c. to reject, to repeal
4. backlash _____ d. negative reaction or response
5. daunting _____ e. seeming difficult to deal with in anticipation; discouraging

Sentences: Try to use the words above in a sentence below. Remember that a word ending may be changed or its figure of speech slightly altered.

6. Kimberly's _____ personality generally leads to alienating her new friends.
7. Many pundits enthusiastically _____ Barack Obama's electoral victory in 2009 because it was an important moment in the history of America.
8. In recent years, there has been a significant increase in the number of people who _____ the idea that vaccines are meant to help people.
9. Reading 300 books in six months is a(n) _____ task, but it must be undertaken if I am to pass my qualifying exams.
10. Bill Clinton received significant _____ when he was sued by Paula Jones for sexual harassment.

Lesson 59

THE ROLE MODEL

NEW WORDS

eminent
ˈemənənt

immerse
iˈmərs

lavish
ˈlaviSH

outmoded
ˌoutˈmōdid

progenitor
prəˈjenətər, prō-

It was the year 2120 and Ethan's rise to **eminence** was all but a certainty. As the **progenitor** of modern space travel, Ethan had recently funded the first functional spaceship by liquidating all of his lifelong assets, thereby allowing people to travel back and forth between Earth and Mars. All the naysayers who frowned upon his decisions and dismissed his spending as **lavish** are now throwing their wealth into the space travel industry. In spite of his fame, Ethan recognizes that he could be quickly **outmoded** by his competitors and continues to be **immersed** in this new industry in order to maintain his monopoly on it for years to come.

Definitions: Try matching the words in the list with the appropriate definitions. If you are stuck, check the glossary in the back of the book or the passage at the top of the page.

1. eminent _____ a. old-fashioned, out of date
2. immerse _____ b. distinguished, well-known
3. lavish _____ c. (adj.) extremely rich, luxurious, or elaborate; (v.) to bestow something in generous or extravagant quantities upon
4. outmoded _____ d. to become deeply involved in something; to become absorbed by something
5. progenitor _____ e. a person or thing from which a person, plant or animal originates; ancestor; parent

Sentences: Try to use the words above in a sentence below. Remember that a word ending may be changed or its figure of speech slightly altered.

6. Certain economists point to President Obama's _____ spending as cause for America's slow recovery from the recession.
7. Linda was so _____ in the television movie that she forgot to do her homework for tomorrow.
8. Scientific theories are continuously _____ due to technological advancement.
9. Albert Einstein is commonly considered the _____ of modern physics, as his ideas on relativity were foundational for this particular field of science.
10. As a renowned comedian and pundit, Jon Stewart is a(n) _____ figure who can influence the majority of young adults in America.

Lesson 60

A QUANDARY

Tom, an adopted boy, received a call a few days ago from a **volatile** woman who claimed to be his biological mother. She quickly burst into tears the moment Tom showed the slightest sign of confusion. In the wake of this sudden **revelation**, Tom was hardly **tentative** in investigating the matter; he began on a journey to find out the identity of the mysterious woman. Doing so triggered his foster parents' fury, perhaps out of fear that their child was being taken away from them. Out of anger, they displayed **enmity** toward Tom's biological mother, citing her lack of responsibility in his development. The matter was resolved peacefully once Tom received the **momentum** he needed to face reality and confront both parties' needs.

NEW WORDS

revelation
ˌrevəˈlāSHən

tentative
ˈtentətiv

volatile
ˈvälətl

momentum
mōˈmentəm, mə-

enmity
ˈenmitē

Definitions: Try matching the words in the list with the appropriate definitions. If you are stuck, check the glossary in the back of the book or the passage at the top of the page.

1. revelation _____ a. prone to change rapidly and unpredictably (often for the worse); prone to display rapid changes of emotion
2. tentative   _____ b. animosity, hatred
3. volatile   _____ c. uncertain, not definite
4. momentum   _____ d. the impetus or driving force behind a cause or action
5. enmity   _____ e. surprise discovery; disclosure

Sentences: Try to use the words above in a sentence below. Remember that a word ending may be changed or its figure of speech slightly altered.

6. Modern America is starting to let go of its _____ toward gay people.
7. The _____ of the Ford Model T automobile completely changed society and brought what was once a luxury to the common people.
8. Tyler's continual support and encouragement provided the needed _____ for Jackie to go back to college and finish her undergraduate degree.
9. The current market trends are _____ and subject to sudden changes in consumer behavior.
10. Due to her _____ nature, Samantha can really explode on her employees when there is even the tiniest amount of inconsistency in their work.

Word Search
Lesson 51-60

```
H S A L K C A B I N V O K E M G
D B E I L L U S O R Y G Z O L J
R R T N T M T E M U N V M L P T
G L L J T W U E G I T E M W L D
N D Z B Y R K N T A N M W T Y Z
I W D Z R O E N D T U H O N D R
N E L I V E U N U A I S N D T Z
N H R E U A T M C M N B S D E Y
U J S U D G K A S H D E R A E D
C L D I D N N I L J E Z R L N W
O G T R V N C A G I B D I D P V
E R Y V D A E M L W A T J T Q W
D R N G L P L Z J L A T P K Y Y
U Z D A W J R P J L W E E W T V
L T D R T Q N B O M D R Z N X R
E J Y R D E Q V Y A G P Z L D R
```

1. ordinary; prosaic
2. to mitigate; to soothe
3. to avoid; to escape
4. to tolerate; to bear
5. playful; comical
6. devious
7. not real; imagined
8. lazy; sluggish
9. to make an attack or assault in return for a similar attack
10. established firmly or solidly
11. to cite or appeal to an authority or a thing for support or action in an argument
12. to elicit; to consciously bring to mind
13. elegant, fancily decorated
14. very skilled or proficient at something
15. negative reaction or response
16. seeming difficult to deal with in anticipation; discouraging
17. (adj.) extremely rich, luxurious, or elaborate; (v.) to bestow something in generous or extravagant quantities upon
18. old-fashioned, out of date
19. prone to change rapidly and unpredictably (often for the worse); prone to display rapid changes of emotion
20. the impetus or driving force behind a cause or action

Vocabulary Review
Lessons 51-60

Directions: Match each word with its best approximate definition. Note that definitions are not necessarily repeated verbatim from the lesson exercises.

1. convoluted _____
2. erudite _____
3. wistful _____
4. chicanery _____
5. mediocre _____
6. awe _____
7. ostensible _____
8. profound _____
9. versatile _____
10. negligent _____
11. naïve _____
12. banal _____
13. empirical _____
14. chronicle _____
15. mercurial _____
16. repudiate _____
17. immerse _____
18. progenitor _____
19. tentative _____
20. enmity _____

a. a fear mixed with shock and wonder (either of something very good or very bad)
b. based on or concerned with experiment or observation rather than pure theory
c. exhibiting a lack of wisdom, experience, or judgment
d. characterized by sudden changes of mood or mind
e. having or feeling a grateful longing
f. active opposition or hostility toward something or someone
g. lacking in originality; obvious; boring
h. not yet fixed; provisional
i. to refuse to accept or be associated with
j. having or showing great knowledge or learning
k. trickery; deceptiveness
l. failing to take proper care in doing something
m. a person or thing from which a person, animal, plant, or movement descends; an ancestor or parent
n. very complex and hard to follow
o. seemingly or stated to be true, but not necessarily so
p. to dip or submerge something completely in liquid; to completely devote oneself to a particular activity or interest
q. very great or intense
r. able to adapt to many functions, environments, or activities
s. of moderate quality; not very good
t. factual written account of historical events in order of their appearance

Word Roots: Unit 6

ROOTS AND THEIR MEANINGS

dys:	faulty, bad	**mal:**	bad
homo:	same	**mis:**	wrong, bad
hetero:	different	**vers/vert:**	to turn
pan:	everywhere, all	**ab/abs:**	away from, against

Here are a few examples of some words that use the above roots:

<u>dys</u>topia: an imagined place where everything is bad; the opposite of a utopia
<u>homo</u>phone: each of two words having the same pronunciation, but with different meanings and spellings
<u>hetero</u>sexual: a person sexually attracted to people of the opposite sex
<u>pan</u>theon: all the gods of a religion collectively; a building where the dead of a nation are collectively honored
<u>mal</u>adjusted: failing to adapt to the demands of a normal social environment
<u>mis</u>anthrope: a person who dislikes mankind and who shuns society
<u>vert</u>igo: a sensation of dizziness or loss of balance, often when looking down from heights
<u>ab</u>erration: an anomaly or departure from what is normally expected

Now try to fill in the table below by finding the appropriate root(s) and interpreting the meaning of each word:

Word	Root(s)	Guessed Meaning	Actual Meaning
abstain			
dysfunction			
homogeneous			
heterodox			
malign			
panacea			
averse			

misnomer			
heterogeneous			
pandemonium			
dyslexic			
maladroit			
mistake			
absolve			
abnegate			

Lesson 61

AN ANNOYING SITUATION

NEW WORDS

nonchalant
ˌnänSHəˈlänt

proximity
präkˈsimətē

loquacious
lōˈkwāSHəs

excerpt
ˈekˌsərpt

quandary
ˈkwänd(ə)rē

As someone with a **loquacious** personality, Nelia's constant communication has often left her peers in a **quandary** as to whether to be her friend. One day, while her English class was analyzing an **excerpt** from *Lord of the Flies*, Nelia could not stop talking about her thoughts on the book. All the students within close **proximity** to her cringed at her incessant talking. The teacher begrudgingly demanded that Nelia stop talking, but it was to no avail: Nelia continued to **nonchalantly** discuss the book while all of her classmates ignored her.

Definitions: Try matching the words in the list with the appropriate definitions. If you are stuck, check the glossary in the back of the book or the passage at the top of the page.

1. nonchalant _____ a. closeness in place, time, occurrence, or relation
2. proximity _____ b. talkative, wordy
3. loquacious _____ c. perplexity about what to do in a tough situation; a difficult situation or dilemma
4. excerpt _____ d. (n.) quotation or passage taken from a film, writing, or broadcast; (v.) to take an extract from a text
5. quandary _____ e. not displaying interest or enthusiasm

Sentences: Try to use the words above in a sentence below. Remember that a word ending may be changed or its figure of speech slightly altered.

6. Jan was left in a _____ when he realized that he had accidentally made a dinner date at the same restaurant and at the same time with two girls.
7. Because Chloe only read a(n) _____ from the book, her analytical essay did not make complete sense.
8. Despite imminent danger presented by a pack of hungry Chihuahuas, Mandy _____ walked home from her work place, believing that she could easily ignore the threat.
9. Kate's perpetual _____ to her boyfriend draws much ire and irritation from her peers.
10. Sharon is an extremely _____ and ebullient person; she constantly makes side conversations in class.

Lesson 62

ORIGIN OF A LEGEND

As she **circumscribes** the map to pinpoint her target, Quynh begins to feel an insurmountable amount of pressure. Living in the shadow of her infamous father, a successful and renowned archaeologist, Quynh has long wanted to prove to the world that she, too, is a prodigy. Her **ostentatious** father has made it even more difficult for her to gain recognition by traveling on dangerous journeys while displaying to the world that he is an **adroit** treasure hunter. Now that he is gone, she feels **encumbered** to overcome his legacy. Taking a deep breath to achieve **equanimity**, Quynh immediately plunged into the dense jungle, gliding towards her target with a fiery spirit.

NEW WORDS

encumber
enˈkəmbər

ostentatious
ˌästənˈtāSHəs

adroit
əˈdroit

circumscribe
ˈsərkəmˌskrīb

equanimity
ˌēkwəˈnimitē, ˌekwə-

Definitions: Try matching the words in the list with the appropriate definitions. If you are stuck, check the glossary in the back of the book or the passage at the top of the page.

1. encumber _____   a. to burden with obligations
2. ostentatious _____   b. adept, ingenious, skillful
3. adroit _____   c. characterized by pretentious or vulgar display, designed to impress or get attention
4. circumscribe _____   d. to limit or confine
5. equanimity _____   e. mental calmness, composure, and evenness of temper, especially in a difficult situation

Sentences: Try to use the words above in a sentence below. Remember that a word ending may be changed or its figure of speech slightly altered.

6. Because they have caused some problems, Alvin's childish pranks are now _____ by school regulations.
7. Marcus exudes a strange sense of _____ in the face of an impending doom brought forth by the arrival of the Martians.
8. Katelyn drove her Rolls Royce _____ around town to let everyone know how luxurious her lifestyle is.
9. Justin is _____ by student loans despite his overwhelming academic success at Harvard University.
10. The first failure is always the most difficult one to overcome, especially when you are a(n) _____ player like Roger.

Lesson 63

SKYDIVING ADVENTURE

NEW WORDS

minuscule/miniscule
ˈminəˌskyool, minˈəsˌkyool

resolute
ˈrezəˌloot, -lət

acronym
ˈakrəˌnim

bereave
biˈrēv

debunk
diˈbəNGk

As dictated by modern culture, the **acronym** YOLO (you only live once) carries the connotation of *carpe diem* (seize the day, from Latin). Gloria decided to make the most of this phrase when she decided to go skydiving. While her parents worried that they would **bereave** her untimely death and implored her not to go skydiving, Gloria was **resolute** in her determination to go. Gloria told her parents that her decision to jump out of an airplane was no **minuscule** choice; rather, it signified her taking control of her life and pushing herself (perhaps literally) to new heights. She also hoped that, after her parents saw her skydive safely, she could **debunk** rumors in their mind that skydiving was a dangerous pastime.

Definitions: Try matching the words in the list with the appropriate definitions. If you are stuck, check the glossary in the back of the book or the passage at the top of the page.

1. miniscule _____ a. firmly resolved or determined
2. resolute _____ b. set of initials representing the name of something
3. acronym _____ c. to expose the falseness of a myth or belief
4. bereave _____ d. very small
5. debunk _____ e. to be deprived of a loved one through profound absence or after the loved one's death

Sentences: Try to use the words above in a sentence below. Remember that a word ending may be changed or its figure of speech slightly altered.

6. Cells are extremely _____ to the point where you would need a magnifying glass to examine them.
7. Recent research demonstrates that a positive correlation between vaccines and autism has been _____.
8. The _____ NASA stands for National Aeronautics and Space Administration.
9. Justin _____ Vu after the latter was shockingly hit by a train the night before driving home from the bar.
10. When Phuong stepped on the court, her lackadaisical personality immediately gave way to a(n) _____ determination for victory.

Lesson 64

AN ENIGMATIC CHILDHOOD FRIEND

As summer approached an inevitable end, Jon – the **paragon** of apathy – mulled over the impending return to his academic life. He knew that his precious **lethargic** days were in serious jeopardy, and he desperately wanted the status quo to remain **immutable** for as long as possible. Fortunately, Jon gave up on his childish behavior as soon as he became **entangled** with Kimberly, his childhood friend who had recently come home for vacation. During an insipid reunion between the two families, Kimberly revealed a **prospectus** for a volunteer seminar held by an obscure organization. Jon accepted the potential invitation to attend, unbeknownst to the fact that he had fallen into a dangerous trap.

NEW WORDS

entangle
enˈtaNGgəl

immutable
iˈmyootəbəl

lethargic
ləˈTHärjik

paragon
ˈparəˌgän, -gən

prospectus
prəˈspektəs

Definitions: Try matching the words in the list with the appropriate definitions. If you are stuck, check the glossary in the back of the book or the passage at the top of the page.

1. entangle _____ a. unchangeable, inflexible
2. immutable _____ b. an outstanding example, epitome
3. lethargic _____ c. document meant to advertise or describe a book, enterprise, or school to clients or investors
4. paragon _____ d. exhibiting a lack of energy or enthusiasm
5. prospectus _____ e. to involve in difficulties, to ensnare

Sentences: Try to use the words above in a sentence below. Remember that a word ending may be changed or its figure of speech slightly altered.

6. Politicians tend to _____ a simple proposal with an exorbitant amount of superfluous additions in order to accomplish their own personal agenda.
7. Risa is the _____ of a model student: she is always organized, always does her homework, dresses appropriately, and respects her teachers.
8. It is imperative that one reads the _____ of an event before attending in order to best manage one's precious time.
9. While cities and people may change, the landscape of the mountains against the ocean seems _____.
10. As someone who is easily influenced by climate, Cameron tends to feel the most _____ on an overcast day.

Lesson 65

NEW WORDS

salvage
ˈsalvij

timorous
ˈtimərəs

weary
ˈwi(ə)rē

ludicrous
ˈloodəkrəs

emphatic
emˈfatik

BIZARRE BEHAVIOR

Day by day, Tomen flies into the endless star ocean and **salvages** the myriad space debris left behind from Galactic War II with his only friend, A.I. Talon. Years in solitude have made him **weary**. He prays every day for a chance to stumble upon something intriguing, albeit suspicious, in this sea of garbage. This day, however, his favorite radio station had replaced music with a girl's perpetual pleas for help. "Given his **timorous** personality, it was surprising that Tomen was **emphatically** commanding me to search for the girl" Talon reported to a man **ludicrously** cladded in all black. Perhaps now, he again felt inspired in life.

Definitions: Try matching the words in the list with the appropriate definitions. If you are stuck, check the glossary in the back of the book or the passage at the top of the page.

1.	salvage	_____	a.	to recover, to reclaim
2.	timorous	_____	b.	ridiculous, laughable
3.	weary	_____	c.	fearful, timid
4.	ludicrous	_____	d.	expressing something forcefully and clearly
5.	emphatic	_____	e.	physically or mentally exhausted

Sentences: Try to use the words above in a sentence below. Remember that a word ending may be changed or its figure of speech slightly altered.

6. With a tinge of condescension and a load of confidence, Nguyen expressed _____ to her friends that she would never fail any English test.

7. Nhung's _____ haircut is a direct result of not spending an appropriate amount of money on a credible stylist.

8. As part of our responsibility to the Earth, we should always _____ materials from electronic waste in order to reduce the ever-increasing toxicity level of our water systems.

9. Brianna may appear to be tough and confident on the outside, but, as recounted by her best friends, she is extremely _____, especially around strangers.

10. Growing _____ of the impending doom resulting from a nuclear war, Ken decided to unleash a series of cyber attacks on all the governments around the world.

Lesson 66

A MYSTERIOUS FATHER

For years, Hawke had been **reverently** asking his father for an explanation regarding the latter's lavish spending on rare metals. The answers he received as to the reasons for such habits were never **frank**, ranging from being a **cathartic** hobby to building an archway to the gods. After a critical accident that claimed both of Hawke's legs, the distressed father donated all of his assets to the community temple, believing that his good deeds would one day ease the gods' wrath. Hawke was bathed in happiness upon hearing about his father's **magnanimity**. During his last day in the hospital, Hawke's father arrived with a big smile on his face and said **ambiguously**: "the gods have answered." Strangely, he then ended Hawke's life.

NEW WORDS

ambiguity
ˌambiˈgyoo-itē

reverent
ˈrev(ə)rənt, ˈrevərnt

magnanimity
ˌmagnəˈnimətē

frank
fraNGk

cathartic
kəˈTHärtik

Definitions: Try matching the words in the list with the appropriate definitions. If you are stuck, check the glossary in the back of the book or the passage at the top of the page.

1. ambiguity _____ a. appreciative, respectful
2. reverent _____ b. relieving of emotional tensions
3. magnanimity _____ c. straightforward, direct
4. frank _____ d. generosity, nobility
5. cathartic _____ e. uncertainty

Sentences: Try to use the words above in a sentence below. Remember that a word ending may be changed or its figure of speech slightly altered.

6. As someone who enjoys order and certainty, Tung tends to become extremely volatile and stressful when faced with _____.
7. Despite years of suffering due to myriad betrayals, Thao continues to display her genuine _____ to strangers, helping them to the best of her ability.
8. Displaying a(n) _____ attitude to the elderly is a great way to obtain their approval.
9. Enjoying a life of debauchery is _____ to Michael, especially after his ongoing struggle against his mean older brother.
10. Being _____ and direct with your best friend may not always be the optimal solution.

Lesson 67

NEW WORDS

endorse
enˈdôrs

parody
ˈparədē

amiable
ˈāmēəbəl

commemorate
kəˈmeməˌrāt

eradicate
iˈradiˌkāt

THE FILMMAKER AND THE CELEBRITY

Donald is well known for his wit. Due to his **amiable** personality, his **parody** videos of many Hollywood celebrities have become popular online. One of his clips was about a celebrity pledging to help **eradicate** global poverty by minimizing her lavish spending and instead making donations to philanthropic organizations. One year later, to **commemorate** her efforts, the celebrity held a big celebration. Needless to say, Donald's satire video conveyed the message that he did not **endorse** her self-aggrandizing behaviors.

Definitions: Try matching the words in the list with the appropriate definitions. If you are stuck, check the glossary in the back of the book or the passage at the top of the page.

1. endorse _____ a. (n.) an imitation of someone, a genre, or a style in a humorous way; (v.) to imitate someone, a genre, or style humorously
2. parody _____ b. to give approval to
3. amiable _____ c. to recall and show respect for someone or something in ceremony; to serve as memorial to
4. commemorate _____ d. to eliminate completely
5. eradicate _____ e. friendly and pleasant to be with

Sentences: Try to use the words above in a sentence below. Remember that a word ending may be changed or its figure of speech slightly altered.

6. Teena is so _____ that almost anyone can get along well with her.
7. The certificates need to be _____ by the principal before they are given to the students.
8. Whether poverty can be completely _____ still remains as a challenge.
9. The monument was built to _____ the soldiers who died in the battle.
10. People who draw cartoons that exaggerate facial features of famous people are intending to _____ these celebrities.

Lesson 68

JAD'S TALENT

Jad is a junior majoring in theater. He joined a performing group in his freshman year and was well known for his creativity and **brevity**. As **decorum** for newcomers, he had to act in the play Romeo & Juliet, which was surprisingly **notorious** for attracting very few audiences. Knowing this, Jad wanted to **alleviate** the anxiety of the production team and to **revitalize** the play. He did so successfully; all of the seats in the theater were filled on opening night.

NEW WORDS

notorious
nəˈtôrēəs, nō-

revitalize
rēˈvītlˌīz

alleviate
əˈlēvēˌāt

brevity
ˈbrevitē

decorum
diˈkôrəm

Definitions: Try matching the words in the list with the appropriate definitions. If you are stuck, check the glossary in the back of the book or the passage at the top of the page.

1. notorious _____ a. to imbue with new life, to rejuvenate
2. revitalize _____ b. well-known or famous for having some bad quality or having done some bad deed
3. alleviate _____ c. concise and exact use of words in writing or in speech
4. brevity _____ d. propriety in manners, etiquette
5. decorum _____ e. to make less severe

Sentences: Try to use the words above in a sentence below. Remember that a word ending may be changed or its figure of speech slightly altered.

6. The government's current policy aims to _____ the economy after a few years of financial crisis.
7. The professor is _____ for never giving A-grades on student assignments because of his exceptionally high expectations.
8. The way you dress may give a great idea of your _____ and modesty.
9. The speech was prepared in a way to maintain its _____ and clarity.
10. One purpose of meditation is to _____ one's suffering and to let go of one's thoughts.

NEW WORDS

envy
ˈenvē

impediment
imˈpedəmənt

libel
ˈlībəl

patronize
ˈpātrəˌnīz, ˈpa-

qualify
ˈkwäləˌfī

Lesson 69

MY SISTER'S ADVICE

My sister Lan once told me, in her paternal and **patronizing** voice, that **envying** others' achievements was a great **impediment** to my development and progress. When I envy others, I tend to **libel** their talents and success as to avoid feeling inferior. When I envy others, I fail to realize my own potential and needs. She told me that I should **qualify** my sentiments of jealousy and focus more on myself.

Definitions: Try matching the words in the list with the appropriate definitions. If you are stuck, check the glossary in the back of the book or the passage at the top of the page.

1. envy _____ a. an obstruction in doing something
2. impediment _____ b. (n.) a published false statement attacking one's reputation; (v.) to defame someone with false statements orally or in writing
3. libel _____ c. to act kindly while displaying a sense of superiority
4. patronize _____ d. 1. to be entitled to a benefit by fulfilling a condition; 2. to make something less absolute; to put reservations or limits on something
5. qualify _____ e. a feeling of discontent and desire caused by someone else's possessions, qualifications, or luck

Sentences: Try to use the words above in a sentence below. Remember that a word ending may be changed or its figure of speech slightly altered.

6. Jake is _____ of his sister because she has a high salary job.
7. Margot spoke to her new puppy in a(n) _____ tone.
8. Sadie's bad reputation is a(n) _____ to her making new friends.
9. The professor _____ his theory by noting all possible objections to it.
10. Try not to _____ a religion even if you oppose its teaching!

Lesson 70

OPPOSITE ENDS

Chang and Hai are partners in a start-up business. Their demeanors are rather contrasting. Chang is a **loner** and **scrupulous** in his work; he tracks details so thoroughly that data will be made easily **tractable** in the future. Hai, on the other hand, prefers the company of others and is more slipshod in his work. One time, Hai accidentally **divulged** a piece of confidential business information to his friends when they were hanging out. Unsurprisingly, Chang got upset with Hai, but it did not take long for Chang's anger to **abate**.

> **NEW WORDS**
>
> **scrupulous**
> ˈskroopyələs
>
> **tractable**
> ˈtraktəbəl
>
> **abate**
> əˈbāt
>
> **loner**
> ˈlōnər
>
> **divulge**
> diˈvəlj, dī-

Definitions: Try matching the words in the list with the appropriate definitions. If you are stuck, check the glossary in the back of the book or the passage at the top of the page.

1. scrupulous _____   a. extremely attentive to details
2. tractable _____   b. to decrease in intensity
3. abate _____   c. someone who avoids the company of others
4. loner _____   d. to disclose, to reveal
5. divulge _____   e. easily managed or controlled

Sentences: Try to use the words above in a sentence below. Remember that a word ending may be changed or its figure of speech slightly altered.

6. James's eccentricity made him a(n) _____ while in high school; people hardly got along with him.
7. I was surprised as my parents _____ the secrets of their past and their love stories.
8. Katharine was _____ in her reading of the paper: she not only looked at the grammar and argument but also checked every footnote.
9. Chloe's anger hardly _____ even though her family tried to calm her down.
10. Unlike Susie, who never learns in class, Xinyi is very _____ and learns everything that her professors teach her in university.

Crossword Puzzle
Lessons 61-70

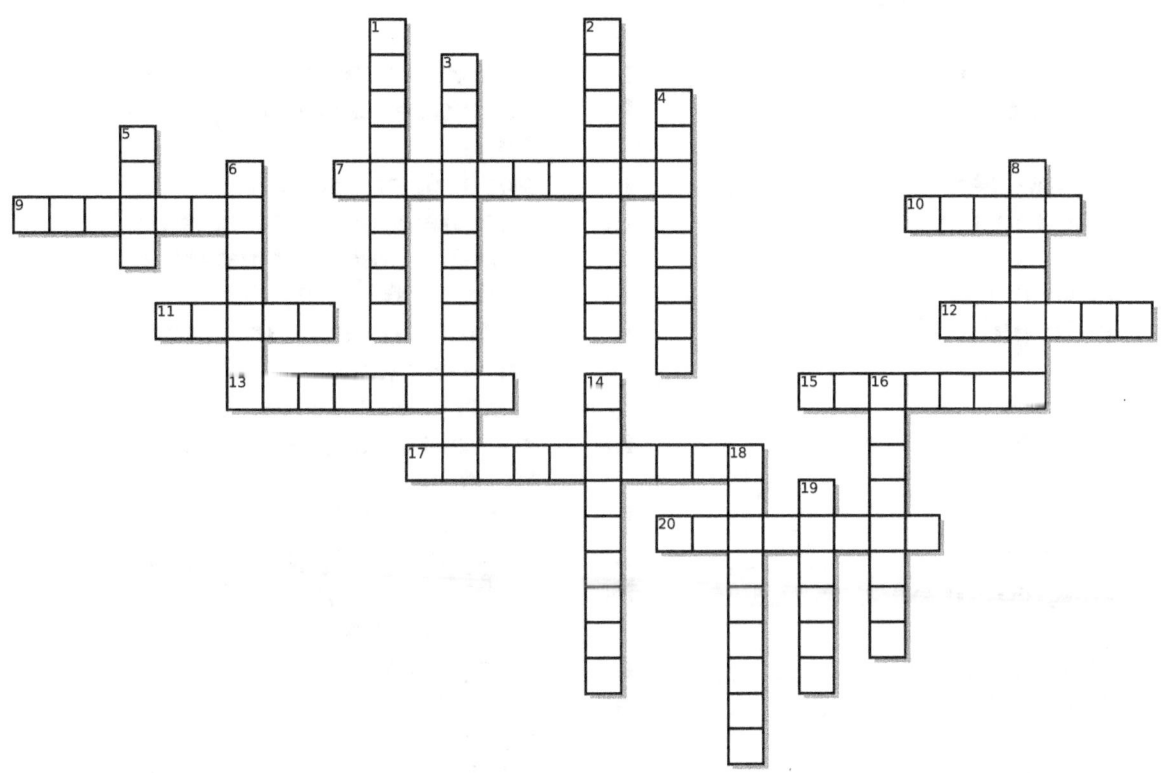

ACROSS

7 not displaying interest or enthusiasm
9 to recover, to reclaim
10 someone who avoids the company of others
11 straightforward, direct
12 (n.) an imitation of someone, a genre, or a style in a humorous way; (v.) to imitate someone, a genre, or style humorously
13 expressing something forcefully and clearly
15 set of initials representing the name of something
17 to imbue with new life, to rejuvenate
20 1. a state of perplexity about what to do in a tough situation; 2. a difficult situation

DOWN

1 to act kindly while displaying a sense of superiority
2 exhibiting a lack of energy or enthusiasm
3 to limit or confine
4 to involve in difficulties, to ensnare
5 a feeling of discontent and desire caused by someone else's possessions
6 to be deprived of a loved one through profound absence or after the loved one's death
8 propriety in manners, etiquette
14 easily managed or controlled
16 appreciative, respectful
18 to eliminate completely
19 adept, ingenious, skillful

Vocabulary Review
Lessons 61-70

Directions: Match each word with its best approximate definition. Note that definitions are not necessarily repeated verbatim from the lesson exercises.

1. proximity _____
2. loquacious _____
3. encumber _____
4. equanimity _____
5. resolute _____
6. debunk _____
7. immutable _____
8. paragon _____
9. timorous _____
10. ludicrous _____
11. magnanimity _____
12. cathartic _____
13. endorse _____
14. amiable _____
15. notorious _____
16. alleviate _____
17. impediment _____
18. libel _____
19. abate _____
20. divulge _____

a. determined; unwavering
b. to prove something to be false
c. absurd, nonsensical
d. nearness in space or time or relationship to something
e. cordial, friendly
f. something that interferes with progress
g. chatty, garrulous, talkative
h. to hold back, restrain, burden
i. having a bad reputation
j. to ease, relieve
k. serving as a perfect embodiment of something
l. to approve or support
m. a trait of generosity and liberality
n. a false statement or making a false statement that damages a person's reputation
o. not susceptible to change
p. nervous or fearful from lack of confidence
q. strongly laxative; emotionally therapeutic or cleansing
r. to disclose, reveal
s. possessing great composure and calmness
t. to become less intense or widespread

Word Roots: Unit 7

ROOTS AND THEIR MEANINGS

neo/nov:	new	**derm:**	skin
carn:	flesh	**equ(i):**	equal
extra:	beyond, outside	**anti:**	against, opposite

Here are a few examples of some words that use the above roots:

neophyte:	a novice, a beginner
carnage:	the killing of a large number of people
extraterrestrial:	from beyond the earth or its atmosphere
dermatologist:	a doctor who diagnoses and treats skin disorders
equivalent:	equal in value, amount, or function
antisocial:	not wanting the company of other people

Now try to fill in the table below by finding the appropriate root(s) and interpreting the meaning of each word:

Word	Root(s)	Guessed Meaning	Actual Meaning
equanimity			
carnal			
extraordinary			
equivocate			
reincarnation			
dermal			
antithetical			
extravagant			
novice			
antithesis			
innovate			

104

Lesson 71

A MEDICAL FIASCO

Yolanda was known to be a **jocular** person who possessed a great talent for making grave situations more **benign**. But one day, she was **manipulated** into making a serious matter worse. When her brother was rushed to the hospital after a motorbike accident, the doctor told her that her brother had passed away (when he was still alive). Upon hearing the sad news, Yolanda **spontaneously** punched the doctor in the face and burst out crying. But upon further inquiry, she realized that the doctor's narrative was not **cohesive** and that her brother was still alive. Joyously, she went to her brother's room and remained by his hospital bed for the rest of the day.

NEW WORDS

benign
bi'nīn

spontaneous
spän'tānēəs

manipulate
mə'nipyə,lāt

jocular
'jäkyələr

cohesive
kō'hēsiv, -ziv

Definitions: Try matching the words in the list with the appropriate definitions. If you are stuck, check the glossary in the back of the book or the passage at the top of the page.

1. benign _____   a. performed by sudden impulse without external stimulus
2. spontaneous _____   b. sticking together (literally or figuratively)
3. manipulate _____   c. not harmful in effect; gentle; kindly
4. jocular _____   d. joking, humorous, or playful
5. cohesive _____   e. to handle or control; to control or influence cleverly, unethically, or unjustly

Sentences: Try to use the words above in a sentence below. Remember that a word ending may be changed or its figure of speech slightly altered.

6. In contrast to Stephen, who has a very serious personality, Todd always has a(n) _____ demeanor.
7. Even though Martha had cancer, her doctors luckily told her that her tumor was _____.
8. Often it is good to be _____ on a first date: rather than planning out a dinner and a movie, it can be beneficial to take chances.
9. Leslie tried to _____ Eileen into going to the casino by stealing her piggy bank and refusing to return it to her unless she accompanied him.
10. Thai's essay lacked any _____ elements: it looked like a bunch of words randomly strung together.

Lesson 72

NEW WORDS

enumerate
iˈn(y)oomə rāt

pretension
priˈtenCHən

apathy
ˈapəTHē

complacent
kəmˈplāsənt

esoteric
ˌesəˈterik

LOTTERY WINNER

After winning the lottery last year, Judy has become somewhat **complacent** with her life. No longer does she strive for career goals, and she seems to have become somewhat **apathetic** about the lives of her colleagues at work. Many of them have distanced themselves from her, complaining that she carries the **pretension** of an elitist individual. Others have simply **enumerated** to Judy all the ways in which she has changed for the worse. About the only aspect of Judy that has not changed is her insatiable desire to learn **esoteric** knowledge.

Definitions: Try matching the words in the list with the appropriate definitions. If you are stuck, check the glossary in the back of the book or the passage at the top of the page.

1. enumerate _____ a. being self satisfied with one's accomplishments
2. pretension _____ b. understood by only a few people with specialized knowledge or interest
3. apathy _____ c. to mention things one by one
4. complacent _____ d. using affectation to try to impress others; ostentatiousness
5. esoteric _____ e. indifference; lack of enthusiasm or concern

Sentences: Try to use the words above in a sentence below. Remember that a word ending may be changed or its figure of speech slightly altered.

6. Only a few brilliant physicists such as Albert Einstein and Stephen Hawking can grasp such _____ ideas as specific minutiae of general relativity.
7. Selena was _____ about Justin's new girlfriend: she did not care who the lady was or whether the couple would be happy.
8. Martin _____ all of the reasons one by one as to why he thought that opening a restaurant would be a bad investment.
9. Jodi has become so _____ that she no longer strives for her medical school ambitions now that she has married a rich man.
10. The party was filled with so much _____ that Lukas pretended to be a millionaire just to fit in.

Lesson 73

LYDIA'S DATING ADVICE

Trying to be **objective** in helping her friend Heather find a partner, Lydia decided to forward along some advice. "Don't be so **aloof** at dinner parties," she urged Heather, "because people will think you are trying to **defy** social conventions." Lydia also advised Heather to quit **romanticizing** her ideas of dating. "Let's face it, you won't marry a real Prince Charming, but you will be able to find someone good enough. There's a large gap between being a prince and being a **bungler** at every social event. I'm sure you'll land the right guy," she said. "Just be realistic about your needs."

NEW WORDS

objective
əb'jektiv

romanticize
rō'mantə‚sīz, rə-

aloof
ə'loof

bungler
'bəNGg(ə)lər

defy
di'fī

Definitions: Try matching the words in the list with the appropriate definitions. If you are stuck, check the glossary in the back of the book or the passage at the top of the page.

1. objective _____ a. to describe idealistically and/or unrealistically
2. romanticize _____ b. to openly resist or refuse to obey
3. aloof _____ c. one who performs tasks clumsily or badly
4. bungler _____ d. not friendly; distant and cool
5. defy _____ e. (adj.) uninfluenced by personal opinions and feelings when representing facts; (n.) a goal or thing sought

Sentences: Try to use the words above in a sentence below. Remember that a word ending may be changed or its figure of speech slightly altered.

6. Sean was surprisingly _____ at last night's party; rather than being the center of attention, he sat in a corner with his nose in a book.
7. Dennis is impressively _____ in his assessment of students: he never lets his feelings get in the way of giving them the grade they deserve.
8. Jason _____ his parents when he snuck out of his house at 2:00 A.M. after they imposed a midnight curfew on him.
9. Known to be a(n) _____, Nancy is always making mistakes when planning weddings, failing to execute properly.
10. When she was little, Nola _____ about having a boyfriend who was the prince of an exotic kingdom.

Lesson 74

LEADING TO DIVORCE

NEW WORDS

epitomize
iˈpitəˌmīz

imperative
imˈperətiv

litigious
ləˈtijəs

paucity
ˈpôsitē

quarrel
ˈkwôrəl, ˈkwä-

Jonathan's parents got in a bad fight last night that ended in their decision to get a divorce. His mother said that it was **imperative** that she be home every afternoon to ensure that Jonathan have family time after school and a healthy dinner. This was especially true because Jonathan's father, who **epitomized** the lifestyle of a workaholic, had a **paucity** of free time available during the week. Jonathan's father retorted that his mother had deliberately damaged his sports car in the garage, a matter that could potentially become **litigious**. Both parents **quarreled** for hours, ultimately acknowledging that the only way to move forward happily was to get a divorce.

Definitions: Try matching the words in the list with the appropriate definitions. If you are stuck, check the glossary in the back of the book or the passage at the top of the page.

1. epitomize _____ a. of vital importance; crucial
2. imperative _____ b. to serve as the perfect example of something
3. litigious _____ c. (n.) a fight or argument; (v.) to fight or argue
4. paucity _____ d. a lack or dearth of something
5. quarrel _____ e. concerning lawsuits; suitable to becoming the subject of a lawsuit

Sentences: Try to use the words above in a sentence below. Remember that a word ending may be changed or its figure of speech slightly altered.

6. Sonja's parents had a large _____ last night and continued fighting over family finances through the wee hours of the morning.
7. Erica is the _____ of a lazy student: she never studies her vocabulary words and expects her tutors to do her homework for her.
8. When Swid's previous employer published untrue things about her, she thought the matter was of a(n) _____ nature and retained an attorney.
9. There is no _____ of words in this book: every page is bristling with new lexicon and ways to use it.
10. It is _____ to watch how many calories you eat every day if you strive to lose weight.

Lesson 75

AN INCREDIBLE THERAPIST

Dr. Pollen is one of the most adept psychologists in town. She has a keen ability to **scrutinize** people's behaviors and body language so that she can advise them. She is excellent at helping individuals give themselves **trenchant** feedback about how they can better their lives without **jeopardizing** their wellness or sanity. She also has a keen eye for letting people know how their **aberrant** behaviors have created problems for them and knows how to help people rectify these issues. Because of these excellent professional skills, I hope to make and **disperse** flyers around town to promote her excellent professional skills.

NEW WORDS

scrutinize
ˈskrootnˌīz

trenchant
ˈtrenCHənt

aberrant
ˈabərənt, əˈber-

jeopardize
ˈjepərˌdīz

disperse
disˈpərs

Definitions: Try matching the words in the list with the appropriate definitions. If you are stuck, check the glossary in the back of the book or the passage at the top of the page.

1. scrutinize _____ a. to inspect closely or thoroughly
2. trenchant _____ b. to endanger
3. aberrant _____ c. departing from norms or typical standards
4. jeopardize _____ d. to spread out
5. disperse _____ e. vigorous or incisive in style; having a sharp edge

Sentences: Try to use the words above in a sentence below. Remember that a word ending may be changed or its figure of speech slightly altered.

6. News of Jessie's tragic breakup with Jake quickly _____ throughout the school; before long every student knew of the melodrama.
7. Mia, who usually gets high grades in math, noted that the "D" she received on her last exam was _____ from her usual performance.
8. Mrs. Willoughby is known to give _____ criticism on student papers: she is always meticulous and criticizes with a keen eye.
9. Fiona _____ her sister's safety when she accidentally opened the car door on the highway while her sister was leaning out the window.
10. It is easy to _____ the behavior of the school president and to find many faults with his decisions.

Lesson 76

NEW WORDS

bewilder
biˈwildər

tenacious
təˈnāSHəs

monotony
məˈnätn-ē

maverick
ˈmav(ə)rik

condescending
ˌkändəˈsendiNG

THE NEW TEACHER

Sheila is something of a **maverick**. Rather than studying from books for her college entrance exams, she believes that her scores will increase by eating cookies. Despite her friends' **condescending** insults at such study habits, she has held **tenaciously** to this theory. Much to the **bewilderment** of her peers, eating cookies improved Sheila's scores drastically. She attributes her success to the joy of eating food over the **monotony** of poring over lessons for hours.

Definitions: Try matching the words in the list with the appropriate definitions. If you are stuck, check the glossary in the back of the book or the passage at the top of the page.

1. bewilder _____ a. lack of variety and interest; repeated same routine
2. tenacious _____ b. to cause confusion
3. monotony _____ c. (adj.) unorthodox; (n.) an unorthodox or independent-minded person
4. maverick _____ d. showing a feeling of patronizing superiority
5. condescending _____ e. keeping a firm hold of something; not relinquishing a plan of action

Sentences: Try to use the words above in a sentence below. Remember that a word ending may be changed or its figure of speech slightly altered.

6. Nora's parents always speak to her in a(n) _____ tone and thus make her feel timorous and anxious to try new things.
7. Most people would dislike the _____ of a data entry job because each day is shockingly like the one preceding it.
8. Luigi is so _____ that he kept professing his feelings for Pearl even after she ended their relationship.
9. Yannick was _____ as to how none of his students could pass their weekly reading quiz.
10. Known to be a(n) _____, James was able to convince his classmates that they could improve their grades by eating cookies every day.

Lesson 77

A BAD POLITICIAN

Our city has a **prominent** politician named Mr. Sneed. He is well known by most of the citizens, but is not so well liked. Many people note that he **equivocates** often when discussing critical social issues, **evades** incisive questions concerning campaign finances, and proposes laws that **infringe** on his constituents' right to free speech. Most citizens **concur** that he should be replaced in the next election with a more forthright person for the job. Nevertheless, Mr. Sneed has no apprehension about the possibility that he will not be reelected.

NEW WORDS

equivocal
iˈkwivəkəl

prominent
ˈprämənənt

infringe
inˈfrinj

concur
kənˈkər

evade
iˈvād

Definitions: Try matching the words in the list with the appropriate definitions. If you are stuck, check the glossary in the back of the book or the passage at the top of the page.

1. equivocal _____ a. 1. to actively break the terms of a law or agreement; 2. to at as if to limit or undermine something; encroach on
2. prominent _____ b. to agree
3. infringe _____ c. 1. important or famous; 2. sticking out or projecting from something
4. concur _____ d. open to multiple interpretations; ambiguous
5. evade _____ e. to avoid

Sentences: Try to use the words above in a sentence below. Remember that a word ending may be changed or its figure of speech slightly altered.

6. Sarath felt that his neighbor was attempting to _____ on his privacy when the latter installed video cameras taping every angle of the former's home.
7. Za is one of the most _____ members of the community: everyone reveres her status and taste for art.
8. Mary's parents _____ that the best way to improve grades is to study more intensely.
9. The charlatan tried to _____ all of my questions as to how he obtained my personal information.
10. Many politicians are accused of being _____ because they change their stance on issues depending on what seems most efficacious.

Lesson 78

NEW WORDS

oblivion
əˈblivēən

sardonic
särˈdänik

amalgam
əˈmalgəm

cantankerous
kanˈtaNGkərəs

dehydrated
dēˈhīdrātid

A SAHARAN DEBACLE

While sorting through an **amalgam** of possibilities for an exotic vacation, Bill decided that he wanted to take a camel tour of the Sahara. He envisioned himself departing toward the exotic as his **cantankerous** friends made **sardonic** remarks and mocked his travel opportunity. But when Bill arrived in the desert, his travel plans were not as blissful as he once thought. His camel passed out and he was left to remain **dehydrated** among the sand dunes. Eventually he died and nobody ever saw him again. Thus his existence in the end was relegated to **oblivion**.

Definitions: Try matching the words in the list with the appropriate definitions. If you are stuck, check the glossary in the back of the book or the passage at the top of the page.

1. oblivion _____ a. parched; losing a large amount of water
2. sardonic _____ b. bad tempered; argumentative; uncooperative
3. amalgam _____ c. a mixture or blend of something
4. cantankerous _____ d. cynical; grimly mocking
5. dehydrated _____ e. the state of being forgotten or unaware of what is happening

Sentences: Try to use the words above in a sentence below. Remember that a word ending may be changed or its figure of speech slightly altered.

6. After wandering through the desert for three days, Momin felt _____ and was enthralled when he arrived at the oasis.
7. When Michael asked Jared how he felt after he failed his chemistry test, the latter said in a(n) _____ tone, "I did a fantastic job."
8. Raccoons often can be _____: if you do not feed them when they beg for food, they may become combative.
9. Khoa's bookshelf has a(n) _____ of different trinkets on it that she has gathered from different facets of her life.
10. After Richard died, his Internet presence was deleted, and his court records were destroyed, his existence was relegated to _____.

Lesson 79

THE UNPREDICTABLE ZELDA

Zelda was constantly **impugned** by her parents for her **erratic** behavior. "Your capriciousness has made life so difficult for us," her mother exclaimed. Her father insisted that Zelda's lack of organization left a sentiment of apprehension that **permeated** throughout the whole family. "We are all very concerned about your choices, Zelda, and we wish there were a way to **quell** the whimsical elements in your character," he said. Together, the three sought **luminous** solutions to understanding Zelda's choices and rectifying her bad habits.

NEW WORDS

erratic
iˈratik

impugn
imˈpyoon

luminous
ˈloomənəs

permeate
ˈpərmēˌāt

quell
kwel

Definitions: Try matching the words in the list with the appropriate definitions. If you are stuck, check the glossary in the back of the book or the passage at the top of the page.

1.	erratic	_____	a.	to spread throughout; pervade
2.	impugn	_____	b.	to put an end to something, usually by use of force; to suppress
3.	luminous	_____	c.	to dispute the truth or validity of; call into question
4.	permeate	_____	d.	not regular or even pattern or movement; unpredictable
5.	quell	_____	e.	full of shedding light; very bright

Sentences: Try to use the words above in a sentence below. Remember that a word ending may be changed or its figure of speech slightly altered.

6. John's behavior was so _____ that nobody could predict what he would do under the stressful circumstances of his sister's untimely death.

7. In order to make the room more _____, Triet installed five additional lamps.

8. The smell of the roast _____ the home as it sat cooking in the oven.

9. In order to _____ Seth's anger, his parents bought him his favorite dinner and told him that he could take a weekend vacation.

10. Fred tried to _____ the capacity of his girlfriend to be a good mother after he saw her ignoring a baby in the supermarket.

Lesson 80

WALDO IN THE WOODS

NEW WORDS

seclusion
siˈklooZHən

trivial
ˈtrivēəl

abridge
əˈbrij

introspection
ˌintrəˈspekSHən

disgruntled
disˈgrəntld

After gaining notoriety for having published three best-selling novels, Waldo became **disgruntled** with the superficiality of everyday life and moved into the woods. He enjoyed a life of **seclusion** there, where he had plenty of time to be **introspective** about his desires and values. For him, moving to the woods was an obvious, if not **trivial**, solution to taking a pause from the rapid pace of life. When he returned from the woods, Waldo decided that, since his books were successful but lengthy, he would try and sell **abridged** versions to the public for extra profit.

Definitions: Try matching the words in the list with the appropriate definitions. If you are stuck, check the glossary in the back of the book or the passage at the top of the page.

1. seclusion _____ a. to shorten a book movie, speech, or text without losing its general meaning
2. trivial _____ b. of little value and importance
3. abridge _____ c. self-reflection; observing one's own mental and emotional process
4. introspection _____ d. being private and away from other people
5. disgruntled _____ e. angry or dissatisfied

Sentences: Try to use the words above in a sentence below. Remember that a word ending may be changed or its figure of speech slightly altered.

6. After publishing *Catcher in the Rye*, J.D. Salinger moved to a house in rural New Hampshire, never wrote for the public again, and lived in _____.

7. It is important to be capable of _____, for without it we cannot ponder the consequences of our actions and hope to learn from them.

8. The _____ version of *Crime and Punishment* is two hundred pages shorter than the original, and its characters are just as well articulated.

9. Terry was so engrossed in pondering _____ matters that nobody ever suspected that he would discuss anything of substance.

10. The worker was so _____ that she insulted all of her colleagues when she did not get what she wanted.

Word Search
Lessons 71-80

```
T R U C N O C E T A R E M U N E J
N L E R R A U Q Y B G I D E F Y T
A M R Y K B J K T Y N D M W M C Z
H T N D J L B L B T L K V P O Y N
C S D M Z M M V A V Z J S H U M M
N U R Q J Y Q R W C B U E T Z G G
E O T D T Q Q L S B O S M R W N N
R R N Y K E A Z D E I V O J L Q E
T E V D N I N M N V C M I I R S V
X K G N V O P A E L A L T U R R O
T N D I R Z T A C N E I U E Q B T
M A R Q R N P O T I G R P S L E Y
W T L M O A J I N I O S R I I T G
R N L P T N C B O O I U V A N O D
R A S H W I B U D D M I S R T L N
J C Y J Z Z S Q T Z O R W R N I V
N V R E W X Y P N N L R L W Y D C
```

1. performed by sudden impulse without external stimulus
2. sticking together (literally or figuratively)
3. to mention things one by one
4. indifference; lack of enthusiasm or concern
5. to describe idealistically and/or unrealistically
6. to openly resist or refuse to obey
7. concerning lawsuits; suitable to becoming the subject of a lawsuit
8. (n.) a fight or argument; (v.) to fight or argue
9. vigorous or incisive in style; having a sharp edge
10. to spread out
11. keep a firm hold of something; not relinquishing a plan of action
12. lack of variety and interest; repeated same routine
13. open to multiple interpretations; ambiguous
14. to agree
15. the state of being forgotten or unaware of what is happening
16. bad tempered; argumentative; uncooperative
17. not regular or even pattern or movement; unpredictable
18. to dispute the truth or validity of; call into question
19. being private and away from other people
20. of little value and importance

Vocabulary Review
Lessons 71-80

Directions: Match each word with its best approximate definition. Note that definitions are not necessarily repeated verbatim from the lesson exercises.

1. benign _____
2. jocular _____
3. complacent _____
4. esoteric _____
5. objective _____
6. aloof _____
7. imperative _____
8. paucity _____
9. scrutinize _____
10. jeopardize _____
11. bewilder _____
12. maverick _____
13. prominent _____
14. evade _____
15. amalgam _____
16. dehydrated _____
17. luminous _____
18. quell _____
19. abridge _____
20. introspection _____

a. lacking water or liquid; parched
b. of vital importance; crucial
c. to escape or avoid (usually by being clever or tricky)
d. joking; humorous; playful
e. bright, shining, shedding light
f. cause to become confused
g. to put an end to something, often by means of force
h. important or famous; projecting from something
i. self-satisfied with oneself or with one's achievements
j. to look over very carefully
k. to examine one's own mental or emotional processes
l. cool and distant
m. a mixture or blend of something
n. only understood by few people with specialized knowledge
o. to endanger or put in harm's way
p. to shorten (usually a movie or text) without losing the main sense
q. gentle; kindly; harmless
r. a dearth or lack of something
s. unorthodox or unconventional independent-minded person
t. uninfluenced by personal feelings or opinions

Word Roots: Unit 8

ROOTS AND THEIR MEANINGS

dign/dian:	worth (value)	in/en/em/im:	into
nai/nas/nat:	to be born	phon:	sound
gen:	type, birth	fac:	to do; to make
ad/at:	to, toward	cli:	to lean

Here are a few examples of some words that use the above roots:

dignity: the state of equality in being worthy of honor or respect
renaissance: the rebirth of something, usually art or music
genotype: the genetic composition of an organism
advance: to move forward or make progress, typically with an expressed purpose
immerse: to submerge in a liquid
incarnate: embodied in human form or in the flesh
telephone: an instrument by which one can communicate with others at a distance
facilitate: to make a process or an action easier
inclination: a natural tendency to act or behave in a certain way

Now try to fill in the table below by finding the appropriate root(s) and interpreting the meaning of each word:

Word	Root(s)	Guessed Meaning	Actual Meaning
factory			
phonetics			
nationality			
proclivity			
nascence			
attain			
genealogy			
engaged			
generic			
engrossing			
decline			

Lesson 81

NEW WORDS

capricious
kəˈpriSHəs, -ˈprē-

ubiquitous
yooˈbikwətəs

penchant
ˈpenCHənt

munificent
myooˈnifəsənt, myə-

conscientious
ˌkänCHēˈenCHəs

QUALITIES OF A GOOD RESEARCHER

Leandra is an excellent researcher. She has a **penchant** for finding solutions to difficult scientific problems and she has **conscientious** study habits. Her colleagues find her to be warm and **munificent**, and appreciate the fact that she is open to helping anyone learn. Just last week, she helped a rather **capricious** coworker focus on a new research question. Now he is investigating the **ubiquitous** nature of nitrogen in the air we breathe.

Definitions: Try matching the words in the list with the appropriate definitions. If you are stuck, check the glossary in the back of the book or the passage at the top of the page.

1. capricious _____ a. strong habitual liking for something or tendency to do something
2. ubiquitous _____ b. wishing to do one's duty well and properly
3. penchant _____ c. very generous
4. munificent _____ d. given to sudden changes of behavior or mood
5. conscientious _____ e. found or appearing everywhere

Sentences: Try to use the words above in a sentence below. Remember that a word ending may be changed or its figure of speech slightly altered.

6. Unlike Alicia, whose behavior is typically predictable, Lark is far more _____: it is hard to put a finger on anything that she will do.
7. Harold studied _____ for his exams, taking meticulous and detailed notes in all of his notebooks and studying for them one hour each day.
8. Mrs. Curry is a(n) _____ host: she always flatters her guests and makes them feel welcome in her home.
9. Motorbikes are _____ throughout Ho Chi Minh City: no matter what street you traverse, the road is full of them.
10. Saby has a(n) _____ for irritating girls on first dates: they almost always walk out on him or ignore him before the date is over.

118

Lesson 82

THE PHILANTHROPIC CRIMINAL

For many, it is hard to **reconcile** the fact that Earl, who volunteers at a soup kitchen, once was imprisoned for stealing money from the poor. It is surprising to imagine that Earl was ever in prison, especially given the **conviction** with which he speaks about helping those in need. Nevertheless, the truth is that he was **exonerated** after it was discovered that he never stole money. Someone **arbitrarily** accused him of stealing several years ago, and the fact that he looked like a wanted criminal only **exacerbated** the erroneous charge. When all the evidence was lined up and Earl was found innocent, his philanthropic life began.

NEW WORDS

exacerbate
igˈzasərˌbāt

reconcile
ˈrekənˌsīl

arbitrary
ˈärbiˌtrerē

conviction
kənˈvikSHən

exonerate
igˈzänəˌrāt

Definitions: Try matching the words in the list with the appropriate definitions. If you are stuck, check the glossary in the back of the book or the passage at the top of the page.

1. exacerbate _____ a. based on random choice or personal whim
2. reconcile _____ b. 1. a formal declaration that one is guilty of a criminal offense; 2. a firmly held belief or opinion
3. arbitrary _____ c. to make (usually a bad situation) worse
4. conviction _____ d. to free from blame or fault in wrongdoing
5. exonerate _____ e. 1. to restore relations between; 2. to make things mentally consistent with each other

Sentences: Try to use the words above in a sentence below. Remember that a word ending may be changed or its figure of speech slightly altered.

6. When Trevor scratched the wound on his wrist, his entire arm and hand became red, thus _____ the inflammation of his skin.
7. It is difficult to _____ Phong's brilliance and high grades with his apathy for school and intellectual endeavors.
8. Drawing someone's name out of a hat to receive a prize is a(n) _____ way to select a winner.
9. When it was discovered that Denise was wrongly accused of murdering the person at the park, she was _____.
10. George vowed to study for his exams with complete _____: he remained focused on his work every day until his exams were done.

Lesson 83

CONTENTIOUS BOOK

NEW WORDS

obscure
əbˈskyoor

smug
sməg

anecdotal
ˌanikˈdōtl

censor
ˈsensər

dejected
diˈjektəd

Harriet found an **obscure** book from a seventeenth century scientist in the municipal library in Rome. Looking through it, she discovered that the Roman Catholic Church had **censored** part of the text by crossing out passages that went against the word of the Bible. Upon further research, she learned that the book was written by a **smug** but **dejected** young man whose family abandoned him. Because he had no form of support, he realized that there was little for him to lose in writing about his scientific views. So, based on perhaps **anecdotal** evidence, he composed a book that challenged the Biblical standards of the day.

Definitions: Try matching the words in the list with the appropriate definitions. If you are stuck, check the glossary in the back of the book or the passage at the top of the page.

1. obscure _____ a. excess pride in oneself or one's successes
2. smug _____ b. (n.) an official who examines pre-released media or printed material to suppress politically contentious or obscene material; (v.) to officially examine (usually a text or movie) and remove unacceptable parts
3. anecdotal _____ c. not necessarily true or reliable
4. censor _____ d. sad and depressed
5. dejected _____ e. (adj.) not discovered or known about; (v.) to make unclear

Sentences: Try to use the words above in a sentence below. Remember that a word ending may be changed or its figure of speech slightly altered.

6. In medieval times, the Catholic Church aimed to _____ all books that were written and to expurgate all passages that contradicted scripture.
7. James felt _____ after Mai dumped him on their anniversary.
8. It is impolite to be _____ and brag about all of your accomplishments to your friends.
9. A(n) _____ detail about the history of Mickey Mouse is that Walt Disney had created another cartoon mouse, Mortimer, prior to Mickey.
10. There is only _____ evidence to suggest that Vu actually likes Mandeville.

Lesson 84

WARRING FAMILIES

With much **malice**, the Smith and the Jones families took each other to court over a property dispute. Both families felt that they owned the island in the middle of the lake on which they resided. The Smith family, who was very outspoken, tried to **indulge** the **quiescent** Jones family into admitting that they did not own the island. The Jones family, however, was **perspicacious** enough not to engage. Luckily, when the issue arrived in court, the judge **eschewed** all claims as bogus and determined that the island was public property.

NEW WORDS

eschew
esˈCHoo

indulge
inˈdəlj

malice
ˈmaləs

perspicacious
ˌpərspiˈkāSHəs

quiescent
kwēˈesnt, kwī-

Definitions: Try matching the words in the list with the appropriate definitions. If you are stuck, check the glossary in the back of the book or the passage at the top of the page.

1. eschew _____ a. period of rest, inactivity, or dormancy
2. indulge _____ b. to deliberately avoid using; abstain from
3. malice _____ c. having insight into the understanding of things
4. perspicacious _____ d. to allow oneself or someone to enjoy the pleasure of something
5. quiescent _____ e. ill-will; intention or desire to do evil

Sentences: Try to use the words above in a sentence below. Remember that a word ending may be changed or its figure of speech slightly altered.

6. Ramona relishes the _____ atmosphere of the library, taking solace in its serene and silent ambience.
7. Drake always writes letters so filled with _____ that the letters' recipients read them in fear.
8. Paul always _____ Justin by taking him to his favorite restaurant when he comes to visit.
9. In order to lose weight, Jarleth _____ chocolate for six months.
10. Shanine is _____ and can generally decipher the intentions of the boys she dates within the first minute of talking to them.

Lesson 85

SCHEMING TEACHER

NEW WORDS

shrewd
SHrood

cacophony
kəˈkäfənē

abstemious
abˈstēmēəs

inundate
ˈinənˌdāt

diatribe
ˈdīəˌtrīb

Mrs. Trehorn was a **shrewd** old woman who enjoyed **inundating** her students with homework assignments. Despite a **cacophony** of whining complaints from students and parents about the inappropriate intensity of her assignments, Mrs. Trehorn refused to lighten the workload. Finally, after ten years of teaching, she met a class who took an **abstemious** approach to her insufferable assignments: the more she assigned, the less they worked. Even her **diatribes** would not convince them to study. In the end, she was left alone with students who did not do their homework; everyone was miserable.

Definitions: Try matching the words in the list with the appropriate definitions. If you are stuck, check the glossary in the back of the book or the passage at the top of the page.

1. shrewd _____ a. having sharp powers of judgment
2. cacophony _____ b. to overwhelm someone with things; to flood
3. abstemious _____ c. non self-indulgent, especially when eating or drinking
4. inundate _____ d. harsh, discordant mixture of sounds
5. diatribe _____ e. a forceful and bitter attack against someone or something

Sentences: Try to use the words above in a sentence below. Remember that a word ending may be changed or its figure of speech slightly altered.

6. The _____ robber was able to steal peoples' money right before their eyes without them even noticing.
7. Because the orchestra had not prepared for the school musical, its opening number sounded more like a(n) _____ than a melodic introduction.
8. Maureen was so _____ with homework assignments that she stayed up all night to complete them.
9. When Minh did not get his favorite toy for Christmas, he launched on a long _____, berating his parents for not giving him his desired gift.
10. Often, a(n) _____ approach to food is the best way to lose weight rapidly.

Lesson 86

JAMES' DATING ADVICE

My schoolmate James seems to give **erroneous** dating advice to his friends. Nevertheless, because he seems to have no difficulty picking up ladies, they believe his tips for finding romance are **plausible**. He always tells people to shy away from discussing **contentious** issues and instead broach **superficial** topics. James notes that the more **uniformly** people follow his advice, the more success they'll have with the opposite sex. Regrettably, however, I have not benefitted at all from his advice!

NEW WORDS

erroneous
iˈrōnēəs

uniform
ˈyoonəˌfôrm

superficial
ˌsoopərˈfiSHəl

plausible
ˈplôzəbəl

contentious
kənˈtenCHəs

Definitions: Try matching the words in the list with the appropriate definitions. If you are stuck, check the glossary in the back of the book or the passage at the top of the page.

1. erroneous _____ a. seeming reasonable, probable, or believable
2. uniform _____ b. (adj.) not changing in form or character; (n.) a distinctive clothing worn by members of a particular organization or profession
3. superficial _____ c. wrong; incorrect
4. plausible _____ d. likely to cause an argument; controversial
5. contentious _____ e. existing or occurring only at the surface; appearing to be true until scrutinized; not having depth of character or understanding

Sentences: Try to use the words above in a sentence below. Remember that a word ending may be changed or its figure of speech slightly altered.

6. It is highly _____ that someone who does not study for his or her college entrance exams will not do well on them.
7. Topics such as uranium enrichment and the manufacture of nuclear weapons are often _____ ones in international talks.
8. There is not a(n) _____ method for dealing with pay raises in Jake's company.
9. Julius found his date to be so _____ as all she could discuss on the date was her perfume and nail polish.
10. The professor who released _____ data for his research was later drummed out of academia for having conjured spurious information.

Lesson 87

LITTLE LOUISE

NEW WORDS

exasperated
igˈzaspəˌrātid

redundant
riˈdəndənt

ascertain
ˌasərˈtān

convivial
kənˈvivēəl, kənˈvivyəl

exotic
igˈzätik

My neighbor Louise is a **convivial** six-year-old girl who enjoys talking about video games and **exotic** adventure movies. Sometimes she forgets what she tells me and delivers **redundant** statements about her interests. Normally, I would be **exasperated** if someone kept repeating the same stories, but I think Louise is an adorable little child, and I like sharing in her joys. Yet despite all of her musings, I still cannot **ascertain** what really inspires her. Hopefully as she grows up she will have a lot of avenues for success open to her.

Definitions: Try matching the words in the list with the appropriate definitions. If you are stuck, check the glossary in the back of the book or the passage at the top of the page.

1. exasperated _____ a. to be intensely irritated; infuriated
2. redundant _____ b. attractive because it is foreign or not ordinary
3. ascertain _____ c. to find something out for certain; to ensure
4. convivial _____ d. no longer needed or useful; superfluous
5. exotic _____ e. friendly, lively, or enjoyable person or environment

Sentences: Try to use the words above in a sentence below. Remember that a word ending may be changed or its figure of speech slightly altered.

6. For many Americans, Asia is a(n) _____ place that lures people because of its eccentric, foreign culture.
7. It is difficult to _____ whether Hung actually read the book without giving him a quiz on the material first.
8. Usually Jeremy's parties are _____: guests enjoy the lively chatting and delicious food.
9. Unless it is for literary style, it would be _____ to repeat the same sentence twice in a paper.
10. Sherry was _____ when she found out that her dog took a poo on her new, white bed sheets.

Lesson 88

TYPEWRITER EULOGY

We are gathered here on this **solemn** day to mourn the loss of the typewriter from world commerce. For decades, the typewriter brought joy and salaries to many secretaries who used it to write letters, bills, and invoices. But now, after suffering a **chronic** battle with the advent of digital word processing, the typewriter has become **obsolete**. As word processors gained fame, people could not be **deluded** into retaining their trusty typewriters. No feelings of **animosity** were held for the esteemed typewriter; instead, the word processor merely was deemed to be more relevant. Thus the typewriter fades into nonexistence as the world marches on.

NEW WORDS

obsolete
ˌäbsəˈlēt

solemn
ˈsäləm

animosity
ˌanəˈmäsitē

chronic
ˈkränik

delude
diˈlood

Definitions: Try matching the words in the list with the appropriate definitions. If you are stuck, check the glossary in the back of the book or the passage at the top of the page.

1. obsolete _____ a. persisting for a long time or constantly recurring (often of illness or habits)
2. solemn _____ b. formal and dignified; serious
3. animosity _____ c. strong hostility toward someone or something
4. chronic _____ d. to mislead someone; to fool, deceive
5. delude _____ e. no longer produced or used; out of date

Sentences: Try to use the words above in a sentence below. Remember that a word ending may be changed or its figure of speech slightly altered.

6. Typewriters are considered nearly _____ now that computer word processors are used in almost every business.
7. Georgia's laziness is a(n) _____ problem and has been affecting her grades in school since she was very little.
8. Unlike parties, which are generally convivial, funerals are typically _____ affairs.
9. There is so much _____ between Isidor and Faisal that they need a mediator when they are put in the same room to talk.
10. The con man _____ his audience into believing that a used car was actually brand new.

Lesson 89

NEW CEO

NEW WORDS

estrange
iˈstrānj

ineffable
inˈefəbəl

mandate
ˈmanˌdāt

pertinent
ˈpərtn-ənt

quizzical
ˈkwizəkəl

My company just hired a new CEO after the board of directors issued a **mandate** that the company have a new leader at the helm. Though the decision to hire a new leader left many **quizzical** expressions on employee faces, the board felt that it was a **pertinent** matter to establish new leadership ethics as the company expands. But what is shocking is the choice of leadership. When employees heard that the new CEO was trained to be a circus clown rather than a businessman, they were **ineffable** about the administration's decisions. They are all convinced that the new CEO will **estrange** himself from the quotidian happenings in business to pursue his clowning adventures.

Definitions: Try matching the words in the list with the appropriate definitions. If you are stuck, check the glossary in the back of the book or the passage at the top of the page.

1. estrange _____ a. an edict, order, or commission to act
2. ineffable _____ b. relevant; germane
3. mandate _____ c. too great or extreme to be verbally expressed
4. pertinent _____ d. showing amused puzzlement
5. quizzical _____ e. to alienate; to no longer be close to someone

Sentences: Try to use the words above in a sentence below. Remember that a word ending may be changed or its figure of speech slightly altered.

6. When Sean, who never acted before, heard that he would be getting the lead in the community play, he had a(n) _____ expression on his face.
7. The tyrant issued a(n) _____ that all female citizens could only have one child.
8. Melanie is _____ from her family and has neither seen them nor spoken to them for eleven years.
9. It is _____ to study business jargon and have an educated vocabulary if you want to be successful in commerce.
10. Yarid was _____ and filled with angst when she saw a spaceship descend on her back lawn.

Lesson 90

MILES THE MENDICANT

One night at a Manhattan café, I saw a financially **insolvent** man named Miles sitting at the front table cutting newspaper clippings. Without trying to be too **solicitous** or to **allude** to his impoverished lifestyle, I wondered why a person without financial means would be making a collage of snippets. Miles told me that, even though he had no formal education, immersing himself in newspaper clippings gave him the feeling of being erudite. Though people could **mar** his social status because he had no degrees, they could not steal the knowledge that he had acquired. I was so impressed with Miles' logic and reasoning that I **truncated** many of his statements off by asking my own questions about what success meant to him. How impressive it was that a man of little means could be so clever!

NEW WORDS

solicitous
səˈlisitəs

truncate
ˈtrəNGˌkāt

mar
mär

insolvent
inˈsälvənt

allusion
əˈlooZHən

Definitions: Try matching the words in the list with the appropriate definitions. If you are stuck, check the glossary in the back of the book or the passage at the top of the page.

1. solicitous _____ a. expression noting something indirectly
2. truncate _____ b. unable to pay debts owed
3. mar _____ c. characterized by showing interest or concern; eager or anxious to do something
4. insolvent _____ d. to shorten by cutting off the top or end
5. allusion _____ e. to sully the appearance, reputation, or quality of someone or something

Sentences: Try to use the words above in a sentence below. Remember that a word ending may be changed or its figure of speech slightly altered.

6. Bankrupt companies are financially _____ and often can no longer afford to stay in business.
7. Because there remained a long line after closing hours, the managers of the ice cream store _____ the queue at the twentieth person.
8. Many of William Faulkner's books have _____ to an underlying panic caused by characters fearing the flattening of time.
9. Laura attempted to _____ her boss' reputation by claiming that the latter was a thief.
10. Many Americans detest _____ behavior from salespeople and feel that such interlopers encroach on their private lives.

Crossword Puzzle
Lessons 81-90

ACROSS

1 (adj.) not discovered or known about; (v.) to make unclear
7 unable to pay debts owed
10 having insight into the understanding of things
11 not necessarily true or reliable
15 to be intensely irritated; infuriated
16 formal and dignified; serious
17 given to sudden changes of behavior or mood
18 showing amused puzzlement
19 having sharp powers of judgment

DOWN

2 to alienate; to no longer be close to someone
3 friendly, lively, or enjoyable person or environment
4 to free from blame or fault in wrongdoing
5 very generous
6 period of rest, inactivity, or dormancy
8 1. existing or occurring only at the surface; 2. not thorough or complete; 3. lacking depth
9 likely to cause or causing an argument; controversial
11 non self-indulgent, especially when eating or drinking
12 to mislead someone; to fool, deceive
13 1. to restore relations between; 2. to make things mentally consistent with each other
14 to shorten by cutting off the top or end

Vocabulary Review
Lessons 81-90

Directions: Match each word with its best approximate definition. Note that definitions are not necessarily repeated verbatim from the lesson exercises.

1. ubiquitous _____
2. penchant _____
3. exacerbate _____
4. arbitrary _____
5. smug _____
6. dejected _____
7. indulge _____
8. malice _____
9. inundate _____
10. diatribe _____
11. erroneous _____
12. plausible _____
13. ascertain _____
14. exotic _____
15. obsolete _____
16. chronic _____
17. ineffable _____
18. mandate _____
19. mar _____
20. allusion _____

a. sad; depressed
b. by random choice or whim
c. outmoded; no longer in use
d. to allow oneself or someone to enjoy the pleasure of
e. speechless; too great or extreme to be verbalized
f. wrong; incorrect
g. excessive pride in oneself or one's achievements
h. to find something out for certain
i. attractive or striking because it is out of the ordinary or geographically distant
j. everywhere, throughout
k. believable, seeming reasonable or probable
l. to damage or impair the quality of someone or something
m. an intention or desire to do evil
n. an expression used to call something to mind without directly referencing it; an indirect or passing reference
o. to flood or overwhelm
p. an official order or command
q. a natural liking or inclination for something
r. persisting for a long time; difficult to eradicate
s. to worsen
t. a long, bitter verbal rant; an invective

Word Roots: Unit 9

ROOTS AND THEIR MEANINGS

cur/cour:	to run	**tens/ten:**	to stretch
ob:	against, toward, in front of	**vor:**	to eat
techn:	tools, skill	**magna/magni:**	big, great

Here are a few examples of some words that use the above roots:

courier:	a messenger who transports goods or documents (eg. carries documents between places)
obviate:	to avoid; prevent; remove a specific difficulty
technology:	the application of scientific knowledge and/or machinery for practical purposes
tenuous:	very weak or slight
voracious:	wanting or devouring great quantities of something, often food
magnanimous:	very generous or forgiving

Now try to fill in the table below by finding the appropriate root(s) and interpreting the meaning of each word:

Word	Root(s)	Guessed Meaning	Actual Meaning
carnivore			
technocracy			
tensile			
attenuate			
obscure			
magnificent			
current			
omnivore			
obstinate			

Lesson 91

ON BEING WORLDLY

One of the qualities that I admire in Marion is her **cosmopolitan** worldview and her **prolific** desire to share it with everyone she meets. Whenever provincially minded strangers attempt to eulogize the advantages of having a narrow worldview, Marion rapidly **undermines** their arguments. She says that locally minded people were important in a bygone era, and that to hold such views in a global society would be downright **anachronistic**. Perhaps it is an **idiosyncrasy** to be so pushy about your global values, but I admire Marion for her convictions.

NEW WORDS

idiosyncrasy
ˌidēəˈsiNGkrəsē

anachronism
əˈnakrəˌnizəm

undermine
ˌəndərˈmīn, ˈəndərˌmīn

prolific
prəˈlifik

cosmopolitan
ˌkäzməˈpälitn

Definitions: Try matching the words in the list with the appropriate definitions. If you are stuck, check the glossary in the back of the book or the passage at the top of the page.

1. idiosyncrasy _____ a. something belonging to a period other than to which it exists in
2. anachronism _____ b. to weaken or erode the foundation of something (often an intellectual argument)
3. undermine _____ c. a mode of behavior peculiar to an individual
4. prolific _____ d. worldly; comfortable in many cultures
5. cosmopolitan _____ e. producing much or many of something

Sentences: Try to use the words above in a sentence below. Remember that a word ending may be changed or its figure of speech slightly altered.

6. One of Antonio's _____ is that he will only eat cake that is green.
7. Having lived in Hong Kong, Istanbul, Paris, Boston, and Nairobi makes Oded one of the most _____ people that I know.
8. Poor logical reasoning often _____ an otherwise sturdy argument.
9. It would be _____ to wear medieval armor to work.
10. Stephen King is a(n) _____ writer, as he has composed over a dozen best-selling horror novels.

Lesson 92

BECOMING A MONK

NEW WORDS

expedition
ˌekspəˈdiSHən

relinquish
riˈliNGkwiSH

ascetic
əˈsetik

corroborate
kəˈräbəˌrāt

extol
ikˈstōl

Jerry decided last year to **relinquish** a life of luxury for a more **ascetic** existence as a Buddhist monk. He decided so after he grew weary of his finance job and had heard a friend at a temple **extol** the values of a humble, peaceful life. So, after hearing such news, Jerry went on an **expedition** to Tibet to see the heart of Buddhism at work. While there, he saw Buddhist practices that **corroborated** his suspicion that a life of religious tolerance and sanctity was the right life for him.

Definitions: Try matching the words in the list with the appropriate definitions. If you are stuck, check the glossary in the back of the book or the passage at the top of the page.

1. expedition _____ a. to confirm or give support to (a statement, finding, or theory)
2. relinquish _____ b. to voluntarily give up something
3. ascetic _____ c. a journey undertaken by people for a purpose
4. corroborate _____ d. to praise enthusiastically
5. extol _____ e. severe self-discipline and abstaining from all forms of indulgence

Sentences: Try to use the words above in a sentence below. Remember that a word ending may be changed or its figure of speech slightly altered.

6. Many politicians like to _____ family values and religion as hallmarks of a stable society.
7. When Alec decided to become a Buddhist monk, he _____ all of his goods to pursue a more _____ existence.
8. Sara's fingerprints on the gun _____ the sheriff's suspicion that she was the key player in the murder of the old man last week.
9. In the seventeenth century, there were many _____ to travel to far-flung places of the globe in search of exotic animals, plants, or stories.

Lesson 93

MACHIAVELLIAN PRINCE

The Florentine statesman Niccolò Macchiavelli (1469-1527) offered advice for princes on how to rule their people in his famed book, *The Prince* (1513). In it, he suggested that **sovereign** rulers like princes must possess a strict and tyrannical **demeanor** to rule. By doing so, he argued, princes can create an **ominous** sense of fear among their subjects, as subjects are more willing to appease a ruler that is feared than one that is loved. Furthermore, a prince should try to **circumvent** many forms of honesty in dealing with subjects, as his primary purpose is not to help his people, but to see his kingdom thrive. Thus, it is best that many of a prince's subjects remain **anonymous** to him rather than to become real intimate entities.

NEW WORDS

ominous
ˈämənəs

sovereign
ˈsäv(ə)rən

anonymous
əˈnänəməs

circumvent
ˌsərkəmˈvent

demeanor
diˈmēnər

Definitions: Try matching the words in the list with the appropriate definitions. If you are stuck, check the glossary in the back of the book or the passage at the top of the page.

1. ominous _____ a. not identified by name; unknown
2. sovereign _____ b. to find a way around an obstacle
3. anonymous _____ c. outward behavior or bearing
4. circumvent _____ d. threatening; showing that something bad may happen
5. demeanor _____ e. supreme ruler or monarch

Sentences: Try to use the words above in a sentence below. Remember that a word ending may be changed or its figure of speech slightly altered.

6. A(n) _____ mood fell over Colleen as she saw a man with a knife try to break in her home.
7. Perhaps out of fear of being discovered and retaliated against, many people prefer to be _____ when leaving criticism.
8. Roger has a cheerful _____ and always smiles when guests enter his sports bar.
9. Many cowardly people prefer to _____ a problem rather than confronting it straight on.
10. Queen Elizabeth I was once the _____ ruler of England.

Lesson 94

HUY THE MAGICIAN

NEW WORDS

eulogy
ˈyoolәjē

inept
iˈnept

maudlin
ˈmôdlin

petulant
ˈpeCHәlәnt

rebellious
riˈbelyәs

One upon a time there lived a **rebellious** young boy named Huy. Huy always interrupted his teachers in class. Because he was so disruptive, his teachers naively assumed that he was academically **inept**. But in reality, he had a secret gift for magic. One day, when he was feeling especially **petulant** after being insulted in class, he whined and screamed until he made his teacher's attendance book disappear. Upon performing this feat, the students were impressed while the excessively **maudlin** teacher cried for hours over the loss of her book. In the end however, all **eulogized** Huy and his amazing magical talent.

Definitions: Try matching the words in the list with the appropriate definitions. If you are stuck, check the glossary in the back of the book or the passage at the top of the page.

1. eulogy _____ a. self-pityingly or tearfully sentimental
2. inept _____ b. showing a desire to resist authority, control, or conventions
3. maudlin _____ c. irascible or ill-tempered like a child
4. petulant _____ d. a speech or piece of writing that praises someone highly
5. rebellious _____ e. having or showing no skill; clumsy

Sentences: Try to use the words above in a sentence below. Remember that a word ending may be changed or its figure of speech slightly altered.

6. Michael _____ his mother so eloquently in his speech at her funeral.
7. The _____ workers refused to do their jobs until their demand for a new boss was addressed.
8. My six-year-old niece becomes _____ when she is not given the ice cream she is promised for dessert: she throws tantrums and cries for hours.
9. It would be _____ to cry for months after your boyfriend abandoned you for another woman.
10. The mathematically _____ student was unable to execute his multiplication tables properly.

Lesson 95

AN ARROGANT MATHEMATICIAN

Sophie likes to show off how smart she is. While she has **innate** mathematical ability, she wants everybody to think that she is a child prodigy. Therefore, she has decided to spend her time trying to **decipher** some of the world's most mysterious mathematical codes with her knowledge. Work in this field has become so hard that Sophie has had to abandon her **gregarious** personality for a persona that **accentuates** isolated scrutiny over complex formulae. Though Sophie claims to have figured out her codes, other mathematicians have been quick to point out the **sophistries** in her reasoning.

NEW WORDS

sophistry
ˈsäfəstrē

gregarious
griˈge(ə)rēəs

accentuate
akˈsenCHooˌāt

innate
iˈnāt

decipher
diˈsīfər

Definitions: Try matching the words in the list with the appropriate definitions. If you are stuck, check the glossary in the back of the book or the passage at the top of the page.

1. sophistry _____ a. fond of company; sociable
2. gregarious _____ b. inborn; natural
3. accentuate _____ c. to convert something encoded into comprehensible, normal language
4. innate _____ d. to make more noticeable or prominent
5. decipher _____ e. the use of fallacious arguments, often with the intention of deceiving

Sentences: Try to use the words above in a sentence below. Remember that a word ending may be changed or its figure of speech slightly altered.

6. Even the famous linguist was unable to _____ the hieroglyphic codes on the pyramids.
7. Most attorneys are trained to locate and disassemble the _____ in their opponents' arguments in court.
8. It seems that Evan's mathematical ability is _____: neither his parents nor his teachers nor his textbooks have made him as adept at math as he is.
9. Harvey is a(n) _____ person who always socializes with his party guests.
10. Tamara's unconventional outfit _____ her weird personality.

Lesson 96

NEW WORDS

digress
dīˈgres

incredulous
inˈkrejələs

empathetic
ˌempəˈTHetik

conspicuous
kənˈspikyooəs

somber
ˈsämbər

PARTY FUNERAL FOR JACKIE

Last Sunday Jackie showed up at her uncle's funeral in Boston. Though it was a **somber** affair, Jackie arrived at the event wearing bright colors and was happy as a clam. Her outfit was surely **conspicuous** among the sea of black suits and dresses, and many of the funeral attendees stared at her with **incredulous** looks on their faces. Such behavior was surely consummate with someone who had no **empathetic** feelings for her late uncle. Many people who began reminiscing nostalgically about Jackie's uncle **digressed** into long discussions of horror about how such a niece could behave so poorly at her uncle's funeral.

Definitions: Try matching the words in the list with the appropriate definitions. If you are stuck, check the glossary in the back of the book or the passage at the top of the page.

1. digress _____ a. gloomy; dark or dull in color or tone
2. incredulous _____ b. standing out so as to be clearly visible
3. empathetic _____ c. the ability to understand and share the feelings of another
4. conspicuous _____ d. to depart from the main subject in speech or writing
5. somber _____ e. unwilling or unable to believe something

Sentences: Try to use the words above in a sentence below. Remember that a word ending may be changed or its figure of speech slightly altered.

6. The events of September 11, 2001 marked a(n) _____ page in American history.
7. It was _____ that Greg had not memorized his lines for the play when he appeared on stage baffled about what to say.
8. Speakers who _____ from their main point often lose their audiences.
9. Mark was _____ when his friend Daniel's cat died because he, too, had once lost a pet.
10. Katy appeared _____ when she heard that Mario used the pages of her new book as wrapping paper for Christmas presents.

Lesson 97

GRIEVING CHAIRMAN MEOW

Paloma's **ebullient** personality makes it difficult for her to be **disillusioned** by many things. No matter what the situation is, she always finds a positive lens upon which to examine things. Take for example, my pet cat, Chairman Meow. Unfortunately, Chairman Meow died last week. Though I was sad, Paloma encouraged me to think of Chairman Meow's **longevity**, reminding me that many cats do not live beyond fifteen years of age. And, though perhaps **unorthodox** to some, she pushed me to get a new cat right away to fill my emptiness. Now that I have my new cat, Hello Catty, I again feel **buoyant**.

NEW WORDS

ebullient
iˈbo͝olyənt, iˈbəlyənt

longevity
lônˈjevətē, län-

unorthodox
ˌənˈôrTHəˌdäks

buoyant
ˈboi-ənt, ˈbo͞oyənt

disillusioned
ˌdisəˈlo͞oZHənd

Definitions: Try matching the words in the list with the appropriate definitions. If you are stuck, check the glossary in the back of the book or the passage at the top of the page.

1. ebullient _____ a. disappointed when something turns out to be less than what was believed or expected
2. longevity _____ b. 1. capable of floating; 2. bubbly and cheerful
3. unorthodox _____ c. unconventional, unusual
4. buoyant _____ d. cheerful and full of energy
5. disillusioned _____ e. concerning having a long life

Sentences: Try to use the words above in a sentence below. Remember that a word ending may be changed or its figure of speech slightly altered.

6. Often solders that return from war feel _____ about notions of progress, victory, or glory after having seen so many citizens slain.
7. Unlike a sinking rock, an ice cube is _____ in water.
8. Shrikirti's _____ study habits baffled her friends; nevertheless, everyone could attest to the fact that reading books with techno music blaring improved her grades.
9. Part of the reason Nicole was elected "Miss Congeniality" was because of her _____ demeanor.
10. While humans have a life expectancy of around eighty years, the _____ of certain turtles is almost twice that amount of time.

Lesson 98

NEW WORDS

hostile
hästl, ˈhä‿stīl

prescient
ˈpreSH(ē)ənt, ˈprē-

vast
vast

assimilate
əˈsiməˌlāt

consummate
ˈkänsəˌmāt

INDRANIL'S ARRANGED MARRIAGE

Though Indranil was originally **hostile** to the idea of having his parents arrange his marriage, he began to change his mind after they introduced him to Prem. How **prescient** they must be, he thought, to pick a girl that I like and to whom I am attracted! And she was pretty, too. Of the **vast** number of possible matches, Indranil became convinced that his parents had found the right partner with whom he could **consummate** his union. And because they came from similar cultural backgrounds, there were very few new rituals and cultural lessons that each had to **assimilate**. What a fortunate pairing!

Definitions: Try matching the words in the list with the appropriate definitions. If you are stuck, check the glossary in the back of the book or the passage at the top of the page.

1. hostile _____ a. having or showing knowledge of events before they take place
2. prescient _____ b. to fully take in information, ideas, or culture
3. vast _____ c. unfriendly; antagonistic
4. assimilate _____ d. (adj.) showing a high degree of flair and skill; (v.) 1. to make a marriage or relationship complete by having sexual intercourse; 2. to complete an action or make perfect
5. consummate _____ e. immense; of a widespread extent or quality

Sentences: Try to use the words above in a sentence below. Remember that a word ending may be changed or its figure of speech slightly altered.

6. If you are talented and hardworking, there should be _____ career options for you.
7. When people move to a new country, they occasionally encounter difficulties in _____ easily to foreign cultures.
8. After Steven insulted Charles at the charity dinner, the latter held _____ feelings toward the former.
9. The awarding of a doctorate is the _____ act to certify that a person can create original knowledge.
10. Though Cleo is regarded by many as _____, others think that her claims of being clairvoyant are nothing but a ruse.

Lesson 99

BAD CHILD

C.J. was known to be an **irreverent** child. Whenever people did not shower him with attention, he would try myriad **novel** methods of attempting to **divert** people's attention away from their duties and onto him. Strangers thought he constantly exhibited **flagrantly** rude manners, and that his parents should get him help. They warned C.J.'s family that if C.J. did not get help soon he would become a menace to society, for there were **precursors** in C.J.'s behavior of a deeply disturbed adult. Sadly, however, C.J.'s relatives were too blind to see his faults and C.J. continued to develop as a problematic individual.

NEW WORDS

divert
di'vərt, dī-

flagrant
'flāgrənt

irreverent
i'rev(ə)rənt

novel
'nävəl

precursor
'prē͵kərsər, pri'kər-

Definitions: Try matching the words in the list with the appropriate definitions. If you are stuck, check the glossary in the back of the book or the passage at the top of the page.

1. divert _____ a. (adj.) new and original; (n.) fictitious prose narrative of book length, often having somewhat realistic characters and actions
2. flagrant _____ b. 1. to cause someone or something to change from one direction or form to another; 2. to distract someone's attention from something
3. irreverent _____ c. showing a lack of respect
4. novel _____ d. blatant; obvious; deliberate
5. precursor _____ e. a forerunner

Sentences: Try to use the words above in a sentence below. Remember that a word ending may be changed or its figure of speech slightly altered.

6. It can be said that a(n) _____ to earthquakes is erratic behavior exhibited by nearby birds and mammals.
7. When Phong pushed Josh on the basketball court to injure him, it was clear that his attempt to harm Josh was _____.
8. Many politicians attempt to _____ attention away from controversial issues by discussing trivial ones instead.
9. Guests were incensed by Ricardo's _____ behavior when he threw confetti and cheered at Monica's funeral.
10. The purpose of a Ph.D. dissertation is to write about a completely _____ idea and break new ground in an academic field.

Lesson 100

FIRE OUT THE WINDOW

NEW WORDS

repent
ri'pent

supercilious
ˌsoopər'silēəs

vanquish
'vaNGkwiSH

indigenous
in'dijənəs

conflagration
ˌkänflə'grāSHən

Last week outside my bedroom window, I saw a **conflagration** in the building next door. I do not know who caused it, but I heard shrieking noises from some of the **indigenous** people loitering nearby. Nevertheless, a **supercilious** firefighter was overly proud of putting it out. "I, and I alone, **vanquished** every flame," he said to the local television broadcaster. Yet when the fireman said this, his colleagues became angry that he did not acknowledge their efforts. Through threats and hostility, they forced him to **repent** for his selfish behavior. Only with repeated pressure were the efforts of all acknowledged.

Definitions: Try matching the words in the list with the appropriate definitions. If you are stuck, check the glossary in the back of the book or the passage at the top of the page.

1. repent _____ a. to defeat thoroughly
2. supercilious _____ b. to express regret for one's sin or wrongdoing
3. vanquish _____ c. originating or occurring naturally in a specific location; native
4. indigenous _____ d. behaving as if one is superior to others
5. conflagration _____ e. gigantic fire

Sentences: Try to use the words above in a sentence below. Remember that a word ending may be changed or its figure of speech slightly altered.

6. Although many people felt that Cheryl had a(n) _____ demeanor, she was, in actuality, a warm hearted, modest person.
7. King Tristan implored his knights to _____ the enemies and to bring indefinite peace to the kingdom.
8. The raccoon is an animal that is _____ to North America.
9. The arrogant oaf refused to _____ for his wrongdoings.
10. Not even three fire trucks could quell the _____ that broke out in the building across the street last night.

Word Search
Lessons 91-100

```
S N Y M W D L N N G J W B L X K Y D Z P N
U V O T S N M Z T T L A D M W W L M Y A L
P I T V T I Z N Z N C S D K Y L V Y T L B
E N T Z E Q N R L C E R U R Y X B I T N L
R N E L M L N O E C R R V O W X L P D N N
C A B J G Y J N R Y I T E J M O R J M G Z
I T U M D B T D D H W T K V P Y Q J G D E
L E L Z B U B X I Q C L E O E J N N R T N
I I L G A X L B G S Q A M H E R B O A N L
O N I T P N M M L Y I S N X T R R L N P K
U D E M L Q W J V Z O L P A E A I I R A W
S I N I N E P T L C Z E L L Y M P E W M R
P G T K Y Y M L B M D R I U I Q S M A Z L
D E M E A N O R Y I L N X S S C R U E L N
K N Y D J D L B T R Q D S X I I D G V J T
T O V J R R Y I M U Y A L E X L O Y J X J
W U M V E Q O R I D K W N R I N L N M N R
P S W B R N N S Y T L T J N Z Q K D E Q L
R N M N K Z H J B T R L P B B R T N K D N
X O L P B R R Y T Y N L N X Y T D W R R
S J J V K N M Y J J W D N L N D B D W K N
```

1. something belonging to a period other than to which it exists
2. worldly; comfortable in many cultures
3. a journey undertaken by people for a purpose
4. to voluntarily give up something
5. not identified by name; unknown
6. outward behavior or bearing
7. having or showing no skill; clumsy
8. self-pityingly or tearfully sentimental
9. to make more noticeable or prominent
10. inborn; natural
11. the ability to understand and share the feelings of another
12. gloomy; dark or dull in color or tone
13. cheerful and full of energy
14. disappointed when something turns out to be less than what was believed or expected
15. having or showing knowledge of events before they take place
16. 1. to absorb and take in information fully; 2. to absorb people, ideas, or a culture into wider society; 3. to cause something to resemble, to liken
17. (adj.) new and original; (n.) a book-length prose narrative, generally with characters and actions that have some element of realism
18. showing a lack of respect
19. behaving as if one is superior to others
20. originating or occurring naturally in a specific location; native

Vocabulary Review
Lessons 91-100

Directions: Match each word with its best approximate definition. Note that definitions are not necessarily repeated verbatim from the lesson exercises.

1.	idiosyncrasy	_____	a.	present or producing in great amounts
2.	prolific	_____	b.	standing out to be clearly visible; attracting attention
3.	ascetic	_____	c.	giving the impression that something bad is about to happen
4.	extol	_____	d.	unfriendly, antagonistic
5.	ominous	_____	e.	conspicuous; obvious
6.	circumvent	_____	f.	a speech or writing that praises someone, often given immediately after his or her death
7.	eulogy	_____	g.	to convert something from a code into comprehensible language
8.	petulant	_____	h.	to defeat thoroughly
9.	gregarious	_____	i.	fond of company; sociable; outgoing
10.	decipher	_____	j.	a person or thing that comes before another of the same kind
11.	digress	_____	k.	to find a way around something; to overcome something, usually in a sneaky way
12.	conspicuous	_____	l.	concerning long life
13.	longevity	_____	m.	to praise
14.	buoyant	_____	n.	of a very great extent or quantity; immense
15.	hostile	_____	o.	a mode of behavior or say of thought peculiar to an individual
16.	vast	_____	p.	able to stay afloat in liquid or gas; bubbly, cheerful
17.	flagrant	_____	q.	childishly sulky or bad-tempered
18.	precursor	_____	r.	a giant fire
19.	vanquish	_____	s.	to wander off topic in speech or writing
20.	conflagration	_____	t.	characterized by severe self-discipline and rejecting all forms of indulgence or excessive material goods

Word Roots: Unit 10

ROOTS AND THEIR MEANINGS

hyper:	over	fic/fig:	to make; to do
epi:	upon	vid/vis:	to see
hypo:	under	dem:	people

Here are a few examples of some words that use the above roots:

hyperactive: abnormally or extremely active
epidemic: widespread occurrence of infectious disease in a community
hypothermia: condition of having a low body temperature
figment: something one believes to be real, but that he or she makes up in imagination
visual: of or related to sight or seeing
demography: the study of populations and changes in populations (especially as related to births, deaths, income, and disease)

Now try to fill in the table below by finding the appropriate root(s) and interpreting the meaning of each word:

Word	Root(s)	Guessed Meaning	Actual Meaning
hypersensitive			
video			
demographics			
hypothyroidism			
fictional			
epithet			
figurative			
epidermis			
hypertension			
figure (v.)			

NEW WORDS

vigorous
ˈvig(ə)rəs

sagacious
səˈgāSHəs

avant-garde
ˌavänt ˈgärd, ˌaväN

punctilious
ˌpəNGkˈtilēəs

invulnerable
inˈvəlnərəbəl

Lesson 101

ADVICE FROM A FASHIONISTA

My friend Caity began writing a blog that celebrates the most **avant-garde** fashion styles in San Francisco. So, in an effort to be more glamorous in my dress, I sought her **sagacious** advice. Caity said that the key to having fashion sense is to be **punctilious** in noting what is innovative in clothing. With this knowledge and **vigorous** attempts to seem sociable, one can be a sartorial icon who is **invulnerable** to the criticisms of peers.

Definitions: Try matching the words in the list with the appropriate definitions. If you are stuck, check the glossary in the back of the book or the passage at the top of the page.

1. vigorous _____ a. concerning new, heterodox ideas or the people introducing them, usually in the arts
2. sagacious _____ b. impossible to harm
3. avant-garde _____ c. showing great attention to detail
4. punctilious _____ d. strong, healthy, energetic; robust
5. invulnerable _____ e. wise; showing keen judgment and discernment

Sentences: Try to use the words above in a sentence below. Remember that a word ending may be changed or its figure of speech slightly altered.

6. My grandfather always gives me _____ advice about how to get my parents to listen to me.
7. It is necessary to stir the ingredients together _____ in a bowl to make batter for brownies.
8. My sister is so _____ in listening to conversations that she will remember exactly whatever someone says weeks after it is said.
9. If you wear armor like a medieval knight, you will feel so _____ that even arrows shot at you will give you no pain.
10. Salvador Dali's work was very _____ for its day: he created novel art forms that permeated the Western psyche.

Lesson 102

HELEN'S COVETED JEWELRY

Due to **unforeseen** circumstances, my aunt Helen passed away last summer. When we were cleaning through her home, we found a chest full of seemingly expensive diamond rings. Because none of us were knowledgeable about these potential treasures, we took them to the local jeweler to appraise them. Initially, he thought us bombarding him with questions was **officious** – so much so that he tried to **curtail** our interest in his expertise by providing **deprecating** remarks. Yet upon seeing the jewelry and deeming it extremely valuable, he concluded that we were not a bunch of **charlatans** presenting him with fake goods in order to rip him off. The jewelry served as a bridge to build a new, unexpected working friendship.

NEW WORDS

charlatan
ˈSHärlətən, ˈSHärlətn

curtail
kərˈtāl

unforeseen
ˌənfôrˈsēn

officious
əˈfiSHəs

deprecate
ˈdepriˌkāt

Definitions: Try matching the words in the list with the appropriate definitions. If you are stuck, check the glossary in the back of the book or the passage at the top of the page.

1. charlatan _____ a. unanticipated; unpredicted
2. curtail _____ b. to express disapproval of
3. unforeseen _____ c. to reduce in quantity or impose restrictions on something
4. officious _____ d. intrusively eager in offering advice or assistance with something
5. deprecate _____ e. a fraud; someone falsely claiming to have knowledge or skill in something

Sentences: Try to use the words above in a sentence below. Remember that a word ending may be changed or its figure of speech slightly altered.

6. Alexander was regarded as a(n) _____ scholar, always offering unsolicited guidance to people with even the slightest interest in research.
7. Nicole's parents hoped that they could _____ her problem with procrastination by forcing her to sit and study in her room every afternoon.
8. Monica has been seen by many as a(n) _____: she constantly is getting paid to teach people piano when she has no musical talent herself!
9. It was a(n) _____ circumstance that James' dad suddenly died in a plane crash.
10. The school bully always makes _____ remarks about his victims.

Lesson 103

IMAGINARY PRINCE

NEW WORDS

demoralize
diˈmôrəˌlīz

invigorate
inˈvigəˌrāt

halting
ˈhôltiNG

sublime
səˈblīm

potentate
ˈpōtnˌtāt

If I were a **potentate** or supreme ruler of my realm, I would do everything I could to make my kingdom amazing. For example, I would **invigorate** my subjects by telling them stories that anyone can become famous and imbuing them with a sense of hope and vision. I would also hope that they felt **sublime** living in my realm, as it would provide them with everything they need to be inspired. Nothing in my kingdom would **demoralize** my citizens or result in any **halting** behaviors. Simply put, it would be a nearly utopian existence.

Definitions: Try matching the words in the list with the appropriate definitions. If you are stuck, check the glossary in the back of the book or the passage at the top of the page.

1. demoralize _____ a. to cause someone to lose hope or spirit
2. invigorate _____ b. a monarch or ruler (often autocratic)
3. halting _____ c. to give strength or energy to
4. sublime _____ d. hesitant, largely due to lack of confidence
5. potentate _____ e. of excellence or beauty to inspire admiration or awe

Sentences: Try to use the words above in a sentence below. Remember that a word ending may be changed or its figure of speech slightly altered.

6. Although Charles is not really a king, he sure acts like a(n) _____ and seems to be given regal privileges wherever he goes.
7. Marianne was in a(n) _____ mood after she won tickets to hear her favorite orchestra perform downtown; she told everyone how excited she was.
8. Though the bully aimed to belittle Martha, she instead felt _____ by his behavior and proceeded to get him in trouble.
9. The troops were _____ about combat after having lost three successive battles in the war.
10. After September 11, 2001, the United States' approach to terrorism has mutated from one of sheer confidence to a more _____ position.

Lesson 104

BELLIGERENT BARNEY

My cousin Barney is a rather **bellicose** young man. No matter what the topic is, nothing seems to **deter** him from becoming combative in discussing it. Sometimes my friends are so afraid to engage Barney that they **feign** illness to avoid the potential of getting into an altercation with him. One friend, in particular, has a **fatalistic** attitude about dealing with Barney, assuming that any interaction with him will always only be negative. Despite the fact that Barney **relishes** a good fight, he is deeply kind on the inside.

NEW WORDS

deter
di'tər

bellicose
'beli͵kōs

feign
fān

relish
'reliSH

fatalistic
͵fātl'istik

Definitions: Try matching the words in the list with the appropriate definitions. If you are stuck, check the glossary in the back of the book or the passage at the top of the page.

1. deter _____ a. belief that all events are predetermined and inevitable
2. bellicose _____ b. aggressive and warlike
3. feign _____ c. to pretend to be affected by something
4. relish _____ d. to discourage someone from doing something, usually by instilling fear or doubt
5. fatalistic _____ e. (n.) 1. great enjoyment; 2. a condiment eaten together with plain food to add flavor; (v.) to enjoy greatly

Sentences: Try to use the words above in a sentence below. Remember that a word ending may be changed or its figure of speech slightly altered.

6. Because of his _____ behavior, Jake's parents grounded him until he felt contrite enough to understand the gravity of beating up his brother.
7. Stephen _____ spending time with his friends at karaoke for his birthday, for he rarely got to see so many of them together in one place.
8. Having a(n) _____ attitude is one definite way to ensure that it will be hard to be successful in the future.
9. In order to avoid taking her midterm at school, Linh _____ illness and got her parents to call in her absence.
10. By hiding June's book before her final exam, Sally hoped to _____ her from preparing to do well and acing the test.

Lesson 105

NEW WORDS

meditation
ˌmedəˈtāSHən

misguided
misˈgīdid

exemplar
igˈzemplər, -ˌplär

insinuate
inˈsinyəˌwāt

renown
riˈnoun

CREEPY YOGA INSTRUCTOR

My cousin Lori met Eddie while he was reading one of his **meditations** about mind-body unity at the local library. He told her he appreciated her coming to his reading, but that her thoughts about spirituality were **misguided**. Only with a dose of yoga, he **insinuated**, could she get a better understanding about his ideas. So Lori signed up for yoga with the **renown** Eddie. But after attending Eddie's yoga class, Lori was disillusioned with her experience. In the end, she concluded that he was hardly an **exemplar**, but rather just a creepy man who liked to flirt with girls.

Definitions: Try matching the words in the list with the appropriate definitions. If you are stuck, check the glossary in the back of the book or the passage at the top of the page.

1. meditation _____ a. a person serving as an excellent model
2. misguided _____ b. to suggest or hint at something indirectly and, perhaps, unpleasantly
3. exemplar _____ c. exhibiting faulty reasoning
4. insinuate _____ d. being known or discussed by many people
5. renown _____ e. 1. the process of reflection; 2. written or spoken discourse expressing one's thoughts on a subject

Sentences: Try to use the words above in a sentence below. Remember that a word ending may be changed or its figure of speech slightly altered.

6. For many people, Marin Luther King, Jr. (1929-1968) is the _____ of an individual who stood up and promoted racial equality.

7. Critics hailed Professor Freiheit's long treatise on capitalism in the twenty-first century as a profound _____ on economic thought.

8. Michael Jordan is reputed to be one of the most _____ basketball players of all time.

9. When my girlfriend sneered at me on Valentine's Day, I interpreted it as a(n) _____ that our relationship may be quickly drawing to a close.

10. I feel that my principal's distrust of me is _____, for I am one of the most honest students in my grade.

Lesson 106

EGOMANIAC PROFESSOR

Students at prestigious universities should be **wary** of egomaniac professors. Though such professors do not constitute the majority of researchers on campus, there is usually a **snob** with a big ego in each department who thinks that he is smarter and more deserving than all of his peers. In order to **discern** which professors behave like this, it is best to pay such individuals **sporadic** visits during office hours to learn how they think. With a little luck, you should be able to unearth what **machinations** these faculty members have for remaining in control of everyone around them so that they can feel like they are the king of their department.

NEW WORDS

sporadic
spəˈradik

machination
ˈmakəˌnāSHən, ˈmaSHə-

wary
ˈwe(ə)rē

snob
snäb

discern
diˈsərn

Definitions: Try matching the words in the list with the appropriate definitions. If you are stuck, check the glossary in the back of the book or the passage at the top of the page.

1. sporadic _____   a. one who thinks his/her tastes or position is superior to those of other people
2. machination _____   b. scheming; engaging in plots or intrigues
3. wary _____   c. occurring at irregular intervals
4. snob _____   d. cautious about possible dangers of things
5. discern _____   e. to perceive or recognize something

Sentences: Try to use the words above in a sentence below. Remember that a word ending may be changed or its figure of speech slightly altered.

6. Shirley's attendance in class is _____: though she is occasionally present, nobody can guess whether she will show up on any given day.
7. For over a year the two criminals were involved in _____ to rob the bank down the street.
8. After Burt was caught cheating on his exam, his teachers were _____ of his study habits and his desire to learn material.
9. Dr. Ahmed is so _____ that he will not even eat in the same room as people who do not have a doctorate.
10. It is difficult to _____ if Laura's sadness is because of her break up or because of her failing her midterm exams.

Lesson 107

NEW WORDS

devoid
di'void

visionary
'viZHə,nerē

corridor
'kôrədər, 'kär-, -,dôr

forestall
fôr'stôl

proliferation
prə,lifə'rāSHən

ELEVATOR PROGNOSTICATOR

Last night I was taking a stroll down my hotel **corridor** when I saw a sleek woman adorned with ribbons and sequins rush toward the elevator. She seemed completely **devoid** of calmness as she sprinted down the hall. Out of curiosity, I began to follow her. I asked her why she seemed so panicked, but she initially would not explain why. She merely said that she was a **visionary** who was in a hurry to **forestall** an attempted robbery across the street. She told me that if she could not apprehend two criminals, there would be a **proliferation** of crimes around town in the next three weeks. Hopefully her visions served her well, as I never saw her ever again afterward.

Definitions: Try matching the words in the list with the appropriate definitions. If you are stuck, check the glossary in the back of the book or the passage at the top of the page.

1. devoid _____ a. long passage in a building with doors to enter rooms
2. visionary _____ b. rapid increase in numbers of something
3. corridor _____ c. (adj.) 1. describing a person who can imagine the future with imagination and wisdom; 2. able to see visions in a dream or as a supernatural apparition; (n.) a person who has ideas about the future or how it may appear
4. forestall _____ d. to prevent or obstruct by taking prior action
5. proliferation _____ e. completely lacking

Sentences: Try to use the words above in a sentence below. Remember that a word ending may be changed or its figure of speech slightly altered.

6. The recent _____ of law schools in the United States has resulted in more lawyers on the job market than there are available jobs.
7. Some deserts receive so little precipitation that they are _____ of any large green plants.
8. One could call my neighbor something of a(n) _____ because he was able to predict the crash of the stock market months before it happened.
9. The anxious students asked their teacher a lot of questions in an attempt to _____ the inevitable quiz that was slated to occur in class.
10. My hotel room is located at the end of the _____ on the right hand side.

Lesson 108

PREDICTING AN EARTHQUAKE

Though it is difficult for humans to **surmise** when an earthquake is about to occur, animals are touted to have far better capabilities of predicting such an event. For example, if an animal that is usually docile acts **irascible**, it is a potential indicator of an impending earthquake. Similarly, if nocturnal animals are unsettled during the day or circadian animals disturbed at night, that is another sign that could **foreshadow** an earthquake. Such behavior occurs regardless of whether the fault line of the quake is active or has been **dormant**, as the geological reactions are similar in both circumstances. Damage from such quakes can potentially render unprotected or uninsured people **indigent** if their homes, businesses, or properties are damaged.

NEW WORDS

indigent
ˈindijənt

irascible
iˈrasəbəl

surmise
sərˈmīz

foreshadow
fôrˈSHadō

dormant
ˈdôrmənt

Definitions: Try matching the words in the list with the appropriate definitions. If you are stuck, check the glossary in the back of the book or the passage at the top of the page.

1. indigent _____ a. to be a warning or indication of a future event
2. irascible _____ b. to guess that something is true without having proper evidence to confirm it
3. surmise _____ c. having a tendency to be easily angered
4. foreshadow _____ d. poor; destitute; needy
5. dormant _____ e. (of an animal) having physical actions suspended for a period of time; (of a volcano temporarily inactive; (of a plant) alive but not growing; (of a disease) no symptoms and uncured, but may recur

Sentences: Try to use the words above in a sentence below. Remember that a word ending may be changed or its figure of speech slightly altered.

6. After sixty years of being _____, the volcano erupted again.
7. It was easy to _____ that Shikha was likely going to get married after we saw her canoodling with her boyfriend in the park.
8. Many young children are so _____ that anything can cause them to become petulant.
9. Famed American author Ernest Hemingway (1899-1981) is well-known for _____ the fate of his protagonists in the opening paragraphs of *A Farewell to Arms*.
10. If you receive a good college education and are pragmatic with your life choices, the probability of being _____ is relatively small.

Lesson 109

PLATO'S CAVE

NEW WORDS

cogent
ˈkōjənt

remnant
ˈremnənt

allegory
ˈaləˌgôrē

chide
CHīd

antagonistic
anˌtagəˈnistik

Perhaps one of the greatest **allegories** is that of the Cave, written by the Greek philosopher Plato. In this allegory, prisoners are shackled in a cave only to see shadows of figures on a wall parading before them. That is their reality. But then, suddenly, one of the prisoners is let free in the cave. He realizes that the shadows are not real; rather, they are the distorted version of reality that he has been trained to believe is true. As the philosopher leaves the cave and sees the sun, he gets a better version of the truth. Excited by what he sees, he hurries back to the cave and **cogently** tells his friends what he has witnessed. Yet his cave friends **chide** him for being weird and see him as an **antagonistic** threat to their reality. Any **remnants** of the freed prisoner's story are immediately discarded, for they pose a threat to the way of life of those imprisoned. The moral of the story: people believe what their reality is.

Definitions: Try matching the words in the list with the appropriate definitions. If you are stuck, check the glossary in the back of the book or the passage at the top of the page.

1. cogent _____ a. having hostile feelings toward someone or something
2. remnant _____ b. small remaining quantity of something
3. allegory _____ c. to scold or castigate
4. chide _____ d. a writing filled with hidden meanings that are moral or political
5. antagonistic _____ e. clear, logical, convincing (concerning an argument)

Sentences: Try to use the words above in a sentence below. Remember that a word ending may be changed or its figure of speech slightly altered.

6. Alexis' _____ speeches helped her get elected as president of the finance club.
7. Some of the deepest and most profound fiction is _____ in nature: the text is replete with allusions to things in real life.
8. Giang's parents _____ her for staying out past her curfew.
9. Anthropologists are always seeking _____ of past civilizations on their excavations.
10. Steven and Peter have a(n) _____ relationship: they are always trying to deprecate and slander each other over many issues.

Lesson 110

LARRY HATES TATOOS

When Larry heard that his daughter Lanie got a tattoo, he became extremely angry. Poor Lanie had to endure her father's **effrontery**, as he despises tattoos and people who have them. For the first five months after hearing of Lanie's tattoo, Larry **exuded** disgust at the thought of his daughter having an **indelible** design etched onto her back. He demanded that she remove the design, but she adamantly refused. He even attempted **covert** ways to get her into surgery to have the object removed, but to no avail. Now that a few years have passed, Larry has grown to accept the tattoo, and the fact that his behavior to remove it was, perhaps, somewhat **precipitous**. The moral of the lesson: a father should judge his daughter by her character and not her looks.

NEW WORDS

indelible
in'deləbəl

exude
ig'zood

effrontery
i'frəntərē

precipitous
pri'sipətəs

covert
kən'vərt

Definitions: Try matching the words in the list with the appropriate definitions. If you are stuck, check the glossary in the back of the book or the passage at the top of the page.

1. indelible _____   a. insolent or impertinent behavior
2. exude _____   b. done suddenly without careful reflection
3. effrontery _____   c. permanent
4. precipitous _____   d. not openly acknowledged or displayed; secretive; stealthy
5. covert _____   e. 1. to discharge a moisture or smell gradually; 2. to display a sentiment or quality openly and intensely

Sentences: Try to use the words above in a sentence below. Remember that a word ending may be changed or its figure of speech slightly altered.

6. Ink used for tattoos is _____ and thus can only be removed through intense medical processes or covered with makeup.
7. Mark's father _____ a sense of pride when he saw his son win the citywide math competition.
8. When waging a war, it is often strategic to be _____ when planning on sabotaging your enemy.
9. It is unwise for teachers to _____ judge their students, for first impressions do not always reflect reality.
10. Only Robert had the _____ to challenge his cousin's choice of spouse at her wedding.

Crossword Puzzle
Lessons 1- 10 11-

ACROSS

2. 1. to discharge a moisture or smell gradually; 2. to display a sentiment or quality openly and intensely
4. (of an animal) having physical actions suspended for a period of time; (of a volcano temporarily inactive; (of a plant) alive but not growing; (of a disease) no symptoms and uncured, but may recur
7. a writing filled with hidden meanings that are moral or political
11. to reduce in quantity or impose restrictions on something
13. belief that all events are predetermined and inevitable
16. rapid increase in numbers of something
17. done suddenly without careful reflection
18. having a tendency to be easily angered
19. (adj.) 1. describing a person who can imagine the future with imagination and wisdom; 2. able to see visions in a dream or as a supernatural apparition; (n.) a person who has ideas about the future or how it may appear

DOWN

1. small remaining quantity of something
3. cautious about possible dangers of things
4. to cause someone to lose hope or spirit
5. 1. the process of reflection; 2. written or spoken discourse expressing one's thoughts on a subject
6. to express disapproval of
8. concerning new, heterodox ideas or the people introducing them, usually in the arts
9. to suggest or hint at something indirectly and, perhaps, unpleasantly
10. to give strength or energy to
12. scheming; engaging in plots or intrigues
14. aggressive and warlike
15. strong, healthy, energetic; robust

Vocabulary Review
Lessons 101-110

Directions: Match each word with its best approximate definition. Note that definitions are not necessarily repeated verbatim from the lesson exercises.

1. sagacious _____
2. punctilious _____
3. charlatan _____
4. officious _____
5. sublime _____
6. potentate _____
7. deter _____
8. relish _____
9. exemplar _____
10. renown _____
11. sporadic _____
12. snob _____
13. devoid _____
14. corridor _____
15. indigent _____
16. surmise _____
17. cogent _____
18. chide _____
19. indelible _____
20. covert _____

a. of such beauty or greatness as to inspire awe
b. to enjoy greatly
c. not openly acknowledged or displayed
d. a person or thing serving as a typical example; a model
e. a person who believes his or her tastes are superior to others and who often regards others with different tastes as lower class
f. wise
g. occurring at irregular intervals or only in a few places; scattered, isolated
h. to scold or rebuke
i. a person falsely claiming to have knowledge or a skill; a fraud
j. poor; needy
k. permanent; cannot be erased
l. being assertive of authority in an overly domineering way; being too eager to help or give advice
m. to suppose something is true without having evidence of it
n. long passage in a building with doors that lead into rooms
o. paying careful attention to detail
p. clear; logical; convincing (of an argument or case)
q. to discourage from doing something by instilling doubt or fear
r. the condition of being known or discussed by many people
s. entirely lacking or free from
t. a monarch or ruler, especially one who is autocratic

Word Roots: Unit 11

ROOTS AND THEIR MEANINGS

pro:	forward, supporting	pon/pos:	to put; to place
eu:	pleasing	voc:	to call
sequ/secu:	to follow	luc/lum:	light, bright

Here are a few examples of some words that use the above roots:

proactive: creating or controlling a situation by being active rather than passive after it has taken place
euphoric: characterized by feeling of intense excitement and happiness
consequential: following as a result or effect of something; important or substantive
deposit (v.): to put or set down something (usually money) in a specific place, often for safekeeping
vocal: expressing feelings loudly
luminous: full of shedding light; very bright

Now try to fill in the table below by finding the appropriate root(s) and interpreting the meaning of each word:

Word	Root(s)	Guessed Meaning	Actual Meaning
sequence			
postpone			
lucid			
provocative			
deposit			
eulogy			
consecutive			

156

Lesson 111

A BAFFLING HISTORY

It was surprising to find out that Hieu, a revered figure of Vietnam, was not exactly a trustworthy **adolescent**. Not only did he violate copious copyright laws that drew the **ire** of various parties, but he also was extremely **deceitful** when it came to interpersonal relationships. Hieu's parents tried to **soothe** people's anger with their opulence, a typical tactic commonly used by the wealthy. Unfortunately, the **tension** became so bad that his parents had no choice but to quickly send him abroad, hoping that he would learn how to become an ethical man. It turned out that their decision was correct.

NEW WORDS

deceitful
di'sētfəl

tension
'tenSHən

adolescent
ˌadl'esənt

ire
ī(ə)r

soothe
sooTH

Definitions: Try matching the words in the list with the appropriate definitions. If you are stuck, check the glossary in the back of the book or the passage at the top of the page.

1. deceitful _____ a. mental or emotional strain
2. tension _____ b. to relieve or comfort
3. adolescent _____ c. intense anger; wrath
4. ire _____ d. (adj.) in the process of developing from a child into an adult; (n.) a young person in between childhood and adulthood
5. soothe _____ e. misleading, fraudulent

Sentences: Try to use the words above in a sentence below. Remember that a word ending may be changed or its figure of speech slightly altered.

6. It is an extremely arduous task to _____ Mary's wrath once it begins: it is neigh unstoppable.
7. Drawing the _____ of the king, Jaime believes he could salvage the situation by killing the evil monster Cerberus.
8. Jon's _____ thesis was finally discredited upon being scrutinized meticulously by the academic board of directors.
9. Part of going through _____ is to experience the rebellious stage where young teenagers always feel the need for self-justification.
10. The _____ between the United States and Russia is becoming more strained every day.

Lesson 112

NEW WORDS

economical
ˌekəˈnämikəl, ˌēkə-

pensive
ˈpensiv

probe
prōb

miraculous
məˈrakyələs

demise
diˈmīz

AN EMINENT DETECTIVE

As a renowned detective, Allen always **probes** the neighbors surrounding the crime scene extensively in order to gather information. Furthermore, he also takes pride in how **economical** his investigations are, making them much more affordable to the public. Where the prominent and loquacious detectives meet their **demise**, the **pensive** Allen makes **miracles**. He is truly an important asset to society.

Definitions: Try matching the words in the list with the appropriate definitions. If you are stuck, check the glossary in the back of the book or the passage at the top of the page.

1. economical _____ a. 1. giving good value in return for one's money, time, or effort; 2. careful not to waste money or resources; 3. using no more of something than necessary
2. pensive _____ b. being able to work wonders; inexplicable
3. probe _____ c. (n.) 1. a small device used for collecting information, often surgically; 2. an unmanned exploratory spacecraft; 3. an investigation of a crime; (v.) to examine thoroughly; to question
4. miraculous _____ d. collapse, downfall
5. demise _____ e. engaged in or involving deep, serious thought

Sentences: Try to use the words above in a sentence below. Remember that a word ending may be changed or its figure of speech slightly altered.

6. The kingdom's ultimate _____ can be attributed to the usurper's relentless attacks.
7. The doctor's _____ surgery allowed his patient to completely recover from a seemingly incurable disease.
8. Kimberly was in a(n) _____ mood yesterday as she was reminded of her youthful high school days.
9. It is a lot more _____ to eat at home than to go out to a restaurant if you're willing to put in the effort to cook.
10. The investigator seeks to _____ the culprit for crime details.

Lesson 113

A MORAL QUANDARY

Ahmed is currently facing the biggest **predicament** of his life. Should he **arrest** this famous pianist whose **melody** is loved and revered in front of her audience? There is no concrete evidence that she is a member of the infamous anti-government group Navi. The original plan was to question her after the concert but now his boss wants an immediate captivity. Cursing his **predecessor** for quitting the job a few weeks ago, Ahmed proceeds into the building, thinking that he has no choice but to **improvise** once inside.

NEW WORDS

predecessor
ˈpredəˌsesər, ˈprē-

arrest
əˈrest

improvisation (improv)
imˌpräviˈzāSHən (imˌpräv)

melodic
məˈlädik

predicament
priˈdikəmənt

Definitions: Try matching the words in the list with the appropriate definitions. If you are stuck, check the glossary in the back of the book or the passage at the top of the page.

1. predecessor _____ a. a creation or execution of an act without preparation
2. arrest _____ b. forbear, ancestor
3. improvisation _____ c. difficult situation, dilemma
4. melodic _____ d. 1. to stop; 2. to take into custody; capture
5. predicament _____ e. pleasant sounding; harmonious

Sentences: Try to use the words above in a sentence below. Remember that a word ending may be changed or its figure of speech slightly altered.

6. For the wealthy Tommy, an everyday _____ involves choosing a country for his next weekend vacation.
7. Upon having the strategy leaked to the opposing team, Ming Ho decided to go scrap the plan and _____ during the match.
8. Despite his _____'s promise 20 years ago, Raynor decided to abolish the peace treaty and launched an attack on the North.
9. Tina's _____ tune allowed her to win over the hearts of her audience at the international music competition.
10. The 9/11 event instilled fear in Americans, allowing the government to expand its power and carry out warrantless _____.

Lesson 114

THE SURPRISING TRUTH

NEW WORDS

salubrious
səˈloobrēəs

exposé
ˌekspōˈzā

vital
ˈvītl

humble
ˈhəmbəl

mythical
ˈmiTHikəl

Daryl wrote a fabulous **exposé** about the key things his town should do to make city life more **salubrious**. He noted that it was **vital** for his town to have better sewage systems and to increase public transit, so as to stop filth and exhaust from ruining the city. It was also important to create initiatives to bring more fresh water to the city. Some of Daryl's critics have claimed that he has a somewhat **mythical** view of what his town ought to look like, but he insists that he is being realistic. The tone of his work is **humble** and pragmatic, and, with a little luck, will be taken seriously by the town alderman.

Definitions: Try matching the words in the list with the appropriate definitions. If you are stuck, check the glossary in the back of the book or the passage at the top of the page.

1. salubrious _____ a. fictitious; imaginary
2. exposé _____ b. a written report about the facts of something, usually something scandalous
3. vital _____ c. modest
4. humble _____ d. essential or crucial for sustenance
5. mythical _____ e. healthy; promoting good health

Sentences: Try to use the words above in a sentence below. Remember that a word ending may be changed or its figure of speech slightly altered.

6. The invention of sewage systems made overcrowded urban areas much more _____ in which to dwell.
7. The dragon is one of the most popular _____ creatures worldwide; it exists in both Western and Eastern cultures.
8. As a(n) _____ man, Vu attributed his success to the support of his peers despite having made the biggest contribution to the project.
9. It is _____ that people who have received poisonous venom from a snake bite be treated immediately; if not, death could be imminent.
10. The recent _____ on Mandy's illegal practices destroyed her company.

Lesson 115

A MAD SCIENTIST

The blight in the country left the soil severely damaged, making it extremely difficult to grow crops. While God's servants **preached** about the impending doom, governments poured a seemingly limitless amount of resources into solving this **conundrum**. An international conference was held shortly afterwards to tackle the problem, but it **excluded** a renowned geneticist named Lisa. **Teeming** with anger from this omission, she designed an **insidious** plan where she discredited every single scientist participating in the conference, plunging the world into even more chaos. Amidst this turmoil, Lisa began to take control of most of the world's food supply with her GMO agenda.

NEW WORDS

conundrum
kəˈnəndrəm

insidious
inˈsidēəs

exclude
ikˈsklood

preach
prēCH

teem
tēm

Definitions: Try matching the words in the list with the appropriate definitions. If you are stuck, check the glossary in the back of the book or the passage at the top of the page.

1. conundrum _____ a. to be full or swarming with something
2. insidious _____ b. proceeding gradually and subtly, and with harmful effects
3. exclude _____ c. to lecture; to deliver a sermon
4. preach _____ d. enigma, riddle
5. teem _____ e. to keep out, to omit

Sentences: Try to use the words above in a sentence below. Remember that a word ending may be changed or its figure of speech slightly altered.

6. James' coach decided to _____ him from the match's lineup because he had committed a school violation a few days ago.
7. The stadium was _____ with people before the big football game.
8. A scientist's struggle entails pursuing _____ that often times appear impossible to solve.
9. Jason enjoys _____ to his friends about the theory of relativity for it is his best subject.
10. Politicians are known to _____ add extra clauses into a bill in order to benefit their own immediate sponsors and corporate backers.

Lesson 116

NEW WORDS

antiquated
ˈantiˌkwātid

terminate
ˈtərməˌnāt

crude
krood

boon
boon

egalitarian
iˌgaləˈterēən

A TRIUMPHANT RETURN

Seung Ho was an extremely outspoken politician who gained his position of power through his family's connections. After **crudely** criticizing Congress for their **antiquated** belief of capitalism, he was immediately **terminated** by the Party. Seung Ho was filled with rage and began to research on the **egalitarianism** structure, which is praised to bring about social and economic equality. He began to plan his next campaign, which would combine both structures. After the election, Seung Ho was voted as the next President and his political movement proved to be a huge **boon** to society.

Definitions: Try matching the words in the list with the appropriate definitions. If you are stuck, check the glossary in the back of the book or the passage at the top of the page.

1. antiquated _____   a. unrefined; vulgar
2. terminate _____   b. blessing; benefit
3. crude _____   c. to abolish; to cease
4. boon _____   d. equal
5. egalitarian _____   e. old-fashioned; archaic

Sentences: Try to use the words above in a sentence below. Remember that a word ending may be changed or its figure of speech slightly altered.

6. Having _____ ideologies makes it difficult for one to assimilate to modern and progressive society.
7. Anything that promotes higher education is a(n) _____ to society.
8. Upon screaming _____ and unrefined remarks at the manager, Clive stormed out of the office angrily, ceasing his employment.
9. We all remember the time when America was a much more _____ country, a republic founded against the notion of royalty.
10. After _____ his enrollment at Harvard University, Mark Zuckerberg went on to found Facebook and became one of the most influential people in the world.

Lesson 117

A COSTLY SACRIFICE

As an undercover agent, Dominick was forced to **conspire** with the drug cartel to set up a trap for a politician who was promoting state-owned drug distribution. He had to **inhibit** the politician's momentum by **maligning** her with fraudulent evidence. The cornered politician tried her best to **dispel** the anger and disappointment of her peers, but to no avail. She was constantly **reprimanded** by her peers and lost her credibility shortly afterwards. Three months later, right before Dominick was able to release the truth, the politician committed suicide in her home.

NEW WORDS

reprimand
ˈreprəˌmand

inhibit
inˈhibit

malign
məˈlīn

dispel
disˈpel

conspirator
kənˈspirətər

Definitions: Try matching the words in the list with the appropriate definitions. If you are stuck, check the glossary in the back of the book or the passage at the top of the page.

1. reprimand _____ a. to restrict; to impede
2. inhibit _____ b. to slander or defame
3. malign _____ c. to scold; to blame
4. dispel _____ d. a schemer
5. conspirator _____ e. to make a doubt, belief, or feeling disappear

Sentences: Try to use the words above in a sentence below. Remember that a word ending may be changed or its figure of speech slightly altered.

6. The presence of advanced medical technology did nothing to _____ the tumor's advancement.
7. The best _____ is the one who pulls the strings without any suspicion.
8. Politicians spend a great deal of effort on _____ their opponents during election season.
9. Not only did Hailey receive strong family _____ for stealing from her aunt, but she also faces a court trial for her misdeeds.
10. It was difficult for Michael to _____ rumors of his drug usage after images of him using steroids went viral.

Lesson 118

A COOKING REVOLUTION

NEW WORDS

revive
ri'vīv

garnish
'gärniSH

nullify
'nələ,fī

polemical
pə'lemikəl

methodical
mə'THädikəl

Cooking was widely accepted as one of humanity's most beautiful arts. Tim loved to cook and he especially enjoyed **garnishing** his food to complement the taste with beautiful sight. He is known for his **methodical** approach to cooking as opposed to the "sensational" style popularized by Gordon Ramsay. Tim's fame led to a **polemical** debate about which is the superior cooking method. Over the years, people began to follow Tim's approach because it was much easier for amateurs. Many chefs around the world wanted to **nullify** Tim's credential and **revive** the traditional practice to bring back their own fame. The controversy continued for many decades.

Definitions: Try matching the words in the list with the appropriate definitions. If you are stuck, check the glossary in the back of the book or the passage at the top of the page.

1. revive _____ a. done systematically according to procedure; a person systematic in thought or behavior
2. garnish _____ b. to revoke; to rescind
3. nullify _____ c. (n.) a decoration or embellishment for something, often food; (v.) 1. to decorate or embellish something, often food; 2. to seize one's salary to settle a debt or claim
4. polemical _____ d. to start again; to revitalize
5. methodical _____ e. concerning something contentious, critical, or disputatious in writing or in speech

Sentences: Try to use the words above in a sentence below. Remember that a word ending may be changed or its figure of speech slightly altered.

6. Gordon Ramsay always _____ his food beautifully, even when he cooks supper for his family at home.
7. Scientists usually are very _____ in their research and experimentation.
8. To be meaningful and impactful, a(n) _____ argument must be persuasive and precise.
9. Most of the athlete's contracts were _____ after his infamous cheating scandal was publicized.
10. Early philosophers and alchemists spent a great deal of time searching for ways to _____ the dead.

Lesson 119

DECEITFUL APPEARANCE

To strangers, the first impressions of Mary is that she is a docile, soft-spoken girl. However, her peers know her as an **acrimonious** person who always tries to **instigate** and amplify conflict in order to prove her superiority, even when it is obvious that the arguments have **facile** solutions. Soon, Mary's actions **disaffected** her peers and she was forced to live a **solitary** lifestyle.

NEW WORDS

facile
ˈfasəl

acrimonious
ˌakrəˈmōnēəs

disaffected
ˌdisəˈfektid

solitary
ˈsäləˌterē

instigate
ˈinstiˌgāt

Definitions: Try matching the words in the list with the appropriate definitions. If you are stuck, check the glossary in the back of the book or the passage at the top of the page.

1. facile _____   a. easy; effortless
2. acrimonious _____ b. alone
3. disaffected _____ c. to influence or provoke
4. solitary _____   d. angry and bitter (often of speech or a debate)
5. instigate _____   e. dissatisfied with those in authority and unwilling to support them any longer

Sentences: Try to use the words above in a sentence below. Remember that a word ending may be changed or its figure of speech slightly altered.

6. Richard "Dick" Proenneke (1916-2003) is famous for his documentary *Alone in the Wilderness* (2004), which depicts his _____ life in Alaska's wilderness.
7. It is baffling when people dismiss one's triumph simply because it was a(n) _____ victory.
8. Professor Snape always acts _____ to Harry Potter despite his secret affection for Harry's mother.
9. Judy _____ the fight by bringing up Katie's horrific childhood.
10. After the president took office, he could not fulfill the majority of his promises while barely keeping the country's economy afloat; this greatly _____ his supporters.

Lesson 120

NEW WORDS

resplendent
riˈsplendənt

satire
ˈsaˌtīr

obstreperous
əbˈstrepərəs, äb-

quaff
kwäf

vile
vīl

THE REALITY OF ADULTHOOD

Often children have **resplendent** ideas of what adulthood is like: a world free of schoolwork and punishment for bad behavior – a world where one can be **obstreperous** about the causes one is passionate about, a world where one can use **satire** to mock others' inanity. In reality, most grown-ups do not have easy or free lives. Many adults work strenuously to make ends meet and have myriad responsibilities in their lives. In order to deal with the **vile** working world, adults need vacations and relationships to survive. Only by **quaffing** life's diversions can many adults have the fortitude to triumph each day.

Definitions: Try matching the words in the list with the appropriate definitions. If you are stuck, check the glossary in the back of the book or the passage at the top of the page.

1. resplendent _____ a. 1. the use of humor, ridicule, exaggeration, or irony to expose people's stupidity or shortcomings; 2. a novel, film, or play that does such; 3. a literary genre that does such
2. satire _____ b. noisy and hard to control
3. obstreperous _____ c. attractive because of being very colorful or splendid
4. quaff _____ d. evil, wicked; extremely unpleasant
5. vile _____ e. to drink heartily

Sentences: Try to use the words above in a sentence below. Remember that a word ending may be changed or its figure of speech slightly altered.

6. Each of Woody Allen's movies can be interpreted as a(n) _____ of death, sex, intellectuals, the media, or politics.
7. My former boss was so _____ that he used to make his nicest employees work fifteen hours a day, seven days a week without overtime pay.
8. On a hot day, there's nothing more enjoyable than to _____ a nice large glass of lemonade.
9. The _____ child threw a tantrum when his parents declined to buy him the chocolate bar that he wanted.
10. Unlike the diner, whose drab interior was a turnoff, the new café charmed visitors with its _____ ambiance.

Word Search
Lessons 111-120

```
R M T R L G D Q L D X Z Z J I N K X C
M V W Q Y N B J T A D B T N L P Q R N
N B M L S O O T H E C R S Z L E U E T
Y L M T N D X D B V D I P B C D L Y N
S U O L U C A R I M D R D O E B N G V
I F N S A T I R E I E A N O M T I P R
N T U L G L Y P O D C O D U H L M B M
H I L C N Y M U E R M K H M A T D D R
I E L M I K S C I I T H R M D Y E Y J
B C I G Q D E M C X C Y G D X T L M Y
I E F L F S O A B A X D X L A T I V K
T D Y F S N L L E X F R W U M W N R N
J Q A O I Z X R E T L A Q Z T B T Z D
Q U R O G Z P X J M W I C T G J T X D
Q M U W T N L Q W J T K T I M P M J R
J S X G P Z D T X N G G G G L D R B J
M N L Y L W N T A K X M Y Q K E B P R
```

1 misleading, fraudulent
2 to relieve or comfort
3 1. giving good value in return for one's money, time, or effort; 2. careful not to waste money or resources; 3. using no more of something than necessary
4 having the power to work wonders; inexplicable
5 forbear, ancestor
6 musical; relating to pleasant sound and harmony
7 essential or crucial for sustenance
8 modest
9 proceeding gradually and subtly, and with harmful effects
10 to lecture; to deliver a sermon
11 old-fashioned; archaic
12 unrefined; vulgar
13 to restrict; to impede
14 to slander or defame
15 to revoke; to rescind
16 1. done according to a systematic or established form of procedure; 2. concerning a person who is orderly or systematic in thought or behavior
17 easy; effortless
18 angry and bitter (typically of a speech or debate)
19 1. the use of humor, ridicule, exaggeration, or irony to expose people's stupidity or shortcomings; 2. a novel, film, or play that does such; 3. a literary genre that does such
20 to drink heartily

Vocabulary Review
Lessons 111-120

Directions: Match each word with its best approximate definition. Note that definitions are not necessarily repeated verbatim from the lesson exercises.

1. adolescent _____
2. ire _____
3. pensive _____
4. demise _____
5. arrest _____
6. predicament _____
7. exposé _____
8. mythical _____
9. conundrum _____
10. teem _____
11. boon _____
12. egalitarian _____
13. reprimand _____
14. conspirator _____
15. revive _____
16. polemical _____
17. solitary _____
18. instigate _____
19. obstreperous _____
20. vile _____

a. anger
b. a blessing; a good thing
c. a report of the facts about something
d. done or existing alone
e. to be full of or swarming with
f. evil; wicked
g. a person's death; the end or failure of an enterprise or institution
h. of, relating to, or involving strongly critical, controversial, or disputatious writing or speech
i. to stop; to capture the attention of
j. noisy and hard to control
k. to restore life
l. in the stage of developing from a child to an adult
m. of or believing the principle that all people are equal and deserve equal rights
n. to bring about, initiate, or provoke an action or event
o. typically occurring in folk tales; idealized with reference to the past
p. a person who partakes in a plan to do something harmful or unlawful
q. a difficult, unpleasant, or embarrassing situation
r. engaged in, involving, or reflecting deep or serious thought
s. a rebuke; to rebuke
t. a confusing or difficult problem or question

Word Roots: Unit 12

ROOTS AND THEIR MEANINGS

her/hes:	to stick	tract:	to drag, pull draw
scrib/script:	to write	port:	to carry
mut:	to change	ven/vent:	to come

Here are a few examples of some words that use the above roots:

co<u>hes</u>ive: the quality of sticking together or forming a united whole
<u>script</u>ed: something written out and then enacted
<u>mut</u>ate: to change or cause to change in form
re<u>tract</u>: to draw or be pulled back in; to withdraw
trans<u>port</u>: to move from one place to another by means of a vehicle
in<u>vent</u>: to create or design (to come upon) an idea

Now try to fill in the table below by finding the appropriate root(s) and interpreting the meaning of each word:

Word	Root(s)	Guessed Meaning	Actual Meaning
immutable			
coherent			
airport			
traction			
convene			
prescribe			
scribal			
portal			

169

Lesson 121

A SIMPLE SOLUTION

NEW WORDS

rudimentary
ˌroodəˈment(ə)rē

winnow
ˈwinō

elicit
iˈlisit

perturbed
pərˈtərbd

multifaceted
ˌməltiˈfasətəd, ˌməltī-

The viral, **multifaceted** disease appeared so suddenly that even the brightest minds around the world were **perturbed** by its sudden outbreak. Copious amounts of research were carried out, yet no treatments could be identified. After months of **winnowing** a mass of research papers, Annie finally came to the surprising conclusion that a **rudimentary** approach was the best way to end this blight. She was able to **elicit** a response from the virus by injecting a stimulating enzyme commonly found in abundance in the tropics. Annie became internationally recognized for her contribution.

Definitions: Try matching the words in the list with the appropriate definitions. If you are stuck, check the glossary in the back of the book or the passage at the top of the page.

1. rudimentary _____ a. to distinguish; to sift out; to separate out
2. winnow _____ b. basic; elementary
3. elicit _____ c. troubled; perplexed
4. perturbed _____ d. versatile; having many aspects
5. multifaceted _____ e. to evoke; to draw out

Sentences: Try to use the words above in a sentence below. Remember that a word ending may be changed or its figure of speech slightly altered.

6. James was extremely _____ by his boss' enigmatic statement regarding his future employment.
7. It is a detective's primary objective to _____ the list of possible suspects in a crime down to one likely culprit.
8. The first step in dealing with a recession is releasing a(n) _____ Stimulus Package that bolsters many aspects of the economy simultaneously.
9. The contraption may appear to be _____ in design, but it is extremely effective in mitigating the impacts of pollution.
10. The movie *Interstellar* (2014) _____ a sense of existential crisis in many of its viewers.

Lesson 122

POETIC JUSTICE

During the **inception** of his restaurant, Ming was a sedulous man, working over ten hours a day and never **procrastinating** on any tasks because he wanted to bathe in opulence. Despite his efforts, business **waxed** and waned for many years. Ming became desperate that his business was not steadily growing and started to **desecrate** the ethics of his competition by demeaning other restaurants on the Internet. His actions led to a huge influx of customers, making him extremely happy. Yet despite having loads of new, **cloying** customers, Ming realized that if he continued to use strong spices in recipes, people would stop frequenting his restaurant.

NEW WORDS

desecration
ˌdesiˈkrāSHən

procrastinate
prəˈkrastəˌnāt, prō-

wax
waks

inception
inˈsepSHən

cloying
kloing

Definitions: Try matching the words in the list with the appropriate definitions. If you are stuck, check the glossary in the back of the book or the passage at the top of the page.

1. desecration _____ a. to delay or put off
2. procrastinate _____ b. to become larger
3. wax _____ c. displeasing because of excess of sweetness or richness or sentiment
4. inception _____ d. blasphemy; violation
5. cloying _____ e. beginning; initiation

Sentences: Try to use the words above in a sentence below. Remember that a word ending may be changed or its figure of speech slightly altered.

6. We know the moon is _____ when the light part grows larger with the passing days, indicating that it is shifting toward a full moon.
7. The act of demolishing historical sites to make way for high-rise office buildings is a _____ of the country's cultural heritage.
8. The _____ of the Internet marked the beginning of contemporary globalization.
9. One of the reasons why most people found *The Twilight Saga* repulsive is because of its _____ romance.
10. It is much preferable to accomplish a given task immediately instead of _____ because the longer you put it off, the harder it is to begin.

Lesson 123

SHATTERED DREAMS

NEW WORDS

dumbfounded
ˈdəmˌfoundid

prune
proon

dither
ˈdiTHər

vicarious
vīˈkerēəs, vi-

reclusive
riˈkloosiv, -ziv

Alexa's parents were **dumbfounded** when they heard that she had not been studying for her college entrance exams. They thought that, because she had become **reclusive**, she must have been hard at work preparing for college; instead, however, she had been sitting in her room **dithering** over which boy she hoped would ask her to prom. How tragic it was for Alexa's parents to discover this, as they had hoped she would be admitted to a prestigious university and that they could **vicariously** experience life at an elite school through her stories. Alas, rather than getting into a stellar collage, Alexa created a landscaping business where she earned her salary by **pruning** trees in the gardens surrounding famous buildings.

Definitions: Try matching the words in the list with the appropriate definitions. If you are stuck, check the glossary in the back of the book or the passage at the top of the page.

1. dumbfounded _____ a. (n.) a plum preserved by drying out; (v.) to trim; to remove the superfluous elements
2. prune _____ b. experienced in the imagination through the actions or feelings of another individual
3. dither _____ c. to be indecisive
4. vicarious _____ d. unsociable; solitary
5. reclusive _____ e. astounded; bewildered

Sentences: Try to use the words above in a sentence below. Remember that a word ending may be changed or its figure of speech slightly altered.

6. It is a fallacy to consider someone _____ just because they're always at home on the computer: there's a whole social world on the Internet.
7. The senator was _____ about during the debate: he did not know what stand to take on income inequality issues.
8. Vietnamese people love to take _____ pride in their peers' accomplishments despite having played no part in the process.
9. Tim was _____ when he found out that his invention – created as a hobby – had become a worldwide phenomenon.
10. In a business environment, reports are to be _____ and kept succinct before submission.

Lesson 124

JUDGMENT LAPSE

Daisy was a really compassionate girl. Because of that, becoming the freshman representative in student congress was a perfectly **viable** option next year; in fact, it was even expected of her. However, upon entering high school, Daisy became obsessed with **enhancing** her intimidating personality, believing that this was her key to gaining popularity. She would make **sarcastic**, and sometimes toxic, remarks to everyone around her. This **miscalculation** led to her being identified by most of her peers as a **delinquent**, destroying the innocent image she once had.

NEW WORDS

sarcastic
sär'kastik

delinquent
di'liNGkwənt

enhance
en'hans

miscalculate
mis'kalkyə‚lāt

viable
'vīəbəl

Definitions: Try matching the words in the list with the appropriate definitions. If you are stuck, check the glossary in the back of the book or the passage at the top of the page.

1. sarcastic _____ a. (adj.) 1. showing a tendency to commit a crime, especially youth; 2. irresponsible; 3. in arrears; (n.) a youth likely to commit a crime
2. delinquent _____ b. applicable; feasible
3. enhance _____ c. 1. to assess a situation wrongly; 2. to measure an amount, distance, or value wrongly
4. miscalculate _____ d. using irony in speech in order to mock or to show contempt
5. viable _____ e. to intensify, increase, or improve the extent, quality, or value thereof

Sentences: Try to use the words above in a sentence below. Remember that a word ending may be changed or its figure of speech slightly altered.

6. Being considered a juvenile _____ can really affect one's future.
7. The snide remarks and _____ tone in the face of the homeless' sufferings suggest a sociopathic inability to feel empathy.
8. While conceding is always a(n) _____ option, those who persist will be met with great rewards.
9. A tiny engineering _____ may make an entire bridge collapse.
10. Not only is it unscrupulous to _____ one's ability with illegal drugs, it is also punishable as a federal offense.

Lesson 125

NEW WORDS

detonate
ˈdetnˌāt

lighthearted
ˈlītˌhärtid

pithy
ˈpiTHē

wane
wān

expropriate
ˌeksˈprōprēˌāt

RUSSIA, CHINA, AGGRESSION

After repeated attempts from powers in Moscow to **detonate** a bomb in Beijing, the Chinese army threatened to **expropriate** all weapons of mass destruction from Russia. In a **pithy** statement, China's leader said, "We will take all weapons from Russia as revenge. This will cause Russia's aggression toward our nation to **wane**." Though the message was grave, the response from Russian authorities was rather **lighthearted**: they simply laughed at the Chinese show of verbal force, unaffected by any threats coming from their neighboring country.

Definitions: Try matching the words in the list with the appropriate definitions. If you are stuck, check the glossary in the back of the book or the passage at the top of the page.

1. detonate _____ a. carefree; jovial
2. lighthearted _____ b. to diminish or lessen
3. pithy _____ c. to explode; to burst
4. wane _____ d. (usually of a government) to seize and take away (usually property) from its owner
5. expropriate _____ e. concise and strongly expressive

Sentences: Try to use the words above in a sentence below. Remember that a word ending may be changed or its figure of speech slightly altered.

6. Unfortunately, the impact of China's 2014 stimulus package _____ quicker than anticipated.
7. Under communist regimes, citizens often have their land and resources _____ by the government in the name of the greater good.
8. After _____ two homemade pressure cooker bombs during the Boston Marathon, the culprits attempted to escape but were quickly identified and arrested.
9. A good businessperson is able to give _____ statements summarizing his or her business plans.
10. The story's _____ beginning quickly devolved into a dark, gritty theme.

Lesson 126

DRINKING PROBLEM

Unfortunately, the city of Harbor Ridge has had an environmental problem that has **menaced** its fresh water reserves. For the past two years, a corporate chemical plant has been dumping its waste into the nearby river, which has made local water no longer **potable**. The city has hired environmental experts to **apprise** them of the gravity of the problem, and also lawyers to inform municipal officials whether the corporate behavior poisoning the drinking water is **illicit**. Chances are high that the city will take action, but surely there will be a **divergence** of views between city representatives and corporate management. Hopefully a solution can be found that will benefit all parties.

NEW WORDS

apprise
əˈprīz

menace
ˈmenəs

illicit
i(l)ˈlisit

diverge
diˈvərj, dī-

potable
ˈpōtəbəl

Definitions: Try matching the words in the list with the appropriate definitions. If you are stuck, check the glossary in the back of the book or the passage at the top of the page.

1. apprise _____ a. (n.) 1. a danger or threat; 2. a person or thing causing a danger or threat; (v.) to threaten in a hostile manner
2. menace _____ b. to inform or advise
3. illicit _____ c. something safe to drink; drinkable
4. diverge _____ d. illegal; prohibited
5. potable _____ e. to separate from a path or route and go in a different direction

Sentences: Try to use the words above in a sentence below. Remember that a word ending may be changed or its figure of speech slightly altered.

6. Humans are sometimes considered as a(n) _____ to the Earth because they are polluting it with their waste.
7. Politicians can tend to _____ from the main topic of discussion to reinforce their own agenda, especially during a debate.
8. Because the tap water in many rural areas is not _____, residents must resort to drinking bottled mineral water to stay hydrated.
9. It is a lawyer's job to _____ his or her clients of the best course of action in a legal quagmire.
10. In order to obtain the necessary evidence to stop any large-scale _____ activities, the national security bodies need to send undercover agents.

Lesson 127

NEW WORDS

foible
ˈfoibəl

reparation
ˌrepəˈrāSHən

venerate
ˈvenəˌrāt

equivocate
iˈkwivəˌkāt

ingenious
inˈjēnyəs

MYSTERIOUS GENIUS

Mark is **venerated** for his **ingenuity** in the field of robotics. He is able to **repair** androids of great intricacy while many of his colleagues fail to understand their basic structure. However, one of his personal **foibles** was that he does not like to share his knowledge. He always **equivocates** when probed about his methods for repairing robots. Mark is truly an enigmatic figure.

Definitions: Try matching the words in the list with the appropriate definitions. If you are stuck, check the glossary in the back of the book or the passage at the top of the page.

1. foible _____ a. to revere; to idolize
2. reparation _____ b. a minor weakness, defect, or eccentricity in someone's behavior
3. venerate _____ c. to use ambiguous language to avoid commitment or to hide the truth
4. equivocate _____ d. clever; brilliant
5. ingenious _____ e. restitution; making amends; paying money to those who have been wronged

Sentences: Try to use the words above in a sentence below. Remember that a word ending may be changed or its figure of speech slightly altered.

6. After a thief was caught on camera stealing $1,800 from Regina's purse at the casino, Regina sued the casino and sought _____ for lost funds.
7. Thanks to Steve Jobs' _____ innovation, Apple was able to become one of the leading electronics corporations in the world.
8. Many politicians _____ on issues instead of addressing problems directly.
9. A husband should love everything about his wife, including her _____.
10. It is fascinating that, to us, the mathematician Galileo Galilei (1564-1642) is a(n) _____ figure, though the Church considered him a social pariah when he was alive.

Lesson 128

INCONGRUENT SISTERS

It was hard to believe that Marilyn and Elizabeth were siblings, for they were totally different in character. Marilyn was extremely **demure** and always kind to those around her. Elizabeth, on the other hand, was **unadorned** with civilities and bluntly told people how she felt. Often Elizabeth would try to **spur** on a quarrel with Marilyn by telling her that she was **hypocritical** in that she never said what she actually thought. Marilyn, however, generally ignored her sister. In Marilyn's view, Elizabeth was harder to stomach than **fetid** produce. Such was the life of two very different sisters.

NEW WORDS

hypocritical
ˌhipəˈkritikəl

unadorned
ˌənəˈdôrnd

fetid
ˈfetid

demure
diˈmyoor

spur
spər

Definitions: Try matching the words in the list with the appropriate definitions. If you are stuck, check the glossary in the back of the book or the passage at the top of the page.

1. hypocritical _____ a. plain and simple, undecorated
2. unadorned   _____ b. smelling extremely unpleasant
3. fetid   _____ c. behaving in a way that indicates someone has higher moral standards than is reality
4. demure   _____ d. to incite or stimulate
5. spur   _____ e. reserved, modest, and shy

Sentences: Try to use the words above in a sentence below. Remember that a word ending may be changed or its figure of speech slightly altered.

6. Despite growing up as a(n) _____ girl, Isabella quickly became pompous after entering university.
7. Sven's excessive opulence definitely served to _____ his egotistical and arrogant personality.
8. It is _____ for a person who smokes five packs of cigarettes each day to extol the value of being cigarette free for health reasons.
9. It is best to relay the truth in a(n) _____ and direct manner.
10. Because Paul had not cleaned the kitchen in nearly two months, a(n) _____ scent emanated from the kitchen space.

Lesson 129

A PERPETUAL STATE

NEW WORDS

avert
əˈvərt

benefactors
ˈbenəˌfaktər, ˌbenəˈfaktər

impoverish
imˈpäv(ə)riSH

proclivity
prōˈklivətē, prə-

reserve
riˈzərv

Politicians always seek strong **benefactors** to sponsor their campaign. However, these wealthy people have the **proclivity** to promote their own personal agenda, **averting** their eyes away from the real social issues. The **impoverished** continue to remain in the slums while the wealthy climb toward the sky, **reserving** a seat next to the gods overlooking the ghettos. As these opulent individuals reign supremely over the country by influencing the politicians, the status quo is maintained.

Definitions: Try matching the words in the list with the appropriate definitions. If you are stuck, check the glossary in the back of the book or the passage at the top of the page.

1. avert _____ a. to prevent or ward off an undesirable occurrence
2. benefactors _____ b. people who give money or other help to a person or a cause
3. impoverish _____ c. avoid
4. proclivity _____ d. to exhaust; to reduce to poverty
5. reserve _____ e. tendency; inclination

Sentences: Try to use the words above in a sentence below. Remember that a word ending may be changed or its figure of speech slightly altered.

6. It is extremely vital to have the correct kind of _____ for any entrepreneurial endeavors.
7. India is one of the many places in the world where the affluent can be seen next to the _____.
8. Tucker called the restaurant to _____ a table for three for dinner.
9. Ulla has a(n) _____ for giving up in the face of adversity, no matter how insignificant.
10. _____ the issue is only delaying the inevitable; people must compromise to effectively solve the problem.

Lesson 130

RESPECTABLE FIGURE

Harshim grew up in the slums of Mumbai, **ostracized** by other children because of his fixation with waste. He went through many periods of **malaise** during childhood, living among the trash. Harshim had only one dream, which was to one day clean the world and provide everyone with a healthy living environment. He worked **sedulously** to make his dream materialize. One day, Harshim created a **receptacle** that could automatically discern the difference between recyclable and non-recyclable rubbish. The simple machine could also sort different types of trash with a special operation that prevents **mischance** from ever occurring. His life has changed completely since then, for he has finally achieved his ultimate goal.

NEW WORDS

sedulous
ˈsejələs

ostracize
ˈästrəˌsīz

mischance
misˈCHans

receptacle
riˈseptikəl

malaise
məˈlāz, -ˈlez

Definitions: Try matching the words in the list with the appropriate definitions. If you are stuck, check the glossary in the back of the book or the passage at the top of the page.

1. sedulous _____ a. to exclude someone from a group
2. ostracize _____ b. assiduous; diligent
3. mischance _____ c. depression, anxiety
4. receptacle _____ d. bad luck
5. malaise _____ e. container; a place for holding or storing

Sentences: Try to use the words above in a sentence below. Remember that a word ending may be changed or its figure of speech slightly altered.

6. Marsha was _____ at the party because she wore a dress that was far too casual for the fancy event.
7. Elon Musk, the CEO of Tesla Motors and SpaceX, is often described as a(n) _____ worker because he spends over 100 hours per week performing occupational tasks.
8. It is a nice gesture to clean the bottles and remove labels before placing them in the recycling _____.
9. A crucial trait of successful entrepreneurs is their ability to overcome the _____ they often feel from experiencing continuous failures in getting a business launched.
10. There should always be auxiliary plans in case a(n) _____ occurs during the original implementation.

Crossword Puzzle
Lessons 121-130

ACROSS

3 to be indecisive
7 something safe to drink; drinkable
11 to evoke; to draw out
14 unsociable; solitary
15 to delay or put off
18 to separate from a path or route and go in a different direction
19 to intensify, increase, or improve the quality, value, or extent of
20 to explode; to burst

DOWN

1 a minor weakness, defect, or eccentricity in someone's behavior
2 beginning; initiation
4 behaving in a way that indicates someone has higher moral standards than is reality
5 to diminish or lessen
6 (adj.) 1. showing a tendency to commit a crime, especially youth; 2. irresponsible; 3. in arrears; (n.) a youth likely to commit a crime
8 to exclude someone from a group
9 people who give money or other help to a person or a cause
10 container; a place for holding or storing
12 tendency; inclination
13 restitution; making amends; paying money to those who have been wronged
16 smelling extremely unpleasant
17 to distinguish; to sift out; to separate out

Vocabulary Review
Lessons 121-130

Directions: Match each word with its best approximate definition. Note that definitions are not necessarily repeated verbatim from the lesson exercises.

1. rudimentary _____
2. multifaceted _____
3. wax _____
4. cloying _____
5. dumbfounded _____
6. vicarious _____
7. sarcastic _____
8. viable _____
9. lighthearted _____
10. pithy _____
11. menace _____
12. illicit _____
13. venerate _____
14. ingenious _____
15. demure _____
16. spur _____
17. avert _____
18. impoverish _____
19. sedulous _____
20. malaise _____

a. to disgust by excess sweetness or richness
b. marked by or given to using irony in order to mock or convey contempt
c. involving or limited to basic principles
d. to give an incentive or encouragement to; to push or propel along
e. a person or thing likely to cause harm or danger or threaten others
f. forbidden by laws, rules, or customs
g. capable of working or living successfully
h. cheerful and carefree
i. clever, original, or inventive
j. experienced in the imagination through the feelings of another
k. reserved, modest, and shy
l. to prevent or ward off
m. a general feeling of discomfort, unease, or illness of which the exact cause is difficult to identify
n. greatly astonished or amazed at or by something
o. regard with great respect; revere
p. to make poor; to exhaust the strength or vitality of
q. having many qualities or faces
r. hard working; diligent
s. to become larger or stronger
t. concise and forcefully expressive

Word Roots: Unit 13

ROOTS AND THEIR MEANINGS

man:	hand	dic:	to say, tell
clu/clo/cla:	to shut	anim:	life, spirit
ten:	hold, keep	esce:	to become

Here are a few examples of some words that use the above roots:

<u>man</u>ual: done by hand; a handbook of instructions for learning to operate something

<u>clo</u>ister: a convent or monastery (a place where one is shut up and shielded from the world for religious duties)

de<u>ten</u>tion: the action of keeping someone in official custody; keeping one in school after hours

<u>dic</u>tate: to lay down authoritatively; to say or read aloud

<u>anim</u>ation: a state of being lively and full of energy; creating a live movement out of successive drawings of things or out of puppets

coal<u>esce</u>: to come together and form a mass or a whole

Now try to fill in the table below by finding the appropriate root(s) and interpreting the meaning of each word:

Word	Root(s)	Guessed Meaning	Actual Meaning
predict			
retentive			
maneuver			
reclusive			
fluorescent			
animal			
claustrophobia			
amanuensis			
tenable			
conclude			

Lesson 131

FALLING APART

For many, the **stereotype** of a student who attends an elite university is that of a child who is **coddled** by his or her parents from the moment he or she is born. Often it is believed that such a student has delusions of **grandeur** and that this individual feels that he or she can do anything in the world. In reality, many students study very hard to attend top universities. They work **expeditiously** on many projects, are intensely involved with activities, and keep abreast of current affairs. Many such students can talk about anything from video games to economic theories to **truces** formed between nations that have ended major conflicts. And still these students work hard to survive. In reality, a good education is not only for the privileged; those who study hard can also achieve academic success.

NEW WORDS

coddle
ˈkädl

stereotype
ˈsterēəˌtīp, ˈsti(ə)r-

grandeur
ˈgranjər, ˈgranˌdyoor

expeditious
ˌekspəˈdiSHəs

truce
ˈtroos

Definitions: Try matching the words in the list with the appropriate definitions. If you are stuck, check the glossary in the back of the book or the passage at the top of the page.

1. coddle _____ a. being quick and still ensuring good result
2. stereotype _____ b. an agreement between opponents to end their conflicts and discuss peace terms
3. grandeur _____ c. to treat with excessive indulgence
4. expeditious _____ d. (n.) commonly held idea or image about a specific group of people; (v.) treat with preconceived notion
5. truce _____ e. quality of being impressive or splendid in style

Sentences: Try to use the words above in a sentence below. Remember that a word ending may be changed or its figure of speech slightly altered.

6. Asians are usually _____ as mathematically gifted in school.
7. The _____ of Angkor, an archaeological site that extends over 400 square kilometers, never fails to amaze tourists from all over the world.
8. The citizens living around the noisy construction site hope that it will be finished _____ so they can resume their peaceful lives.
9. Unlike European systems, Singapore's government does not _____ its citizens with welfare services and provides public assistance to the needy only sparingly.
10. Although a bilateral _____ between the two ethnic groups has been signed, it can be broken easily.

Lesson 132

A DILEMMA

NEW WORDS

animate
ˈanəˌmit (adj.); ˈanəˌmāt (v.)

canvass
ˈkanvəs

gargantuan
gärˈganCHooən

lax
laks

dilemma
diˈlemə

I looked around with caution, making sure that nobody was around while Madeline laboriously **canvassed** the **gargantuan** workroom of her fiancé. The security in the mansion was unusually **lax** tonight, so we had easily sneaked in. Madeline suspected that her fiancé had proposed to her solely out of guilt: he was a lawyer and he made a mistake in the past that led to her father's death. I knew how much Madeline loved her father; she always appeared **animated** whenever she talked about him. Madeline's **dilemma** was that she loved her fiancé, but was unsure whether she could forgive his past mistakes. But Madeline's doubt would remain unsubstantiated until she could find some legal evidence while rummaging through the room.

Definitions: Try matching the words in the list with the appropriate definitions. If you are stuck, check the glossary in the back of the book or the passage at the top of the page.

1. animate _____ a. a difficult situation requiring a choice between two or more equally unfavorable options
2. canvas _____ b. slipshod, not sufficiently strict or careful
3. gargantuan _____ c. (adj.) alive or having life; (v.) 1. to bring to life or enliven; 2. to give renewed inspiration or encouragement to something
4. lax _____ d. of great quantity; huge, giant
5. dilemma _____ e. 1. to try to obtain or request something, especially votes from people; 2. to try to get someone's opinion; 3. to discuss thoroughly

Sentences: Try to use the words above in a sentence below. Remember that a word ending may be changed or its figure of speech slightly altered.

6. At night, Uncle Alan usually goes out to _____ construction sites for empty used bottles he collects and sells.
7. Uyen is faced with a(n) _____: she has to choose between going to her best friend's wedding anniversary or her boyfriend's birthday party.
8. Studying for final exams has triggered Tuan's _____ appetite for sweets, which help him release his stress.
9. Looking at Lily's _____ eyes when admiring sculptures, one can sense her love for the art form.
10. The condominium is thought to have _____ security because there have been only a few thieves who have managed to get away.

Lesson 133

RANDOMNESS

Christina chose an interesting hostel for our vacation in Penang: its interior design was primitive and ancient. Furthermore, some infrastructure was awfully **outdated**. When I asked Christina why she had chosen this hostel, she was **overt** about her intentions. She said that she wanted to **abstain** from a luxurious, modern lifestyle for a while. Then she went on to tell me that she had married a local man who would travel with her to Egypt and the Middle East. I was surprised by this **tangent**, but convinced that any story about marrying a random man had to be **fallacious**. But when Nasser walked into the room, I knew she was not lying.

> **NEW WORDS**
>
> **outdated**
> ˌoutˈdātid
>
> **abstain**
> abˈstān
>
> **tangent**
> ˈtanjənt
>
> **overt**
> ōˈvərt, ˈōvərt
>
> **fallacious**
> fəˈlāSHəs

Definitions: Try matching the words in the list with the appropriate definitions. If you are stuck, check the glossary in the back of the book or the passage at the top of the page.

1. outdated _____ a. to resist doing something or to resist being tempted by something
2. abstain _____ b. obsolete; no longer in trend
3. tangent _____ c. done or shown openly; readily apparent
4. overt _____ d. something based on a mistaken belief
5. fallacious _____ e. a digression from the main topic

Sentences: Try to use the words above in a sentence below. Remember that a word ending may be changed or its figure of speech slightly altered.

6. Although many people write on their personal computers, a notebook and a pen will never become _____.
7. There are certain kinds of food you need to _____ from in your diet if you want to obtain a lean physique.
8. Dominique is very _____ about her feelings toward Nathan, although she tells her friends that she has no interest in him.
9. Bored of talking about the scientific names of organic molecules, Tai decided to go off on a(n) _____ and discuss the history of chemistry.
10. Because Malkah believed the _____ claim that it was Roman's birthday, she showed up with a birthday cake for him, to his bafflement.

Lesson 134

A QUIET CHARACTER

NEW WORDS

stoic
ˈstō-ik

acquiesce
ˌakwēˈes

posthumous
ˈpäsCHəməs, pästˈ(h)yooməs

synopsis
səˈnäpsis

misanthrope
ˈmisənˌTHrōp, ˈmiz

Those who have only known Juan for a short time think of him as either a very **stoic** character or a **misanthrope**. He is not very vocal about his thoughts, but he expresses himself profusely in his writings. I had a chance to read a **synopsis** of one of his books and it has taught me more about Juan than a two-hour conversation with him. I know from his writing that Juan does not **acquiesce** to the social norms and he detests the idea of striving for **posthumous** fame as a writer.

Definitions: Try matching the words in the list with the appropriate definitions. If you are stuck, check the glossary in the back of the book or the passage at the top of the page.

1. stoic _____ a. one who dislikes people in general
2. acquiesce _____ b. calm, seemingly emotionless
3. posthumous _____ c. to agree or give in
4. synopsis _____ d. a brief summary or outline of a text
5. misanthrope _____ e. happening after a person's death

Sentences: Try to use the words above in a sentence below. Remember that a word ending may be changed or its figure of speech slightly altered.

6. The novel *The Love of The Last Tycoon* written by American author F. Scott Fitzgerald (1896-1940) was published _____ in 1941.
7. Few people know how tough and _____ Tammy is because they are fooled by her petite figure and geniality.
8. Despite Ray's wealth, he decided not to _____ to his wife's rising demand – she wanted a million dollar house.
9. Trung is a full-scale _____: he never talks to people.
10. "Here is the _____ of my play. I hope to hear your feedback."

Lesson 135

WHEN THINGS TURN SULLEN

Kyle was standing on the **precipice** contemplating jumping off. Those of us who watched knew that Kyle was depressed, and we **unanimously** begged him not to take the plunge. We told him that, with our support, he would **persevere** over any difficulties he may face in life. But Kyle did not listen and sent himself over the ledge. We all wept in silence, **conjoining** our sadness with a hope that the afterlife would provide Kyle more comfort. Then, suddenly, a miracle happened: Kyle floated through the air back up toward us. A **talisman** had given him the power of flight! We couldn't believe our eyes and rejoiced at the lucky trinket that Kyle beheld.

NEW WORDS

unanimous
yooˈnanəməs

precipice
ˈpresəpəs

persevere
ˌpərsəˈvi(ə)r

talisman
ˈtalismən, -iz-

conjoin
kənˈjoin, kän-

Definitions: Try matching the words in the list with the appropriate definitions. If you are stuck, check the glossary in the back of the book or the passage at the top of the page.

1. unanimous _____ a. to persist, to refuse to stop despite obstacles
2. precipice _____ b. two or more people in complete agreement, held by everyone involved
3. persevere _____ c. a very tall and steep cliff (literal or figurative)
4. talisman _____ d. to connect, to join
5. conjoin _____ e. an object (usually a stone, ring, or necklace) thought to possess magical powers

Sentences: Try to use the words above in a sentence below. Remember that a word ending may be changed or its figure of speech slightly altered.

6. Despite having been rejected by over thirty companies, Tung _____ and eventually landed his dream internship.
7. When standing at the _____ of the Grand Canyon, one can take beautiful pictures of the rock valleys, rivers, and ravines.
8. After deliberation, the jurors decided on a(n) _____ verdict to sentence the defendant.
9. According to a recent statistic, _____ twins occur about once in every 200,000 births.
10. Leandra found a(n) _____ that had the amazing ability to turn anything it directed its energy toward into gold.

Lesson 136

A MAN OF MEANS

NEW WORDS

discerning
di'sərniNG

convergence
kən'vərjəns

ambition
am'biSHən

affluence
'aflooəns

transgression
trans'greSHən, tranz-

Tai is an extremely bright businessman who has a knack for **discerning** lucrative opportunities that people usually overlook. His enormous **affluence** is undoubtedly due to a **convergence** of his great talents and his **ambition** to make lots of money. Yet Tai is by no means a greedy man. In fact, he holds venerable ethics and values and has never fallen into any **transgressions** during his pursuit of great wealth. He deems money only as a means to gain personal autonomy and to pursue worthy philanthropic endeavors.

Definitions: Try matching the words in the list with the appropriate definitions. If you are stuck, check the glossary in the back of the book or the passage at the top of the page.

1. discerning _____ a. great wealth
2. convergence _____ b. an act that violates a rule, law, or principle; an offense
3. ambition _____ c. the act of coming together
4. affluence _____ d. a strong desire to succeed
5. transgression _____ e. perceptive, having good judgment; able to detect great subtlety

Sentences: Try to use the words above in a sentence below. Remember that a word ending may be changed or its figure of speech slightly altered.

6. Beneath the global image of a(n) _____ Singapore, many citizens, especially those of the older generation, still suffer from great poverty.
7. Hung and Alex do not get along well because there is no _____ of interests.
8. Delilah's _____ sometimes exhausts her because she is always working hard to achieve her goals.
9. Having practiced art for several years, Uyen has developed a(n) _____ eye for color.
10. Having an affair is an unforgiveable _____ in a relationship.

Lesson 137

THE ODD ONE OUT

Having made many **concessions** to the demands of social norms, Jackson felt **jaded** and alienated from his true nature. He thought what is considered a social standard was **stymieing** his self-expression. Whenever he tried to be creative in **formulating** his unique lifestyle, he was met with **detractors** who called him an eccentric outcast.

NEW WORDS

formulate
ˈfôrmyəˌlāt

stymie
ˈstīmē

detractor
diˈtraktər

concession
kənˈseSHən

jaded
ˈjādid

Definitions: Try matching the words in the list with the appropriate definitions. If you are stuck, check the glossary in the back of the book or the passage at the top of the page.

1. formulate _____ a. tired, lacking enthusiasm, or bored, usually after having too much of something
2. stymie _____ b. to create methodically; articulate, express
3. detractor _____ c. something granted in response to demands; a preferential allowance given by an organization or government
4. concession _____ d. to hinder the progress of
5. jaded _____ e. a person who criticizes or belittles the value of something

Sentences: Try to use the words above in a sentence below. Remember that a word ending may be changed or its figure of speech slightly altered.

6. Writing essays all day long can leave even the most enthusiastic writer _____, depleted and uninspired.
7. Vietnam's economic potential may be greatly _____ if the number of talented youth seeking opportunities overseas keeps increasing.
8. Whenever I propose a new marketing idea, Joshua always finds fault in it and diminishes its effectiveness. What a(n) _____!
9. Singapore's senior citizens and students can use public transportation at cheaper fares thanks to various transport _____ programs.
10. It is difficult to _____ an opinion on the topic without knowing all of the facts.

Lesson 138

NEW WORDS

compilation
ˌkämpəˈlāSHən

torpid
ˈtôrpid

summon
ˈsəmən

impressionistic
imˌpreSHəˈnistik

swarthy
ˈswôrTHē

A PRACTICAL APPROACH

Ying has no **impressionistic** ideal of love and does not jump hastily into romance. After knowing that she is attracted to someone, Ying makes a thorough **compilation** of that person's history and personal strengths to see how he might fit into her life. Then she arranges to meet him regularly to ensure that he's not **torpid**, but rather lively during their conversations and activities together. After knowing for sure he is the right one (preferably a **swarthy** man), she **summons** up the courage to confess to him. Ying's approach may seem time-consuming at first but it helps her limit unproductive relationships in the long run.

Definitions: Try matching the words in the list with the appropriate definitions. If you are stuck, check the glossary in the back of the book or the passage at the top of the page.

1. compilation _____ a. based on unsystematic, subjective reactions
2. torpid _____ b. dark-skinned
3. summon _____ c. mentally or physically inactive; sluggish
4. impressionistic _____ d. a process or act of assembling different sources to put together something
5. swarthy _____ e. 1. to authoritatively or urgently call on someone or something to be present; 2. to call people to attend a meeting; 3. to urgently demand help; 4. to bring to the surface a quality or reaction from within oneself

Sentences: Try to use the words above in a sentence below. Remember that a word ending may be changed or its figure of speech slightly altered.

6. Alena made a potion and recited a mantra to _____ the spirits of her ancestors.
7. The record is a(n) _____ of my favorite soundtracks.
8. It is often easier to give _____ views than rational judgments.
9. When you compare citizens of Sweden to those of Sri Lanka, the Nordic people look much paler than their more _____ comrades in the tropics.
10. Kim has to _____ her courage in order to approach random strangers on the street to do her educational surveys.

Lesson 139

CONSOLATION

My heart and my head are inconsistent and sometimes are even in **disputation**. I wish to search for peace, but I act in a way that creates conflict. Sometimes, the consequences of my actions are so crushing that I become too emotionally affected. My mother would then remind me that it is only **mandatory** for the thunderstorm to come when there is an imbalance of electric charges and that after a gloomy night I can appreciate a **vividly** bright day better. For that, whenever I **wince** in time of great **despair**, I tell myself that a new source of joy, or direction, is about to arise.

NEW WORDS

wince
wins

despair
di'spe(ə)r

vivid
'vivid

mandatory
'mandə,tôrē

disputation
,dispyoo'tāSHən

Definitions: Try matching the words in the list with the appropriate definitions. If you are stuck, check the glossary in the back of the book or the passage at the top of the page.

1. wince _____ a. hopelessness, pessimism
2. despair _____ b. (n.) a facial or bodily response to suggest pain, distress; (v.) to recoil, draw back due to pain or fear
3. vivid _____ c. required by rule, compulsory
4. mandatory _____ d. debate or argument
5. disputation _____ e. suggesting a clear and lively image; evoking strong feeling; intense in color

Sentences: Try to use the words above in a sentence below. Remember that a word ending may be changed or its figure of speech slightly altered.

6. A(n) _____ illustration alongside a newspaper article can make the long reading appear less intimidating.
7. It is _____ for international students to have immunization shots before coming to the United States for their studies.
8. Don't give up in times of _____: things are not as bad as they seem at first.
9. I _____ while trying to gulp down the blackish, pungent liquid that my parents called Chinese medicinal herbs but tasted to me like charcoal.
10. It is surprising that Tung and An are dating because they used to be in constant _____.

NEW WORDS

muster
ˈməstər

haphazard
ˌhapˈhazərd

recessive
riˈsesiv

obdurate
ˈäbd(y)ərit

affable
ˈafəbəl

Lesson 140

NATURE VERSUS NURTURE

While a trait such as attached earlobes is **recessive** in human beings, other qualities are not so definitively genetic. Take, for example, personality. Many people believe that, although genetics may play a role, it is much more likely that one's tendency to be **affable** or **obdurate** is governed by his or her upbringing and social experiences. As a result, psychologists and social workers have stressed the importance of making sure that children are reared in stable families where their emotional well-being is nurtured in a structured way. If a child is raised in a home with **haphazard** emotional organization, it will require that child additional effort to **muster** his or her strength to succeed in the world as an adult. Such goes the argument for those who believe that nurture, how one is raised, trumps nature, one's genetic inheritance, in society.

Definitions: Try matching the words in the list with the appropriate definitions. If you are stuck, check the glossary in the back of the book or the passage at the top of the page.

1. muster _____ a. to assemble a group of people; to call up (a) feeling(s), emotion(s), or response(s)
2. haphazard _____ b. genetic trait that is exhibited only when inherited from both parents
3. recessive _____ c. unplanned, lacking organization
4. obdurate _____ d. friendly, cordial
5. affable _____ e. stubborn, resistant to change

Sentences: Try to use the words above in a sentence below. Remember that a word ending may be changed or its figure of speech slightly altered.

6. Jin Hee is such a(n) _____ girl; everyone loves talking to her.
7. The desired crystal structure cannot be obtained if the synthesis procedure is carried out _____ without order.
8. She took a deep breath, _____ up her confidence, and entered the interview room.
9. The two old men have been quarreling for months: a(n) _____ silence between them has persisted for weeks.
10. Having blue eyes is a genetically _____ trait: unless both parents pass along an allele for blue eyes, a child will not have them.

Word Search
Lessons 131-140

```
N A E T A L U M R O F P R T
O C B C Q R U A C O O T L Q
I Q J M O S O A M S V D N S
T U P T T M N T T M I E U Y
A I U E Y V P H C S E O R Y
T E R N A D U I C A I L X T
U S O S A M A E L C R G I N
P C S B O N R M A A R T A D
S E D U D N I L B A T M E C
I E S I I U L M N I S I O D
D P C N P A R D O I T D O T
Q R G N F R E A L U D I L N
B M P N I U O A T L S R O G
B J K D R W T T E E W M K N
```

1. to treat with excessive indulgence
2. quality of being impressive or splendid in style
3. 1. to try to obtain or request something, especially votes from people; 2. to try to get someone's opinion; 3. to discuss thoroughly
4. a difficult situation requiring a choice between two or more equally unfavorable options
5. done or shown openly; readily apparent
6. something based on a mistaken belief
7. to agree or give in
8. happening after a person's death
9. two or more people in complete agreement, held by everyone involved
10. an object (usually a stone, ring, or necklace) thought to possess magical powers
11. perceptive, having good judgment; able to detect great subtlety
12. a strong desire to succeed
13. to create methodically; articulate, express
14. a person who criticizes or belittles the value of something
15. a process or act of assembling different sources to put together something
16. mentally or physically inactive; sluggish
17. (n.) a facial or bodily response to suggest pain, distress; (v.) to recoil, draw back due to pain or fear
18. debate or argument
19. to assemble a group of people; to call up (a) feeling(s), emotion(s), or response(s)
20. stubborn, resistant to change

Vocabulary Review
Lessons 131-140

Directions: Match each word with its best approximate definition. Note that definitions are not necessarily repeated verbatim from the lesson exercises.

1. stereotype _____
2. truce _____
3. gargantuan _____
4. lax _____
5. outdated _____
6. abstain _____
7. synopsis _____
8. misanthrope _____
9. precipice _____
10. persevere _____
11. affluence _____
12. transgression _____
13. stymie _____
14. jaded _____
15. summon _____
16. swarthy _____
17. vivid _____
18. mandatory _____
19. haphazard _____
20. affable _____

a. a very tall, steep rock face or cliff
b. extremely large
c. wealth
d. to continue successfully in course of action, even with little hope of success
e. friendly, likeable
f. lacking any principle of organization; disorganized
g. to refrain oneself from doing or enjoying something
h. required
i. a brief summary of something
j. a widely held and oversimplified idea of a particular type of person or thing
k. to thwart; to hinder the progress of
l. to call on something; to demand; to call people to attend
m. an act that goes against the law or a code of conduct
n. dark-skinned
o. not strict with rules
p. bright, sharp, or clear
q. an agreement between enemies to stop fighting for a certain time
r. a person who dislikes humankind or who avoids human society
s. tired, bored, or lacking enthusiasm after having had too much of something
t. obsolete; out of date

Word Roots: Unit 14

ROOTS AND THEIR MEANINGS

dis:	apart, away from, not	pun/pen:	to pay, punish, compensate
nom/nym:	name	us/ut:	to use
gno:	to know	un/non:	not

Here are a few examples of some words that use the above roots:

<u>dis</u>engaged:	emotionally unattached
homo<u>nym</u>:	two or more words having the same spelling but different meanings
a<u>gno</u>stic:	a person who claims neither faith nor nonbelief in God
<u>pun</u>itive:	inflicting or intended to be punishment; a charge or tax that is exorbitantly high
<u>ut</u>ensil:	an implement for household usage
<u>un</u>inspired:	lacking in imagination, commitment, or originality
<u>non</u>committal:	not willing to stick to a definite course of action

Now try to fill in the table below by finding the appropriate root(s) and interpreting the meaning of each word:

Word	Root(s)	Guessed Meaning	Actual Meaning
nomenclature			
penalty			
diagnostic			
unintelligent			
disrespectful			
reusable			
ignorant			
nonessential			
pseudonym			

NEW WORDS

rigorous
ˈrigərəs

blare
ble(ə)r

deluge
ˈdel(y)ooj

melodramatic
ˌmelədrəˈmatik

panorama
ˌpanəˈramə, -ˈrämə

Lesson 141

MOOD BREAKER

After hours of **rigorous** climbing, Chelsea and I finally reached the top of the mountain. A feeling of triumph swept over me as I gasped at the magnificent **panorama** in front of my eyes. The air was still and I felt almost engulfed by the vastness of the universe. Suddenly, Chelsea uttered in her usual **melodramatic** tone, "I've had a **deluge** of sweat and my feet are having peripheral oedema!" I turned to quiet her. In the serenity of nature, human voices sound like **blaring** car horns.

Definitions: Try matching the words in the list with the appropriate definitions. If you are stuck, check the glossary in the back of the book or the passage at the top of the page.

1. rigorous _____   a. a wide, continuous view; an overall picture or thorough survey of something
2. blare _____   b. (n.) a large amount of something coming at the same time; (v.) to flood with something
3. deluge _____   c. painstaking and exact; demanding, harsh
4. melodramatic _____   d. to make a loud, harsh noise
5. panorama _____   e. exaggerated and overemotional

Sentences: Try to use the words above in a sentence below. Remember that a word ending may be changed or its figure of speech slightly altered.

6. An ambitious student, Jake is always _____ with heavy schoolwork and club meetings.
7. Marcus has a habit of wearing earphones that _____ loud music all the time, so he often cannot hear his friends when they call him from afar.
8. Annabelle is usually pleasant, but her tendency to be a(n) _____ drama queen can be unbearable sometimes.
9. To evaluate the significance of an artwork, one should consider the _____ of the work's historical context.
10. Margaret Thatcher went through an academically _____ program in Chemistry at Oxford University before starting her career in politics.

Lesson 142

SERENDIPITY

Anh and Yuen met by serendipity. In a foreign city full of polished locals, they both dressed **slovenly** and thus quickly recognized each other as lone travelers. They came together and immediately clicked. They were able to **conjure** up **scintillating** conversations that energized each other's mind and to use their individual wisdom to **placate** each other's anxiety. They decided to keep accompanying one another because they both had a **prophetic** sense that a journey together would be more exciting and fulfilling.

NEW WORDS

conjure
kənˈdʒʊ(ə)r

scintillating
ˈsin(t)lˌātiNG

placate
ˈplākāt

slovenly
ˈsləvənlē, ˈslä-

prophetic
prəˈfetik

Definitions: Try matching the words in the list with the appropriate definitions. If you are stuck, check the glossary in the back of the book or the passage at the top of the page.

1. conjure _____ a. to calm, soothe, appease
2. scintillating _____ b. ill-groomed and untidy; careless, negligent
3. placate _____ c. shining brightly; clever and brilliant
4. slovenly _____ d. accurately predictive of the future
5. prophetic _____ e. to gather, to bring something into existence

Sentences: Try to use the words above in a sentence below. Remember that a word ending may be changed or its figure of speech slightly altered.

6. Estelle knew that her sister Harriet was difficult to _____, but it seemed that a trip to the baseball stadium had some effect on appeasing the latter.
7. Unlike Paula's _____ scholarship, which dazzles readers with ideas, Maureen's work is flat and boring.
8. Julia's living quarters were _____: dirty clothes were strewn about, stale food was left on the floor, and the bed sheets smelled foul.
9. People say that Jodi's words are _____ because her predictions have come true; but I'd rather think her warnings are based on rigorous reasoning.
10. It takes time for me to _____ up my courage to express my feelings for someone.

Lesson 143

A SUPPORTING HAND

NEW WORDS

preponderance
priˈpändərəns

abject
ˈabˌjekt, abˈjekt

culpable
ˈkəlpəbəl

dissipate
ˈdisəˌpāt

subversive
səbˈvərsiv

She was sobbing uncontrollably. Tears welled up in her eyes which filled with a **preponderance** of **abject** sorrow. It had been one hour and her wails showed no sign of **dissipating**. I had never seen her so weak and vulnerable. She was always cool and composed. Something must have happened, a **subversive** event that sapped her usual vim. I asked her who was **culpable** of causing such sadness, but she refused to talk. Feeling helpless, I squeezed the side of her shoulder to offer my emotional support and she closed her eyes as she relished the feeling of compassion.

Definitions: Try matching the words in the list with the appropriate definitions. If you are stuck, check the glossary in the back of the book or the passage at the top of the page.

1. preponderance _____ a. being greater in number, importance, or quantity
2. abject _____ b. to be guilty and blameworthy for
3. culpable _____ c. to disperse; to waste away
4. dissipate _____ d. (adj.) attempting to undermine an established system; (n.) a revolutionist, insurgent
5. subversive _____ e. extremely miserable and unfortunate; contemptible, self-abashing

Sentences: Try to use the words above in a sentence below. Remember that a word ending may be changed or its figure of speech slightly altered.

6. There was a(n) _____ of chili peppers in my Thai dish; it was so spicy that I could barely eat it.
7. The evidence corroborated that Evan was indeed _____ of the crime.
8. Friction can cause energy to _____ in the form of heat.
9. Unfortunately, the national government is wary of _____ groups trying to overthrow or dislodge its power.
10. People flock to big cities like Saigon to search for new economic opportunities that will hopefully lift them up from _____ poverty.

Lesson 144

A WAY OF LIFE

Keefe is obsessed with handsome residences. He used to have a gorgeous house but he sold it to buy a cottage, and then sold the cottage for a villa where he is now living lavishly in **manorial** style. Keefe's parents are **enraged** by his spending habits and often advise him to find a less **obtrusive** way to show off his wealth. But Keefe has an **obstinate** view that money should be circulated instead of being hoarded. The **denotation** of money, to him, is only a medium of exchange. He believes he is exchanging papers for a lifestyle that makes him happy.

NEW WORDS

obstinate
ˈäbstənit

obtrusive
əbˈtroosiv, äb-

enrage
enˈrāj

manorial
məˈnôrēəl

denotation
ˌdēnōˈtāSHən

Definitions: Try matching the words in the list with the appropriate definitions. If you are stuck, check the glossary in the back of the book or the passage at the top of the page.

1. obstinate _____ a. stubbornly persistent, unwilling to yield
2. obtrusive _____ b. of or pertaining to a large country house with lands or the principal home of a landed estate (often in medieval times)
3. enrage _____ c. noticeable or prominent in an unwelcome manner
4. manorial _____ d. to make angry
5. denotation _____ e. indication of something using words or symbols; the primary meaning of a word

Sentences: Try to use the words above in a sentence below. Remember that a word ending may be changed or its figure of speech slightly altered.

6. Khang was a(n) _____ child who insisted on having his ways.
7. Misophonia is a neuropsychiatric disorder in which specific sounds can _____ or disgust people who have the condition.
8. Distinct from emotional connotation of words, _____ is their logical meaning.
9. The best brand designs display subtlety and the logo is often not _____ showed.
10. The _____ system, which was practiced in medieval Western societies, included the relationship between a landlord and a group of dependent peasants.

Lesson 145

A PURSUIT OF PERFECTION

NEW WORDS

connotation
ˌkänəˈtāSHən

knell
nel

espouse
iˈspouz

penitent
ˈpenitnt

refined
riˈfīnd

Yvonne **espouses** perfection because it energizes her. As such, she walks and behaves in a way that exudes an aura of **refined** elegance. Yvonne covets beautiful little things and scrutinizes everything she does and every word she says. For these reasons, she has built her brand, and the name Yvonne has a **connotation** among people around her. But Yvonne is a lonely soul. Men come and go because they are chased away by her unrealistic standards of perfection. For some, dating her is like tolling the death **knell** for their social lives. Nevertheless, even though Yvonne occasionally feels **penitent** about her choices, she has decided that she cannot give up her way of life.

Definitions: Try matching the words in the list with the appropriate definitions. If you are stuck, check the glossary in the back of the book or the passage at the top of the page.

1. connotation _____ a. an idea or feeling that is implied or evoked by a term
2. knell _____ b. to adopt and promote a cause, theory, or belief
3. espouse _____ c. the sound of a bell, usually in reference to the dead or a funeral
4. penitent _____ d. cultivated in manner, appearance, taste; free from impurities
5. refined _____ e. repentant, regretful

Sentences: Try to use the words above in a sentence below. Remember that a word ending may be changed or its figure of speech slightly altered.

6. The word "cancer" certainly does not have a positive _____.
7. In regard to his taste for intellectual food, Tai is undeniably a very _____ man.
8. A man and a woman should have similar family values that both _____ to ensure a stable marriage.
9. Dinesh felt _____ because he lied to his mother, claiming that he took her money to pay for a college course when he actually burned the cash at a casino.
10. In the town of Salem, the _____ of the church bell signals that a citizen has just passed away.

Lesson 146

UNCERTAINTY

When I agreed to go on that trip with him, I had a **presentiment** that it would not be all gain and no pain. I had **disjointed** ideas of who he was and he wasn't very **outspoken** about his feelings and thoughts. "Does he kidnap? Is he a good person? What will I do if bad things happen?" I was **plagued** with uncertainties because a few weeks of knowing him were insufficient to evaluate his character. Still, I could not possibly foresee every **contingency** that might take place during our trip. The only way to find out how things would turn out was to go ahead.

NEW WORDS

disjointed
disˈjointid

plague
plāg

presentiment
priˈzentəmənt

outspoken
ˌoutˈspōkən

contingency
kənˈtinjənsē

Definitions: Try matching the words in the list with the appropriate definitions. If you are stuck, check the glossary in the back of the book or the passage at the top of the page.

1. disjointed _____ a. (n.) a thing or person that causes trouble and unhappiness; (v.) to cause distress
2. plague _____ b. expressing one's opinion freely and frankly
3. presentiment _____ c. divided, lacking continuity or organization
4. outspoken _____ d. a possible event that might happen in the future; a provision for an unforeseen circumstance
5. contingency _____ e. a gut feeling about the future, likely one of a foreboding nature

Sentences: Try to use the words above in a sentence below. Remember that a word ending may be changed or its figure of speech slightly altered.

6. Tina is _____ about her opinions so some of her colleagues do not like her.
7. We should have a(n) _____ plan if plan A does not work out.
8. I have a(n) _____ that our relationship will not last long due to our differences in characters and beliefs.
9. Keeping too much to oneself for a prolonged period of time might _____ one's emotional wellbeing.
10. Michael may sound smart and knowledgeable when talking about ecology but his understanding of the field is rather _____.

Lesson 147

A FUTILE ATTEMPT

NEW WORDS

remiss
ri′mis

dispassionate
dis′paSHənit

temperate
′temp(ə)rət

seduce
si′d(y)oos

brouhaha
′broohä͵hä, broo′hähä

We sat next to each other, an icy silence hovering between us. She tried to break the ice by **seducing** me with food, but I remained **temperate**. She tried to get me talking by gossiping over some celebrity **brouhaha**, but I remained **dispassionate**. She tried to probe my thoughts by asking me questions, but I only nodded in silence. She then gave up and berated me for being aloof and **remiss** in politeness. Maybe she couldn't fathom how exhausted I felt as she was always energetic, or how deeply hurt I was that my blank mind couldn't muster up a response.

Definitions: Try matching the words in the list with the appropriate definitions. If you are stuck, check the glossary in the back of the book or the passage at the top of the page.

1. remiss _____ a. uninfluenced by strong emotions
2. dispassionate _____ b. negligent, careless in one's duty
3. temperate _____ c. excited public response to something
4. seduce _____ d. to lure someone into inadvisable courses of action or belief
5. brouhaha _____ e. moderate; restrained in one's behavior

Sentences: Try to use the words above in a sentence below. Remember that a word ending may be changed or its figure of speech slightly altered.

6. Joanie is trying to _____ Jake with her new line of perfume.
7. Phong's teacher gave a lecture that was extremely _____: throughout the entire talk, Phong could hardly become engaged in the talk.
8. "I don't care what other people think about my decisions", Ngoc said in a cold and _____ voice.
9. We know we are _____ by distracting ourselves with movies and popcorn, but the writing assignments are too monotonous and unbearably dull.
10. There was a(n) _____ over Julian's speech; it was full of wit but too casual and flippant for someone running for the student council's presidency.

Lesson 148

AMERICAN WOMEN'S VOTING RIGHTS

During her **grandiloquent** 1848 speech in Seneca Falls, New York, Elizabeth Cady Stanton (1815-1902) promoted a Declaration of Sentiments that would set in motion America's women's **suffrage** movement. This Declaration of Sentiments served as a **catalyst** that manifested a national movement to give women voting rights. As decades rolled on, ardent feminists **marshaled** support from fellow women and even some men to get equal political representation. Women finally were guaranteed voting rights in the United States in 1920. No longer a **prophecy**, women could actually begin voting in American elections after that year.

NEW WORDS

prophecy
ˈpräfəsē

marshal
ˈmärSHəl

suffrage
ˈsəfrij

catalyst
ˈkatl-ist

grandiloquent
granˈdiləkwənt

Definitions: Try matching the words in the list with the appropriate definitions. If you are stuck, check the glossary in the back of the book or the passage at the top of the page.

1. prophecy _____ a. stimulus to make change happen
2. marshal _____ b. prediction of future event
3. suffrage _____ c. pompous in style or manner; designed in a way to impress
4. catalyst _____ d. the right to vote
5. grandiloquent _____ e. (n.) 1. an officer of the highest rank in the armed forces in certain countries; 2. a municipal officer or head of a police department; 3. an official responsible for supervising public events; (v.) to arrange or assemble in order

Sentences: Try to use the words above in a sentence below. Remember that a word ending may be changed or its figure of speech slightly altered.

6. My aunt believes blindly in _____; she is willing to pay lots of money to see a fortune-teller for half an hour.
7. Although many people enjoy hearing the politician's _____ speeches, I am turned off by the excessive indulgence of his parlance.
8. Iron is a commonly used _____ in organic chemical reactions.
9. For the past three months, the defendant's legal team has been attempting to _____ evidence proving that the defendant is indeed innocent.
10. Susan B. Anthony, an American social reformer, played an essential role in the women's _____ movement.

Lesson 149

CHARLES DARWIN

NEW WORDS

anthropological
anTHrəpəˈläjikə

rousing
ˈrouziNG

complicity
kəmˈplisitē

archipelago
ˌärkəˈpeləˌgō

exacting
igˈzaktiNG

Charles Darwin (1809-82) studied medicine and then divinity at Cambridge but neither discipline had as **rousing** an appeal to him as geology. In 1831, Darwin set off to the Galapagos Islands aboard the *HMS Beagle*, taking five weeks to make **exacting** charts of the **archipelago**. The voyage to the islands helped Darwin develop his theories of evolution, which he disclosed in his most famous book, *The Origin of Species* (1859). The implication of his theories led to the idea of Social Darwinism, an application of natural selection to sociology and politics, unfortunately without Darwin's full **complicity**. Also, Darwin's discussions on human evolution in his later books helped provide a foundation for modern biological **anthropology**.

Definitions: Try matching the words in the list with the appropriate definitions. If you are stuck, check the glossary in the back of the book or the passage at the top of the page.

1. anthropological _____ a. relating to the study of humankind
2. rousing _____ b. demanding great attention to detail
3. complicity _____ c. inciting enthusiasm, full of energy
4. archipelago _____ d. involvement with others in a crime or something illegal
5. exacting _____ e. a group of islands

Sentences: Try to use the words above in a sentence below. Remember that a word ending may be changed or its figure of speech slightly altered.

6. Indonesia is a(n) _____ consisting of over 17,000 different islands.
7. After a(n) _____ celebration with her friends at the club, Kate went home and immersed herself in the stillness of the night.
8. Next week, our class is embarking on a(n) _____ expedition in northern India to investigate the local religious beliefs and practices.
9. I turned to his direction and signaled a wink of _____ between us.
10. One must give _____ attention to alignment and spacing in order to create an effective poster design.

Lesson 150

UNHAPPY LIFE

We love our auntie, except for her frequent and **irksome** lamenting. Auntie had enjoyed a privileged life, well protected by her loving parents, until she met my Uncle, who was raised in less **propitious** environment. Very often, she feels sore because her life is not **progressive**, and envious of her siblings because their wealth has greatly **surpassed** hers. Auntie's dissatisfaction with her current situation seems to make her more **peevish** nowadays.

NEW WORDS

progressive
prəˈgresiv

peevish
ˈpēviSH

surpass
sərˈpas

propitious
prəˈpiSHəs

irksome
ˈərksəm

Definitions: Try matching the words in the list with the appropriate definitions. If you are stuck, check the glossary in the back of the book or the passage at the top of the page.

1. progressive _____ a. advancing gradually
2. peevish _____ b. annoying in a tiresome way
3. surpass _____ c. bad-tempered, tending to complain
4. propitious _____ d. to go beyond expectations
5. irksome _____ e. favorable; likely to result in success

Sentences: Try to use the words above in a sentence below. Remember that a word ending may be changed or its figure of speech slightly altered.

6. As you study vocabulary diligently every day, you should see a(n) _____ trend in your ability to read academic and intellectual work.
7. Francis's intuition and intellectual capacity for Physics far _____ that of his peers.
8. I find it really _____ when my brother keeps repeating one thing over and over again.
9. Song Woo is the most _____ woman I have ever met: almost everything can get under her skin.
10. Solid substrates in aquatic environment are _____ for the growth of fungus.

Crossword Puzzle
Lessons 141-150

ACROSS

2 negligent, careless in one's duty
5 to gather, to bring something into existence
8 (n.) 1. an officer of the highest rank in the armed forces in certain countries; 2. a municipal officer or head of a police
12 to disperse; to waste away
14 accurately predictive of the future
15 (adj.) attempting to undermine an established system; (n.) a revolutionist, insurgent
17 an idea or feeling that is implied or evoked by a term
18 relating to the study of humankind
19 a possible event that might happen in the future; a provision for an unforeseen circumstance
20 to adopt and promote a cause, theory, or belief

DOWN

1 to lure someone into inadvisable courses of action or belief
3 prediction of future event
4 of or pertaining to a large country house with lands or the principal home of a landed estate (often in medieval times)
6 demanding great attention to detail
7 to go beyond expectations
9 favorable; likely to result in success
10 a wide, continuous view; an overall picture or thorough survey of something
11 stubbornly persistent, unwilling to yield
13 a gut feeling about the future, likely one of a foreboding nature
16 painstaking and exact; demanding, harsh

Vocabulary Review
Lessons 141-150

Directions: Match each word with its best approximate definition. Note that definitions are not necessarily repeated verbatim from the lesson exercises.

1. blare _____ a. not influenced by strong emotion so as to be impartial and rational
2. deluge _____ b. a flood of something
3. scintillating _____ c. feeling sorrow or regret for having done something wrong
4. slovenly _____ d. noticeable or prominent in an intrusive way
5. preponderance _____ e. irritating; annoying
6. culpable _____ f. to cause continual distress to; to pester and harass repeatedly
7. obtrusive _____ g. elegant and cultured in appearance, manner, or taste
8. enrage _____ h. a noisy, overexcited reaction in response to something
9. penitent _____ i. a group of islands
10. refined _____ j. a loud noise
11. plague _____ k. favoring social/cultural reform of new, liberal ideas
12. outspoken _____ l. the quality of being greater in quality, importance, or amount of something
13. dispassionate _____ m. a person or thing that precipitates an event
14. brouhaha _____ n. frank in stating one's opinions, especially if they're controversial
15. suffrage _____ o. blameworthy, deserving of blame
16. catalyst _____ p. the right to vote
17. rousing _____ q. messy and dirty (usually of a person and his/her appearance)
18. archipelago _____ r. exciting; stirring
19. progressive _____ s. to make very angry
20. irksome _____ t. sparkling or shining brightly

Word Roots: Unit 15

ROOTS AND THEIR MEANINGS

spec:	to look, appear	de:	away from, opposite of
gyn:	woman	tact:	touch
sed/sid:	to sit, be still	corp:	body

Here are a few examples of some words that use the above roots:

spectacle: a visually striking performance or play
misogynistic: referring to a hatred of women
sedentary: tending to spend much time seated down; inactive or inert
depart: to leave, often in order to embark on a journey
tactile: of or related to the sense of touch; tangible
corpse: a dead human body

Now try to fill in the table below by finding the appropriate root(s) and interpreting the meaning of each word:

Word	Root(s)	Guessed Meaning	Actual Meaning
deposit			
androgynous			
sediment			
corpus			
speculate			
preside			
contact			
detract			
retrospect			

208

Lesson 151

A CONCERN

"Do you think the media is reflecting our society in all its facets and complexity? I personally doubt that media **pluralism** is really free from influence."

"Why are you concerned?" Yadas responded.

"It is our right as citizens of a democratic society to be informed with news and perspectives, unaffected by political agenda and government **intrusion**." I **bemoaned**.

Yadas just shrugged his shoulders, saying nothing. I felt that it is only **pernicious** for societal development when we, the citizens, are disinterested and **lackadaisical**.

NEW WORDS

pluralism
ˈploorəˌlizəm

bemoan
biˈmōn

intrusion
inˈtrooZHən

pernicious
pərˈniSHəs

lackadaisical
ˌlakəˈdāzikəl

Definitions: Try matching the words in the list with the appropriate definitions. If you are stuck, check the glossary in the back of the book or the passage at the top of the page.

1. pluralism _____ a. to lament; to grieve
2. bemoan _____ b. co-existence of groups of different backgrounds within one society
3. intrusion _____ c. lacking enthusiasm or effort
4. pernicious _____ d. unwelcome entrance which disturbs; something unwelcome
5. lackadaisical _____ e. causing great harm, malicious

Sentences: Try to use the words above in a sentence below. Remember that a word ending may be changed or its figure of speech slightly altered.

6. There is no use _____ the amount of homework you are assigned; just get started and it will be all done in no time.

7. Taking advantage of people to make money may be lucrative at first but socially _____ in the long run.

8. How can Ziyi expect to get into a competitive medical school given her _____ attitude toward her studies?

9. I was aware of my _____ in Joanne's family but I had nowhere else to stay for the night and it was pouring outside.

10. In Montreal, there is cultural _____: people who speak French and people who speak English coexist and thrive in a beautiful metropolis.

Lesson 152

DISPARITY

NEW WORDS

stringent
ˈstrinjənt

decorous
ˈdekərəs, diˈkôrəs

pliable
ˈplīəbəl

vaccine
vakˈsēn

yen
yen

"Why are you always **decorous**? I find your **stringent** adherence to rules really boring," she said.

"You just want everyone to be **pliable** and playful and follow your wildness." I responded.

"Isn't it fun? Don't you have a **yen** to break free?"

"I am free within the constraints of my own principles."

"I find principles suffocating and pathogenic."

"Maybe you need a **vaccine**."

Definitions: Try matching the words in the list with the appropriate definitions. If you are stuck, check the glossary in the back of the book or the passage at the top of the page.

1. stringent _____ a. keeping with good propriety and taste; polite and restrained
2. decorous   _____ b. rigorous, strictly controlled
3. pliable   _____ c. (n.) a strong yearning for something; (v.) to yearn for something
4. vaccine   _____ d. flexible, easily bent or molded
5. yen   _____ e. substance used to provide immunity against certain diseases; protective software

Sentences: Try to use the words above in a sentence below. Remember that a word ending may be changed or its figure of speech slightly altered.

6. Dr. Lai is a(n) _____ lab technician: she practices safety vigorously and follows experimental procedures strictly.
7. Vy always portrays a(n) _____ image of herself: she wears pretty dresses and acts extremely polite – even when she only goes shopping in the supermarket.
8. I am open-minded, but my value system is in no way _____.
9. It is advisable to have a full meal before taking doses of _____ so that your body has energy to fight the viruses.
10. Tien has always had a(n) _____ to work as an art director.

Lesson 153

A LOVE FOR ORGANIC CHEMISTRY

Dr. Li, now the mother of two, often told her children about her time as a chemist at a **prestigious** research institution. She optimized mechanisms to synthesize **organic** compounds found in nature so they can be used in the medicinal industry. She recalled having to **maneuver** through a maze of possible intermediate pathways in order to produce the desired product. The synthesis procedure was rigorous; any **slipshod** handling of chemicals and miscalculations would result in considerable waste of time and resources. Although her job was demanding, Dr. Li found her discoveries and contributions to research **immensely** rewarding.

NEW WORDS

organic
ôrˈganik

immense
iˈmens

slipshod
ˈslipˌSHäd

maneuver
məˈnoovər

prestigious
preˈstijəs, -ˈstē-

Definitions: Try matching the words in the list with the appropriate definitions. If you are stuck, check the glossary in the back of the book or the passage at the top of the page.

1. organic _____ a. done in a careless manner
2. immense _____ b. (n.) 1. a movement or series of movements requiring care and skill; 2. a carefully planned scheme often using deception; (v.) 1. to manipulate; 2. to turn or move skillfully
3. slipshod _____ c. 1. relating to living things; 2. produced without the use of chemical agents; 3. constitutional, essential as parts of a whole
4. maneuver _____ d. having great reputation
5. prestigious _____ e. extremely strong, in great quantity

Sentences: Try to use the words above in a sentence below. Remember that a word ending may be changed or its figure of speech slightly altered.

6. Instead of enjoying learning at his own pace, Zhang viewed high school as a rat race to earn an acceptance letter from a(n) _____ university.
7. I have never seen any scholarship application essay that was written in such a(n) _____ manner!
8. Anh cried, unable to hide her _____ and happy emotions when she reunited with her son after four years.
9. Food that is labeled _____ is sold at a higher price, but its actual nutritional contents may just be as good as the non-organic food.
10. Koh has a knack for _____ people to do what she wants; be careful when you are with her.

Lesson 154

AN EPICUREAN

NEW WORDS

laborious
lə'bôrēəs

averse
ə'vərs

adhere
ad'hi(ə)r

spate
spāt

hedonistic
ˌhēdn'istik

Joel is an undisciplined and **hedonistic** spirit. He takes great delight in sensuous enjoyment of food and drinks and treats every day as a vacation. He is **averse** to **laborious** tasks that require great effort from him. Although Joel has many creative ideas for his independent projects, whenever a **spate** of work arises, he would procrastinate by distracting himself with movies and would be unable to **adhere** to any disciplined schedule to get his projects accomplished. With such attitude, Joel is currently unemployed. I wonder how he can fund his pursuit of pleasures.

Definitions: Try matching the words in the list with the appropriate definitions. If you are stuck, check the glossary in the back of the book or the passage at the top of the page.

1. laborious _____ a. to stick to firmly; to follow through
2. averse _____ b. seeking pleasure, especially for self-indulgence
3. adhere _____ c. arduous, demanding great effort and time
4. spate _____ d. strongly opposed to
5. hedonistic _____ e. a large number or amount of something happening in quick succession

Sentences: Try to use the words above in a sentence below. Remember that a word ending may be changed or its figure of speech slightly altered.

6. Singapore Architecture students often spend _____ hours in the design studios and thus are seldom present at social events.
7. A(n) _____ wife is difficult to please: she always wants more clothes, shoes and expensive vacations.
8. It is important to _____ strictly to the laboratory safety rules to minimize the risks of accidents.
9. A(n) _____ of consecutive failed attempts really challenges one's patience and tenacity.
10. Don't be _____ to constantly challenging your comfort zone because that attitude will help you grow.

Lesson 155

A TASTELESS MEAL

We had a habit of discussing work over meals because eating good food was our outlet to regain clarity of thought. Somehow this time, the **succulent** dishes provided little help to our **unhinged** minds.
"The legal case we are handling is particularly **tedious**. Right now, we only have **presumptive** evidence, but it's neither conclusive nor sufficient to file our lawsuit. We need more time to investigate. It's easy to lapse into a **provincial** perspective under time pressure."
He said while I nodded in agreement, thinking how tasteless the food was.

NEW WORDS

succulent
ˈsəkyələnt

provincial
prəˈvinSHəl

presumptive
priˈzəmptiv

unhinge
ˌənˈhinj

tedious
ˈtēdēəs

Definitions: Try matching the words in the list with the appropriate definitions. If you are stuck, check the glossary in the back of the book or the passage at the top of the page.

1. succulent _____ a. taking something to be true or adopting a particular attitude toward something
2. provincial _____ b. juicy and tasty
3. presumptive _____ c. 1. to make someone mentally unbalanced; 2. to deprive of stability or fixity; 3. to take a door off its hinges
4. unhinge _____ d. boring and tiresome due to dull repetition
5. tedious _____ e. narrow-minded, unsophisticated

Sentences: Try to use the words above in a sentence below. Remember that a word ending may be changed or its figure of speech slightly altered.

6. Making a good moussaka can be a really _____ task: there are more than 10 intermediate steps in the recipe before the final dish is prepared.
7. I'm having a craving for a(n) _____ salmon fillet carpeted in cream mushroom sauce accompanied by a glass of champagne for dinner.
8. After Claire had received a phone call from her cousin, her mind became _____ and she couldn't focus on her work any more.
9. He found the people in the city ostentatious, and they found him _____, uneducated, and detached.
10. Tal was _____ in assuming that her housemate had stolen her money without having searched her room for the lost cash.

Lesson 156

NEW WORDS

audacious
ôˈdāSHəs

exempt
igˈzem(p)t

alienate
ˈālēəˌnāt, ˈālyə-

faction
ˈfakSHən

disparity
diˈsparitē

UNSPOKEN DISCONTENT

In a few hours, I will know which **faction** I belong to: the gifted or the mediocre. Our school divides the kids into these two classes of great **disparity** by an aptitude test so that the teachers can best cater to our different needs. I am not in a position to challenge this established system, but I feel that the students in one group are **alienated** from those in the other. The teachers also tend to be more lenient and make more **exemptions** for the gifted ones. There are probably students who have similar views but none of us is **audacious** enough to voice our opinions.

Definitions: Try matching the words in the list with the appropriate definitions. If you are stuck, check the glossary in the back of the book or the passage at the top of the page.

1. audacious _____ a. to make someone feel isolated or estranged
2. exempt _____ b. bold, daring
3. alienate _____ c. a small dissenting group within a larger group, especially in politics
4. faction _____ d. a great difference between things
5. disparity _____ e. (adj.) free from liability or obligation imposed on others; (n.) a person who is free of liability for something, usually paying tax; (v.) to free a person from an obligation or liability imposed on others

Sentences: Try to use the words above in a sentence below. Remember that a word ending may be changed or its figure of speech slightly altered.

6. Artists are thought to have _____ souls because they seem to be in their world and away from the public while creating their best work.
7. When you compare Yolanda's elegant mansion to Mark's dilapidated bungalow, the _____ between the quality of the two homes is unmistakable.
8. As a foreign student studying in Singapore, I was _____ from taking a course in a second language.
9. Jacob had a lot of _____ to throw confetti and play celebration music at his uncle's funeral.
10. Stereotyping and a lack of understanding can lead to _____ within a group.

Lesson 157

A CHILDHOOD GAME

As children, my brother and I liked to role-play. One time, we assumed ourselves to be imaginative political characters **segregated** by different ideologies. One of us was kind and pro-environment while the other, acting with great **turpitude**, had no issue destroying nature's wonders. We debated hotly over how to manage our **parched** national forests. But we were only children. Because we were young, our discussion hardly **elucidated** any important environmental questions and our proposed solutions were too simple to solve any complex problems. Sometimes we fell into disputations so intense that our mother had to step in for **mediation**. My brother is now in law school, perhaps due to the influence of our childhood experience.

NEW WORDS

segregation
ˌsegriˈgāSHən

mediation
ˌmēdēˈāSHən

parch
pärCH

elucidate
iˈloosiˌdāt

turpitude
ˈtərpiˌt(y)ood

Definitions: Try matching the words in the list with the appropriate definitions. If you are stuck, check the glossary in the back of the book or the passage at the top of the page.

1. segregation _____ a. to clarify; to illuminate
2. mediation _____ b. act of intervention to resolve conflicts
3. parch _____ c. depravity; wickedness
4. elucidate _____ d. to dry something completely through heat
5. turpitude _____ e. separation into groups

Sentences: Try to use the words above in a sentence below. Remember that a word ending may be changed or its figure of speech slightly altered.

6. Rosanne's language is esoteric and philosophical and I often need to ask her to _____ what she means.

7. Some believe that peace in the Middle East is still possible, but only through unbiased _____.

8. An effective leader will encourage inclusiveness and avoid _____ among his people.

9. Saigon's weather in April is so hot that I feel as if my skin will be as _____ as dried weed if I go out under the sun.

10. The dictator's _____ shocked everyone: any citizen that disagreed with his views was swiftly executed.

NEW WORDS

acoustic
əˈkoostik

doctrinaire
ˌdäktrəˈner

impecunious
ˌimpəˈkyoonēəs

plunge
plənj

escalate
ˈeskəˌlāt

Lesson 158

FROM ACADEMIA TO BUSINESS

Marge spent eight years in graduate school studying **acoustic** patterns in medieval Celtic music. But when she finished her degree, she was unable to find an academic job. Under such circumstances, she was forced to take a **plunge** into a pragmatic career. Initially, employers had no interest in hiring Marge because her **doctrinaire** interview answers held little practicality. As a result, Marge grew anxious because she feared that she would never be hired and that she would live an **impecunious** lifestyle for decades. So she **escalated** her efforts to get a job by learning some practical technical skills. Now she is the CFO of a large technology company in California.

Definitions: Try matching the words in the list with the appropriate definitions. If you are stuck, check the glossary in the back of the book or the passage at the top of the page.

1. acoustic _____ a. insistent on using theory or doctrine without considering practicality
2. doctrinaire _____ b. relating to sound, hearing
3. impecunious _____ c. to become more serious and intense
4. plunge _____ d. having little or no money
5. escalate _____ e. (n.) a jump or dive into water; 2. a swift and drastic fall in value or amount; (v.) 1. to move downward or drop steeply; 2. to embark on something with vigor

Sentences: Try to use the words above in a sentence below. Remember that a word ending may be changed or its figure of speech slightly altered.

6. Some people prefer _____ renditions of pop songs to their original versions.
7. A trivial disagreement between a bus driver and a passenger quickly _____ into a serious dispute.
8. Morton led a(n) _____ lifestyle; he saved endlessly for items because he could barely afford to survive.
9. When Tom saw snow for the first time, he got super excited and immediately _____ into that thick white blanket.
10. Unlike Ethan, who was very pragmatic in his approach to solving traffic problems, Carlo maintained a(n) _____ mindset.

Lesson 159

ANOTHER WAY

I joked and she laughed. I could tell from her outbursts of **mirth** that she was in a **transitory** state of joy. But her deep grey eyes possessed a **perpetual** sadness. Eyes don't lie; they have an **intrinsic** ability to converse in a way words alone cannot convey. I wanted to connect with her beyond our laughter so I reached out for her hands and my eyes fixated at hers, as if inviting a more **holistic** conversation.

NEW WORDS

holistic
hō'listik

intrinsic
in'trinzik, -sik

mirth
mərTH

perpetual
pər'peCHooəl

transitory
'transi,tôrē, 'tranzi-

Definitions: Try matching the words in the list with the appropriate definitions. If you are stuck, check the glossary in the back of the book or the passage at the top of the page.

1. holistic _____ a. considering all factors, all-inclusive
2. intrinsic _____ b. fleeting, not lasting
3. mirth _____ c. amusement – often expressed by laughter
4. perpetual _____ d. inherent, innate, essential
5. transitory _____ e. occurring repeatedly; lasting forever

Sentences: Try to use the words above in a sentence below. Remember that a word ending may be changed or its figure of speech slightly altered.

6. Colleges claim that undergraduate admission is _____: not only grades and test scores are assessed, but essays, activities, references, and character also play a role in accepting an applicant.
7. Apart from external motives, it is important that one find _____ joy and meaning in what one does.
8. The city seems to be in _____ transformation: there is always something new every now and then.
9. Happiness is only a(n) _____ feeling.
10. Everyone loves to be with people who bring laughter and _____.

Lesson 160

AUNT KARINA

NEW WORDS

incidental
ˌinsiˈdentl

linchpin
ˈlinCHˌpin

commend
kəˈmend

surmount
sərˈmount

fouled
fould

Aunt Karina was the **linchpin** that held the family together. It seemed like, with her support, there was no obstacle that I or my siblings could not **surmount**. Even with only **incidental** information about our travesties, Karina could give us fabulous guidance. Each of us in the family **commended** her for her prescience and kindness to help us navigate rough waters. Her reputation among members of our family never **fouled**.

Definitions: Try matching the words in the list with the appropriate definitions. If you are stuck, check the glossary in the back of the book or the passage at the top of the page.

1. incidental _____ a. occurring as a consequence; secondary, subordinate
2. linchpin _____ b. made dirty, defiled, or soiled
3. commend _____ c. to overcome; to get over something
4. surmount _____ d. to praise; to endorse
5. fouled _____ e. a person or thing vital to a business or an organization

Sentences: Try to use the words above in a sentence below. Remember that a word ending may be changed or its figure of speech slightly altered.

6. Lindy is seen as the _____ that holds her billiards team together: if she quit, then the entire team would dissolve.
7. Intense physical attraction is only _____ to building a stable and meaningful relationship.
8. Don't make contemptible decisions that will make your reputation become _____.
9. Being clear of the upcoming challenges that have to be _____ in order to achieve your goals will get you ready mentally.
10. Amy should be _____ for the countless hours that she has devoted to helping the poor in New York City.

Word Search
Lessons 151-160

```
S Z B T R R N V Z T L Y J D F Q T
V U D R X B N G G K E N V A M Q W
S U O I N U C E P M I D C M Z D X
Y P T I M M K R D N V T I P W T R
D R E T G Q Y Q L U I B D O Y Z Z
E D O R X I L B C O T E G N U L P
C T Z T P G T A N I X I Z B L S T
O T I Y I E J S B N N M P L B P R
R P H N P S T N E O N A G R P B S
O M C P T E N U I R R M G L U U T
U E R Y T R E A A P P I U R R T E
S X A A D N U B R L H R O M O G J
Z E P J I T N S G T A C O U N B Q
Y S N C L Q W M I L N U N I S J Q
L Y C L R J Q J I O N J H I V L P
G A M W P N L S Y T N N R D L Y D
V P K Z J Z M J G B U T W M Z L Y
```

1 co-existence of groups of different backgrounds within one society
2 unwelcome entrance which disturbs; something unwelcome
3 keeping with good propriety and taste; polite and restrained
4 substance used to provide immunity against certain diseases; protective software
5 1. relating to living things; 2. produced without the use of chemical agents; 3. constitutional, essential as parts of a whole
6 having great reputation
7 arduous, demanding great effort and time
8 a large number or amount of something happening in quick succession
9 1. to make someone mentally unbalanced; 2. to deprive of stability or fixity; 3. to take a door off its hinges
10 boring and tiresome due to dull repetition
11 (adj.) free from liability or obligation imposed on others; (n.) a person who is free of liability for something, usually paying tax; (v.) to free a person from an obligation or liability imposed on others
12 a small dissenting group within a larger group, especially in politics
13 to dry something completely through heat
14 depravity; wickedness
15 having little or no money
16 (n.) a jump or dive into water; 2. a swift and drastic fall in value or amount; (v.) 1. to move downward or drop steeply; 2. to embark on something with vigor
17 occurring repeatedly; lasting forever
18 fleeting, not lasting
19 a person or thing vital to a business or an organization
20 to overcome; to get over something

Vocabulary Review
Lessons 151-160

Directions: Match each word with its best approximate definition. Note that definitions are not necessarily repeated verbatim from the lesson exercises.

1. pernicious _____
2. lackadaisical _____
3. stringent _____
4. pliable _____
5. immense _____
6. maneuver _____
7. averse _____
8. hedonistic _____
9. succulent _____
10. provincial _____
11. audacious _____
12. alienate _____
13. segregation _____
14. elucidate _____
15. doctrinaire _____
16. escalate _____
17. holistic _____
18. mirth _____
19. incidental _____
20. fouled _____

a. lazy; lacking enthusiasm and determination
b. easily bent or influenced; flexible
c. to cause to become more intense or serious
d. in the pursuit of self-pleasure, usually self-indulgent
e. accompanying but not a major part of something
f. having a strong dislike or opposition to something
g. the act of setting someone or something apart from others
h. cause someone to feel isolated or estranged
i. seeking to impose a belief in a circumstance without regard to practical considerations
j. characterized by the parts being referenced or explicable only in consideration of the whole
k. having a harmful effect, especially in a gradual or subtle way
l. amusement, often expressed by laughter
m. bold and daring, perhaps with a lack of respect
n. concerning a person or place: narrow minded or unsophisticated
o. to twist, turn, or manipulate
p. strict, precise, and exacting (of regulations and conditions)
q. to make something clear; explain
r. extremely large or great, especially in scale or degree
s. offensive smelling; wicked or immoral
t. juicy, tender, or tasty (of a food)

Word Roots: Unit 16

ROOTS AND THEIR MEANINGS

retro:	backward, behind	**simil/simul:**	likeness, imitation
cis:	to cut	**am:**	to love
urb:	city	**co/com/con:**	with, together

Here are a few examples of some words that use the above roots:

retrograde: movement that is directed backward
scissors: implement or instrument used to cut materials
urban: concerning or relating to a city or a town
simultaneous: occurring, happening, or operating at the same time
amorous: showing, feeling, or relating to sexual desire
connect: to join together so that a link (either literally or figuratively) is established

Now try to fill in the table below by finding the appropriate root(s) and interpreting the meaning of each word:

Word	Root(s)	Guessed Meaning	Actual Meaning
simulate			
combine			
retroactive			
cooperate			
retrospect			
amicable			
suburbia			
incision			

Lesson 161

NEW WORDS

morass
mə'ras, mô-

auditory
'ôdi͵tôrē

refract
ri'frakt

adamant
'adəmənt

righteous
'rīCHəs

MITCHELL'S MADNESS

Mitchell went to his doctor and **adamantly** demanded that the latter terminate his prescription medication, as the side effects made him feel nauseous. The doctor reminded him that the last time Mitchell had stopped taking his medication, his psychotic symptoms had quickly returned, leaving him in a **morass** of delusional problems. For example, Mitchell would notice that light would **refract** to create face-like shadows on the wall, and he would also hear **auditory** hallucinations of angry voices from the wall shouting at him. After being reminded of this, Mitchell began to second-guess himself. He knew that his doctor was a trustworthy professional and a **righteous** man, who only wanted what was best for his patients, so Mitchell agreed to continue taking his medication despite the unwanted side-effects.

Definitions: Try matching the words in the list with the appropriate definitions. If you are stuck, check the glossary in the back of the book or the passage at the top of the page.

1. morass _____   a. to make a ray of light change direction when it enters a medium at an angle goes through at an angle
2. auditory _____   b. morally right or justifiable
3. refract _____   c. 1. an area of boggy ground; 2. a complicated or confusing situation
4. adamant _____   d. relating to the sense of hearing
5. righteous _____   e. refusing to be persuaded

Sentences: Try to use the words above in a sentence below. Remember that a word ending may be changed or its figure of speech slightly altered.

6. Although his colleagues pointed out many flaws in his business plan, Adam remained _____ about going through with it.
7. The physics teacher amazed his students when he showed them how lenses _____ light differently depending on what they are made of.
8. Harold navigated through the _____ of having both of his ex-girlfriends tell him that he was a bad boyfriend at once every night for a week.
9. Helen was a visual learner; she could remember everything she read but could not seem to absorb _____ information at all.
10. A(n) _____ person can be trusted to make fair decisions even in difficult situations.

Lesson 162

YEAR OF THE GOAT

Residents of New York City's Chinatown recently hosted a parade for the Chinese New Year, an event that celebrates the rich cultural **heritage** of the Chinese people. However, in an act of deplorable **jingoism**, a group of intolerant citizens attempted to ruin the celebration by trying to **dislodge** the head of a goat (a **figurative** manifestation of the new year) that had been constructed for the parade. Much to the jingoists' **chagrin**, police stopped them before they succeeded, and the parade continued as planned.

NEW WORDS

dislodge
dis'läj

chagrin
SHə'grin

jingoism
'jiNGgō,izəm

heritage
'heritij

figurative
'figyərətiv

Definitions: Try matching the words in the list with the appropriate definitions. If you are stuck, check the glossary in the back of the book or the passage at the top of the page.

1. dislodge _____ a. distress or embarrassment at having failed or been humiliated
2. chagrin _____ b. 1. property that is inherited; 2. objects or traditions, values, historical buildings or countryside passed down from previous generations
3. jingoism _____ c. to knock or force out of position
4. heritage _____ d. metaphorical, not literal
5. figurative _____ e. extreme patriotism

Sentences: Try to use the words above in a sentence below. Remember that a word ending may be changed or its figure of speech slightly altered.

6. The death of his father was heartbreaking, but the property he received as part of his _____ would keep him financially afloat while he grieved.
7. Max managed to _____ one of his teeth after getting hit in the mouth with a basketball during recess.
8. Owen's acne problem was a constant source of _____ throughout his high school years.
9. My comment wasn't supposed to be taken literally! I was speaking in a(n) _____ manner in order to illustrate my point more powerfully.
10. Having national pride may sometimes be admirable, but _____ can result in negative attitudes towards certain nationalities.

Lesson 163

ARTHRITIC GARY

NEW WORDS

stimulate
ˈstimyəˌlāt

rigid
ˈrijid

predilection
ˌpredlˈekSHən, ˌprēdl-

tenet
ˈtenit

palliate
ˈpalēˌāt

Gary had a strong desire to take up Buddhist meditation, as he believed that following the **tenets** and practices of Buddhism would give him more peace in his life and help him reduce his **predilections** towards unhealthy habits. However, his arthritis caused his knees to hurt whenever he tried to fold his **rigid** legs into a cross-legged seated position. His physician told him that regular stretching to **stimulate** his knees daily would help ease the pain when getting into this position. Indeed, the stretching exercises did **palliate** the situation, but the arthritis was still there, so Gary decided to try lying-down meditation instead.

Definitions: Try matching the words in the list with the appropriate definitions. If you are stuck, check the glossary in the back of the book or the passage at the top of the page.

1. stimulate _____ a. a preference or special liking for something
2. rigid _____ b. to make less severe or unpleasant without removing the cause
3. predilection _____ c. a principle or belief
4. tenet _____ d. to make (something) more active or excited
5. palliate _____ e. unable to bend or be forced out of shape

Sentences: Try to use the words above in a sentence below. Remember that a word ending may be changed or its figure of speech slightly altered.

6. The cat's body became as _____ as a board when it heard the neighbor's dog let out a vicious bark.
7. Before she even asked him where he would like to eat, Lindsey knew Jim would suggest a Mexican restaurant due to his _____ for spicy tacos.
8. Leyla joined a yoga class in hopes of _____ her chronic back pain, but she knew she would need surgery if she wanted to get rid of it permanently.
9. According to the Bible, the Ten Commandments are eternal _____ that serve as a guide to basic morality.
10. The children became very _____ and could not be calmed down after eating all of their holiday candy at once.

Lesson 164

LOUIE MISSES NEW YORK

As a child of lower Manhattan, Louie never enjoyed living in Texas. He grew **disenchanted** with Texas' rustic lifestyle and yearned to return to the big city. One day he grew **despondent** enough to listen to his friend Janet, a fellow New Yorker who had been **appraising** his unfortunate situation. "I'll tell you what," she said. **Blandishing** him with an offer, she continued, "It seems like life here is **noxious** for you. If you come to New York, I will give you half off rent in my apartment." Louie was enthralled and Janet was too, for she had a secret crush on Louie and still earned money off of a business transaction.

NEW WORDS

disenchanted
ˌdisenˈCHantid

despondence
diˈspändəns

appraise
əˈprāz

blandish
ˈblandiSH

noxious
ˈnäkSHəs

Definitions: Try matching the words in the list with the appropriate definitions. If you are stuck, check the glossary in the back of the book or the passage at the top of the page.

1. disenchanted _____ a. to assess the value or quality of
2. despondence _____ b. harmful; poisonous; extremely unpleasant
3. appraise _____ c. to coax with kind words or flattery
4. blandish _____ d. a state of low spirits due to loss of hope or courage
5. noxious _____ e. disappointed by someone or something previously respected or admired

Sentences: Try to use the words above in a sentence below. Remember that a word ending may be changed or its figure of speech slightly altered.

6. Tom tried to _____ his tutor into telling his parents he was a responsible student when he did not do his work.
7. Fans became _____ with the band after the release of their new album, which was drastically different in sound compared to their previous work.
8. Often people find the smell of a skunk to be _____; it is extremely odorous and unsettling.
9. Paulina's _____ over the loss of her beloved pet dog showed no sign of letting up anytime soon.
10. Michael was known for _____ potential employees rather stringently during their interviews.

Lesson 165

TURNING THINGS AROUND

NEW WORDS

luxury
ˈləkSH(ə)rē, ˈləgZH(ə)-

vulgar
ˈvəlgər

decisive
diˈsīsiv

aggrandize
əˈgranˌdīz

precede
priˈsēd

Liam grew up in a poor family that lived a **vulgar**, destitute life. Even simple things that many people take for granted, such as having heat during the winter, were **luxuries** for them. However, as Liam grew up, he took **decisive** action in order to **aggrandize** his and his family's situation. Unlike the generations in his family that **preceded** him, Liam decided to take his education seriously so that he could attend university and eventually start his own business to support himself and help his struggling parents.

Definitions: Try matching the words in the list with the appropriate definitions. If you are stuck, check the glossary in the back of the book or the passage at the top of the page.

1. luxury _____ a. able to make choices quickly and/or confidently
2. vulgar _____ b. to happen or come before (in time)
3. decisive _____ c. 1. a state of extravagant living; 2. an inessential desirable item that is expensive
4. aggrandize _____ d. lacking sophistication or good taste
5. precede _____ e. to make great or greater

Sentences: Try to use the words above in a sentence below. Remember that a word ending may be changed or its figure of speech slightly altered.

6. Although their children love listening to rap music, many parents find the _____ language prevalent in rap lyrics to be offensive.
7. When appointing a leader, it is important to choose a(n) _____ person that can act without worrying about every possible consequence.
8. The townspeople hoped that the newly elected mayor would be more effective than the person that _____ him.
9. Jay dreamed of the life of _____ he would lead if he were ever lucky enough to win the lottery.
10. The president hoped that his new healthcare policy would _____ his public image.

Lesson 166

ALIEN ATTACK

Steven's favorite movie is an indie sci-fi film called *Attack of the Blobs*. The movie is about the introduction of an **invasive** alien species on Earth that eventually brings about an **apocalypse**. When the aliens first land on the planet, they are tiny, seemingly harmless creatures that are incapable of causing even the smallest **mischief**. However, over the span of a few days, their bodies grow into gigantic, **amorphous** blobs that destroy the streets and buildings with which they came into contact. After **zealously** sending in military forces to successfully halt alien destruction, the government enacted a new policy that involved the immediate termination of any foreign species that arrived upon domestic soil.

NEW WORDS

apocalypse
əˈpäkəˌlips

mischief
ˈmisCHif

zealous
ˈzeləs

invasive
inˈvāsiv

amorphous
əˈmôrfəs

Definitions: Try matching the words in the list with the appropriate definitions. If you are stuck, check the glossary in the back of the book or the passage at the top of the page.

1. apocalypse _____ a. extremely passionate about or devoted to (sometimes in a negative way)
2. mischief _____ b. 1. a great disaster; 2. the end of the world
3. zealous _____ c. without clearly defined shape or form
4. invasive _____ d. playful misbehavior or troublemaking
5. amorphous _____ e. tending to spread undesirably or harmfully

Sentences: Try to use the words above in a sentence below. Remember that a word ending may be changed or its figure of speech slightly altered.

6. Children will often get into _____ if there is no one watching them.
7. Pete's new band had a(n) _____ lineup; it was constantly changing and had no permanent members.
8. Scientists are trying their best to warn the world of the inclement environmental _____ that will occur if global warming is not taken seriously.
9. As one of the most _____ Fleetwood Mac fans I know, Stevie has band posters, tickets, and albums posted all over her room.
10. The sound of the construction was quite _____ and could be heard in every building on the block.

Lesson 167

NEW WORDS

libertine
ˈlibərˌtēn

cerebral
səˈrēbrəl, ˈserəbrəl

deplete
diˈplēt

extemporize
ikˈstempəˌrīz

humane
(h)yooˈmān

FAVORITE FILM

Christian was an avid fan of many genres of film, but he particularly fancied **cerebral** movies that made him think deeply about certain issues or that delve into the psychology of a character. For example, he absolutely loved *American Psycho* (2000), a film about an investment banker with an ostentatious and shallow lifestyle who hides his psychopathic ego and **libertine** fantasies from his co-workers and friends. As the movie progresses, he begins to escalate deeper into his fantasies, and his actions become less and less **humane**. He begins going on a murdering rampage and kills many people, including his co-worker (in a scene which was heavily **extemporized**.) By the end of the film, the character's sanity seems to be completely **depleted**, and the audience is left unsure of what is real and what is not.

Definitions: Try matching the words in the list with the appropriate definitions. If you are stuck, check the glossary in the back of the book or the passage at the top of the page.

1. libertine _____ a. to use up the supply or resources of
2. cerebral _____ b. having or showing compassion or benevolence
3. deplete _____ c. intellectual and not emotional
4. extemporize _____ d. characterized by a disregard for morality
5. humane _____ e. to improvise; to create and perform spontaneously and without preparation

Sentences: Try to use the words above in a sentence below. Remember that a word ending may be changed or its figure of speech slightly altered.

6. Clyde prefers to read _____ novels that make him think about important philosophical questions.
7. Miles often did not prepare much for his jazz performances, choosing to _____ a majority of the time that he was on stage.
8. If we are not mindful of the way we use the Earth's resources, they may be _____ sooner than we expect.
9. Stacy's veterinary clinic was respected for its _____ methods of euthanizing sick animals.
10. Kevin's willingness to indulge himself at the expense of others was indicative of his _____ attitude.

Lesson 168

TEAMWORK MAKES THE DREAM WORK

Jenna and Helga were working together to create a **diorama** of the solar system for their science class. Jenna had hoped to make the project intricate and **dynamic** with many moving parts to demonstrate the rotation and revolution of the planets, but the project was due the next day and the girls had barely even begun! The girls did not make a very effective team — Jenna tended to be **domineering**, ordering Helga to complete tasks without consulting her first, whereas Helga was quite lazy. She refused to put in any actual effort because, in her **odious** attitude, she believed that if they were meant to get a good grade on the project, they would get it regardless of how much work they put into it. Their lack of teamwork was the biggest **obstruction** to their productivity, and they ended up receiving a failing grade for their shoddy project.

NEW WORDS

odious
ˈōdēəs

diorama
ˌdīəˈramə, -ˈrä-

dynamic
dīˈnamik

obstruction
əbˈstrəkSHən, äb-

domineering
ˌdämə'ni(ə)riNG

Definitions: Try matching the words in the list with the appropriate definitions. If you are stuck, check the glossary in the back of the book or the passage at the top of the page.

1. odious _____ a. a thing that impedes or prevents passage or progress
2. diorama _____ b. overly controlling
3. dynamic _____ c. a three-dimensional model of a scene
4. obstruction _____ d. extremely unpleasant
5. domineering _____ e. always changing or active

Sentences: Try to use the words above in a sentence below. Remember that a word ending may be changed or its figure of speech slightly altered.

6. It would be _____ to invite the thieves who robbed your best friend's home over for coffee in your living room.
7. One of the reasons why Albert decided to quit was because of his boss's _____ personality, which made it difficult to enjoy work.
8. After the hurricane, many of the homeowners in the neighborhood worked together to clear fallen trees and other _____ from the road.
9. Ralph decided to create a realistic _____ of a scene from his favorite book for his art project.
10. Due to the _____ work environment, there was never a dull moment at the office.

Lesson 169

BAD DECISIONS

NEW WORDS

resignation
ˌrezigˈnāSHən

foresight
ˈfôrˌsīt

elongated
iˈlôNGˌgātid, iˈläNG-

havoc
ˈhavək

tacit
ˈtasit

With much **resignation**, Brandon, a former lieutenant in the Baltimore police department, accepted the fact that he was going to be dismissed. He did not want to give up his position, but he did not have much of a choice. He had recently been involved in a drunk driving accident, which had caused much **havoc** at a busy intersection. Brandon wished that he had had the **foresight** to see the consequences of his bad decision, but this was not the case. After word got out that he had been the cause of the accident, the chief of police made the **tacit** suggestion that Brandon should take responsibility for his actions and resign rather than force the department to fire him directly. Brandon reluctantly agreed, displaying an **elongated** frown and a tear in his eye.

Definitions: Try matching the words in the list with the appropriate definitions. If you are stuck, check the glossary in the back of the book or the passage at the top of the page.

1. resignation _____
2. foresight _____
3. elongated _____
4. havoc _____
5. tacit _____

a. the ability to predict what will happen in the future
b. understood or implied without being stated
c. widespread destruction, confusion, or disorder
d. unusually long in relation to its width
e. 1. an act of retiring or giving up a position; 2. the acceptance of something undesirable but inevitable

Sentences: Try to use the words above in a sentence below. Remember that a word ending may be changed or its figure of speech slightly altered.

6. If John had not had the _____ to bring his raincoat, he would have gotten drenched during the sudden downpour.
7. The house fire caused much _____ within the normally peaceful neighborhood.
8. Bruce met the fact that he was going to be fired with _____: there was nothing he could do to prevent being dismissed.
9. A lack of response will be regarded as a(n) _____ agreement.
10. The _____ necks of giraffes allow them to eat leaves on high branches almost effortlessly.

Lesson 170

MARRIAGE TROUBLES

Sally had started to become worried about her husband's behavior. Over the past couple of months, Harry had begun to lead a more **dissolute** lifestyle and would often come home after work quite intoxicated. He had also seemed to become more emotionally distant from Sally, giving **terse** responses to her questions and sometimes ignoring her altogether. This was in **stark** contrast to the way he used be – full of energy, enthusiasm, and a zeal for life that had drawn Sally to him in the first place. Harry's progressively worsening behavior prompted Sally to seek the help of a marriage counselor to try and **fortify** their relationship, hoping to **ameliorate** the situation before it became unsalvageable.

NEW WORDS

dissolute
ˈdisəˌloot

stark
stärk

ameliorate
əˈmēlyəˌrāt, əˈmēlēə-

fortify
ˈfôrtəˌfī

terse
tərs

Definitions: Try matching the words in the list with the appropriate definitions. If you are stuck, check the glossary in the back of the book or the passage at the top of the page.

1. dissolute _____ a. to strengthen
2. stark _____ b. brief and direct in a way that may seem unfriendly
3. ameliorate _____ c. severe or bare in appearance; sharply clear
4. fortify _____ d. lax in morals
5. terse _____ e. to make something bad, unfortunate, or unsatisfactory better

Sentences: Try to use the words above in a sentence below. Remember that a word ending may be changed or its figure of speech slightly altered.

6. Although they were siblings, there was a(n) _____ difference in the way the two brothers behaved.
7. The workers _____ the house with extra support to protect it from severe weather.
8. It was difficult to have a conversation with Richard, who was an unusually quiet person that often responded in a(n) _____ manner.
9. The drunken man often offended others with his _____ actions.
10. Jerry volunteered much of his time to the local orphanage in hopes of _____ the unfortunate situations of the children there.

Crossword Puzzle
Lessons 161-170

ACROSS

2. lacking sophistication or good taste
6. 1. a state of extravagant living; 2. an inessential desirable item that is expensive
7. to knock or force out of position
10. to make something bad, unfortunate, or unsatisfactory better
11. to make less severe or unpleasant without removing the cause
15. relating to the sense of hearing
16. a state of low spirits due to loss of hope or courage
17. overly controlling
18. characterized by a disregard for morality
19. 1. a great disaster; 2. the end of the world
20. unusually long in relation to its width

DOWN

1. to coax with kind words or flattery
3. 1. property that is inherited; 2. objects or traditions, values, historical buildings or countryside passed down from previous generations
4. extremely passionate about or devoted to (sometimes in a negative way)
5. morally right or justifiable
8. to improvise; to create and perform spontaneously and without preparation
9. 1. an act of retiring or giving up a position; 2. the acceptance of something undesirable but inevitable
12. unable to bend or be forced out of shape
13. always changing or active
14. brief and direct in a way that may seem unfriendly

Vocabulary Review
Lessons 161-170

Directions: Match each word with its best approximate definition. Note that definitions are not necessarily repeated verbatim from the lesson exercises.

1. morass _____
2. adamant _____
3. chagrin _____
4. jingoism _____
5. stimulate _____
6. tenet _____
7. disenchanted _____
8. noxious _____
9. aggrandize _____
10. precede _____
11. mischief _____
12. amorphous _____
13. cerebral _____
14. humane _____
15. odious _____
16. diorama _____
17. havoc _____
18. tacit _____
19. stark _____
20. fortify _____

a. disappointed by someone or something that was previously esteemed
b. distress and/or embarrassment for having failed or been humiliate
c. to increase the power, wealth, status, or reputation of
d. intellectual (as opposed to emotional or physical)
e. a boggy or swampy area; a difficult or complicated situation
f. widespread destruction; great confusion or disorder
g. playful and often troublemaking misbehavior, especially in children
h. severe in appearance; complete
i. extremely unpleasant; repulsive
j. harmful, poisonous, or very unpleasant
k. implied or understood without being stated
l. a model representing a scene with three dimensional figures
m. a key principle or belief
n. to come before or ahead of another in time or position
o. to make someone or something more active or excited
p. to strengthen physically or mentally
q. refusing to be persuaded to change one's mind
r. showing kindness and compassion
s. lacking a clearly defined shape or form
t. extreme and hostile patriotism

Literary and Drama Terms

> Whether you have a passion for literature or you feel forced to learn it for exams, there are terms that you should know. Below is a list of major literary terms that will help you better understand how literature operates.

alliteration: the use of the same letter or sound at the beginning of adjacent or nearly connected words

analogy: a comparison between two things, usually for the purpose of instruction or clarification

anecdote: a short, catchy story about an intriguing incident or person

eulogy: a speech or writing that praises someone excessively, often after that person's death

foreshadow: something that serves as a warning or indication of a future event

hyperbole: claims or statements that are so exaggerated as to not be able to be taken literally in a serious manner

irony: a set of affairs or circumstances that seems to be the exact opposite of what one would expect, thus resulting in amusement

foil (n.): a character or object used for contrast in order to emphasize and enhance the qualities of another

metaphor: a figure of speech where a word or phrase is applied to an action to which it cannot in reality or literally be applied; a thing that is regarded as symbolic or representative of something else

onomatopoeia: the use of a word that sounds exactly like its name (e.g. ding dong, boom, cuckoo)

personification: the attribution of human characteristics to something that is nonhuman; giving some abstract entity humanlike attributes

plot: the main events of a novel, play, or other work presented in some form of sequence

pseudonym: a fictitious name used by an author of a work, almost always because the author does not want to reveal his or her identity

setting: the place and time in which a novel, short story, play, or other event takes place

simile: a figure of speech comparing one thing with another using "like" or "as" in the comparison

soliloquy: often used in a play, the act of speaking or reading one's feelings aloud – regardless of whether other people are present

synopsis: a brief summary of a piece of writing, drama, film, or other piece of art

Lesson 171

PROPHECIES REVEALED

NEW WORDS

veiled
vāld

manifest
ˈmanəˌfest

dismantle
disˈmantl

flourish
ˈfləriSH

oracle
ˈôrəkəl

Roland had recently been feeling lost and despondent. Hoping to find some direction and happiness in his life, he decided to visit someone who claimed to be an **oracle** that could see what one's future holds. When Roland arrived at the home of the self-proclaimed prophet, the oracle was sitting in a dimly lit room with his face **veiled** underneath a sheer cloth. With a **flourish,** the oracle made a gesture at Roland to take a seat. After listening to Roland's troubles, the oracle advised Roland that in order to find his inner path he must **dismantle** his preconceived notion of what happiness is. Only then, when he looked inside himself and understood what it meant for him to be "happy," would the truth **manifest** itself so Roland could follow a meaningful path in life.

Definitions: Try matching the words in the list with the appropriate definitions. If you are stuck, check the glossary in the back of the book or the passage at the top of the page.

1. veiled _____ a. (n.) 1. a bold or extravagant gesture; 2. an ornamental flowing curve in writing; (v.) to grow or develop in a healthy or vigorous way
2. manifest _____ b. to take something apart
3. dismantle _____ c. covered or concealed
4. flourish _____ d. a person with great wisdom; someone believed to communicate with a deity
5. oracle _____ e. (n.) a customs document listing the people and contents of a ship, train, or plane; (v.) 1. to show or demonstrate clearly; 2. to be evidence of, to prove; 3. (of a ghost or an illness) to appear

Sentences: Try to use the words above in a sentence below. Remember that a word ending may be changed or its figure of speech slightly altered.

6. Bri felt that she had the flu as early symptoms began to _____.
7. If you want your garden to _____, you must make sure the plants receive plentiful water and sunlight.
8. Many people turned to the _____ in times of need, hoping that he could give them a divine answer to their problems.
9. Larry looked at his enemy with thinly _____ contempt.
10. Dylan _____ his computer in an attempt to diagnose the issues he was having with it.

Lesson 172

PIRATE THREAT

Back in the sixteenth century, the town of Cabral constantly feared **predation** by pirates. Citizens of the town saw the pirates sporadically, as they were **itinerant** on the high seas. But when they came to town, they were **pugnacious** and robbed everyone of their cherished and expensive goods. Often the pirates were so terrifying as to harm people. Though citizens begged for **clemency**, the pirates usually attacked them and robbed them blind. In the event someone was neither assaulted nor robbed, the case was surely deemed **anomalous**, and that person was deemed to be very lucky. Only after Cabral received more advanced weaponry in the following century was it able to ward off its seafaring enemies.

NEW WORDS

clemency
ˈklemənsē

predation
priˈdāSHən

anomalous
əˈnämələs

pugnacious
pəgˈnāSHəs

itinerant
īˈtinərənt, iˈtin-

Definitions: Try matching the words in the list with the appropriate definitions. If you are stuck, check the glossary in the back of the book or the passage at the top of the page.

1. clemency _____
2. predation _____
3. anomalous _____
4. pugnacious _____
5. itinerant _____

a. eager or quick to argue or fight
b. deviating from what is normal or expected
c. traveling from place to place
d. lenience or mercy
e. the act of preying on other animals; attacking or plundering

Sentences: Try to use the words above in a sentence below. Remember that a word ending may be changed or its figure of speech slightly altered.

6. The _____ results of the experiment baffled scientists.
7. Due to his _____ nature, you never knew where in the world Gus might be at any given time of the year.
8. Ralph's _____ personality made it difficult for him to make close friends.
9. Joshua's parents granted little _____ in punishing him for not doing his homework: they scolded him at length and forced him to study more.
10. The spines on a porcupine's back are an effective defense against _____.

Lesson 173

A NICE CHIANTI

NEW WORDS

aroma
əˈrōmə

brusque
brəsk

imposter
imˈpästər

renew
riˈn(y)oo

intermittent
ˌintərˈmitnt

As a wine connoisseur, Jordan made sure to attend the **intermittent** wine festivals in his city whenever they were held. He had a liking for wine that probably stemmed from being raised by parents that made and bottled their own wine. Each time he went to the local wine festival, it would remind him of his childhood years and **renew** his love for the fermented beverage. Unfortunately, some of the dishonest wine-sellers at these festivals spoke to him in a **brusque** manner, trying to sell him lower quality, **imposter** wines. They, however, were never able to fool Jordan, who was an expert at identifying authentic wines by their unique **aromas**.

Definitions: Try matching the words in the list with the appropriate definitions. If you are stuck, check the glossary in the back of the book or the passage at the top of the page.

1. aroma _____ a. occurring at irregular intervals
2. brusque _____ b. a distinctive, pleasant smell
3. imposter _____ c. offhand or abrupt in speech or manner
4. renew _____ d. a person who deceives others by pretending to be someone else
5. intermittent _____ e. to make new, fresh, or strong again

Sentences: Try to use the words above in a sentence below. Remember that a word ending may be changed or its figure of speech slightly altered.

6. Matthew's _____ comments on the speech came as a surprise to everyone because he usually is reserved and thinks things through before he talks.

7. The _____ rests that Michelle needed to take during her morning run indicated to her that she needed to exercise more regularly.

8. Stewart claimed to be an experienced pilot, but he turned out to be a(n) _____ who had never stepped foot in a cockpit.

9. The depressed man decided to go on a meditation retreat to see if he could _____ his sense of purpose in his life.

10. The satisfying _____ of fresh bread brought back memories of when Lisa used to work in a bakery.

Lesson 174

CAPTIVATED BY CALAMITY

Although Martha was an outwardly cheerful and **congenial** person, she had a dark obsession with **catastrophes**. She loved reading newspaper articles about natural disasters, and her favorite novels were those that contained **motifs** of death and destruction. She was particularly fascinated by the Hindenburg disaster, in which the **voluptuous** frame of an airship caught fire as it **hovered** about 100 meters above where it was supposed to land and then crashed to the ground, killing 36 people.

NEW WORDS

motif
mō'tēf

hover
'həvər

congenial
kən'jēnyəl

catastrophe
kə'tastrəfē

voluptuous
və'ləpCHəwəs

Definitions: Try matching the words in the list with the appropriate definitions. If you are stuck, check the glossary in the back of the book or the passage at the top of the page.

1. motif _____ a. to remain in one place in the air
2. hover _____ b. a terrible disaster
3. congenial _____ c. a theme that is repeated through a book, story, etc.; a decorative pattern
4. catastrophe _____ d. suggesting sensual pleasure by fullness and beauty of form
5. voluptuous _____ e. suitable or appropriate; pleasant

Sentences: Try to use the words above in a sentence below. Remember that a word ending may be changed or its figure of speech slightly altered.

6. Wendy's _____ crimson dress accentuated her natural beauty.
7. The helicopter _____ noisily over the helipad as it prepared to land.
8. The residents of the coastal town prepared for a(n) _____ after hearing the news that a hurricane might pass in its vicinity.
9. Abnormal distortions in mundane objects are a recurring _____ in the artist's works.
10. The quality that Anthony liked most about Winona was her _____ personality, which made her easy to talk to.

Lesson 175

A MISUSE OF POWER

NEW WORDS

autocrat
ˈôtəˌkrat

debris
dəˈbrē, ˌdā-

debacle
diˈbakəl, -ˈbäkəl

delusion
diˈlooZHən

recluse
ˈrekˌloos, riˈkloos, ˈrekˌlooz

Everybody in the office loathed Dwight, the assistant regional manager at the paper company. Whenever the **reclusive** manager was away, which was often, Dwight became the stand-in boss, though his coworkers thought he acted more like an **autocrat**. He seemed to be under the **delusion** that he had complete control over the workings of the office and was immune to the general etiquette that governed acceptable work behavior. He had a short temper and became quickly enraged when people did not follow his directions exactly. One day, in a short fit of rage, Dwight kicked over a desk in the office, covering the room with **debris**. Luckily for Dwight's coworkers, once the manager found out about the **debacle**, he demoted Dwight to a position with less power, as Dwight could clearly not handle this level of responsibly.

Definitions: Try matching the words in the list with the appropriate definitions. If you are stuck, check the glossary in the back of the book or the passage at the top of the page.

1. autocrat _____ a. a complete failure
2. debris _____ b. scattered fragments
3. debacle _____ c. one who lives a solitary existence and who often avoids people
4. delusion _____ d. a ruler who has absolute power
5. recluse _____ e. a belief that is not true; a false idea

Sentences: Try to use the words above in a sentence below. Remember that a word ending may be changed or its figure of speech slightly altered.

6. Frank knew it was probably a(n) _____, but he constantly had the feeling that he was being watched.

7. After the _____ that was his first musical, Hugh had difficulty finding a theater that would show his new performance piece.

8. Phil's boss acted like a(n) _____ and always ignored any input from his employees.

9. Though he was once very sociable, Phillip became something of a(n) _____ after his mother's death: he spoke to few people and was no longer much involved in anything.

10. It will take weeks to clean up all of the _____ that the earthquake created.

Lesson 176

MELANCHOLY MITCH

Mitch used to be a happy and energetic man, but ever since the death of his wife he had become **lugubrious**. He was so downtrodden that his friends saw him as the **incarnation** of sadness itself. They no longer enjoyed spending time with him because he would become very **querulous** and argumentative when they were around him. His friends **postulated** that this meant that he did not want to be around them, but this isolation only made Mitch's sorrow grow worse. Mitch finally decided to visit a psychiatrist, who prescribed him antidepressants to combat his depressive symptoms. After a few weeks of taking the medication, Mitch's friends noticed some **salutary** effects in his demeanor, although the depression still had not fully gone away.

NEW WORDS

querulous
ˈkwer(y)ələs

postulate
ˈpäsCHələt (n.) ˈpäsCHəˌlāt (v.)

lugubrious
ləˈg(y)oobrēəs

salutary
ˈsalyəˌterē

incarnation
ˌinkärˈnāSHən

Definitions: Try matching the words in the list with the appropriate definitions. If you are stuck, check the glossary in the back of the book or the passage at the top of the page.

1. querulous _____ a. full of sadness or sorrow
2. postulate _____ b. a person who represents a quality or idea
3. lugubrious _____ c. complaining in an annoyed way
4. salutary _____ d. (n.) a thing assumed to be true as the basis for reasoning; (v.) to assume the truth or basis of something for the basis of reasoning or belief
5. incarnation _____ e. having a good or helpful result (especially after something unpleasant has happened)

Sentences: Try to use the words above in a sentence below. Remember that a word ending may be changed or its figure of speech slightly altered.

6. Many people believe that the serial killer was the _____ of evil itself.
7. Susan _____ that it would be difficult to have a discussion about Judaism without first accepting that there is a unique, Jewish God.
8. The car accident was tragic but served as a(n) _____ reminder to be more careful on the road.
9. Betsy's eight-year-old son became insufferably _____ whenever he didn't get what he wanted.
10. Nick tried to hide his depression from his friends, but they knew something was wrong by the sound of his _____ voice.

Lesson 177

BIPOLAR BEAUTY

NEW WORDS

antipathy
anˈtipəTHē

durable
ˈd(y)oorəbəl

gratuitous
grəˈt(y)ooitəs

euphoria
yooˈfôrēə

perennial
pəˈrenēəl

Kay's bipolar disorder was both a source of **perennial** distress as well as endless inspiration. As an artist, Kay used both the positive and negative aspects of her disorder to create her works. The intense moments of **euphoria** she felt periodically sent her on a frenzied high that aroused within her a passionate desire to express these powerful emotions. On the other hand, art gave Kay an outlet to work out the **antipathy** and **gratuitous** anger she felt during her low periods. There was a sharp contrast in her work between the pieces she created during her highs and those made during her lows, but Kay believed that all of her works as a whole were a depiction of the volatile yet **durable** spirit that defined her life.

Definitions: Try matching the words in the list with the appropriate definitions. If you are stuck, check the glossary in the back of the book or the passage at the top of the page.

1. antipathy _____ a. able to withstand wear, pressure or damage
2. durable _____ b. intense happiness and excitement
3. gratuitous _____ c. 1. existing or continuing in the same way for a long time; 2. (of people) appearing permanently engaged in a specified way of life; 3. (of plants) living for several years
4. euphoria _____ d. not necessary or appropriate
5. perennial _____ e. a strong feeling of dislike

Sentences: Try to use the words above in a sentence below. Remember that a word ending may be changed or its figure of speech slightly altered.

6. Evan has had countless joyous moments in his life, but nothing could surpass the _____ he felt when he first fell in love.
7. It is better to buy something expensive and _____ rather than something cheap and easily breakable.
8. The lack of manners that many children display was the main factor contributing to David's _____ for little kids.
9. Theresa refused to buy the video game for her son because of the _____ violence that it contained.
10. A(n) _____ problem of the struggling artist was the difficulty in keeping her original inspiration alive.

Lesson 178

REGGIE'S REVENGE

Reggie was a dynamic, **kinetic** boy. He liked to ride his bicycle around town, but the bullies at the school made this difficult to do. They made fun of him and the **hovel** he lived in and regularly deflated the air in Reggie's bike tires, thus **hampering** Reggie's curiosity for exploration. Feeling sad about his son's plight, Reggie's father advised him that in order to stop the bullies from bothering him, Reggie would have to stand up for himself. Although he had some **misgivings** about his father's advice, Reggie decided to follow it. The next day, when someone tried to let the air out of Reggie's bike tires, Reggie became the **embodiment** of fury and unleashed his deep-seated rage on his tormentor. His retaliation sent the bully to the nurse's office and also sent Reggie to detention, but it was worth it because no one ever messed with him again.

NEW WORDS

embodiment
emˈbädēmənt, im-

misgiving
misˈgiviNG

kinetic
kəˈnetik

hovel
ˈhəvəl, ˈhävəl

hamper
ˈhampər

Definitions: Try matching the words in the list with the appropriate definitions. If you are stuck, check the glossary in the back of the book or the passage at the top of the page.

1. embodiment _____ a. of, resulting from, or pertaining to motion
2. misgiving _____ b. someone or something that perfectly represents a certain quality, idea, or feeling
3. kinetic _____ c. to slow the movement, progress, or action of someone or something
4. hovel _____ d. a feeling of doubt or anxiety about the consequences or outcome of something
5. hamper _____ e. a small, squalid, and unpleasant dwelling

Sentences: Try to use the words above in a sentence below. Remember that a word ending may be changed or its figure of speech slightly altered.

6. Despite his original agreement to go through with the plan, Daniel had some _____ about his friends' idea to skip school.

7. Paul has an extremely _____ personality: he is always on the go and looking to explore new places.

8. Quinn's dream of becoming a famous novelist was _____ by his frequent bouts of laziness.

9. With the long hours that Angelica put into volunteering at the soup kitchen, she seemed to be a living _____ of selflessness.

10. It was surprising to see that Sean, such a refined and dapper man, lived in a(n) _____.

Lesson 179

RICK'S REPENTANCE

NEW WORDS

flout
flout

unremitting
ˌənriˈmitiNG

indeterminate
ˌindiˈtərmənit

exultation
ˌeksəlˈtāSHən, ˌegzəl-

sacrilege
ˈsakrəlij

Rick prayed quietly in front of a statue of Jesus Christ as the **unremitting** gaze of the holy figure stared down at him. Rick remembered with deep regret the days when he would shamelessly **flout** the religious practices that his family devotedly followed. The embarrassment and humiliation that Rick caused his family eventually got to him, and he decided to repent for his past **sacrilege**. Although the future effects of his atonement were **indeterminate** at the moment, the **exultation** Rick felt when he finally accepted Jesus as his savior was freeing.

Definitions: Try matching the words in the list with the appropriate definitions. If you are stuck, check the glossary in the back of the book or the passage at the top of the page.

1. flout _____   a. not exactly known, defined, or established
2. unremitting _____   b. a feeling of triumphant happiness
3. indeterminate _____   c. to openly disregard (a rule, law or convention)
4. exultation _____   d. a violation or misuse of what is regarded as holy or sacred
5. sacrilege _____   e. never stopping or lessening

Sentences: Try to use the words above in a sentence below. Remember that a word ending may be changed or its figure of speech slightly altered.

6. The vintage guitar collector considered the act of destroying one's guitar after a performance to be _____.
7. The _____ that Donna felt after finishing the race was euphoric.
8. Although Tim didn't do so well on the final exam, the professor still rewarded him with an A in the course for his _____ effort throughout the semester.
9. The secret society had a(n) _____ amount of members; nobody knew how big it truly was.
10. Nobody liked hanging out with Jack, who regularly _____ basic manners.

Lesson 180

GUITAR SHOP

Kirk and Russell made custom guitars for a living and loved even the most menial parts of the guitar-building process, such as **interleaving** the sheets of wood for each guitar top. They completed each task with **alacrity** and care. The two friends also had a certain **synergy** when working together that allowed them to work very efficiently. However, despite their dedication and skill, Kirk and Russell were having trouble **consigning** their guitars to the local guitar store, which only sold guitars from well-known brands. Their inability to find a store to sell their guitars **stunted** their business's growth, so they decided to open their own shop instead.

NEW WORDS

consign
kənˈsīn

stunted
stəntid

interleave
ˌintərˈlēv

alacrity
əˈlakritē

synergy
ˈsinərjē

Definitions: Try matching the words in the list with the appropriate definitions. If you are stuck, check the glossary in the back of the book or the passage at the top of the page.

1. consign _____ a. an eagerness or cheerful readiness
2. stunted _____ b. to insert pages between other pages; to put something in between the layers of
3. interleave _____ c. someone or something whose development or progress is hindered
4. alacrity _____ d. to deliver something in a person's custody; to send (something) to a person to be sold; to assign permanently
5. synergy _____ e. increased effectiveness resulting from combined action

Sentences: Try to use the words above in a sentence below. Remember that a word ending may be changed or its figure of speech slightly altered.

6. Brett and Owen had an amazing _____ when they played music together.
7. The plant's growth was _____ by the insecticides used on it.
8. Winnie _____ four of her best paintings to the local art gallery.
9. Ronald _____ the pages of his storybooks with colorful illustrations.
10. Vincent read his acceptance from his dream university with _____.

Word Search
Lessons 171 - 180

```
Q D N V K B M D M Q N L S N P P J M J N
U E Y L N P J L D Q I U M X K W B X M M
E B Y Q R N T W T M O X L Y R V R C Y N
R A N L X Q L J P L N Y J X X K A V R W
U C T J N N B O A D I S M A N T L E J B
L L Z D Q M S M R Q A L Y G A B D K Y J
O E L N D T O N J L D H T S M Z G J B J
U N E Y E N N M A M T V T K R N E D N P
S X T R A R X C I A Z R R E I X N Z B L
K J A J Y T R Y P S O Y C T U N Y Y K X
B R L G P I N I B P G L T L Z D E P W K
Z L U N T N T A H P U I T E L J N T T N
J Z T Y G N A E R S M A V M U M N R I M
N M S L A I V I E E T D L I G Q J Y V C
M H O V E R S T R I N T E B N P S N B V
R R P L Z J L N O O N I N L D G Q U W M
Y J Y T W G U N O L H R T L I Q J T R Z
T V Q R Q M Q Z N C D P J I K E Z P L B
Z T D T W L Z N R Q W T U L V T V J X K
X P G P Q R Y Z J D Y T J E T R T Z B M
```

1. covered or concealed
2. to take something apart
3. deviating from what is normal or expected
4. traveling from place to place
5. offhand or abrupt in speech or manner
6. a person who deceives others by pretending to be someone else
7. to remain in one place in the air
8. a terrible disaster
9. a complete failure
10. one who lives a solitary existence and who often avoids people
11. complaining in an annoyed way
12. (n.) a thing assumed to be true as the basis for reasoning; (v.) to assume the truth or basis of something for the basis of reasoning or belief
13. a strong feeling of dislike
14. intense happiness and excitement
15. a feeling of doubt or anxiety about the consequences or outcome of something
16. of, resulting from, or pertaining to motion
17. never stopping or lessening
18. a feeling of triumphant happiness
19. to deliver something in a person's custody; to send (something) to a person to be sold; to assign permanently
20. an eagerness or cheerful readiness

Vocabulary Review
Lessons 171-180

Directions: Match each word with its best approximate definition. Note that definitions are not necessarily repeated verbatim from the lesson exercises.

1. flourish _____
2. oracle _____
3. clemency _____
4. pugnacious _____
5. aroma _____
6. intermittent _____
7. motif _____
8. voluptuous _____
9. autocrat _____
10. debris _____
11. lugubrious _____
12. incarnation _____
13. durable _____
14. perennial _____
15. hovel _____
16. hamper _____
17. flout _____
18. sacrilege _____
19. interleave _____
20. synergy _____

a. inclined to quarrel or fight; combative
b. to openly disregard
c. a person or place noted for carrying a divine prophecy
d. existing for a long or infinite time; constantly recurring
e. to grow or develop in a healthy, vigorous manner
f. a small, filthy, unpleasant dwelling
g. to insert pages between blank pages in a book; to insert layers between other layers of something
h. looking or sounding sad and dismal
i. a person who embodies in the flesh a sprit, idea, or abstract quality of something
j. characterized by luxury and evoking sensual pleasure
k. the interaction of two or more entities producing a greater effect when combined than when acting alone
l. occurring at irregular intervals
m. a decorative design or pattern
n. violating or misusing something regarded as sacred
o. a ruler with absolute power
p. a distinctive, typically pleasant smell
q. to hinder or impede the progress of something
r. able to withstand wear, pressure, or damage
s. mercy; lenience
t. scattered fragments of something wrecked or destroyed

A Crowd of "ISMs": A-L

> When reading literature, history, art history, social sciences, politics, or philosophy, you are likely to encounter academic words ending in "ism." Here we wish to briefly define some of these meanings. This list is hardly exhaustive, but is intended to give you a sense of some common words you may see appearing in materials that you read.

abolitionism: a belief system that favors of getting rid of institutions, especially that of (formerly) slavery or capital punishment

capitalism: an economic system in which a country's trade and industry are controlled through free market exchange of wealth

communism: a model of society in which all property is publically owned and in which each person works according to his/her abilities or needs

conservatism: a belief system that supports sustaining traditional attitudes and values; in American government, it is often tied to the Republican party, which favors small government, lower taxation, and religious and family values

fascism: a nationalistic, right-wing, authoritarian system of government most widely associated with Benito Mussolini (1883-1945) in Italy.

federalism: a system of government in which powers are divided between a central (usually national) authority and smaller divisional powers

feudalism: the social system that was in place in medieval Europe, in which a lord held lands from the Crown in exchange for protection, and in which peasants and serfs lived on a lord's land and worked for him in exchange for military protection

globalism: a mode of thought or policy that envisions the whole world as a sphere of political or social influence

imperialism: a policy whereby nations expand their power into other parts of the world, often through the use of force and/or diplomacy

liberalism: a belief system associated with free political institutions and/or religious toleration together with supporting a large governmental influence in regulating capitalism and social welfare matters

libertarianism: a political philosophy that advocates only minimal public intervention in the lives of citizens

Lesson 181

NEW WORDS

sensationalism
senˈsāSHənlˌizəm

rancor
ˈraNGkər

virtuoso
ˌvərCHooˈōsō

precarious
priˈke(ə)rēəs

inherent
inˈhi(ə)rənt, -ˈher-

AN UNLUCKY TALENT

Cilius Mobik is a **virtuoso** with an **inherent** talent in playing the piano. However, he is greatly underrated, and his agency is trying to do everything to put him in the spotlight where he deserves to be. The agency has started to spend big money on promoting his records and to write articles about him in several magazines. To their dismay, it has been all to no avail. The agency then decided to use **sensationalism** as a marketing tactic, making bombastic music videos of Cilius and arranging interviews where he can show off his techniques in the hope of making him famous. However, Cilius has only extracted **rancor** from the public as evidence of his natural talent remains **precarious**.

Definitions: Try matching the words in the list with the appropriate definitions. If you are stuck, check the glossary in the back of the book or the passage at the top of the page.

1. sensationalism _____   a. innate; native; inbred
2. rancor _____   b. unstable, unsure; uncertain; dubious
3. virtuoso _____   c. the use of shocking details to cause excitement
4. precarious _____   d. anger or dislike for someone
5. inherent _____   e. one who excels in something especially art, or music

Sentences: Try to use the words above in a sentence below. Remember that a word ending may be changed or its figure of speech slightly altered.

6. She answered her accusers politely without a trace of _____.
7. It is debatable whether Victor can be considered a(n) _____ as he possesses great skills but lacks soul in his playing.
8. He could mimic printed text with alarming accuracy and dissociate the shapes and lines from their _____ meanings.
9. The cheap tabloids relied on _____ to increase their circulation.
10. For years, the legalization of same-sex marriage in America was on _____ footing, but the Supreme Court ruled in favor of it in 2015.

Lesson 182

CARLA'S UNEMPLOYMENT FIASCO

Though Carla lost her job for a **legitimate** reason — she was constantly late to work — her lack of punctuality set off a bad chain of events. First, she had to contend with her boss' **reproach** for her unprofessional behavior. Then, she had to seek **remuneration** from the government so that she could have an unemployment paycheck until she found a new job. Meanwhile, she had to adopt a **frugal** lifestyle because she was earning less than before, which alienated her from her immediate family members who expected her to continue supporting them financially. Much to their **consternation**, they could not figure out why Carla spent hours looking for her dream job rather than one that would put food on the table. Lucky for Carla, she soon found an exciting job at the local bank and stabilized her occupational and family relations.

NEW WORDS

reproach
ri'prōCH

legitimate
li'jitəmit

consternation
ˌkänstər'nāSHən

frugal
'froogəl

remuneration
riˌmyoonə'rāSHən

Definitions: Try matching the words in the list with the appropriate definitions. If you are stuck, check the glossary in the back of the book or the passage at the top of the page.

1. reproach _____ a. compensation; pay for a service
2. legitimate _____ b. rebuke; disapproval; discredit
3. consternation _____ c. sparing economically
4. frugal _____ d. legal; valid; sanctioned
5. remuneration _____ e. a strong feeling of surprise or sudden disappointment that causes confusion

Sentences: Try to use the words above in a sentence below. Remember that a word ending may be changed or its figure of speech slightly altered.

6. After decades of service for the army, all he gets now is a small _____ that is just enough for him to make ends meet.
7. When you're young, it is often wise to be _____ and save money rather than to spend it on lavish things.
8. They completely disregarded her request, even though it was an invariably _____ one.
9. Much to my _____, she kneeled down and proposed to me after only one awkward date.
10. Mandeville felt that he was above _____ and thus felt no compunction about stealing fifty dollars from his father's wallet.

Lesson 183

A GREEDY BROTHER

NEW WORDS

felicity
fəˈlisətē

beneficiaries
ˌbenəˈfiSHēˌerē

meddle
ˈmedl

fraudulent
ˈfrôjələnt

fortitude
ˈfôrtəˌtood

After Piper's father died, her brother wanted to take all the heritage and make it his own property. The family lawyer, not doing what he should have done, **meddled** in the matter and helped the brother make a **fraudulent** will deriving all money from Piper. Piper knew what the lawyer and her despicable brother were doing; she investigated the case on her own and later sent all the evidence and proof of fraud of her brother to the district prosecutor. Her **fortitude** paid off when the judge ruled that Piper was indeed one of the legitimate **beneficiaries** of her father's fortune. Piper felt **felicity** at the time the judge's decision was announced, for justice had been served. Yet she felt sorry for her brother as he was sentenced to five years in prison.

Definitions: Try matching the words in the list with the appropriate definitions. If you are stuck, check the glossary in the back of the book or the passage at the top of the page.

1. felicity _____ a. cheating; dishonest
2. beneficiaries _____ b. 1. great happiness; 2. a talent for speaking or writing
3. meddle _____ c. mental strength in facing adversity
4. fraudulent _____ d. people that benefit from something, usually a trust or will
5. fortitude _____ e. to be involved in activities of other people, especially when they do not want your involvement

Sentences: Try to use the words above in a sentence below. Remember that a word ending may be changed or its figure of speech slightly altered.

6. The store on the corner is being investigated by federal investigators after reports of _____ business activities.
7. America likes to _____ in other nations' business, sending troops to other countries and participating in all kinds of international disputes.
8. Tony's sudden death made all of his _____ millionaires.
9. Despite his belief of marriage being the end of romance, Dang is experiencing an unprecedented kind of _____ after marrying this woman.
10. Never once did her _____ waver during that long illness.

Lesson 184

THE ROVING AND UNFOCUSED STUDENT

Alison was a smart girl who was **exuberant** about going on lots of adventures. This enthusiasm was organic and resulted in many excursions; however, it prevented her from stopping to ponder the **thesis** of her history research paper. Two weeks after her professor had read this paper, he called Alison into his office and spoke to her in an **avuncular** tone. "Alison, you're a smart student, but this paper is not clear. I am going to have to give you a poor grade." Alison's eyes filled with tears as he continued. "If you persist with a life of **liberation** from your studies by traveling frequently, your grades will remain low. Going on lots of trips is not a **panacea** for all of your worries in life. Only hard word will get you academic success." Alison took the advice, quit wandering, and researched hard for her papers henceforth.

NEW WORDS

avuncular
əˈvəNGkyələr

thesis
ˈTHēsis

liberation
ˌlibəˈrāSHən

exuberant
igˈzoobərənt

panacea
ˌpanəˈsēə

Definitions: Try matching the words in the list with the appropriate definitions. If you are stuck, check the glossary in the back of the book or the passage at the top of the page.

1. avuncular _____ a. the act of freeing someone from slavery, imprisonment or oppression; a release
2. thesis _____ b. filled with energy and enthusiasm
3. liberation _____ c. like an uncle
4. exuberant _____ d. a remedy for all disease; a solution to all problems
5. panacea _____ e. a statement that someone wants to discuss or prove

Sentences: Try to use the words above in a sentence below. Remember that a word ending may be changed or its figure of speech slightly altered.

6. Love is the _____ for all sorrows.
7. Many African-Americans look at the 1960s as a key moment in their _____: finally, after decades of subservience, they were granted the same privileges as Caucasians in the United States.
8. Assuming thoroughly his _____ role, Nadim takes his nephew to the movies each week.
9. My _____ will discredit classical economics, proving its self-adjusting nature to be false.
10. The _____ crowd rushed to greet the returning national champions in collegiate basketball.

Lesson 185

NEW WORDS

unkempt
ˌənˈkem(p)t

bankrupt
ˈbaNGkˌrəpt, -rəpt

missive
ˈmisiv

aplomb
əˈpläm, əˈpləm

plight
plīt

BERNIE'S PREDICAMENT

Once upon a time there was an **unkempt** merchant from New Hampshire named Bernie. Every day, Bernie donned a rumpled shirt and trotted into his office. One day, Bernie went into the safe near his office to look for his important papers, and discovered that all of the money he hid there was gone. "I'm practically **bankrupt**," he murmured to himself in angst. Not sure how to handle his situation, Bernie sent **missives** to his family, friends, and local authorities to articulate his **plight**. Few people were willing to assist Bernie in any way. Yet despite these setbacks, Bernie pressed on with **aplomb**. He took up three extra jobs, saved extensively for two years, and concluded that one day he might be able to have a comfortable retirement.

Definitions: Try matching the words in the list with the appropriate definitions. If you are stuck, check the glossary in the back of the book or the passage at the top of the page.

1. unkempt _____ a. a written message; letter
2. bankrupt _____ b. a dangerous, unfortunate, or difficult situation
3. missive _____ c. confidence and skill shown especially in a difficult situation
4. aplomb _____ d. having an untidy or disheveled appearance
5. plight _____ e. (adj.) 1. describing a person or organization unable to pay debts; 2. depleted or impoverished; 3. completely lacking in a particular quality or value; (n.) a person deemed to be insolvent by the court system (v.) to reduce a person or organization to insolvency

Sentences: Try to use the words above in a sentence below. Remember that a word ending may be changed or its figure of speech slightly altered.

6. To blog from behind bars, Gioeli begins by writing a(n) _____ by hand.
7. Many people claimed that the senator was _____ because he wore rumpled clothes and his uncombed hair danced in the wind.
8. Lehman Brothers declared _____ due to their risky involvement in the derivatives market and subprime mortgage crisis.
9. She had seen the _____ of hundreds of people and was no stranger to death.
10. It is his _____ that salvages the firm in a time of such crisis.

Lesson 186

A HISTORY PARK

Alexander is trying to **tout** the investors into building a park with **archaic**-looking buildings. The park is aimed to serve people who have a **bent** for old things and history, bringing them back to the high and late medieval period when Gothic architecture was **prosperous.** Alexander suggests that the buildings need not be fully authentic, because that would involve a great deal of complex designing; they can be **derivative** from real existing Gothic buildings.

NEW WORDS

derivative
di'rivətiv

bent
bent

archaic
är'kāik

prosperous
'prē'pres

tout
tout

Definitions: Try matching the words in the list with the appropriate definitions. If you are stuck, check the glossary in the back of the book or the passage at the top of the page.

1. derivative _____ a. flourishing; successful; thriving
2. bent _____ b. antiquated; ancient
3. archaic _____ c. to persuade; to promote; to talk up
4. prosperous _____ d. a strong inclination; talent
5. tout _____ e. made up of parts from something else

Sentences: Try to use the words above in a sentence below. Remember that a word ending may be changed or its figure of speech slightly altered.

6. She can't help but feel nostalgic and perplexed standing in this marvelous castle, beholding its _____ furniture.
7. After a(n) _____ year, Apple stock share prices shot up by 30%.
8. The headquarters facility was _____ as the best in the country.
9. Paul, a man of religious _____, traveled around the world to spread the messages of Christ.
10. They say that the book lacks originality and seems to be too _____ from other similar works.

Lesson 187

NEW WORDS

parameters
pəˈramitərz

purify
ˈpyoorəˌfī

mediate
ˈmēdēˌāt

savanna
səˈvanə

formulaic
ˌfôrmyəˈlāik

THE FRAMEWORK ISSUE

GreenCo and Aquapump are negotiating a deal where both firms will **purify** water from nearby water streams so that tribes in the **savanna** can utilize it for both agricultural production and everyday use. GreenCo wants to use their **formulaic** standard in controlling the quality of water which is similar to ones that GreenCo uses in other projects it has in other parts of the world. However, Aquapump refuses and insists on using original **parameters** as the standard. Without this issue, the deal would go on smoothly. Thus, to push the contract process, the firms will hire an intermediary to **mediate** this issue.

Definitions: Try matching the words in the list with the appropriate definitions. If you are stuck, check the glossary in the back of the book or the passage at the top of the page.

1. parameters _____ a. to make unadulterated or clear; to free from guilt or dirt
2. purify _____ b. to intervene between people in a dispute in order to bring about a resolution or agreement
3. mediate _____ c. a grassy plain with few trees usually found in tropical or subtropical areas
4. savanna _____ d. produced in accordance with a followed rule or style
5. formulaic _____ e. guidelines that control what something is or how something should be done

Sentences: Try to use the words above in a sentence below. Remember that a word ending may be changed or its figure of speech slightly altered.

6. It is strict policy that the water here is _____ before it is drunk.
7. My aunt had to _____ the heated dispute between my parents.
8. Temperature, pressure, and density are used as _____ for determining the conditions of the atmosphere.
9. Unlike with math problems, there is no _____ way to solve interpersonal problems.
10. Sitting in his jeep looking out at the _____, John saw the lion fatally strike the feeble zebra.

Lesson 188

THE TAXATION MATTER

In Arizona, Republicans are trying to pass an act that would raise income tax on the middle class without raising corporate tax, which shows the politicians' **propensity** to favor the rich. Although this act is **feasible** as no problem will occur in the implementation of it, it is **deleterious** to the state's economy as most people will have less money to consume and further invest; it also will widen the income gap between the rich and the poor. Many opposing lobbyists, as well as politicians, are trying to stop this act from passing. If it is passed, it will be very arduous to **repeal**, and other **contiguous** states may make the same mistake.

NEW WORDS

propensity
prəˈpensətē

contiguous
kənˈtigyooəs

feasible
ˈfēzəbəl

deleterious
ˌdeliˈti(ə)rēəs

repeal
riˈpēl

Definitions: Try matching the words in the list with the appropriate definitions. If you are stuck, check the glossary in the back of the book or the passage at the top of the page.

1. propensity _____ a. to revoke or annul (a vote or congressional act)
2. contiguous _____ b. capable of being done, effected
3. feasible _____ c. damaging or harmful
4. deleterious _____ d. touching; adjacent
5. repeal _____ e. a strong natural tendency to do something

Sentences: Try to use the words above in a sentence below. Remember that a word ending may be changed or its figure of speech slightly altered.

6. Your plan sounds ideal, but whether it is _____ is another story.
7. The imposition of tariffs can be _____ to one's economy as it creates both production and consumption distortion.
8. The United States is _____ with Canada and Mexico, but not with Italy and Mongolia.
9. The homophobic Westboro Baptist Church wants the legalization of same-sex marriage _____.
10. Marginal _____ to consume shows how much a population is willing to spend given a level of income.

Lesson 189

ACCOMPLICE BETRAYAL

NEW WORDS

somnolent
ˈsämnələnt

coward
ˈkou-ərd

unerring
ˌənˈəriNG, -ˈer-

conspire
kənˈspīr

meager
ˈmēgər

Chuck was a very poor guy, trying to get by every day on his **meager** paycheck. One day, he thought of robbing a bank so that he could get rich. He then held a talk with some of his close poor friends, asking if any of them wanted to be his partner in crime. He **conspired** with them to come up with a plan. Sadly, the meeting was **somnolent** because he thought his plan was **unerring** and didn't listen to anyone's opinions. All of the friends left, except one. On the day of the robbery, the plan went wrong, and they were arrested. While being interrogated, his friend **cowardly** said that Chuck was the master of the plan so as to get less time in jail. Chuck really regretted what he had done, but it was too late.

Definitions: Try matching the words in the list with the appropriate definitions. If you are stuck, check the glossary in the back of the book or the passage at the top of the page.

1. somnolent   _____   a. deficient in quantity or quality
2. coward   _____   b. to secretly plan to something harmful or illegal
3. unerring   _____   c. likely to induce sleep
4. conspire   _____   d. a person who shows a shameful lack of courage
5. meager   _____   e. always right or accurate

Sentences: Try to use the words above in a sentence below. Remember that a word ending may be changed or its figure of speech slightly altered.

6. Thriftymart pays its part-time employees a(n) _____ $7.25 an hour.
7. The television series *Game of Thrones* is so twisted and full of people who _____ to replace their king with someone easily influenceble.
8. Cheating on his girlfriend and abandoning her when she is pregnant proves that Khoa is just another despicable _____.
9. The sermon was so _____ that even the most eager listeners quickly dozed off after it was underway.
10. With _____ conviction, Samuel knew that pursuing a second doctorate was a good career move for him.

Lesson 190

AN UNEXPECTED SUCCESS

Britney had always been known as a little **obtuse** and lazy. She did not study well, and people thought she would amount to nothing in life. But Britney dreamed of being a fashion store owner, and her **intuition** told her that she could pursue this dream. Despite opposition from her family and friends, Britney decided to use her savings to open a clothing store selling **ersatz** brand name clothing. For her dream, Britney became a determined and **diligent** young lady, working very hard to run her store and never losing faith despite the first few months of sporadic sales. Later on, her hard work did pay off, and people were **nonplussed** to see that her store was the most popular store for young working women in town.

> **NEW WORDS**
>
> **intuition**
> ˌint(y)ooˈiSHən
>
> **obtuse**
> əbˈt(y)oos, äb-
>
> **diligent**
> ˈdiləjənt
>
> **nonplussed**
> nänˈpləst
>
> **ersatz**
> ˈerˌsäts, -ˌzäts, erˈzäts

Definitions: Try matching the words in the list with the appropriate definitions. If you are stuck, check the glossary in the back of the book or the passage at the top of the page.

1. intuition _____ a. painstaking; assiduous
2. obtuse _____ b. utterly perplexed
3. diligent _____ c. being a usually artificial and inferior substitute
4. nonplussed _____ d. stupid or unintelligent
5. ersatz _____ e. quick and ready insight; the ability to know something without having proof

Sentences: Try to use the words above in a sentence below. Remember that a word ending may be changed or its figure of speech slightly altered.

6. Despite meticulous instruction from the lecturer, Hieu is simply too _____ to comprehend the model.
7. "How on earth did you know he was going to ask you out?" "Just my _____."
8. Chinese companies are gifted at manufacturing _____ goods and selling them at cheap prices.
9. Justin was utterly _____ when he learned that his work had become the fourteenth most read paper in the field.
10. Daddy teaches me to be _____, persevering through all the storms that life might bring.

Crossword Puzzle
Lessons 181-190

ACROSS

1. confidence and skill shown especially in a difficult situation
8. a strong inclination; talent
9. compensation; pay for a service
11. to persuade; to promote; to talk up
12. one who excels in something especially art, or music
13. to intervene between people in a dispute in order to bring about a resolution or agreement
16. cheating; dishonest
17. capable of being done, effected
18. touching; adjacent
19. stupid or unintelligent
20. a written message; letter

DOWN

2. guidelines that control what something is or how something should be done
3. a strong feeling of surprise or sudden disappointment that causes confusion
4. always right or accurate
5. unstable, unsure; uncertain; dubious
6. the act of freeing someone from slavery, imprisonment or oppression; a release
7. quick and ready insight; the ability to know something without having proof
10. mental strength in facing adversity
14. to secretly plan to something harmful or illegal
15. a statement that someone wants to discuss or prove

Vocabulary Review
Lessons 181-190

Directions: Match each word with its best approximate definition. Note that definitions are not necessarily repeated verbatim from the lesson exercises.

1. rancor _____
2. inherent _____
3. legitimate _____
4. frugal _____
5. felicity _____
6. meddle _____
7. avuncular _____
8. panacea _____
9. unkempt _____
10. plight _____
11. archaic _____
12. prosperous _____
13. purify _____
14. savanna _____
15. propensity _____
16. deleterious _____
17. coward _____
18. meager _____
19. diligent _____
20. nonplussed _____

a. anger or dislike for someone
b. innate; native; inbred
c. thrifty; economical
d. causing harm or damage
e. very old or old-fashioned; no longer in use but used to convey an old-fashioned flavor
f. materialistically or intellectually successful; doing well financially
g. like an uncle
h. showing care and consciousness in one's responsibilities
i. to interfere in something that is generally not one's concern
j. lacking in quality or quantity
k. to remove contaminants from something
l. an inclination or natural tendency to behave in a particular way
m. a dangerous, hard, or very unfortunate situation
n. so surprised and confused that one does not know how to react
o. conforming to the law or rules; able to be defended with justification
p. a person who lacks the courage to endure unpleasant things
q. a grassy plain typically found in tropical and subtropical climate zones
r. having an untidy or disheveled appearance
s. extreme happiness
t. a solution or remedy for all illnesses or problems

A Crowd of "ISMs": M-Z

> Here we continue our list of important "ism" words often found in intellectual literature.

modernism: a style or movement in the arts or architecture that breaks with classical forms

nationalism: patriotic feelings in support of a particular country, often as superior over other countries

nihilism: rejecting all religious and moral principles, often associated with the belief that life has no meaning

postmodernism: an intellectual style and concept in arts and intellectual scholarship that represents a departure from modernism, often revealing a general distrust of grand theories and ideologies

realism: the belief in representing people, situations, or things in such a way that appears true to life

socialism: a theory in economics and politics emphasizing that the production, distribution, and exchange of goods should be regulated by the whole community; a transitional state between capitalism and communism

structuralism: a belief that in human cognition, behavior, and culture, there is an underlying pattern or structure

	that organizes and reflects patterns and contrasts underneath a superficial diversity
surrealism:	a movement in early twentieth century art and literature aimed at juxtaposing things irrationally in order to stimulate creative thought
totalitarianism:	a system of government that is heavily centralized and with a dictator which requires total subservience to the state

Lesson 191

NEW WORDS

induce
inˈd(y)oos

extract
ikˈstrakt

thwart
THwôrt

lingering
ˈliNGg(ə)riNG

ogle
ˈōgəl

AN OBSTINATE WITCH

Manny was not very good at getting dates with girls in college. Every day, he would sit in the cafeteria and **ogle** the most attractive ladies he saw. Then he would come up to their table and ask them out on a romantic date. Regularly they **thwarted** his attempts to secure a date, and told him that he was **inducing** a sense of nausea in them. Still, Manny retained a **lingering** hope that one day he would actually get a date with one of these pretty girls. Finally, on his last dinner at college, Manny was able to **extract** the phone number of Lauren, a girl he'd been thinking about for years, in a conversation. Quickly realizing that she had accidentally given Manny her phone number, Lauren ran to the store after dinner and immediately changed her number. Manny, as usual, was left hopeless.

Definitions: Try matching the words in the list with the appropriate definitions. If you are stuck, check the glossary in the back of the book or the passage at the top of the page.

1. induce _____ a. to frustrate or baffle; to oppose
2. extract _____ b. staying beyond expected time
3. thwart _____ c. to stare at in a manner showing sexual desire
4. lingering _____ d. 1. to remove or take out; 2. to obtain a substance or resource by a special method
5. ogle _____ e. to cause someone to do something

Sentences: Try to use the words above in a sentence below. Remember that a word ending may be changed or its figure of speech slightly altered.

6. Many radical groups in the world use torture to _____ information from people they suspect of crimes.
7. Even though Shonté was dumped by her boyfriend, there remained a(n) _____ hope in her mind that he would one day return for her.
8. Harvey _____ the young girl because he liked her but was too socially insecure to ask her out.
9. If you want people to do things for you, you have to _____ them by giving incentives.
10. The Republicans consistently try to _____ any plan that Democrats posit by giving falsified facts to the public.

Lesson 192

A REGRETTABLE DISOBLIGATION

After a God-defying **impertinence,** the city of Oglipayas was cursed into a **moribund** state where all resources and water suddenly ran out. Herculias, the hero of the city, tried to save the day by finding the long lost holy diamond ring and offering it to their god in a **consecrated** ceremony. Their god read the Oglipayans' **cognitive** thoughts and judged that they all earnestly sought forgiveness, so their god rescinded his curse, making the city return to its normal state. The Oglipayans were so **jubilant** that they held parties for 300 consecutive days. They never disobeyed their god again.

NEW WORDS

cognitive
ˈkägnətiv

impertinence
imˈpərtnəns

consecrated
ˈkänsiˌkrāt

moribund
ˈmôrəˌbənd, ˈmär-

jubilant
ˈjoobələnt

Definitions: Try matching the words in the list with the appropriate definitions. If you are stuck, check the glossary in the back of the book or the passage at the top of the page.

1. cognitive _____ a. dedicated to a sacred purpose
2. impertinence _____ b. rejoicing; triumphant; joyous
3. consecrated _____ c. irrelevance, inappropriateness, or absurdity
4. moribund _____ d. involving conscious mental activities
5. jubilant _____ e. no longer active or effective; very sick; close to death

Sentences: Try to use the words above in a sentence below. Remember that a word ending may be changed or its figure of speech slightly altered.

6. Fred was _____ when he heard that his team had won the state soccer match.
7. Everybody could feel the _____ mood radiating from the duchess when her baby was declared a prince.
8. A solid course in buyer behavior will walk students through all the _____ stages that a customer goes through before he or she purchases a good.
9. Writing with this kind of _____ won't get you anywhere in the real world.
10. People have seen Courtney going to various auditions recently; she must be trying to revive her _____ career.

Lesson 193

A VENERABLE PROFESSION

NEW WORDS

avarice
ˈavəris

inertia
iˈnərSHə

engrossing
enˈgrōsiNG

arduous
ˈärjoōəs

pedagogy
ˈpedəˌgäjē, -ˌgägē

Pedagogy is a profession that is **engrossing** for many who like academics. It is so captivating because teachers have to be altruistic and passionate about their job. Teachers generally lack **avarice** as well — even though they work long and **arduous** hours, they do not expect to be paid big money. Teachers sometimes feel tired and frustrated too, but they never show any **inertia**. They always try to be energetic and dedicated to their students.

Definitions: Try matching the words in the list with the appropriate definitions. If you are stuck, check the glossary in the back of the book or the passage at the top of the page.

1. avarice _____ a. very difficult; challenging
2. inertia _____ b. greed
3. engrossing _____ c. the art, science, or profession of teaching
4. arduous _____ d. 1. a tendency to do nothing or remain unchanged; resistance to change in some physical property; 2. (in physics) a property where an object remains in its existing rest state or in straight line motion unless acted upon by an external force
5. pedagogy _____ e. absorbing all of one's attention and interest

Sentences: Try to use the words above in a sentence below. Remember that a word ending may be changed or its figure of speech slightly altered.

6. Governmental _____ in structural reforms has cost Vietnam further potential GDP growth.
7. To get where he is now, Justin had to go through a great deal of turmoil and tons of _____ work.
8. His knowledge of _____ was displayed when he spoke at length about the various theories about teaching small classes of students.
9. The new book was so _____ that I sat for six hours straight and read it in its entirety.
10. Many CEOs are plagued by _____ and a thirst for power.

Lesson 194

A PRESIDENTIAL UPSET

Everyone thought that the president would win reelection because he was an **incumbent** who had done an excellent job leading during his first term. He also had **recourse** to a lot of wealthy donors who wished to **perpetuate** his image as the appropriate leader to continue fighting for their rights. But his rival, an upstart from Boston, had a **vibrant** message of how to strengthen the economy and democracy in the country by helping the lower and middle classes. His speeches **astounded** voters and, in the end, the incumbent lost the election. The support of the masses allowed for a sea change in politics.

> **NEW WORDS**
>
> **astound**
> əˈstound
>
> **recourse**
> ˈrēˌkôrs, riˈkôrs
>
> **vibrant**
> ˈvībrənt
>
> **incumbent**
> inˈkəmbənt
>
> **perpetuate**
> pərˈpeCHo͞oˌāt

Definitions: Try matching the words in the list with the appropriate definitions. If you are stuck, check the glossary in the back of the book or the passage at the top of the page.

1. astound _____ a. showing great life, activity, and energy; very bright and strong
2. recourse _____ b. someone currently holding office
3. vibrant _____ c. to astonish; to flabbergast; to amaze
4. incumbent _____ d. 1. to make something continue indefinitely; 2. to preserve something valued from oblivion or extinction
5. perpetuate _____ e. an opportunity or choice to use or do something in order to deal with a problem or situation

Sentences: Try to use the words above in a sentence below. Remember that a word ending may be changed or its figure of speech slightly altered.

6. Often it is easier for a(n) _____ to win reelection because he or she is currently in office and has experience with his or her position.
7. The professor _____ teaching his impractical method at the cost of the department's reputation.
8. What _____ me the most is how a department in such a prestigious university can treat its students so unprofessionally and unfairly.
9. The dispute was settled without _____ to law.
10. Freddie Mercury is widely regarded as the best live performer of his era for being consistently _____ at his events.

Lesson 195

NEW WORDS

pundit
ˈpəndit

unflappable
ˌənˈflapəbəl

amenable
əˈmēnəbəl, əˈmen-

miscreant
ˈmiskrēənt

belabor
biˈlābər

AN OUTSPOKEN, DISCONTENTED CITIZEN

Isaac is an expert in current affairs, and he is not **amenable** to the way the government has handled many recent issues. With the support of multitude of people in academia and the political world, Isaac has begun giving speeches that **belabor** how incompetent the government is. The **pundits** who defend the government, however, depict him as a **miscreant**. With great aplomb, Isaac seems to be **unflappable** in his steadfast commitment to his beliefs; he carries on with his series of speeches, demanding that the government do its job right.

Definitions: Try matching the words in the list with the appropriate definitions. If you are stuck, check the glossary in the back of the book or the passage at the top of the page.

1. pundit _____ a. to repeat an idea or argument to emphasize it
2. unflappable _____ b. a person who behaves badly or in a way that breaks the law
3. amenable _____ c. an expert who usually gives speeches in public
4. miscreant _____ d. open and responsive to suggestion
5. belabor _____ e. imperturbable; to be able to remain calm in a difficult situations

Sentences: Try to use the words above in a sentence below. Remember that a word ending may be changed or its figure of speech slightly altered.

6. While some professors are _____ to giving take-home final exams, others insist on taking a three-hour test in class.
7. Some _____ could always be found to comment, and imagination supplied what newspapers feared to print.
8. He just likes to show that he can do magic and then _____ the point through talking excessively about his skill.
9. People could not believe that Jane dated a(n) _____ like James.
10. He prided himself on being _____ in even the most chaotic situation.

Lesson 196

FREE-MINDED ARCHAEOLOGIST

Erica was a **neophyte** archaeologist who recently has been on her first dig to unearth part of an **extinct** civilization located near the Euphrates River. Together with a team, Erica **traversed** over forty square kilometers hoping to excavate something important. Nothing was found, however, and the team leader intimated that his colleagues had become **indolent**. But Erica thought she had seen an artifact along the way. Her team leader did not want to hear her queries, and insisted on her **subordination** to his commands. But Erica broke with the team and began to dig. Amazingly, she unearthed a talisman from a long departed civilization!

NEW WORDS

subordination
sə͵bôrdnˈāSHən

neophyte
ˈnēəˌfīt

indolent
ˈindələnt

extinct
ikˈstiNG(k)t

traverse
trəˈvərs

Definitions: Try matching the words in the list with the appropriate definitions. If you are stuck, check the glossary in the back of the book or the passage at the top of the page.

1. subordination _____ a. lazy
2. neophyte _____ b. to cross; to cut across
3. indolent _____ c. no longer existing
4. extinct _____ d. a beginner, greenhorn, tyro
5. traverse _____ e. the act of placing in a lower rank or position

Sentences: Try to use the words above in a sentence below. Remember that a word ending may be changed or its figure of speech slightly altered.

6. Unlike Samuel, who had been a seasoned member of congress, Barry was a(n) _____ only beginning his first term.
7. Many of the factory workers here are _____: they snooze on the job rather than produce the widgets that we had hoped they would create.
8. That homosexuality will make the human race _____ is an unqualified argument.
9. The refusal to allow women to be educated was part of society's long history of _____ of women to men.
10. The candidates _____ the state throughout the campaign.

Lesson 197

NEW WORDS

emblem
ˈembləm

trepidation
ˌtrepiˈdāSHən

Byzantine
ˈbizənˌtēn, bəˈzan-, -ˌtīn

disrepute
ˌdisrəˈpyoot

vagary
ˈvāgərē

THE CHANGE OF IMAGE

Nina fell into **disrepute** after her company was found to be guilty of ethical misconduct. The firm decided to change its old image by changing its **emblem**. The process of designing a new emblem had to be deliberately and carefully planned; it could not be just a **vagary** that popped out of someone's mind. After extensive rumination, Nina finally contrived a new emblem to represent her company. This new emblem was **Byzantine**, having a lot of complicated patterns and tiny details. It is completely different stylistically from the old logo. Nina hopes that the new sign will help revive her business, but she has some **trepidation** about whether a new tag can truly resurrect her company.

Definitions: Try matching the words in the list with the appropriate definitions. If you are stuck, check the glossary in the back of the book or the passage at the top of the page.

1. emblem　_____　a.　lack of good reputation
2. trepidation　_____　b.　whim; unusual idea
3. Byzantine　_____　c.　a person or thing that represents an idea
4. disrepute　_____　d.　labyrinthine; intricate
5. vagary　_____　e.　feeling of fear that something may happen

Sentences: Try to use the words above in a sentence below. Remember that a word ending may be changed or its figure of speech slightly altered.

6. With much _____, the circus clown jumped through a ring of fire.
7. The President fell into _____ after multiple allegations of extramarital affairs.
8. Captain America is the _____ of the United States of America: disciplined, responsible, and perseverant.
9. It really is Mother Nature's _____ if the temperature drops to zero degrees one summer night.
10. Day after day, tape after tape, I became more enthralled with the _____ plot of his life.

Lesson 198

THE MOTIVATION REGENERATION

After the death of the beloved former CEO, the firm's employees fell into a **morbid** state. They worked with lethargy and discouragement. The Board of Directors could not let this situation **habituate** for they knew if it did it would make the firm **founder**. Thus, they started to look for a new CEO who not only was excellent in strategic management but also could bring a renewed **vitality** to the firm. The Board was **elated** to find a new CEO who satisfied what they were looking for in only two weeks. The employment of the new CEO gave the employees a revived motivation and a sense of direction.

NEW WORDS

founder
ˈfoundər

vitality
vīˈtalitē

morbid
ˈmôrbəd

habituate
həˈbiCHooˌāt

elate
iˈlāt

Definitions: Try matching the words in the list with the appropriate definitions. If you are stuck, check the glossary in the back of the book or the passage at the top of the page.

1. founder _____ a. cheerless; unpleasant; morose
2. vitality _____ b. (n.) someone who establishes an institution or settlement; (v.) 1. to collapse or fail (of a plan or endeavor); 2. to fill with water and sink (of a ship)
3. morbid _____ c. to make or become accustomed or used to something
4. habituate _____ d. to make (someone) extremely happy
5. elate _____ e. vigorousness; exuberance

Sentences: Try to use the words above in a sentence below. Remember that a word ending may be changed or its figure of speech slightly altered.

6. "This is such a marvelous and joyous wedding! Look at how _____ the couple is!"
7. The chief difficulty experienced by the administration was to _____ the Arabs and Nubas, both naturally warlike, to a state of peace.
8. After the death of the lead guitarist, it was clear to see that the band had lost its _____.
9. I have a(n) _____ fear of spiders.
10. Opening a new campus on the other side of town doesn't make sense with the fact that their training programs are _____.

Lesson 199

A SUPERFICIAL GUY

NEW WORDS

astonishing
əˈstäniSHiNG

sparing
ˈspe(ə)riNG

fragrant
ˈfrāgrənt

perseverance
ˌpərsəˈvi(ə)rəns

mimic
ˈmimik

Chuck is a poor guy, but he always tries so hard to do shallow things. He **mimics** celebrities' behaviors and spends almost everything he has on perfumes so that he can be **fragrant** all the time. In spending on other things in life, however, he is very **sparing**, calculating every possible way to save some money. It is **astonishing** to see how he uses his **perseverance** to earn very little money then squanders it on unnecessary things. People wish that he would one day wake up and become pragmatic.

Definitions: Try matching the words in the list with the appropriate definitions. If you are stuck, check the glossary in the back of the book or the passage at the top of the page.

1. astonishing _____ a. aromatic; perfumed; scented
2. sparing _____ b. to imitate; to copy
3. fragrant _____ c. economical; frugal; meager
4. perseverance _____ d. determination; endurance
5. mimic _____ e. startling; stunning; amazing

Sentences: Try to use the words above in a sentence below. Remember that a word ending may be changed or its figure of speech slightly altered.

6. The mortgage officer showed reluctance to make a loan to the _____ couple who are trying to save up enough for a house.
7. Even if you are smart, lacking _____ and grit will not bring you success.
8. Despite coming across as child-like at first, Peter has shown to have _____ compassion and consideration for others.
9. She has a talent for _____ famous actresses; she now makes a living out of impersonation.
10. The soup was _____ with herbs and spices.

Lesson 200

SAILING RECOLLECTION

After an **exhaustive** day sailing through stormy waters, our ship finally was **becalmed** as the winds off the Florida coast subsided. The ship's captain, too, **severed** his relationship with two lazy crewmen who did not appropriately manage the boat facilities. With this newfound tranquility, the passengers on our sailboat finally began to delight in their time at sea. Sleeping on a boat was never something that I suspected that I would like, but my initial **leery** feelings about this endeavor dissipated amidst this spell of tranquility. Gleefully I "commiserated" with my sailing buddies as I soaked up the sun. How I wished I could stay on this boat forever relaxing while a **proxy** did my work back at home.

NEW WORDS

exhaustive
igˈzôstiv

sever
ˈsevər

becalm
biˈkä(l)m

leery
ˈli(ə)rē

proxy
ˈpräksē

Definitions: Try matching the words in the list with the appropriate definitions. If you are stuck, check the glossary in the back of the book or the passage at the top of the page.

1. exhaustive _____ a. suspicious; wary
2. sever _____ b. to deprive (a ship) of wind necessary to move it
3. becalm _____ c. the authority to represent someone else, especially in voting
4. leery _____ d. complete; comprehensive; full-scale
5. proxy _____ e. 1. to divide by cutting or slicing; 2. to terminate or break off a connection or relationship

Sentences: Try to use the words above in a sentence below. Remember that a word ending may be changed or its figure of speech slightly altered.

6. Quan was _____ of her neighbors for they were acting dubiously.
7. _____ at sea, the ship sat motionless for hours.
8. When representing your clients in court, you have to use an appropriate _____ or else your case will not be coherent.
9. After a(n) _____ search of our house, we still had not found the cat.
10. After breaking up with Annie, John blocked her phone number and disengaged with all of their mutual friends, thus _____ all connections with her.

Word Search
Lessons 191-200

```
S E V I T S U A H X E P B L
U T R E P I D A T I O N Q B
B G N I S S O R G N E L V Y
O C O N S E C R A T E D E N
R V I T D I I M E T N L G F
D I Z N M N E N A D B T R N
I T S I C L U U D A N A T B
N A M U B U T B P O G U E T
A L Y M O E M P I R L I O E
T I E X P U A B A R A E C F
I T M R O L D N E B O U N E
O Y E R F R T R O N D M L T
N P T N J J P R A N T G M V
M B U N W N J P I L O M T M
```

1. to cause someone to do something
2. to stare at in a manner showing sexual desire
3. dedicated to a sacred purpose
4. no longer active or effective; very sick; close to death
5. absorbing all of one's attention and interest
6. very difficult; challenging
7. someone currently holding office
8. 1. to make something continue indefinitely; 2. to preserve something valued from oblivion or extinction
9. imperturbable; to be able to remain calm in a difficult situations
10. to repeat an idea or argument to emphasize it
11. the act of placing in a lower rank or position
12. lazy
13. a person or thing that represents an idea
14. feeling of fear that something may happen
15. (n.) someone who establishes an institution or settlement; (v.) 1. to collapse or fail (of a plan or endeavor); 2. to fill with water and sink (of a ship)
16. vigorousness; exuberance
17. aromatic; perfumed; scented
18. to imitate; to copy
19. complete; comprehensive; full-scale
20. the authority to represent someone else, especially in voting

Vocabulary Review
Lessons 191-200

Directions: Match each word with its best approximate definition. Note that definitions are not necessarily repeated verbatim from the lesson exercises.

1.	thwart	_____	a.	full of energy or enthusiasm; colorful
2.	lingering	_____	b.	a beginner, novice, greenhorn, tyro
3.	cognitive	_____	c.	to shock or surprise immensely
4.	jubilant	_____	d.	an unexpected change in a situation or in someone's behavior
5.	avarice	_____	e.	steadfastness in something despite difficulty or delay in achieving success
6.	pedagogy	_____	f.	lasting for a long time, staying or hanging around
7.	astound	_____	g.	no longer in use or existence
8.	vibrant	_____	h.	an expert in a field who frequently has his or her opinions solicited
9.	pundit	_____	i.	to become ecstatically happy
10.	miscreant	_____	j.	greed
11.	neophyte	_____	k.	the method of practice of teaching
12.	extinct	_____	l.	cautious due to realistic suspicions
13.	disrepute	_____	m.	to frustrate or baffle; to oppose
14.	vagary	_____	n.	characterized by an interest in unpleasant things such as death and disease
15.	morbid	_____	o.	held in low esteem by the public
16.	elate	_____	p.	feeling or expressing great happiness; triumphant
17.	astonishing	_____	q.	to divide by cutting off
18.	perseverance	_____	r.	a person who is ill-behaved or who breaks the law
19.	sever	_____	s.	extremely surprising or amazing; impressive
20.	leery	_____	t.	concerning the process of acquiring, assessing, and assimilating knowledge

Long Live Latin!

Though Latin is, for all intents and purposes, a dead language outside of Vatican City, many of its phrases still show up in modern English texts (though less frequently on standardized tests). Below is a list of some common Latin phrases that are used in English together with their meanings.

a posteriori:	reasoning from effects to causes
a priori:	reasoning from causes to effects
ad hoc:	for this purpose (for a specific purpose)
ad hominem:	a specific attack on an individual's values based on emotion rather than on reason
ad nauseum:	to a sickening extent
bona fide:	in good faith; sincerely
carpe diem:	seize the day
ceteris paribus:	all things being equal
et cetera (etc.):	and the rest; and so forth
ex libris:	from the library (of...)
habeas corpus:	writing saying someone has been brought legally before a court to decide whether detaining such an individual is legal
ibid.:	in the same place in a book (short for Latin ibidem)
in loco parentis:	in the place of a parent
in situ:	in position; in its original place
in vitro:	in a test tube (literally: in glass)
in vivo:	within a living organism
inter alia:	amongst other things
mea culpa:	through my own fault
non sequitur:	a conclusion or inference that doesn't follow from its premises (literally: it does not follow)
per annum:	by the year
per capita:	by the heads; for each person taken individually
per diem:	by the day; per day; for each day
per se:	by or in itself
post mortem:	an autopsy (literally: after death)
prima facie:	at first sight; on the face of it

quid pro quo: one thing for another; something for something
semper fidelis: always faithful
sine qua non: indispensible
vice versa: the positions being reversed; if the positions were reversed

Idiomatic Expressions I

Idiomatic expressions are phrases whose meaning does not convey the literal sense of the words in the expression. For example, telling someone to "break a leg" does not convey that you wish someone to have a personal injury. Rather, the phrase "break a leg" means "good luck," and is typically said to someone before a theatrical or musical performance. English has hundreds of idioms, and many native speakers only know a fraction of them. Below and in two additional Idiomatic Expressions sections is a list of some common English idiomatic expressions. These lists are by no means exhaustive, but should help you get a sense of some commonly said idioms.

Idiomatic Expression	Meaning/Example
to break a leg	Said to wish someone good luck in a musical or theatrical performance. My mother told me to break a leg before I played the lead role in my school play.
to go postal	Going completely insane, often involving violence A man went postal last week and punched three grocery store clerks in the face for no apparent reason
to break the ice	To initiate social interaction or conversation After three minutes of sitting in silence in the theater group, Laura broke the ice and asked how everyone's day was.
once in a blue moon	Rarely, not very often. Suzanna is into fitness and eats ice cream only once in a blue moon.

to get up on the wrong side of the bed	To feel irritable; to be in a bad mood; to have a bad day from the moment it begins Marylou must have gotten up on the wrong side of the bed; normally she is very friendly, but she seems to be screaming at everyone today.
crocodile tears	Showing emotion insincerely. The politician showed crocodile tears at his electoral opponent's funeral. He wasn't truly sad to see his opponent die; on the contrary, he was thrilled to have less competition!
piece of cake	Finding a task to be extremely easy. Today's calculus test was a piece of cake; I know I got 100% and the test only took fifteen minutes to complete!
(every cloud has a) silver lining	No matter how bleak a situation is, there is always some positive element in it. Even though Nitu lost her corporate job and was unemployed for three months, she saw the silver lining around her circumstances, discovered a newfound love for comedy, and is now a successful comedian.
to pass the buck	To not assume responsibility for something and designate that responsibility to someone else. Rather than assuming responsibility for explaining corporate losses, the CEO passed the buck to his CFO to explain the downturn.
to throw a curve(ball)	To confuse someone by doing something tricky or unexpected. Sean threw his brothers a curve when his date for prom was not the girl that they expected but rather his best male friend.

to hit the sack/hit the hay	**To fall asleep** After a long day of walking around the amusement park, the kids hit the hay as soon as they arrived at home.
to bring down the house	**To evoke heavy applause and cheers** Jessica's singing brought down the house last night; everyone was captivated by her amazing voice.
to leave no stone unturned	**To search every possible place for something.** Shri left no stone unturned in the hotel when she looked for her keys that had gone missing.
back to the drawing board	**Time to start from the beginning again** When all of Kel's plans to get a date with Liz failed, he went back to the drawing board to ponder new ideas to get her on a date.
to spill the beans	**To reveal a secret or surprise** Jason spilled the beans when he told his sister that everyone was throwing her a surprise birthday party at 6PM at her favorite restaurant.
out to lunch	**Not alert, uninformed, giddy** I think Linda was out to lunch at the business conference on Friday; she did not follow a single rule that employees were commanded to follow at the meeting.
to feather one's nest	**To acquire wealth for oneself, usually by exploiting others to obtain said wealth.** The CEO feathered his nest by taking key employees out to lunch and flattering them in order to win their approval.

to let sleeping dogs lie	**To not instigate trouble; to not incite something that could cause trouble.** Martha encouraged her brother to let sleeping dogs lie and not provoke the school bully, who already had been expelled from school for beating her up.
to take with a grain of salt	**To not take seriously** Everyone takes Mrs. Angotti's criticisms with a grain of salt, for she exaggerates everything she says.
to pull one's weight	**To do one's fair share of the work** In a healthy team project each team member must pull his or her (own) weight.
to show one's hand	**To reveal one's true intentions** Nobody believed that Alice really loved James; she showed her hand when she admitted to her friends that James was only a good boyfriend because he had money to buy her all of the expensive clothes that she wanted.
left holding the bag	**Left to take all the blame for something** Paula and James jointly robbed a bank. But when the police arrived, Paula quickly escaped out the back door and left James holding the bag as the sole culprit in the robbery.
ivory tower	**A place that feels sealed off from the real world** Many people argue that professors live in an ivory tower because their research often centers strictly on theoretical issues rather than pragmatic ones.

to cut corners	**To take shortcuts or find easier or cheaper ways of doing things** **A bad business will try and cut corners on its budget by using staff and resources of subpar quality and charging full price for its services.**

Lesson 201

STRICT HISTORY TEACHER

My history teacher, Mr. Knee, is a **stickler** for details. He is very concerned about ensuring that students remember dates of all major historical events and will **harangue** students who forget to do their homework or who cannot remember famous quotes **verbatim**. He is also not **moderate** in his class rules, for students who arrive late without an excuse note will automatically receive a detention. Trying to cut corners in Mr. Knee's class is a challenge for the **guileless**: one needs to truly be an expert at deception to get away with anything in this class.

NEW WORDS

stickler
ˈstik(ə)lər

verbatim
vərˈbātəm

guileless
ˈgīlis

moderate
ˈmäd(ə)rət (adj.; n.); ˈmäd(ə)rāt (v.)

harangue
həˈraNG

Definitions: Try matching the words in the list with the appropriate definitions. If you are stuck, check the glossary in the back of the book or the passage at the top of the page.

1. stickler _____ a. (adj. and adv.) in exactly the same words as used originally
2. verbatim _____ b. a person who demands a certain quality or type of behavior
3. guileless _____ c. to lecture at length in an aggressive, critical manner
4. moderate _____ d. (adj.) 1. average in amount, intensity, or degree; 2. not politically radical; (n.) a person who does not hold radical views; (v.) 1. to make less extreme, intense or violent; 2. to preside over
5. harangue _____ e. innocent and without deception

Sentences: Try to use the words above in a sentence below. Remember that a word ending may be changed or its figure of speech slightly altered.

6. Leon was a(n) _____ for details: he needed to hear precise details about all of his business plans.
7. Kiet's father _____ him to do his homework since he was lazy.
8. Most animals prefer _____ weather to extreme heat or cold.
9. Court stenographers are supposed to copy peoples' statements in court _____, thus creating an exact transcript of what transpired.
10. The _____ entrepreneur was easily duped by his competitors.

Lesson 202

DROUGHT CONCERNS

NEW WORDS

verbalize
ˈvərbəˌlīz

bliss
blis

queer
kwi(ə)r

dilate
ˈdīˌlāt, dīˈlāt

arable
ˈarəbəl

It is a little **queer** that Juan, who usually has difficulty **verbalizing** his feelings, was so fiery and articulate in articulating his thoughts on the recent drought. He told us all that months without rain had made local **arable** land unsuitable for farming, and that citizens in the agricultural valley may be toiling away for at least three years after the drought ends before they could have any **blissful** experience in reaping a giant harvest. His anger over the lack of hydration seems to have **dilated** his blood vessels, for Juan was flush red when he stated his views.

Definitions: Try matching the words in the list with the appropriate definitions. If you are stuck, check the glossary in the back of the book or the passage at the top of the page.

1. verbalize _____ a. suitable for growing crops
2. bliss _____ b. to make wider or larger; to open
3. queer _____ c. to express ideas or feelings in words, often by speaking out loud
4. dilate _____ d. strange; odd
5. arable _____ e. perfect happiness; great joy

Sentences: Try to use the words above in a sentence below. Remember that a word ending may be changed or its figure of speech slightly altered.

6. Because they receive so little rainfall, most desert lands are not _____.
7. When I go to the eye doctor, he puts drops in my eye to _____ my pupil and examine my widened eyes better.
8. I always feel _____ when I am eating my favorite chocolate cake and vanilla ice cream.
9. It can be difficult to date someone who has difficulty _____ his or her feelings: it is important to express how we feel so that others understand us.
10. It is definitely _____ to wear a bathing suit to a state funeral.

Lesson 203

RESTAURANT RELOCATION

I fear that my favorite restaurant's seemingly **impromptu** decision to move from an urban location to a rural hideaway may be a **retrograde** step for the establishment. Currently the restaurant is flourishing downtown, where many people admire its savory dishes. A sudden move away from the city is **consonant** neither with the restaurant's metropolitan ambience nor with its clientele's cosmopolitan mindset. And it seems like the restaurant may have to **exhort** its customers to travel far if it wants to sustain business. Many people find the restaurant's decision to move to be **blasphemous** for a business whose stated mission is to make city life more relaxing.

NEW WORDS

consonance
ˈkänsənəns

exhort
igˈzôrt

retrograde
ˈretrəˌgrād

blasphemous
ˈblasfəməs

impromptu
imˈpräm(p)ˌt(y)oo

Definitions: Try matching the words in the list with the appropriate definitions. If you are stuck, check the glossary in the back of the book or the passage at the top of the page.

1. consonance _____ a. to urge or encourage one to do something
2. exhort _____ b. (adj. and adv.) done without being planned, organized, or rehearsed
3. retrograde _____ c. agreement or compatibility between opinions or actions
4. blasphemous _____ d. directed or moving backwards; reversed
5. impromptu _____ e. sacrilegious; against God or sacred things

Sentences: Try to use the words above in a sentence below. Remember that a word ending may be changed or its figure of speech slightly altered.

6. It is _____ to pick your nose and eat your boogers before the Queen of England.
7. To an observer on Earth, most planets occasionally exhibit _____ motion: occasionally they travel backward on their path.
8. Rather than preparing his speech, Jason spoke in _____ form.
9. Mark _____ his sister to run for mayor because so many people felt that she was the right person for the job.
10. Dylan is an excellent businessman because his behaviors are always _____ with his vows: he always follows through on his word.

Lesson 204

NEW WORDS

proponent
prəˈpōnənt

dismissive
disˈmisiv

mystified
ˈmistəˌfīd

glutton
ˈglətn

distressed
disˈtrest

WOMEN'S RIGHTS ACTIVIST

I am **mystified** about how Cassandra, a **proponent** of women's rights, could be so **dismissive** of her feminist peers. Because my curiosity urged me to explore the issue, I decided to probe Cassandra on her views. Cassandra intimated that she was **distressed** by many of her feminist peers because they valued advancing women's rights at the cost of curtailing men's rights. For Cassandra, who was a **glutton** for equality on all issues, the best type of female advocate is one who recognizes that men and women are equals: bringing down the status of one sex to boost the other was, to her, downright terrible.

Definitions: Try matching the words in the list with the appropriate definitions. If you are stuck, check the glossary in the back of the book or the passage at the top of the page.

1. proponent _____ a. (for someone) to be utterly bewildered or perplexed
2. dismissive _____ b. a person who is usually fond of or eager for something (often food)
3. mystified _____ c. a person who advocates a project, cause, or theory
4. glutton _____ d. suffering from anxiety, sorrow, or pain
5. distressed _____ e. feeling that something is unworthy of consideration

Sentences: Try to use the words above in a sentence below. Remember that a word ending may be changed or its figure of speech slightly altered.

6. My neighbor was _____ by how roses grew on my lawn in the middle of January.
7. Huey is a(n) _____ for chocolate; he cannot resist cocoa.
8. A good teacher is never _____ of his/her students' intellectual needs, for teachers should always look to ensure that a student is challenged.
9. Amber was _____ when she heard the sad news that her boyfriend had been injured in a train accident.
10. As a major _____ of the movement to abolish fast food restaurants in Italy, Gianna pushed to have all chain restaurants in Milan closed.

Lesson 205

TEMPLE VISIT FAILURE

Because the threat of an avalanche was **imminent**, we were unable to take the **serpentine** road up to the mountain temple. This was particularly disappointing, for the temple contains a **replica** of a famous fourth century statue of a local deity. My brother, despite **fulsome** remarks to our tour guide, was unable to reschedule the temple visit to the next week, which made him depressed. The circumstances are truly unfortunate because our travel agency, which is renown for its **unimpeachable** commitment to satisfying tourist wishes, was unable to make a temple trip materialize during our journey.

NEW WORDS

serpentine
ˈsərpənˌtēn, -ˌtīn

imminent
ˈimənənt

unimpeachable
ˌənimˈpēCHəbəl

fulsome
ˈfoolsəm

replica
ˈreplikə

Definitions: Try matching the words in the list with the appropriate definitions. If you are stuck, check the glossary in the back of the book or the passage at the top of the page.

1. serpentine _____ a. unable to be doubted or questioned; entirely trustworthy
2. imminent _____ b. flattering to an excessive degree
3. unimpeachable _____ c. winding or twisting
4. fulsome _____ d. an exact model or copy of something
5. replica _____ e. about to happen

Sentences: Try to use the words above in a sentence below. Remember that a word ending may be changed or its figure of speech slightly altered.

6. The road up the mountain is _____ and turns endlessly.
7. The brilliant François built a breathtaking _____ of the Eiffel Tower out of toothpicks.
8. Most Americans revere president Abraham Lincoln (1809-1865) for his candor and _____ behavior.
9. Judging from the sky's rapidly darkening color, a storm is likely _____.
10. While giving compliments can be nice, excessively _____ behavior is usually not a good quality.

Lesson 206

GOLDEN PALACE

NEW WORDS

immaterial
ˌi(m)məˈti(ə)rēəl

insulate
ˈins(y)əˌlāt

unsolicited
ˌənsəˈlisitid

lodging
ˈläjiNG

gilded
ˈgildid

Because all of the objects in the king's palace are **gilded**, **lodging** in the palatial estate is restricted to people only of noble birth. Furthermore, because of the exorbitant price of these objects, the palace is **insulated** by scores of guards who, every hour, prevent thieving commoners from showing up **unsolicited**. It is **immaterial** whether one's intentions are genuine or conniving, as nobody who is not regal is welcome beyond the palace gates.

Definitions: Try matching the words in the list with the appropriate definitions. If you are stuck, check the glossary in the back of the book or the passage at the top of the page.

1.	immaterial	_____	a.	to use a material to protect something from the elements or heat loss
2.	insulate	_____	b.	unimportant under the circumstances; irrelevant
3.	unsolicited	_____	c.	covered thinly with gold leaf or gold paint
4.	lodging	_____	d.	not requested; done voluntarily
5.	gilded	_____	e.	a place where someone lives or stays temporarily

Sentences: Try to use the words above in a sentence below. Remember that a word ending may be changed or its figure of speech slightly altered.

6. When taking a long road trip it is helpful to find _____ for each night to sleep in.
7. Many homes in cold climates have material in their attics to _____ them from the cold.
8. Many people find Claudia offensive because she always offers _____ advice to people on how to live their lives.
9. Many objects in the Sultan of Brunei's palace are _____; because of their high value, common people are not allowed to touch them.
10. Whether you are rich or poor is _____ to whether you will be faithful in a relationship.

Lesson 207

THEATRICAL DEBUT

After memorizing all of her lines and reading through the **minutiae** of the play script, Janine was finally ready to go on stage. She was to play a major role in *Frankenstein*, a piece that embodied the spirit of **romanticism** at its height. As she awaited the stagehand's **cue** to go on a stage, she could feel a sense of excitement **pervading** the auditorium. In five minutes she would be on stage reciting her lines, waiting for the **stimulus** of the orchestra to get her dancing after her initial soliloquy was complete.

NEW WORDS

minutiae
mə'n(y)ooSHē,ē, -SHē,ī

pervade
pər'vād

cue
kyoo

romanticism
rō'mantə,sizəm, rə-

stimulus
'stimyələs

Definitions: Try matching the words in the list with the appropriate definitions. If you are stuck, check the glossary in the back of the book or the passage at the top of the page.

1. minutiae _____ a. a thing said or done that serves as a signal for action
2. pervade _____ b. the state or quality of expressing feelings, inspiration, and subjectivity over reason
3. cue _____ c. to spread through and be perceived in all parts of a place
4. romanticism _____ d. small, precise, or trivial details of something
5. stimulus _____ e. 1. a signal or event that evokes a reaction by a tissue or organ; 2. a thing that rouses activity in someone or something; 3. an exciting or interesting quality

Sentences: Try to use the words above in a sentence below. Remember that a word ending may be changed or its figure of speech slightly altered.

6. A skunk's odor often _____ through entire neighborhoods.
7. Neil is so lazy; he only works if provided with a major _____.
8. Most CEOs of giant corporations do not like to have countless hours of their time wasted pouring over _____ of their business.
9. Books that emphasize feeling and passion over reason are said to deal with hallmark ideas of the _____ movement.
10. Alice is to go on stage and sing as soon as Harry gives her the _____ to perform.

NEW WORDS

crux
krəks, krooks

piecemeal
ˈpēsˌmēl

relegate
ˈreləˌgāt

innuendo
ˌinyooˈendō

prevalent
ˈprevələnt

Lesson 208

ACADEMIC INTEGRITY

Cheating has become a **prevalent** problem at many of America's top universities. Academic officials have noted the increased sense of academic misconduct, and think that a growing apathy for scholarly values lay at the **crux** of the problem. Students, they believe, have **relegated** pursuing knowledge to a lower priority than developing a professional identity. Many of academicians' **innuendos** reveal a great disgust at this trend. Sadly, efforts to restore academic integrity on campuses have been **piecemeal** and have resulted in no large-scale revival of scholarly values. We can only hope that students will once again begin to cherish their studies.

Definitions: Try matching the words in the list with the appropriate definitions. If you are stuck, check the glossary in the back of the book or the passage at the top of the page.

1. crux _____ a. to consign to an inferior mark or position
2. piecemeal _____ b. widespread in a particular area at a particular time
3. relegate _____ c. a suggestive, allusive, often disparaging remark
4. innuendo _____ d. characterized by unsystematic partial measures taken over a period of time
5. prevalent _____ e. the decisive or most important point at issue

Sentences: Try to use the words above in a sentence below. Remember that a word ending may be changed or its figure of speech slightly altered.

6. In many Southeast Asian countries, motorbikes are _____: they constitute well over half of the vehicles on the roads.
7. Ho Chi Minh City has grown through _____ development projects over the last two decades.
8. Though Shad's argument was replete with details, the _____ of his point was that California taxes must be lowered.
9. It was hard for Monica to ignore Theodore's _____ to come to his room for a little private chat.
10. Many intellectual snobs often _____ lowbrow humor to pure puerile crap.

Lesson 209

CHEMICAL POLLUTANT BILL

Next week congress is set to **ratify** a bill that will implement a new **taxonomy** for classifying poisonous liquid chemicals. The reason for this change is that many environmentalists think that the current scheme to identify chemicals is not clear enough to provide **prognoses** for many hazardous toxic situations. Because so many liquid chemicals **contaminate** our waters, we need a more explicit system for identifying the chemicals by their potency. Supporters of the new bill have expressed **unbounded** enthusiasm for it and are eager to see it implemented immediately.

NEW WORDS

contaminate
kənˈtaməˌnāt

prognosis
prägˈnōsəs

taxonomy
takˈsänəmē

ratify
ˈratəˌfī

unbounded
ˌənˈboundid

Definitions: Try matching the words in the list with the appropriate definitions. If you are stuck, check the glossary in the back of the book or the passage at the top of the page.

1. contaminate _____ a. to sign or give formal consent to a contract, treaty, or agreement to make it formally valid
2. prognosis _____ b. to make impure by adding a polluting substance
3. taxonomy _____ c. limitless
4. ratify _____ d. forecasted outcome of a situation or disease
5. unbounded _____ e. branch of science dealing with the classification of organisms; the classification of something; a scheme of classification

Sentences: Try to use the words above in a sentence below. Remember that a word ending may be changed or its figure of speech slightly altered.

6. In order for the bill to be _____, a majority of the senators must vote in favor of it.
7. Carl Linnaeus (1707-1778) is the father of our _____ system; in creating it, he assigned two Latin words to classify each living organism he knew.
8. Tanya had _____ enthusiasm for the equestrian show: nothing could limit her passion for horses and their riders.
9. The doctor's fortunate _____ was that Bruce did not have cancer as he initially expected.
10. Chemicals from the nearby factory have _____ drinking water to the point of it being non-potable.

Lesson 210

PROBOSCIS MONKEYS

NEW WORDS

reprieve
ri'prēv

interminable
in'tərmənəbəl

uncouth
ˌənˈkooTH

varied
've(ə)rēd

inhabit
in'habit

After what seemed like an **interminable** two years of working on her dissertation, Ivona was thrilled to get a month-long break. It was something of a necessary **reprieve** for her, as she was finally able to **inhabit** a space other than her university library. So she decided to go to Hawaii for that month. Her vacation reminded her that, aside from research, she had such **varied** interests as scuba diving, theater, rock climbing, and fine dining. But after having been sheltered away from people for so long, some fellow tourists that she met on her vacation found her to be a bit **uncouth**. Such experiences reminded Ivona that, even though she is inundated with academic work, it is important to maintain a social life.

Definitions: Try matching the words in the list with the appropriate definitions. If you are stuck, check the glossary in the back of the book or the passage at the top of the page.

1. reprieve _____ a. to live in or occupy a place or environment
2. interminable _____ b. lacking good manners, refinement, or grace
3. uncouth _____ c. showing a number of different types of elements
4. varied _____ d. unending; unceasing
5. inhabit _____ e. (n.) a cancellation or postponement of punishment; (v.) to cancel or postpone the punishment of someone

Sentences: Try to use the words above in a sentence below. Remember that a word ending may be changed or its figure of speech slightly altered.

6. After thirty weeks of work, six days a week, Shalina was happy to receive a(n) _____ so she could relax.
7. Three different Native American tribes once _____ this region of upstate New York.
8. Florin has such _____ interests as scuba diving, cooking, reading medieval French poetry, and stamp collecting.
9. It is _____ to belch in the middle of a wedding ceremony.
10. The baby's crying felt _____: for twenty straight minutes, the little boy on the bus whined incessantly.

Crossword Puzzle
Lessons 201-210

ACROSS

3 branch of science dealing with the classification of organisms; the classification of something; a scheme of classification
10 forecasted outcome of a situation or disease
13 a place where someone lives or stays temporarily
15 (for someone) to be utterly bewildered or perplexed
16 lacking good manners, refinement, or grace
17 directed or moving backwards; reversed
18 innocent and without deception
19 unable to be doubted or questioned; entirely trustworthy
20 not requested; done voluntarily

DOWN

1 the decisive or most important point at issue
2 a thing said or done that serves as a signal for action
4 to consign to an inferior mark or position
5 about to happen
6 (adj. and adv.) in exactly the same words as used originally
7 small, precise, or trivial details of something
8 to make wider or larger; to open
9 suffering from anxiety, sorrow, or pain
11 (adj. and adv.) done without being planned, organized, or rehearsed
12 unending; unceasing
14 to express ideas or feelings in words, often by speaking out loud

Vocabulary Review
Lessons 201-210

Directions: Match each word with its best approximate definition. Note that definitions are not necessarily repeated verbatim from the lesson exercises.

1. stickler _____
2. harangue _____
3. bliss _____
4. arable _____
5. exhort _____
6. blasphemous _____
7. proponent _____
8. glutton _____
9. serpentine _____
10. replica _____
11. insulate _____
12. gilded _____
13. pervade _____
14. cue _____
15. innuendo _____
16. prevalent _____
17. contaminate _____
18. ratify _____
19. reprieve _____
20. inhabit _____

a. twisting; winding
b. to lecture someone in a lengthy and aggressive manner
c. an allusive or indirect remark or hint
d. to make something impure by adding a substance
e. to make a piece of legislation (contract, treaty, etc.) officially valid
f. a person who advocates a theory, proposal, or project
g. to spread through and exist in every part of a region
h. a person who is excessively fond of something, especially food
i. a thing said or done to serve as a signal – often in acting
j. land suitable for growing crops
k. to live in or occupy a place
l. a person who insists on a certain quality or type of behavior
m. sacrilegious or profane
n. to protect from the loss of heat or entry of sound; to protect from the unpleasant elements of something
o. covered thinly with gold leaf or paint
p. to strongly encourage someone to act
q. widespread in a certain area at a particular time
r. total joy or happiness
s. a short rest from an undesirable situation
t. an exact copy or model of something

Idiomatic Expressions II

This list is a continuation of common idiomatic expressions. It is the second unit in a three-part sequence.

Idiomatic Expression	Meaning/Example
sour grapes	Something that one cannot have and, as a consequence, one disparages it as if it were not desirable. Even though Ann fairly lost the debate for which she had spent months preparing, others perceived her subsequent dismissal of it as being meaningless as sour grapes.
wouldn't be caught dead	To never do something because it would be too embarrassing to be caught doing it Ahuva said she wouldn't be caught dead eating food out of a garbage can.
to cost an arm and a leg	To be very expensive Hamburgers at the new restaurant cost an arm and a leg. They're at least twice as expensive as any other burger in town.
writing on the wall	Likelihood that something bad will happen I could see the writing on the wall concerning Horatio's divorce when he and his wife began fighting every day.

to go up in smoke	**To be spoiled or wasted** Martha's secret plans to retire went up in smoke after Hailey announced them to the entire office staff.
on the dot	**Exactly on time** Marcus is always punctual for afternoon meetings; he always shows up for his scheduled 2PM appointment at 2:00 on the dot.
tongue in cheek	**To say something without serious intention** Gene said tongue in cheek that he would date Kelly, but when Kelly actually asked him out he felt somewhat uncomfortable.
through thick and thin	**Through good times and bad times** Fair-weather friends will leave someone in times of trouble, but a good friend will stand by your side through thick and thin.
to keep a stiff upper lip	**To not let unfortunate things upset you; to not act upset (even if you might be)** Even though Eileen's sister burned all of her textbooks before her final exams, Eileen kept a stiff upper lip and was civil to her sister. She also went to the library to study her notes and to use books available to the public in order to prepare for her tests.

not playing with a full deck	**Not operate in a rationally or mentally sound manner** When Tom told his boss that cookies were not selling because they were too expensive and his boss decided to raise the sale price of cookies in an attempt to boost sales, Tom became convinced that his boss was not playing with a full deck.
to burn the midnight oil	**Stay up very late at night working** Chris burned the midnight oil cramming formulas into his head for Fridays' physics exam.
to wear one's heart on one's sleeve	**To reveal one's emotions too clearly** Marco wore his heart on his sleeve when he told his bosses how depressed he was at work and how his coworkers were stealing pencils from his desk.
Achilles heel	**A(n) (often deadly) weakness in spite of a great strength** Although Greg was an eloquent speaker, his Achilles heel was public oratory: he stuttered when speaking to large groups.
off the beaten path	**Not well known or popular with many people** Eddie's Diner is a fabulous restaurant that is off the beaten path: since it is four miles from the highway and in the middle of the countryside, only locals and well-informed travelers are aware of its splendor.
to lay one's cards on the table	**To reveal one's true intentions; to be candid about one's position on an issue** Rather than trying to defend her brother's sloth, Barbara lay her cards on the table concerning her brother's indolence: "My brother is lazy and cannot finish tasks on time," she bluntly told his clientele.

Idiom	Definition and Example
without rhyme or reason	For no rational purpose or reason Yolanda is a pretty unpredictable person. Often she will lose her temper and become violent without rhyme or reason.
at the drop of a hat	Immediately, instantly The king expected his chefs to serve him a five-course meal at the drop of a hat: he expected that if he merely snapped his fingers, plates of meat and vegetables would be on their way to his throne.
to make a long story short	To get to the point; to avoid a longwinded explanation Though Elena was sick of her boyfriend dating other girls and flirting with random people, she preferred brevity when she addressed the problem to him. Rather than delineating her complaints, she said, "To make a long story short, you're not faithful. That's why our relationship is now over."
to bring home the bacon	To earn a salary or bring home money earned on a job Lukas took a big job at a consulting firm so that he could bring home the bacon and support his family.
to carry the day	To be successful; to win a competition Even though Martin pointed out a fallacy in Fred's logic, Fred's overall argument carried the day.
on pins and needles	Anxious or in suspense Scott was on pins and needles waiting for his exam results to get posted.

to steal someone's thunder	To take the credit and accolades for something that another person does Although Derek wrote a brilliant paper with penetrating insights into the causes of the Industrial Revolution, his adviser stole Derek's thunder and accepted much intellectual credit for guiding Derek's thought processes.
to have the upper hand	To have a position of power and control over someone else Even though Rajib worked hard and wanted a raise, he was tactful in requesting one from his boss, who held the upper hand in making decisions about the former's salary.

Lesson 211

NEW WORDS

recriminations
ri͵krimәˈnāSHәnz

expound
ikˈspound

devour
diˈvou(ә)r

mawkish
ˈmôkiSH

aural
ˈôrәl

RESTAURANT DRAMA

People came from far and wide to **devour** the excellent food prepared by Andreas. His Dutch restaurant was thriving, and people **expounded** in great detail their perceived reasons for his success. One day, however, a client ordered a bowl of bean soup from Andreas, but she received a plate of apple strudel instead. Having very little patience, the client mocked Andreas' **aural** skills. She accused Andreas of being mean-spirited and ignorant, and he responded with **recriminations** that she was being overly hostile and insensitive. She then sat in the restaurant crying for over an hour, worrying Andreas that her **mawkish** nature was a real problem. Only when Andreas offered her a free coffee did the customer cheer up and recant for overreacting.

Definitions: Try matching the word in the box with the appropriate definition. If you are stuck, check the glossary in the back of the book or the passage at the top of the page.

1. recriminations _____ a. to explain and present a theory or idea systematically and in detail
2. expound _____ b. to eat or read with great intensity and in large quantity
3. devour _____ c. accusations in response to those from someone else
4. mawkish _____ d. of or related to the ear or sense of hearing
5. aural _____ e. sentimental in a feeble or discomforting way

Sentences: Try to use the words above in a sentence below. Remember that a word ending may be changed or its figure of speech slightly altered.

6. Though Archie can read and write Japanese well, his _____ skills need some work; listening exercises remain a challenge for him.
7. Good lawyers are able to _____ upon their arguments with ease in a courtroom.
8. When the students accused their teacher of grading them unfairly, the teacher made _____ about her students' poor study habits to the principal.
9. We watched Jimmy _____ three pizzas and two ice cream sundaes for lunch; he must have been very hungry!
10. People accused Jerry of being _____ when she cried nearly every day for six months after her boyfriend dumped her.

Lesson 212

AN ACADEMIC CALLING

Emily's primary choice for a **vocation** was to become a university history professor. When she was in college, she **inquired** regularly about which new academic books had just appeared on the market. During her graduate school career, nothing could satiate her **craving** for reading new books and writing analyses of them. Many professors heralded her doctoral thesis on the Great Depression as a **masterful** work that profoundly impacted how scholars see economic trends in modern America. Before long, and perhaps somewhat **unwittingly**, a somewhat green Emily found herself receiving tenure track offers at many of the world's most prestigious universities because of her sustained scholarly labor.

NEW WORDS

masterful
ˈmastərfəl

unwitting
ˌənˈwitiNG

inquire
inˈkwīr

vocation
vōˈkāSHən

craving
ˈkrāviNG

Definitions: Try matching the word in the box with the appropriate definition. If you are stuck, check the glossary in the back of the book or the passage at the top of the page.

1. masterful _____
2. unwitting _____
3. inquire _____
4. vocation _____
5. craving _____

a. a person not aware of the full facts; not done purposefully
b. a powerful desire for something
c. a strong feeling of suitability for a career or occupation; a person's employment or job
d. powerful and able to control others; performed or performing extremely skillfully
e. to ask information from someone

Sentences: Try to use the words above in a sentence below. Remember that a word ending may be changed or its figure of speech slightly altered.

6. Dale was a(n) _____ accomplice in yesterday's bank robbery. She did not know that her friend hid stolen money in the trunk of her car.
7. Choosing a(n) _____ can be an ordeal for someone who is extremely talented and has several possible prosperous career paths.
8. Hilda had a(n) _____ for a hamburger and drove to the local diner at four in the morning in order to have one.
9. If you are allergic to peanuts, it is imperative that you _____ whether peanut products are used to make the meals that you order at a restaurant.
10. Shayna did a(n) _____ job in the school debate: the other candidates simply could not challenge her or find any aporiae in her arguments.

Lesson 213

NEW WORDS

placebo
plə'sēbō

voluminous
və'loomənəs

microcosm
'mīkrə,käzəm

simulate
'simyə,lāt

gaffe
gaf

FAYE'S SPEAKNG PROBLEM

Faye is a brilliant woman, but she has difficulty speaking in public. Though her intentions are genuine, she is prone to making **gaffes** that obstruct her ability to forge a stellar environmental science career. This is especially painful, as she has done a **voluminous** amount of research on carbon emissions and has **simulated** dozens of experiments in her lab to bolster her findings. If her department at the local university can be seen as a **microcosm** of the academic field at large, then she surely will not be advancing far on her career path because of her verbal blunders. Her friends claimed to give her pills to help her become a better speaker, but in fact these pills were merely **placebos**: they were only a thoughtful means of motivating her to have the courage to present. With a little luck, Faye will garner the courage to deliver better talks soon.

Definitions: Try matching the word in the box with the appropriate definition. If you are stuck, check the glossary in the back of the book or the passage at the top of the page.

1. placebo _____ a. large in volume; occupying much space
2. voluminous _____ b. a harmless pill prescribed for psychological benefit rather than for physiological effect
3. microcosm _____ c. an unintentional remark or act lavishing embarrassment on its originator; a blunder
4. simulate _____ d. a community, situation, or place regarded as encapsulating key qualities of something larger
5. gaffe _____ e. to imitate the character or appearance of

Sentences: Try to use the words above in a sentence below. Remember that a word ending may be changed or its figure of speech slightly altered.

6. Brian believed that the pills he took helped him lose weight, but in actuality they were merely _____; he shed pounds from keeping a strict diet.
7. Before trekking into outer space, potential astronomers are often placed into man-made structures that _____ an environment devoid of gravity.
8. Many shareholders suspect that Shaolaine will not be made the company's new CEO because she is prone to making _____ at public events.
9. Yetta's dissertation is _____: it is over 600 pages long.
10. It would be unfair to call New York City a(n) _____ of American life because a large country's values cannot be appropriately reflected by the people and behaviors of a single city.

Lesson 214

SKILLED MARRIAGE COUNSELOR

Gerald is a **veteran** marriage counselor who, in the course of his thirty-year career, has guided many dissatisfied couples away from divorce. Usually he can sense when a couple is on the verge of falling apart by honing in on their **semantics** during therapy sessions. He can also tell when at least one member of a couple assumes a fake or hostile **persona** to incite agitation. Many of the couples he has seen reconcile their problems, and claim that he is among the shrewdest **arbitrators** of relationships that they know. If you feel that you are approaching the **advent** of divorce, you should contact Gerald for help.

NEW WORDS

veteran
ˈvetərən, ˈvetrən

advent
ˈadˌvent

persona
pərˈsōnə

semantic
səˈmantik

arbitrator
ˈärbiˌtrātər

Definitions: Try matching the word in the box with the appropriate definition. If you are stuck, check the glossary in the back of the book or the passage at the top of the page.

1. veteran _____ a. the aspect of one's character presented to or perceived by others
2. advent _____ b. related to meaning in logic or language
3. persona _____ c. an independent person or body appointed to settle a dispute
4. semantic _____ d. the arrival of a notable thing, person, or event
5. arbitrator _____ e. 1. a person experienced in a particular field; 2. a person who has served in the military

Sentences: Try to use the words above in a sentence below. Remember that a word ending may be changed or its figure of speech slightly altered.

6. Businessmen much prefer looking at cold, hard data to analyzing _____ terms that saturate academic studies of management.
7. Though this is my first time playing paintball, I have received good advice on how to play from my friend Jake, who is a(n) _____ at the sport.
8. Historians note that the _____ of computers dates back to the calculating machine that French mathematician Blaise Pascal (1623-62) made in 1642.
9. Because they were unable to negotiate peaceably, Carla and Erik required a(n) _____ to help dissolve their estate following their divorce.
10. Even though Jeanne was not a very friendly person, her job as a customer service representative forced her to adopt an affable _____ at work.

Lesson 215

NEW WORDS

deficient
diˈfiSHənt

fetter
ˈfetər

inordinate
iˈnôrdn-it

flora
ˈflôrə

natty
ˈnatē

TROUBLE IN BIOLOGY CLASS

Jacob was a good student overall, but he was often **deficient** in science skills. Because of this, he spent an **inordinate** amount of time reviewing notes and rereading his textbook for botany class. Sometimes he would even spend the majority of a weekend practically **fettered** to his desk so that he could absorb the content of his coursework. Now, with an intricate test on **flora** classification on the horizon, Jacob is more worried than ever. He knows that, even if he studies voraciously, gets a good night sleep, and wears **natty** clothes to his exam, he may still not succeed. But with a little fortitude and inspiration, he should have some success in botany.

Definitions: Try matching the word in the box with the appropriate definition. If you are stuck, check the glossary in the back of the book or the passage at the top of the page.

1. deficient _____ a. smart and fashionable (usually of a person or of clothing)
2. fetter _____ b. unusually or disproportionally large; excessive
3. inordinate _____ c. the plants of a particular region, habitat, or geological period
4. flora _____ d. to restrain with chains or manacles (literally or metaphorically)
5. natty _____ e. lacking in a specified ingredient, ability, or quality

Sentences: Try to use the words above in a sentence below. Remember that a word ending may be changed or its figure of speech slightly altered.

6. Despite being brothers, the _____ gap between Mark and Larry's intellectual abilities is remarkable.
7. Nothing could _____ Tran's insatiable thirst for money.
8. It is shocking how, although Bali and Lombok are only about 35 kilometers apart, their _____ differs significantly.
9. Students who are not educated in quality schools are often _____ in their verbal and mathematics skills.
10. All of the ladies in the retirement home fawned over Jason's _____ appearance and charming personality.

Lesson 216

CONTENTIOUS CARTOONIST

Just this past year a new cartoonist has had a strip appear in the local newspaper. The cartoons, which feature an **anthropomorphized** cat, have caused quite a stir. Initially, elderly people became **incensed** when the cartoon cat stated derogatory things about old people. More recently, handicapped citizens have adopted a **surly** attitude toward the cartoonist after the fictitious cat mocked people with dyslexia and agoraphobia. At the rate things are going, this cartoon cat may cause a major **upheaval** at the local newspaper office. I am unclear as to why the local press has not ceased printing the cartoon, especially since its editors **profess** to be egalitarian and humane people.

NEW WORDS

upheaval
ˌəpˈhēvəl

anthropomorphize
ˌanTHrəpəˈmôrˌfīz

incensed
inˈsenst

surly
ˈsərlē

profess
prəˈfes, prō-

Definitions: Try matching the word in the box with the appropriate definition. If you are stuck, check the glossary in the back of the book or the passage at the top of the page.

1. upheaval _____ a. a violent or sudden disruption to something
2. anthropomorphize _____ b. to attribute human characteristics to the behavior of an animal, object, or god
3. incensed _____ c. very angry; enraged
4. surly _____ d. bad-tempered and unfriendly
5. profess _____ e. to claim openly (and often falsely) that one possesses a certain feeling or quality

Sentences: Try to use the words above in a sentence below. Remember that a word ending may be changed or its figure of speech slightly altered.

6. Unlike Silas, who has a pleasant disposition, Louisa is often quite _____.

7. Kwame was _____ when he heard that his brother had stolen his favorite pair of shoes and sold them for extra spending money on spring break.

8. It is easy to _____ to be an altruistic person; it is much harder to actually be so in real life.

9. Artists almost always _____ cartoon characters: usually such creatures wear human clothes, stand upright, and/or speak human languages.

10. Because of the recent _____ in the Middle East, travelers are being urged to avoid taking leisure trips in that region.

Lesson 217

NEW WORDS

waft
wäft, waft

authenticate
ô'THenti͵kāt

grotesque
grō'tesk

multifarious
͵məlt(ə)'fe(ə)rēəs

incision
in'siZHən

PLASTIC SURGERY DILEMMA

Generally speaking, Kylie was a pretty girl with **multifarious** likeable traits, yet there was one physical handicap that served as a hindrance: she had a gigantic, bulbous nose. People openly mocked this **grotesque** facial feature, thus causing Kylie to feel insecure about her appearance. As a result, she decided to undergo rhinoplasty. For weeks she tried to **authenticate** the credentials of the best surgeons in town before finally going under the knife. With skill and care, the town's best surgeon made an **incision** near Kylie's nose and began work. Kylie looks very different now, and I can enjoy watching her drink hot cocoa as the steam from her piping hot drink **wafts** out of its cup across her face. Not everyone with a big nose need remain ugly forever!

Definitions: Try matching the word in the box with the appropriate definition. If you are stuck, check the glossary in the back of the book or the passage at the top of the page.

1. waft _____ a. many and of various different types
2. authenticate _____ b. comically or repulsively ugly; incongruous to a shocking degree
3. grotesque _____ c. a surgical cut made into the skin or flesh
4. multifarious _____ d. to prove or show something to be genuine
5. incision _____ e. to pass or cause gently to pass through the air

Sentences: Try to use the words above in a sentence below. Remember that a word ending may be changed or its figure of speech slightly altered.

6. It is often an elaborate task to _____ a copy of a rare antique book.
7. The doctor made a(n) _____ into the patient's chest at the beginning of the surgery.
8. Most colleges are _____ institutions: they have many different parts and aspects to them.
9. On a clear day, I can see steam out of factory chimneys _____ through the air.
10. In recent decades, income disparity in the United States has become _____: the rich now have so much while the poor have so little.

306

Lesson 218

THE TOUCHING NOVELLA

When my friend was in college, he wrote an autobiographical novella about a romantic endeavor that he had. The work tells the story of a man who met a woman in a café, and, after **numerous** exchanges, asked her out on a date. But the two were opposites in their lifestyles: he led a **Spartan** existence while she bathed in opulence. Initially they got along well, but gradually the **reciprocity** between them broke down and their relationship ended. In order to savor the moment, my friend wrote a beautiful **vignette** about the experience, for if he could not have the girl he could at least have a beautiful piece of writing to encapsulate his experience. And to prevent being ridiculed or scrutinized, he penned the work under a **pseudonym**.

NEW WORDS

reciprocity
ˌresəˈpräsətē

pseudonym
ˈsoodn-im

Spartan
ˈspɑːt(ə)n

vignette
vinˈyet

numerous
ˈn(y)oom(ə)rəs

Definitions: Try matching the word in the box with the appropriate definition. If you are stuck, check the glossary in the back of the book or the passage at the top of the page.

1. reciprocity _____ a. characterized by austerity or lack of comfort or luxury
2. pseudonym _____ b. many; abundant; great in number
3. Spartan _____ c. a fictitious name, often used by authors
4. vignette _____ d. the process of exchanging with others for mutual benefit
5. numerous _____ e. a brief, evocative account or description

Sentences: Try to use the words above in a sentence below. Remember that a word ending may be changed or its figure of speech slightly altered.

6. Bethany's short story was a beautiful _____ that served as a window into her thoughts, feelings, and soul.
7. Buddhist monks usually live a(n) _____ lifestyle: they exist in a(n) world largely devoid of material goods and luxuries.
8. Because the novelist did not want her identity revealed to the public, she created a(n) _____ under which she published her romance books.
9. One cannot have a healthy relationship without _____: if people do not share, they cannot grow.
10. To my knowledge, there are _____ activities to do on a first date; the possibilities seem endless!

Lesson 219

SHERIFF MATT

NEW WORDS

asphyxiate
asˈfiksēˌāt

catapult
ˈkatəˌpəlt, -ˌpoolt

compelled
kəmˈpel

detritus
diˈtrītəs

predominant
priˈdämənənt

Compelled by a persistent sense of enforcing justice, Matt decided to become a sheriff. Law enforcement in the small town of Midland was often a mundane task, especially since the **predominant** types of crime in down were misdemeanors and small infractions. But when someone in town **asphyxiated** a six-year-old girl, Matt knew that an important crime needed to be solved. Sifting through the **detritus** and other evidence from the crime scene, Matt eventually surmised that the murderer was a fugitive criminal. When Matt got his colleagues to apprehend the killer and bring him to justice, he **catapulted** from obscurity to fame.

Definitions: Try matching the word in the box with the appropriate definition. If you are stuck, check the glossary in the back of the book or the passage at the top of the page.

1. asphyxiate _____ a. present as the main or most salient element
2. catapult _____ b. waste or debris of any kind
3. compelled _____ c. to kill someone by depriving them of air
4. detritus _____ d. to feel forced or obliged to do something
5. predominant _____ e. (n.) a device that allows one to launch someone or something in a direction; (v.) to launch someone or something in a direction

Sentences: Try to use the words above in a sentence below. Remember that a word ending may be changed or its figure of speech slightly altered.

6. Kelsey felt _____ to take Alistair to dinner after she heard that he had been eating alone for two weeks.
7. Even though I like the buildings on campus, the _____ reason that I am attending this university is because of its stellar professors.
8. The once clean town now is crumbling and its streets are filled with _____ from crumbling infrastructure and waste.
9. After solving an outstanding problem in the field of mathematics, the unknown professor was _____ to fame.
10. The murderer placed a garbage bag over his victim in an attempt to _____ him, thus ending his life.

Lesson 220

A FICTITIOUS COLONIAL AMERICAN BIOGRAPHY

One could surmise that John Smith led the life of a typical American colonist. In the early seventeenth century, he began the **emigration** process of leaving England and sailing across the Atlantic Ocean to come to America. He arrived on with a contract of **indenture**, which bound him to a cobbler for seven years to train him in the art of shoemaking. But after four years of hard work, John could no longer **brook** his supervisor's guidance, as his mentor was not skilled at his job. Worried that he was being trained by an **imbecile**, John violated his contract and sought employment elsewhere. But most of John's fellow colonists found his personality **grating** and difficult, so John never amounted to anything in his environment.

NEW WORDS

indenture
inˈdenCHər

emigration
ˌemiˈgrāSHən

imbecile
ˈimbəsəl, -ˌsil

brook
brook

grating
ˈgrātiNG

Definitions: Try matching the word in the box with the appropriate definition. If you are stuck, check the glossary in the back of the book or the passage at the top of the page.

1. indenture _____ a. a formal legal agreement, contract, or document, often tying an apprentice to a master for a fixed term
2. emigration _____ b. a stupid person
3. imbecile _____ c. (n.) a small stream; (v.) to tolerate or allow
4. brook _____ d. sounding harsh and unpleasant; annoying
5. grating _____ e. the process of leaving one's country to settle elsewhere

Sentences: Try to use the words above in a sentence below. Remember that a word ending may be changed or its figure of speech slightly altered.

6. During the latter decades of the nineteenth century there was mass _____ from Eastern Europe to the United States.
7. Despite Marylou's high tolerance, it was difficult for her to _____ Kyle's manic, suicidal behavior in her class.
8. Only a(n) _____ would hand out his or her life savings freely to strangers.
9. Often doctoral students feel like they are living a life of _____ because they serve for years under a thesis adviser before becoming professors.
10. It is hard to study with such _____ noise coming from the machines outside running incessantly.

Word Search

Lessons 1 - - 10

```
M D E L L E P M O C G X R Y R
S E R U T N E D N I E K T B S
O W R N U Q I P N R P I Z U L
C M L B L P T N I U C Z O N T
O Q M G P L H U C O O I L L G
R A Y E T N Q E R E R P U T B
C M R Q M N O P A A N P X K P
I Y I B I I I F V A S B E N
M N N T I C G I T T A F E P Q
A O C A E T T R A A E L L D Y
W D I R D L R C A T C A K T Y
K U S D U V V A T T C O T M J
I E I M W Q E E T E I A V D Y
S S O Y V Y R N B O N O G K W
H P N M Q R J O T M R T N V L
```

1. to explain and present a theory or idea systematically and in detail
2. sentimental in a feeble or discomforting way
3. to ask information from someone
4. a strong feeling of suitability for a career or occupation; a person's employment or job
5. a harmless pill prescribed for psychological benefit rather than for physiological effect
6. a community, situation, or place regarded as encapsulating key qualities of something larger
7. the arrival of a notable thing, person, or event
8. an independent person or body appointed to settle a dispute
9. to restrain with chains or manacles (literally or metaphorically)
10. smart and fashionable (usually of a person or of clothing)
11. a violent or sudden disruption to something
12. very angry; enraged
13. many and of various different types
14. a surgical cut made into the skin or flesh
15. the process of exchanging with others for mutual benefit
16. a fictitious name, often used by authors
17. (n.) a device that allows one to launch someone or something in a direction; (v.) to launch someone or something in a direction
18. to feel forced or obliged to do something
19. a formal legal agreement, contract, or document, often tying an apprentice to a master for a fixed term
20. the process of leaving one's country to settle elsewhere

Vocabulary Review
Lessons 211-220

Directions: Match each word with its best approximate definition. Note that definitions are not necessarily repeated verbatim from the lesson exercises.

1. devour _____
2. aural _____
3. masterful _____
4. craving _____
5. simulate _____
6. gaffe _____
7. veteran _____
8. persona _____
9. deficient _____
10. flora _____
11. surly _____
12. profess _____
13. waft _____
14. grotesque _____
15. Spartan _____
16. vignette _____
17. asphyxiate _____
18. detritus _____
19. imbecile _____
20. brook _____

a. a stupid person
b. characterized by austerity; sparing in comfort or luxury
c. ill-tempered and unfriendly
d. a brief, evocative account of something; a small illustration or portrait photo that fades into the background without an explicit border
e. lacking in a quality, skill, or ingredient
f. a person with much experience in a particular field; a person who has served in the military
g. to tolerate or allow something
h. powerful enough to control others; done very skillfully
i. to kill someone by suffocation or depriving them of air
j. to imitate the character or appearance of something
k. comically or repulsively ugly; inappropriate to a shocking degree
l. waste or debris
m. a powerful or insatiable desire for something
n. to pass gently or easily through the air
o. relating to the ear or a sense of hearing
p. to eat ravenously and quickly
q. an unintentional remark or act that causes embarrassment to its originator
r. to claim openly and often untruthfully that one has a certain feeling or quality
s. the plants of a particular region, habitat, or period
t. an aspect of someone's character that is perceived or presented to ve others

Idiomatic Expressions III

This list is a culmination of common idiomatic expressions. It is the final unit in a three-part sequence. Note that these three units are hardly exhaustive of English language idioms.

Idiomatic Expression	Meaning/Example
to know the ropes	To understand the details of a situation or task. Even though it was Vy's first day at Central High, she knew the ropes of how to teach chemistry because she earned a chemistry degree and had taught it before at five schools.
to save face	To avoid humiliation or embarrassment in an attempt to save dignity When Trang was accused of not paying her employees, she quietly paid them but said nothing to them in order to save face.
to strike while the iron is hot	Seize an opportunity while you have the chance. Kendra, whose research on black holes was fascinating, struck while the iron was hot and applied to Harvard when she heard that the astronomy department was seeking a researcher who had expertise in black holes.

Pyrrhic victory	A victory for someone, but at significant and often detrimental personal cost. Shirley succeeded at getting the management fired at her company, but it was a Pyrrhic victory because she hurt her reputation and lost her job in doing so.
ball is in someone's court	The decision to act is that of the person whose court the ball is in After Uyen told Antonio that she did not want to date him, he told her that the ball was in her court to articulate whether she wanted a friendship with him as a result.
to tilt at windmills	To fight against imaginary enemies or to fight a battle that cannot be won When Ellen said that she was on the quest to develop a medicine that would allow humans to live to be 10000 years old, her friends told her that her quest for immortality was tilting at windmills.
to go out on a limb	To state an opinion or defend a perspective that is very different from other people's All of the professors except Mario thought the student was an idiot, but Mario went out on a limb and defended the student's intelligence.
to put the cart before the horse	To have things in the wrong order; to have things confused or mixed up. Dante put the cart before the horse when he bought movie tickets for his date with Diana before asking her out.

bitter pill to swallow	An unpleasant fact that has to be accepted It was a bitter pill for Micah to swallow that her cat died in the earthquake and would never again comfort her with its endearing purr.
devil's advocate	To deliberately argue against a position in order to assess the validity of an argument Even though I supported Vu marrying his girlfriend, I played devil's advocate and presented all of the reasons why he might not want to get married to see if a wedding was indeed a good choice for him.
to take/grab the bull by the horns	To take control of a situation and be proactive about it Both Jake and Eric dreamed of being movie stars, but Eric was successful because he grabbed the bull by the horns at every opportunity he could to advance his career.
to have an axe to grind	To have a strong opinion about something and to convince other people that your opinion is correct Sheryl had an axe to grind with the local ice cream store: she told all of its employees that they were rude and that their food was awful; then she attempted to convince all of her friends to boycott the store and its products.
to have cold feet	To have anxiety or reservations about something Even though Stephen was madly in love with Bethany, he had cold feet and cancelled their wedding the day before the actual event.

to feel (a bit) under the weather	**To feel a bit sick** Mary felt a bit under the weather so she decided not to go to school.
to take the wind out of one's sails	**To deflate one's ego** Sam took the wind out of Corli's sails when he showed her that, contrary to her expectation, she was not the best swimmer on the team.
to upset the apple cart	**To ruin carefully laid plans** When Justin revealed that Mario was secretly planning to quit his job, he upset the apple cart for Mario, who wanted nobody to know of his plans.
a cold shower	A surprisingly chilly or unpleasantly shocking reception or reaction. Huy had a cold shower when he received his exam results: after months of studying, his score was uncomfortably low.
to make ends meet	To manage so that one's finances are enough for survival. Timothy worked three jobs just to make ends meet so that he could support his family.
to miss the boat	**To have made an error or been wrong** Peter missed the boat on his algebra test; he made the same mistakes over and over again on each exam question.
to take under one's wing	**To protect and mentor somebody** Jay took the talented student under his wing and trained him to become an excellent writer.

ANSWER KEY

Lesson 1

1. c
2. d
3. a
4. e
5. b
6. pragmatic
7. prosaic
8. altruistic
9. astute
10. Indignant

Lesson 2

1. b
2. d
3. e
4. c
5. a
6. cryptic
7. reminiscence
8. extravagant
9. curative
10. autonomy

Lesson 3

1. c
2. e
3. a
4. b
5. d
6. clandestine
7. squandered
8. appease
9. paramount
10. fastidious

Lesson 4

1. e
2. c
3. b
4. a
5. d
6. excavated
7. ingenuous
8. migrate
9. philanthropic
10. demography

Lesson 5

1. c
2. a
3. e
4. b
5. d
6. recanted
7. tyranny
8. soporific
9. garrulous
10. indicted

Lesson 6

1. d
2. a
3. b
4. e
5. c
6. lamented
7. ambivalent
8. bolster
9. articulate
10. provocative

Lesson 7

1. c
2. e
3. d
4. a
5. b
6. facetious
7. retract
8. derided
9. decried
10. bane

Lesson 8

1. c
2. e
3. a
4. b
5. d
6. pedantic
7. fervent
8. subdue
9. commiserate
10. apportion

Lesson 9

1. b
2. c
3. a
4. e
5. d
6. exemplify
7. innocuous
8. denounce
9. pilfer
10. miser

Lesson 10

1. d
2. c
3. b
4. e
5. a
6. stagnant

7. underscore
8. rectitude
9. resigned
10. inane

Crossword Puzzle: Lessons 1-10

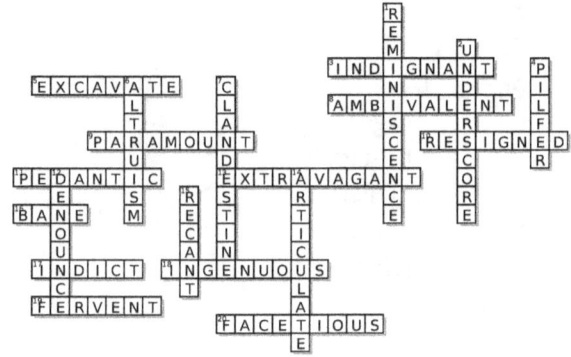

Review: Lessons 1-10

1. p
2. n
3. q
4. b
5. j
6. a
7. d
8. l
9. m
10. r
11. g
12. s
13. i
14. c
15. o
16. k
17. t
18. e
19. h
20. f

Lesson 11

21. e
22. b
23. d
24. a
25. c
26. replicate
27. nostalgia
28. bombast
29. austere
30. paradox

Lesson 12

1. a
2. b
3. d
4. c
5. e
6. scorn
7. deference
8. imperious
9. beguile
10. dilettante

Lesson 13

1. c
2. b
3. a
4. e
5. d
6. comprehensive
7. forbear
8. apprehensive
9. pedestrian
10. subjective

Lesson 14

1. e
2. a
3. c
4. d
5. b
6. pivotal
7. misnomer
8. dexterous
9. expedient
10. insolent

Lesson 15

1. b
2. c
3. a
4. e
5. d
6. immune
7. respite
8. stipulated
9. redolent
10. unequivocally

Lesson 16

1. e
2. c
3. a
4. b
5. d
6. anecdote
7. callous
8. resilient
9. aesthetic
10. conciliate

Lesson 17

1. b
2. e
3. d
4. c
5. a
6. serendipity
7. castigated
8. impetuously
9. diminutive
10. belied

Lesson 18

1. a
2. d
3. b
4. c
5. e
6. compunction
7. penetrate
8. apt
9. substantiate
10. forgo/forego

Lesson 19

1. e
2. a
3. b
4. d
5. c
6. instill
7. plastic
8. dilatory
9. fabricated
10. mitigate

Lesson 20

1. b
2. e
3. c
4. d
5. a
6. strenuous
7. hubris
8. unprecedented
9. refuted
10. reluctant

Word Search: Lessons 11–20

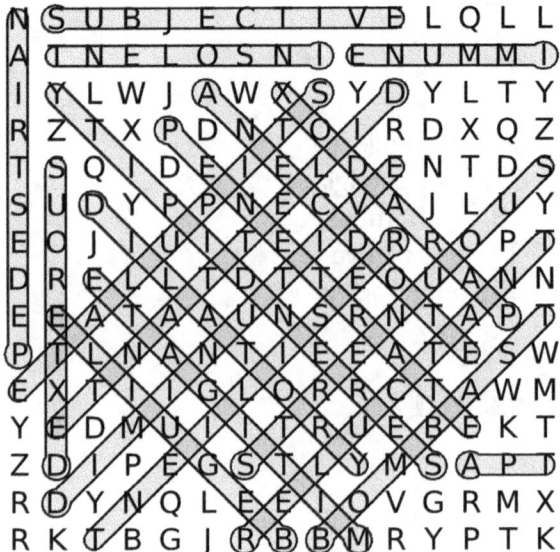

Review: Lessons 11–20

1. a
2. d
3. c
4. q
5. p
6. r
7. e
8. o
9. b
10. h
11. k
12. i
13. f
14. j
15. n
16. t
17. m
18. g
19. l
20. s

Lesson 21

1. b
2. a

3. e
4. d
5. c
6. rhetoric
7. condemned
8. conventional
9. reticent
10. circumspect

Lesson 22

1. c
2. e
3. a
4. b
5. d
6. defunct
7. serene
8. incongruent
9. belligerent
10. dismay

Lesson 23

1. e
2. c
3. d
4. a
5. b
6. arcane
7. conceal
8. perfunctorily
9. frivolous
10. suppress

Lesson 24

1. d
2. e
3. a
4. b
5. c
6. mollify
7. interloper
8. diplomatic
9. platitudes
10. fertile

Lesson 25

1. a
2. e
3. d
4. b
5. c
6. strident
7. unstinting
8. quarantined
9. regressive
10. harbinger

Lesson 26

1. c
2. a
3. e
4. b
5. d
6. conjectured
7. diffident
8. connoisseur
9. cynical
10. robust

Lesson 27

1. b
2. c
3. a
4. e
5. d
6. docile
7. detached
8. benevolent
9. steadfast
10. inscrutable

Lesson 28

1. c
2. d
3. e
4. a
5. b

6. artifice
7. synthesize
8. pioneer
9. futile
10. concord

Lesson 29

1. e
2. d
3. f
4. a
5. b
6. c
7. momentous
8. intrepid
9. discrete
10. finesse
11. discreet
12. poignant

Lesson 30

1. d
2. e
3. a
4. c
5. b
6. unswerving
7. succinct
8. fortuitous
9. reinforce
10. protégé

Crossword Puzzle: Lessons 21-30

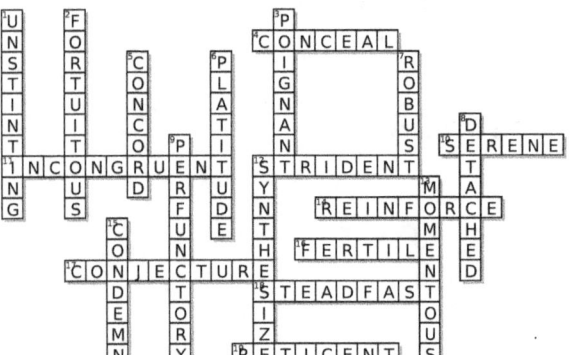

Review: Lessons 21-30

1. b
2. i
3. s
4. m
5. t
6. c
7. p
8. f
9. e
10. q
11. r
12. o
13. d
14. a
15. g
16. h
17. n
18. l
19. k
20. j

Lesson 31

1. d
2. e
3. a
4. b
5. c
6. dubious
7. deliberate
8. consensus
9. skeptical
10. eccentric

Lesson 32

1. d
2. a
3. b
4. e
5. c
6. supplanted
7. duplicitous

8. lauded
9. didactic
10. brooding

Lesson 33

1. b
2. c
3. e
4. a
5. d
6. aspiration
7. hackneyed
8. placid
9. condoned
10. tenuous

Lesson 34

1. b
2. c
3. e
4. a
5. d
6. disseminated
7. myopically
8. flagged
9. precocious
10. ironic

Lesson 35

1. c
2. e
3. d
4. b
5. a
6. reiterate
7. fathomed
8. sullen
9. vacuous
10. primitive

Lesson 36

1. b
2. d
3. a
4. e
5. c
6. inevitable
7. disparaged
8. enigma
9. superfluous
10. dearth

Lesson 37

1. b
2. a
3. d
4. e
5. c
6. eclectic
7. cajoled
8. lucid
9. vexed
10. disingenuous

Lesson 38

1. b
2. d
3. a
4. e
5. c
6. infatuated
7. contemptible
8. prodigy
9. verbose
10. augmented

Lesson 39

1. e
2. a
3. b
4. c
5. d
6. flamboyant
7. downplaying
8. judicious

9. predisposed
10. nuance

Lesson 40

1. b
2. d
3. a
4. e
5. c
6. reprehensible
7. vapid
8. surreptitious
9. extrapolate
10. perplexed

Word Search: Lessons 31-40

Review: Lessons 31-40

1. c
2. m
3. i
4. s
5. k
6. a
7. t
8. l

9. p
10. n
11. g
12. r
13. e
14. f
15. q
16. b
17. h
18. d
19. o
20. j

Lesson 41

1. b
2. a
3. d
4. e
5. c
6. partisan
7. flippant
8. melancholy
9. abstruse
10. disdain

Lesson 42

1. c
2. a
3. d
4. e
5. b
6. mendacity
7. vindicated
8. egotism
9. censured
10. divisive

Lesson 43

1. b
2. a
3. d
4. e
5. c

6. lackluster
7. vindictive
8. prohibitive
9. corruption
10. auspicious

Lesson 44

1. c
2. e
3. a
4. b
5. d
6. ecstasy
7. juxtaposition
8. foster
9. obfuscate
10. pristine

Lesson 45

1. b
2. d
3. a
4. c
5. e
6. tactful
7. vehement
8. onerous
9. euphemisms
10. resurgence

Lesson 46

1. d
2. c
3. b
4. a
5. e
6. meticulously
7. indulgent
8. candid
9. elite
10. apologetic

Lesson 47

1. d
2. e
3. a
4. b
5. c
6. nebulous
7. eloquent
8. effusive
9. vulnerabilities
10. charisma

Lesson 48

1. b
2. a
3. d
4. c
5. e
6. lucrative
7. voracious
8. prudent
9. credulity
10. aversion

Lesson 49

1. a
2. c
3. b
4. e
5. d
6. iconoclastic
7. edifying
8. laconic
9. prodigious
10. obsequious

Lesson 50

1. b
2. d
3. a
4. e
5. c

6. resuscitating
7. veracity
8. entrepreneur
9. tangential
10. nomad

3. b
4. a
5. c
6. convoluted
7. intricate
8. assuage
9. mundane
10. erudite

Crossword Puzzle: Lessons 41-50

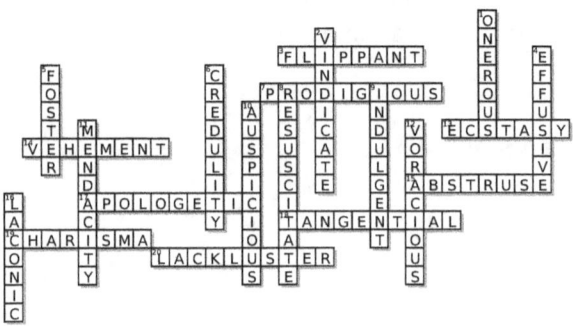

Lesson 52

1. b
2. a
3. d
4. c
5. e
6. elude
7. opulent
8. wistful
9. chicanery
10. endure

Review: Lessons 41-50

1. n
2. t
3. f
4. p
5. a
6. i
7. k
8. c
9. r
10. e
11. b
12. s
13. o
14. q
15. l
16. j
17. d
18. h
19. m
20. g

Lesson 53

1. e
2. d
3. c
4. a
5. b
6. mediocre
7. rebut
8. whimsical
9. awe
10. cunning

Lesson 54

1. a
2. e
3. c
4. d
5. b
6. emboldened
7. illusory
8. languid
9. ostensible
10. profound

Lesson 51

1. d
2. e

Lesson 55

1. d
2. a
3. e
4. b
5. c
6. taunting
7. negligent
8. versatile
9. retaliated
10. entrenched

Lesson 56

1. e
2. a
3. d
4. b
5. c
6. embellished
7. naïve
8. invoked
9. evoke
10. banal

Lesson 57

1. d
2. e
3. b
4. a
5. c
6. ornate
7. chronicles
8. adept
9. ephemeral
10. empirical

Lesson 58

1. b
2. c
3. a
4. d
5. e
6. mercurial
7. acclaimed
8. repudiate
9. daunting
10. backlash

Lesson 59

1. b
2. d
3. c
4. a
5. e
6. lavish
7. immersed
8. outmoded
9. progenitor
10. eminent

Lesson 60

1. e
2. c
3. a
4. d
5. b
6. enmity
7. revelation
8. momentum
9. tentative
10. volatile

**Word Search:
Lessons 51-60**

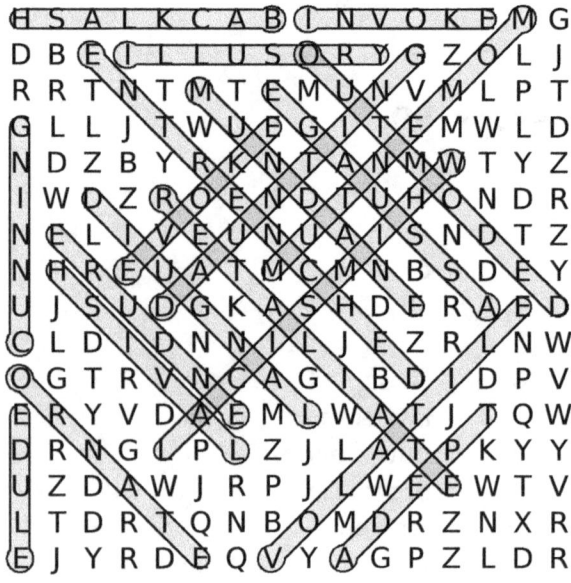

Review: Lessons 51-60

1. n
2. j
3. e
4. k
5. s
6. a
7. o
8. q
9. r
10. l
11. c
12. g
13. b
14. t
15. d
16. i
17. p
18. m
19. h
20. f

Lesson 61

1. e
2. a
3. b
4. d
5. c
6. quandary
7. excerpt
8. nonchalantly
9. proximity
10. loquacious

Lesson 62

1. a
2. c
3. b
4. d
5. e
6. circumscribed
7. equanimity
8. ostentatiously
9. encumbered
10. adroit

Lesson 63

1. d
2. a
3. b
4. e
5. c
6. minuscule/miniscule
7. debunked
8. acronym
9. bereaved
10. resolute

Lesson 64

1. e
2. a
3. d
4. b
5. c
6. entangle
7. paragon
8. prospectus
9. immutable
10. lethargic

Lesson 65

1. a
2. c
3. e
4. b
5. d
6. emphatically
7. ludicrous
8. salvage
9. timorous
10. weary

Lesson 66

1. e
2. a
3. d
4. c
5. b
6. ambiguity
7. magnanimity
8. reverent
9. cathartic
10. frank

Lesson 67

1. b
2. a
3. e
4. c
5. d
6. amiable
7. endorsed
8. eradicated
9. commemorate
10. parody

Lesson 68

1. b
2. a
3. e
4. c
5. d
6. revitalize
7. notorious
8. decorum
9. brevity
10. alleviate

Lesson 69

1. e
2. a
3. b
4. c
5. d
6. envious
7. patronizing
8. impediment
9. qualified
10. libel

Lesson 70

1. a
2. e
3. b
4. c
5. d
6. loner
7. divulged
8. scrupulous
9. abated
10. tractable

Crossword Puzzle: Lessons 61-70

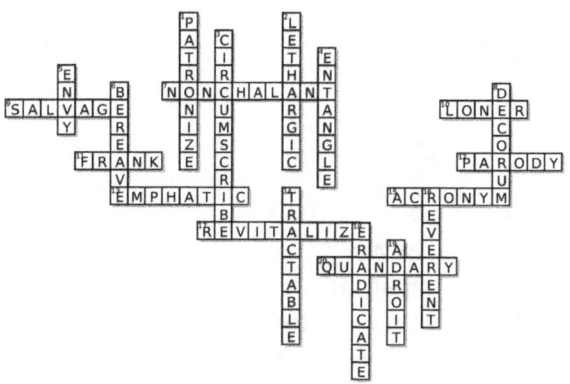

Review: Lessons 61-70

1. d
2. g
3. h
4. s
5. a
6. b
7. o
8. k
9. p
10. c
11. m
12. q
13. l
14. e
15. i
16. j
17. f
18. n
19. t
20. r

Lesson 71

1. c
2. a
3. e
4. d
5. b
6. jocular
7. benign
8. spontaneous
9. manipulate
10. cohesive

Lesson 72

1. c
2. d
3. e
4. a
5. b
6. esoteric
7. apathetic
8. enumerated
9. complacent
10. pretension

Lesson 73

1. e
2. a
3. d
4. c
5. b
6. aloof
7. objective
8. defied
9. bungler
10. romanticized

Lesson 74

1. b
2. a
3. e
4. d
5. c
6. quarrel
7. epitome
8. litigious
9. paucity
10. imperative

Lesson 75

1. a
2. e
3. c
4. b
5. d
6. dispersed
7. aberrant
8. trenchant
9. jeopardized
10. scrutinize

Lesson 76

1. b
2. e
3. a
4. c
5. d

6. condescending
7. monotony
8. tenacious
9. bewildered
10. maverick

Lesson 77

1. d
2. c
3. a
4. b
5. e
6. infringe
7. prominent
8. concurred
9. evade
10. equivocal

Lesson 78

1. e
2. d
3. c
4. b
5. a
6. dehydrated
7. sardonic
8. cantankerous
9. amalgam
10. oblivion

Lesson 79

1. d
2. c
3. e
4. a
5. b
6. erratic
7. luminous
8. permeated
9. quell
10. impugn

Lesson 80

1. d
2. b
3. a
4. c
5. e
6. seclusion
7. introspection
8. abridged
9. trivial
10. disgruntled

Word Search: Lessons 71-80

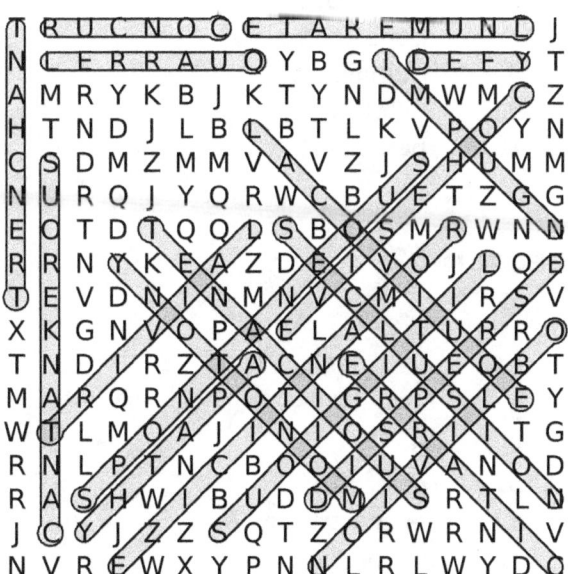

Review: Lessons 71-80

1. q
2. d
3. i
4. n
5. t
6. l
7. b
8. r
9. j
10. o
11. f
12. s

13. h
14. c
15. m
16. a
17. e
18. g
19. p
20. k

Lesson 81

1. d
2. e
3. a
4. c
5. b
6. capricious
7. conscientiously
8. munificent
9. ubiquitous
10. penchant

Lesson 82

1. c
2. e
3. a
4. b
5. d
6. exacerbating
7. reconcile
8. arbitrary
9. exonerated
10. conviction

Lesson 83

1. e
2. a
3. c
4. b
5. d
6. censor
7. dejected
8. smug
9. anecdotal
10. obscure

Lesson 84

1. b
2. d
3. e
4. c
5. a
6. quiescent
7. malice
8. indulges
9. eschewed
10. perspicacious

Lesson 85

1. a
2. d
3. c
4. b
5. e
6. shrewd
7. cacophony
8. inundated
9. diatribe
10. abstemious

Lesson 86

1. c
2. b
3. e
4. a
5. d
6. plausible
7. contentious
8. uniform
9. superficial
10. erroneous

Lesson 87

1. a
2. d
3. c
4. e

5. b
6. exotic
7. ascertain
8. convivial
9. redundant
10. exasperated

Lesson 88

1. e
2. b
3. c
4. a
5. d
6. obsolete
7. chronic
8. solemn
9. animosity
10. deluded

Lesson 89

1. e
2. c
3. a
4. b
5. d
6. quizzical
7. mandate
8. estranged
9. pertinent
10. ineffable

Lesson 90

1. c
2. d
3. e
4. b
5. a
6. insolvent
7. truncated
8. allusions
9. mar
10. solicitous

Crossword Puzzle: Lessons 81-90

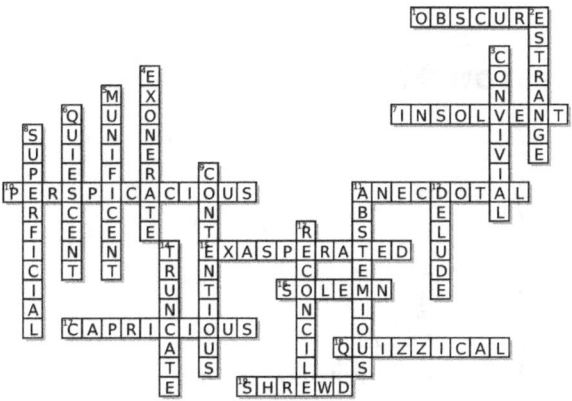

Review: Lessons 81-90

1. j
2. q
3. s
4. b
5. g
6. a
7. d
8. m
9. o
10. t
11. f
12. k
13. h
14. i
15. c
16. r
17. e
18. p
19. l
20. n

Lesson 91

1. c
2. a
3. b
4. e
5. d
6. idiosyncrasies
7. cosmopolitan

332

8. undermines
9. anachronistic
10. prolific

Lesson 92

1. c
2. b
3. e
4. a
5. d
6. extol
7. relinquished, ascetic
8. corroborated
9. expeditions

Lesson 93

1. d
2. e
3. a
4. b
5. c
6. ominous
7. anonymous
8. demeanor
9. circumvent
10. sovereign

Lesson 94

1. d
2. e
3. a
4. c
5. b
6. eulogized
7. rebellious
8. petulant
9. maudlin
10. inept

Lesson 95

1. e
2. a
3. d
4. b
5. c
6. decipher
7. sophistries
8. innate
9. gregarious
10. accentuates

Lesson 96

1. d
2. e
3. c
4. b
5. a
6. somber
7. conspicuous
8. digress
9. empathetic
10. incredulous

Lesson 97

1. d
2. e
3. c
4. b
5. a
6. disillusioned
7. buoyant
8. unorthodox
9. ebullient
10. longevity

Lesson 98

1. c
2. a
3. e
4. b
5. d
6. vast
7. assimilating
8. hostile
9. consummate
10. prescient

Lesson 99

1. b
2. d
3. c
4. a
5. e
6. precursor
7. flagrant
8. divert
9. irreverent
10. novel

Lesson 100

1. b
2. d
3. a
4. c
5. e
6. supercilious
7. vanquish
8. indigenous
9. repent
10. conflagration

Word Search: Lessons 91-100

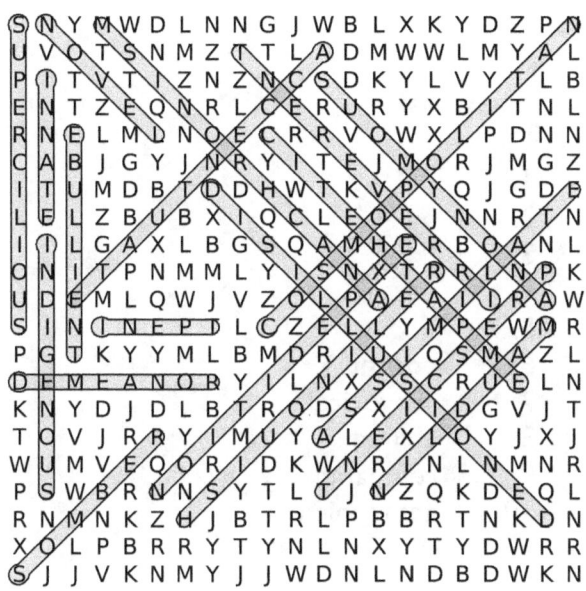

Review: Lessons 91-100

1. o
2. a
3. t
4. m
5. c
6. k
7. f
8. q
9. i
10. g
11. s
12. b
13. l
14. p
15. d
16. n
17. e
18. j
19. h
20. r

Lesson 101

1. d
2. e
3. a
4. c
5. b
6. sagacious
7. vigorously
8. punctilious
9. invulnerable
10. avant-garde

Lesson 102

1. e
2. c
3. a
4. d
5. b
6. officious
7. curtail
8. charlatan
9. unforeseen
10. deprecating

334

Lesson 103

1. a
2. c
3. d
4. e
5. b
6. potentate
7. sublime
8. invigorated
9. demoralized
10. halting

Lesson 104

1. d
2. b
3. c
4. e
5. a
6. bellicose
7. relished
8. fatalistic
9. feigned
10. deter

Lesson 105

1. e
2. c
3. a
4. b
5. d
6. exemplar
7. meditation
8. renowned
9. insinuation
10. misguided

Lesson 106

1. c
2. b
3. d
4. a
5. e
6. sporadic
7. machinations
8. wary
9. snobby/snobbish
10. discern

Lesson 107

1. e
2. c
3. a
4. d
5. b
6. proliferation
7. devoid
8. visionary
9. forestall
10. corridor

Lesson 108

1. d
2. c
3. b
4. a
5. e
6. dormant
7. surmise
8. irascible
9. foreshadowing
10. indigent

Lesson 109

1. e
2. b
3. d
4. c
5. a
6. cogent
7. allegorical
8. chided
9. remnants
10. antagonistic

Lesson 110

1. c
2. e
3. a
4. b
5. d
6. indelible
7. exuded
8. covert
9. precipitously
10. effrontery

Crossword Puzzle: Lessons 101-110

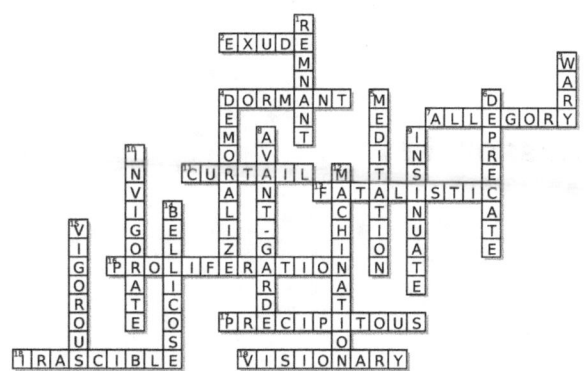

Review: Lessons 101-110

1. f
2. o
3. i
4. l
5. a
6. t
7. q
8. b
9. d
10. r
11. g
12. e
13. s
14. n
15. j
16. m
17. p
18. h
19. k
20. c

Lesson 111

1. e
2. a
3. d
4. c
5. b
6. soothe
7. ire
8. deceitful
9. adolescence
10. tension

Lesson 112

1. a
2. e
3. c
4. b
5. d
6. demise
7. miraculous
8. pensive
9. economical
10. probe

Lesson 113

1. b
2. d
3. a
4. e
5. c
6. predicament
7. improvise
8. predecessor
9. melodic
10. arrests

336

Lesson 114

1. e
2. b
3. d
4. c
5. a
6. salubrious
7. mythical
8. humble
9. vital
10. exposé

Lesson 115

1. d
2. b
3. e
4. c
5. a
6. exclude
7. teeming
8. conundrums
9. preaching
10. insidiously

Lesson 116

1. e
2. c
3. a
4. b
5. d
6. antiquated
7. boon
8. crude
9. egalitarian
10. terminating

Lesson 117

1. c
2. a
3. b
4. e
5. d
6. inhibit
7. conspirator
8. maligning
9. reprimands
10. dispel

Lesson 118

1. d
2. c
3. b
4. e
5. a
6. garnishes
7. methodical
8. polemical
9. nullified
10. revive

Lesson 119

1. a
2. d
3. e
4. b
5. c
6. solitary
7. facile
8. acrimoniously
9. instigated
10. disaffected

Lesson 120

1. c
2. a
3. b
4. e
5. d
6. satire
7. vile
8. quaff
9. obstreperous
10. resplendent

Word Search: Lessons 111-120

Review: Lessons 111-120

1. l
2. a
3. r
4. g
5. i
6. q
7. c
8. o
9. t
10. e
11. b
12. m
13. s
14. p
15. k
16. h
17. d
18. n
19. j
20. f

Lesson 121

1. b
2. a
3. e
4. c
5. d
6. perturbed
7. winnow
8. multifaceted
9. rudimentary
10. elicited

Lesson 122

1. d
2. a
3. b
4. e
5. c
6. waxing
7. desecration
8. inception
9. cloying
10. procrastinating

Lesson 123

1. e
2. a
3. c
4. b
5. d
6. reclusive
7. dithering
8. vicarious
9. dumbfounded
10. pruned

Lesson 124

1. d
2. a
3. e
4. c
5. b
6. delinquent
7. sarcastic
8. viable
9. miscalculation
10. enhance

Lesson 125

1. c
2. a
3. e
4. b
5. d
6. waned
7. expropriated
8. detonating
9. pithy
10. lighthearted

Lesson 126

1. b
2. a
3. d
4. e
5. c
6. menace
7. diverge
8. potable
9. apprise
10. illicit

Lesson 127

1. b
2. e
3. a
4. c
5. d
6. reparations
7. ingenious
8. equivocate
9. foibles
10. venerated

Lesson 128

1. c
2. a
3. b
4. e
5. d
6. demure
7. spur
8. hypocritical
9. unadorned
10. fetid

Lesson 129

1. c
2. b
3. d
4. e
5. a
6. benefactors
7. impoverished
8. reserve
9. proclivity
10. averting

Lesson 130

1. b
2. a
3. d
4. e
5. c
6. ostracized
7. sedulous
8. receptacle
9. malaise
10. mischance

Crossword Puzzle: Lessons 121-130

Review: Lessons 121-130

1. c
2. q
3. s
4. a
5. n
6. j
7. b
8. g
9. h
10. t
11. e
12. f
13. o
14. i
15. k
16. d
17. l
18. p
19. r
20. m

Lesson 131

1. c
2. d
3. e
4. a
5. b
6. stereotyped
7. grandeur
8. expeditiously
9. coddle
10. truce

Lesson 132

1. c
2. e
3. d
4. b
5. a
6. canvas
7. dilemma
8. gargantuan
9. animate
10. lax

Lesson 133

1. b
2. a
3. e
4. c
5. d
6. outdated
7. abstain
8. overt
9. tangent
10. fallacious

Lesson 134

1. b
2. c
3. e
4. d
5. a
6. posthumously
7. stoic
8. acquiesce
9. misanthrope
10. synopsis

Lesson 135

1. b
2. c
3. a
4. e
5. d
6. persevered
7. precipice
8. unanimous
9. conjoined
10. talisman

Lesson 136

1. e
2. c
3. d
4. a
5. b

6. affluent
7. convergence
8. ambition
9. discerning
10. transgression

Lesson 137

1. b
2. d
3. e
4. c
5. a
6. jaded
7. stymied
8. detractor
9. concession
10. formulate

Lesson 138

1. d
2. c
3. e
4. a
5. b
6. summon
7. compilation
8. impressionistic
9. swarthy
10. torpid

Lesson 139

1. b
2. a
3. e
4. c
5. d
6. vivid
7. mandatory
8. despair
9. winced
10. disputation

Lesson 140

1. a
2. c
3. b
4. e
5. d
6. affable
7. haphazardly
8. mustered
9. obdurate
10. recessive

Word Search: Lessons 131-140

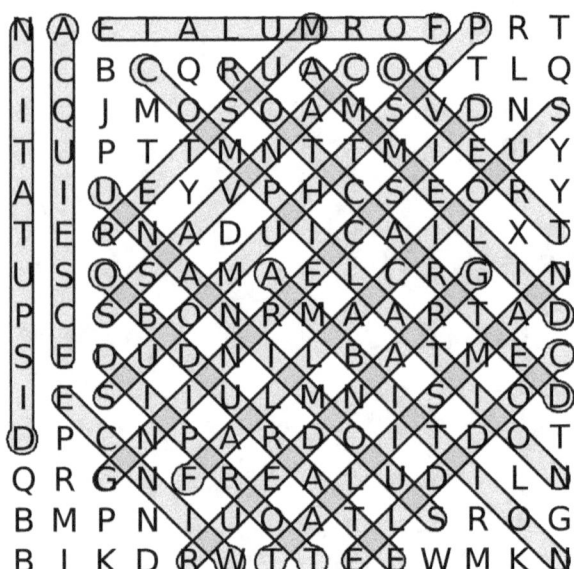

Review: Lessons 131-140

1. j
2. q
3. b
4. o
5. t
6. g
7. i
8. r
9. a
10. d
11. c
12. m

13. k
14. s
15. l
16. n
17. p
18. h
19. f
20. e

Lesson 141

1. c
2. d
3. b
4. e
5. a
6. deluged
7. blare
8. melodramatic
9. panorama
10. rigorous

Lesson 142

1. e
2. c
3. a
4. b
5. d
6. placate
7. scintillating
8. slovenly
9. prophetic
10. conjure

Lesson 143

1. a
2. e
3. b
4. c
5. d
6. preponderance
7. culpable
8. dissipate
9. subversive
10. abject

Lesson 144

1. a
2. c
3. d
4. b
5. e
6. obstinate
7. enrage
8. denotation
9. obtrusively
10. manorial

Lesson 145

1. a
2. c
3. b
4. e
5. d
6. connotation
7. refined
8. espouse
9. penitent
10. knell

Lesson 146

1. c
2. a
3. e
4. b
5. d
6. outspoken
7. contingency
8. presentiment
9. plague
10. disjointed

Lesson 147

1. b
2. a

3. e
4. d
5. c
6. seduce
7. dispassionate
8. temperate
9. remiss
10. brouhaha

Lesson 148

1. b
2. e
3. d
4. a
5. c
6. prophecies
7. grandiloquent
8. catalyst
9. marshal
10. suffrage

Lesson 149

1. a
2. c
3. d
4. e
5. b
6. archipelago
7. rousing
8. anthropological
9. complicity
10. exacting

Lesson 150

1. a
2. c
3. d
4. e
5. b
6. progressive
7. surpasses
8. irksome
9. peevish
10. propitious

Crossword Puzzle: Lessons 141-150

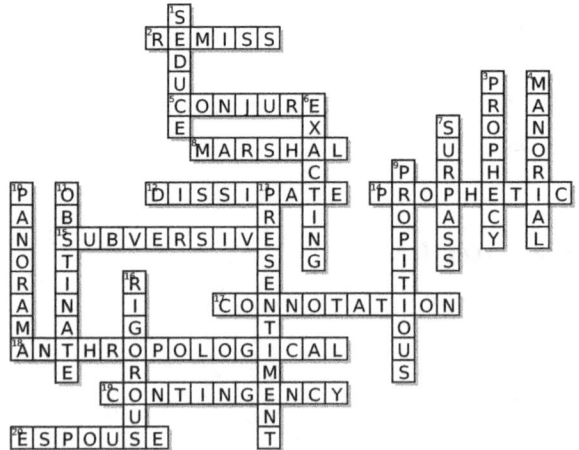

Review: Lessons 141-150

1. j
2. b
3. t
4. q
5. l
6. o
7. d
8. s
9. c
10. g
11. f
12. n
13. a
14. h
15. p
16. m
17. r
18. i
19. k
20. e

Lesson 151

1. b
2. a
3. d
4. e
5. c

6. bemoaning
7. pernicious
8. lackadaisical
9. intrusion
10. pluralism

Lesson 152

1. b
2. a
3. d
4. e
5. c
6. stringent
7. decorous
8. pliable
9. vaccines
10. yen

Lesson 153

1. c
2. e
3. a
4. b
5. d
6. prestigious
7. slipshod
8. immense
9. organic
10. maneuvering

Lesson 154

1. c
2. d
3. a
4. e
5. b
6. laborious
7. hedonistic
8. adhere
9. spate
10. averse

Lesson 155

1. b
2. e
3. a
4. c
5. d
6. tedious
7. succulent
8. unhinged
9. provincial
10. presumptive

Lesson 156

1. b
2. o
3. a
4. c
5. d
6. alienated
7. disparity
8. exempt
9. audacity
10. factions

Lesson 157

1. e
2. b
3. d
4. a
5. c
6. elucidate
7. mediation
8. segregation
9. parched
10. turpitude

Lesson 158

1. b
2. a
3. d
4. e
5. c

6. acoustic
7. escalated
8. impecunious
9. plunged
10. doctrinaire

Lesson 159

1. a
2. d
3. c
4. e
5. b
6. holistic
7. intrinsic
8. perpetual
9. transitory
10. mirth

Lesson 160

1. a
2. e
3. d
4. c
5. b
6. linchpin
7. incidental
8. fouled
9. surmounted
10. commended

Word Search: Lessons 151-160

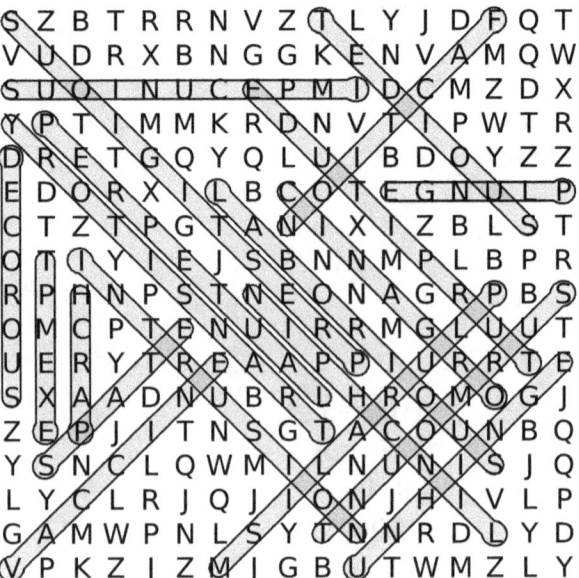

Review: Lessons 151-160

1. k
2. a
3. p
4. b
5. r
6. o
7. f
8. d
9. t
10. n
11. m
12. h
13. g
14. q
15. i
16. c
17. j
18. l
19. e
20. s

Lesson 161

1. c
2. d
3. a
4. e
5. b
6. adamant
7. refract
8. morass
9. auditory
10. righteous

Lesson 162

1. c
2. a
3. e
4. b
5. d
6. heritage
7. dislodge
8. chagrin
9. figurative
10. jingoism

Lesson 163

1. d
2. e
3. a
4. c
5. b
6. rigid
7. predilection
8. palliating
9. tenets
10. stimulated

Lesson 164

1. e
2. d
3. a
4. c
5. b
6. blandish
7. disenchanted
8. noxious
9. despondence
10. appraising

Lesson 165

1. c
2. d
3. a
4. e
5. b
6. vulgar
7. decisive
8. preceded
9. luxury
10. aggrandize

Lesson 166

1. b
2. d
3. a
4. e
5. c
6. mischief
7. amorphous
8. apocalypse
9. zealous
10. invasive

Lesson 167

1. d
2. c
3. a
4. e
5. b
6. cerebral
7. extemporize
8. depleted
9. humane
10. libertine

Lesson 168

1. d
2. c
3. e
4. a
5. b
6. odious
7. domineering
8. obstructions
9. diorama
10. dynamic

Lesson 169

1. e
2. a
3. d
4. c
5. b
6. foresight
7. havoc
8. resignation
9. tacit
10. elongated

Lesson 170

1. d
2. c
3. e
4. a
5. b
6. stark
7. fortified
8. terse
9. dissolute
10. ameliorating

Crossword Puzzle: Lessons 161-170

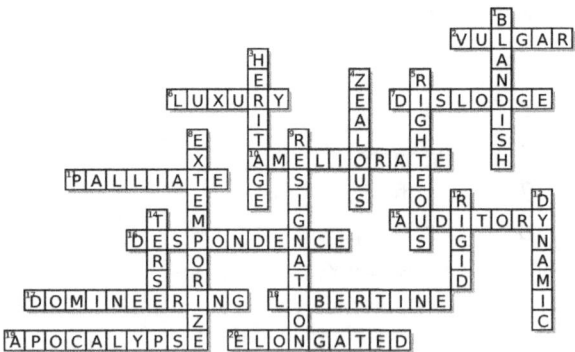

Review: Lessons 161-170

1. e
2. q
3. b
4. t
5. o
6. m
7. a
8. j
9. c
10. n
11. g
12. s
13. d
14. r
15. i
16. l
17. f
18. k
19. h
20. p

Lesson 171

1. c
2. e
3. b
4. a
5. d
6. manifest
7. flourish
8. oracle

9. veiled
10. dismantled

Lesson 172

1. d
2. e
3. b
4. a
5. c
6. anomalous
7. itinerant
8. pugnacious
9. clemency
10. predation

Lesson 173

1. b
2. c
3. d
4. e
5. a
6. brusque
7. intermittent
8. imposter
9. renew
10. aroma

Lesson 174

1. c
2. a
3. e
4. b
5. d
6. voluptuous
7. hovered
8. catastrophe
9. motif
10. congenial

Lesson 175

1. d
2. b
3. a
4. e
5. c
6. delusion
7. debacle
8. autocrat
9. recluse
10. debris

Lesson 176

1. c
2. d
3. a
4. e
5. b
6. incarnation
7. postulated
8. salutary
9. querulous
10. lugubrious

Lesson 177

1. e
2. a
3. d
4. b
5. c
6. euphoria
7. durable
8. antipathy
9. gratuitous
10. perennial

Lesson 178

1. b
2. d
3. a
4. e
5. c

6. misgivings
7. kinetic
8. hampered
9. embodiment
10. hovel

Lesson 179

1. c
2. e
3. a
4. b
5. d
6. sacrilegious
7. exultation
8. unremitting
9. indeterminate
10. flouted

Lesson 180

1. d
2. c
3. b
4. a
5. e
6. synergy
7. stunted
8. consigned
9. interleaved
10. alacrity

Word Search: Lessons 171-180

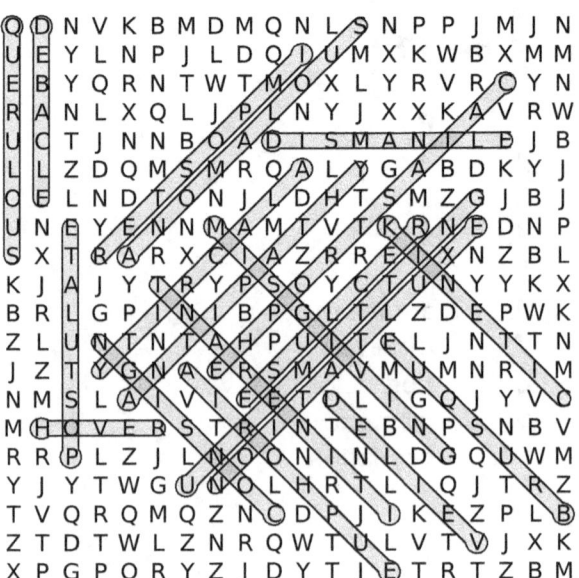

Review: Lessons 171-180

1. e
2. c
3. s
4. a
5. p
6. l
7. m
8. j
9. o
10. t
11. h
12. i
13. r
14. d
15. f
16. q
17. b
18. n
19. g
20. k

Lesson 181

1. c
2. d
3. e
4. b
5. a
6. rancor
7. virtuoso
8. inherent
9. sensationalism
10. precarious

Lesson 182

1. b
2. d
3. e
4. c
5. a
6. remuneration
7. frugal
8. legitimate
9. consternation
10. reproach

Lesson 183

1. b
2. d
3. e
4. a
5. c
6. fraudulent
7. meddle
8. beneficiaries
9. felicity
10. fortitude

Lesson 184

1. c
2. e
3. a
4. b
5. d
6. panacea
7. liberation
8. avuncular
9. thesis
10. exuberant

Lesson 185

1. d
2. e
3. a
4. c
5. b
6. missive
7. unkempt
8. bankruptcy
9. plight
10. aplomb

Lesson 186

1. e
2. d
3. b
4. a
5. c
6. archaic
7. prosperous
8. touted
9. bent
10. derivative

Lesson 187

1. e
2. a
3. b
4. c
5. d
6. purified
7. mediate
8. parameters
9. formulaic
10. savanna

Lesson 188

1. e
2. d
3. b
4. c
5. a
6. feasible
7. deleterious
8. contiguous
9. repealed
10. propensity

Lesson 189

1. c
2. d
3. e
4. b
5. a
6. meager
7. conspire
8. coward
9. somnolent
10. unerring

Lesson 190

1. e
2. d
3. a
4. b
5. c
6. obtuse
7. intuition
8. ersatz
9. nonplussed
10. diligent

Crossword Puzzle: Lessons 181-190

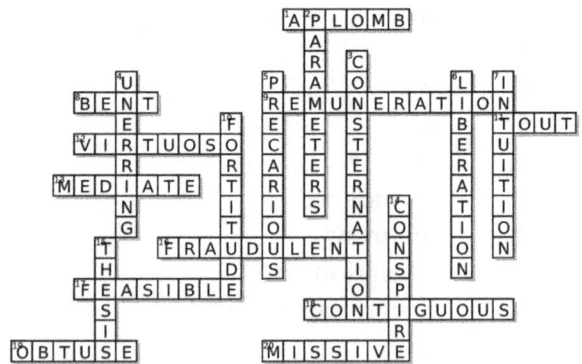

Review: Lessons 181-190

1. a
2. b
3. o
4. c
5. s
6. i
7. g
8. t
9. r
10. m
11. e
12. f
13. k
14. q
15. l
16. d
17. p
18. j
19. h
20. n

Lesson 191

1. e
2. d
3. a
4. b
5. c
6. extract
7. lingering
8. ogled

9. induce
10. thwart

Lesson 192

1. d
2. c
3. a
4. e
5. b
6. jubilant
7. consecrated
8. cognitive
9. impertinence
10. moribund

Lesson 193

1. b
2. d
3. e
4. a
5. c
6. inertia
7. arduous
8. pedagogy
9. engrossing
10. avarice

Lesson 194

1. c
2. e
3. a
4. b
5. d
6. incumbent
7. perpetuates
8. astounds
9. recourse
10. vibrant

Lesson 195

1. c
2. e
3. d
4. b
5. a
6. amenable
7. pundits
8. belabors
9. miscreant
10. unflappable

Lesson 196

1. e
2. d
3. a
4. c
5. b
6. neophyte
7. indolent
8. extinct
9. subordination
10. traversed

Lesson 197

1. c
2. e
3. d
4. a
5. b
6. trepidation
7. disrepute
8. emblem
9. vagary
10. Byzantine

Lesson 198

1. b
2. e
3. a
4. c
5. d

6. elated
7. habituate
8. vitality
9. morbid
10. foundering

Lesson 199

1. e
2. c
3. a
4. d
5. b
6. sparing
7. perseverance
8. astonishing
9. mimicking
10. fragrant

Lesson 200

1. d
2. e
3. b
4. a
5. c
6. leery
7. Becalmed
8. proxy
9. exhaustive
10. severing

Word Search: Lessons 191-200

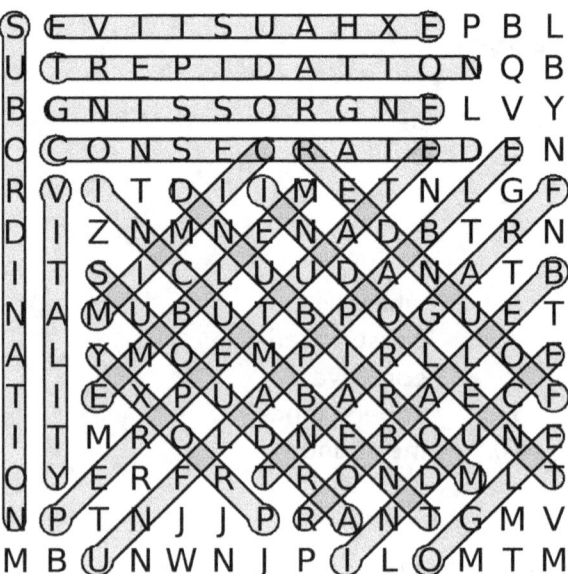

Review: Lessons 191-200

1. m
2. f
3. t
4. p
5. j
6. k
7. c
8. a
9. h
10. r
11. b
12. g
13. o
14. d
15. n
16. i
17. s
18. e
19. q
20. l

Lesson 201

1. b
2. a
3. e
4. d
5. c
6. stickler
7. harangued
8. moderate
9. verbatim
10. guileless

Lesson 202

1. c
2. e
3. d
4. b
5. a
6. arable
7. dilate
8. blissful
9. verbalizing
10. queer

Lesson 203

1. c
2. a
3. d
4. e
5. b
6. blasphemous
7. retrograde
8. impromptu
9. exhorted
10. consonant

Lesson 204

1. c
2. e
3. a
4. b
5. d
6. mystified
7. glutton
8. dismissive
9. distressed
10. proponent

Lesson 205

1. c
2. e
3. a
4. b
5. d
6. serpentine
7. replica
8. unimpeachable
9. imminent
10. fulsome

Lesson 206

1. b
2. a
3. d
4. e
5. c
6. lodging
7. insulate
8. unsolicited
9. gilded
10. immaterial

Lesson 207

1. d
2. c
3. a
4. b
5. e
6. pervades
7. stimulus
8. minutiae
9. Romantic
10. cue

Lesson 208

1. e
2. d
3. a
4. c
5. b
6. prevalent
7. piecemeal
8. crux
9. innuendo
10. relegate

Lesson 209

1. b
2. d
3. e
4. a
5. c
6. ratified
7. taxonomic/taxonomical
8. unbounded
9. prognosis
10. contaminated

Lesson 210

1. e
2. d
3. b
4. c
5. a
6. reprieve
7. inhabited
8. varied
9. uncouth
10. interminable

Crossword Puzzle: Lessons 201-210

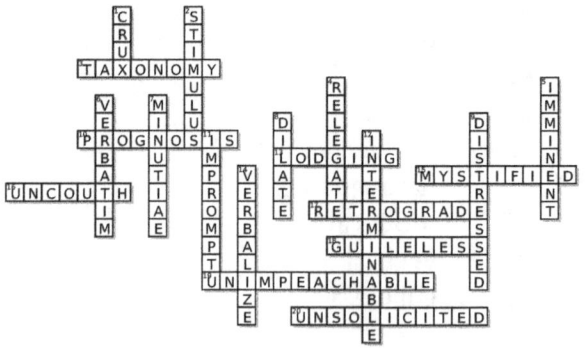

Review: Lessons 201-210

1. l
2. b
3. r
4. j
5. p
6. m
7. f
8. h
9. a
10. t
11. n
12. o
13. g
14. i
15. c
16. q
17. d
18. e
19. s
20. k

Lesson 211

1. c
2. a
3. b
4. e
5. d
6. aural
7. expound
8. recriminations

9. devour
10. mawkish

Lesson 212

1. d
2. a
3. e
4. c
5. b
6. unwitting
7. vocation
8. craving
9. inquire
10. masterful

Lesson 213

1. b
2. a
3. d
4. e
5. c
6. placebos
7. simulate
8. gaffes
9. voluminous
10. microcosm

Lesson 214

1. e
2. d
3. a
4. b
5. c
6. semantic
7. veteran
8. advent
9. arbitrator
10. persona

Lesson 215

1. e
2. d
3. b
4. c
5. a
6. inordinate
7. fetter
8. flora
9. deficient
10. natty

Lesson 216

1. a
2. b
3. c
4. d
5. e
6. surly
7. incensed
8. profess
9. anthropomorphize
10. upheaval

Lesson 217

1. e
2. d
3. b
4. a
5. c
6. authenticate
7. incision
8. multifarious
9. wafting
10. grotesque

Lesson 218

1. d
2. c
3. a
4. e
5. b
6. vignette

7. Spartan
8. pseudonym
9. reciprocity
10. numerous

Lesson 219

1. c
2. e
3. d
4. b
5. a
6. compelled
7. predominant
8. detritus
9. catapulted
10. asphyxiate

Lesson 220

1. a
2. e
3. b
4. c
5. d
6. emigration
7. brook
8. imbecile
9. indenture
10. grating

Word Search: Lessons 211-220

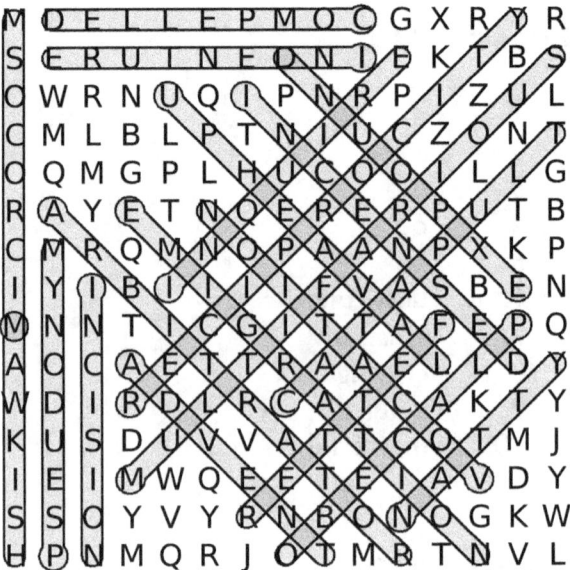

Review: Lessons 211-220

1. p
2. o
3. h
4. m
5. j
6. q
7. f
8. t
9. e
10. s
11. c
12. r
13. n
14. k
15. b
16. d
17. i
18. l
19. a
20. g

GLOSSARY

This glossary contains definitions of the new words from every lesson contained in this book. Please note that not every meaning of each word is contained in this glossary. Generally, only the most commonly used meanings of the words below are defined.

All entries in the glossary take the following form:

word (lesson): (part of speech) definition

Key for parts of speech:
adj. = adjective   adv. = adverb   n. = noun   v. = verb

A

abate (70): (v.) to decrease in intensity

aberrant (75): (adj.) departing from norms or typical standards

abject (143): (adj.) extremely miserable and unfortunate; contemptible, self-abashing

abridge (80): (v.) to shorten a book movie, speech, or text without losing its general meaning

abstain (133): (v.) to resist doing something or to resist being tempted by something

abstemious (85): (adj.) non self-indulgent when eating or drinking

abstruse (41): (adj.) understood by only a few, esoteric

accentuate (95): (v.) to make more noticeable or prominent

acclaim (58): (v.) to give approval, to laud

acoustic (158): (adj.) relating to sound, hearing

acquiesce (134): (v.) to agree or give in

acrimonious (119): (adj.) angry and bitter (often of speech or a debate)

acronym (63): (n.) set of initials representing a name of something

adamant (161): (adj.) refusing to be persuaded

adept (57): (adj.) very skilled or proficient at something

adhere (154): (v.) to stick to firmly; to follow through

adolescent (111): (adj.) in the process of developing from a child into an adult; (n.) a young person in between childhood and adulthood

adroit (62): (adj.) adept, ingenious, skillful

advent (214): (n.) the arrival of a notable thing, person, or event

aesthetic (16): (adj.) considering or pertaining to art or beauty

affable (140): (adj.) friendly, cordial

affluence (136): (n.) great wealth

aggrandize (165): (v.) to make great or greater

alacrity (180): (n.) an eagerness or cheerful readiness

alienate (156): (v.) to make someone feel isolated or estranged

allegory (109): (n.) a writing filled with a hidden meaning or hidden meanings that are moral or political

alleviate (68): (v.) make less severe

allusion (90): (n.) expression noting something indirectly

aloof (73): (adj.) not friendly; distant and cool

altruism (1): (n.) disinterested or selfless concern for others

amalgam (78): (n.) a mixture or blend of something

ambiguity (66): (n.) uncertainty

ambition (136): (n.) a strong desire to succeed

ambivalent (6): (adj.) having mixed feelings about something

ameliorate (170): (v.) to make something bad, unfortunate, or unsatisfactory better

amenable (195): (adj.) open and responsive to suggestion

amiable (67): (adj.) friendly and pleasant to be with

amorphous (166): (adj.) without clearly defined shape or form

anachronism (91): (n.) something belonging to a period other than which it exists

anecdotal (83): (adj.) not necessarily true or reliable

anecdote (16): (n.) a short story or tale to explain something

animate (132): (adj.) alive or having life; (v.) 1. to bring to life or enliven; 2. to give renewed inspiration or encouragement to something

animosity (88): (n.) strong hostility toward someone or something

anomalous (172): (adj.) deviating from what is normal or expected

anonymous (93): (adj.) not identified by name; unknown

antagonistic (109): (adj.) having hostile feelings toward someone or something

anthropological (149): (adj.) relating to the study of humankind

anthropomorphize (216): (v.) to attribute human characteristics to the behavior of an animal, object, or god

antipathy (177): (n.) a strong feeling of dislike

antiquated (116): (adj.) old-fashioned; archaic

apathy (72): (n.) indifference; lack of enthusiasm or concern

aplomb (185): (n.) confidence and skill shown especially in a difficult situation

apocalypse (166): (n.) 1. a great disaster; 2. the end of the world

apologetic (46): (adj.) 1. regretfully excusing or acknowledging a failure or offense; 2. concerning a reasoned argument or writing in justification of something

appease (3): (v.) to calm, quell, assuage

apportion (8): (v.) to divide, distribute

appraise (164): (v.) to assess the value or quality of

apprehensive (13): (adj.) anxious; hesitant about something

apprise (126): (v.) to inform or advise

apt (18): (adj.) 1. appropriate or suitable in circumstances; 2. having tendency to do something; 3. quick to learn

arable (202): (adj.) suitable for growing crops

arbitrary (82): (adj.) based on random choice or personal whim

arbitrator (214): (n.) an independent person or body appointed to settle a dispute

arcane (23): (adj.) understood by few; mysterious; secret

archaic (186): (adj.) antiquated; ancient

archipelago (149): (n.) a group of islands

arduous (193): (adj.) very difficult; challenging

aroma (173): (n.) a distinctive, pleasant smell

arrest (113): (v.) 1. to stop; 2. to take into custody; capture

articulate (6): (adj.) written or spoken clearly and/or persuasively; (v.) to express oneself in speech or writing clearly and/or persuasively

artifice (28): (n.) something designed to trick or deceive

ascertain (87): (v.) to find something out for certain; to ensure

ascetic (92): (adj.) of severe self-discipline and abstaining from all forms of indulgence

asphyxiate (219): (v.) to kill someone by depriving them of air

aspiration (33): (n.) a great desire to achieve something

assimilate (98): (v.) to fully take in information, ideas, or culture

assuage (51): (v.) to mitigate; to soothe

astonishing (199): (adj.) startling; stunning; amazing

astound (194): (v.) to astonish; to flabbergast; to amaze

astute (1): (adj.) having keen judgment or insight

audacious (156): (adj.) bold, daring

auditory (161): (adj.) relating to the sense of hearing

augment (38): (v.) to increase, add to something so that it becomes greater

aural (211): (adj.) of or related to the ear or sense of hearing

auspicious (43): (adj.) promising, propitious

austere (11): (adj.) severe or strict in manner or attitude; plain in style or appearance; having little luxury

authenticate (217): (v.) to prove or show something to be genuine

autocrat (175): (n.) a ruler who has absolute power

autonomy (2): (n.) the right of self-government; freedom

avant-garde (101): (adj.) concerning new, heterodox ideas or the people introducing them, usually in the arts

avarice (193): (n.) greed

averse (154): (adj.) strongly opposed to

aversion (48): (n.) strong dislike

avert (129): (v.) to prevent or ward off an undesirable occurrence

avuncular (184): (adj.) like an uncle

awe (53): (n.) amazement; astonishment

B

backlash (58): (n.) negative reaction or response

banal (56): (adj.) mundane; hackneyed

bane (7): (n.) a cause of distress or destruction

bankrupt (185): (adj.) 1. describing a person or organization unable to pay debts; 2. depleted or impoverished; 3. completely lacking in a particular quality or value; (n.) a person deemed to be insolvent by the court system (v.) to reduce a person or organization to insolvency

becalm (200): (v.) to deprive (a ship) of wind necessary to move it

beguile (12): (v.) to charm or enchant in a deceptive way

belabor (195): (v.) to repeat an idea or argument to emphasize it

belie (17): (v.) to fail to give a true impression of something; disguise or contradict

bellicose (104): (adj.) aggressive and warlike

belligerent (22): (adj.) hostile; warlike; aggressive

bemoan (151): (v.) to lament; to grieve

benefactors (129): (n.) people who give money or other help to a person or a cause

beneficiaries (183): (n.) people that benefit from something, usually a trust or will

benevolent (27): (adj.) kind and caring; well-intentioned

benign (71): (adj.) not harmful in effect; gentle; kindly

bent (186): (n.) a strong inclination; talent

bereave (63): (v.) to deprive someone of something, usually a loved one after a death

bewilder (76): (v.) to cause confusion

blandish (164): (v.) to coax with kind words or flattery

blare (141): (v.) to make a loud, harsh noise

blasphemous (203): (adj.) sacrilegious; against God or sacred things

bliss (202): (n.) perfect happiness; great joy

bolster (6): (v.) to support, strengthen

bombast (11): (n.) high-sounding language with little meaning

boon (116): (n.) blessing; benefit

brevity (68): (n.) concise and exact use of words in writing or in speech

brood (32): (v.) to think deeply about something, often something that makes one unhappy

brook (220): (n.) a small stream; (v.) to tolerate or allow

brouhaha (147): (n.) excited public response to something

brusque (173): (adj.) offhand or abrupt in speech or manner

bungler (73): (n.) one who performs tasks clumsily or badly

buoyant (97): (adj.) 1. capable of floating; 2. bubbly and cheerful

Byzantine (197): (adj.) labyrinthine; intricate

C

cacophony (85): (n.) harsh, discordant mixture of sounds

cajole (37): (v.) to coax, persuade someone to do something through flattery and pleasing words

callous (16): (adj.) insensitive and a bit cruel

candid (46): (adj.) frank, honest, straightforward

cantankerous (78): (adj.) bad tempered; argumentative; uncooperative

canvass (132): (v.) 1. to try to obtain or request something, especially votes from people; 2. to try to get someone's opinion; 3. to discuss thoroughly

capricious (81): (adj.) given to sudden changes of behavior or mood

castigate (17): (v.) to lambaste; to criticize harshly

catalyst (148): (n.) stimulus to make change happen

catapult (219): (n.) a device that allows one to launch someone or something in a direction; (v.) to launch someone or something in a direction

catastrophe (174): (n.) a terrible disaster

cathartic (66): (adj.) relieving of emotional tensions

censor (83): (n.) an official who examines pre-released media or printed material to suppress politically contentious or obscene material; (v.) to officially examine (usually a text or movie) and remove unacceptable parts

censure (42) (n.) an expression of formal disapproval; (v.) to express severe disapproval of someone or something, often formally

cerebral (167): (adj.) intellectual and not emotional

chagrin (162): (n.) distress or embarrassment at having failed or been humiliated

charisma (47): (n.) personal charm or quality that enables a person to attract and influence other people

charlatan (102): (n.) a fraud; someone falsely claiming to have knowledge or skill in something

chicanery (52): (n.) deception; dishonesty

chide (109): (v.) to scold or castigate

chronic (88): (adj.) persisting for a long time or constantly recurring (often of illness or habits)

chronicle (57): (n.) 1. a factual written account of historical events in chronological order; 2. a writing that describes a series of events; (v.) to record events in a factual and detailed way

circumscribe (62): (v.) to limit or confine

circumspect (21): (adj.) wary and unwilling to take risks

circumvent (93): (v.) to find a way around an obstacle

clandestine (3): (adj.) secretive

clemency (172): (n.) lenience or mercy

cloying (122): (adj.) displeasing because of excess of sweetness or richness or sentiment

coddle (131): (v.) to treat with excessive indulgence

cogent (109): (adj.) clear, logical, convincing (concerning an argument)

cognitive (192): (adj.) involving conscious mental activities

cohesive (71): (adj.) sticking together (literally or figuratively)

commemorate (67): (v.) to recall and show respect for someone or something in ceremony; to serve as memorial to

commend (160): (v.) to praise; to endorse

commiserate (8): (v.) to feel or express sympathy or pity

compelled (219): (v.) to feel forced or obliged to do something

compilation (138): (n.) a process or act of assembling different sources to put together something; something that is compiled

complacent (72): (adj.) self satisfaction with one's accomplishments

complicity (149): (n.) involvement with others in a crime or something illegal

comprehensive (13): (adj.) thorough; covering all aspects

compunction (18): (n.) feeling guilt or sorrow for poor behavior

conceal (23): (v.) to hide or cover up something

concession (137): (n.) something granted in response to demands; a preferential allowance given by an organization or government

conciliate (16): (v.) to stop someone from being angry or discontented; placate; pacify

concord (28): (v.) to agree or put in agreement

concur (77): (v.) to agree

condemn (21): (v.) to express public disapproval of; censure

condescending (76): (adj.) showing a feeling of patronizing superiority

condone (33): (v.) to overlook, allow or forgive something

conflagration (100): (n.) gigantic fire

congenial (174): (adj.) suitable or appropriate; pleasant

conjecture (26): (n.) 1. an opinion or conclusion based on incomplete information; 2. an unproven math theorem; (v.) to form an opinion about something based on incomplete information

conjoin (135): (v.) to connect, to join

conjure (142): (v.) to gather, to bring something into existence

connoisseur (26): (n.) an expert at something (usually the arts or cuisine)

connotation (145): (n.) an idea or feeling that is implied or evoked by a term

conscientious (81): (adj.) wishing to do one's duty well and properly

consecrated (192): (adj.) dedicated to a sacred purpose

consensus (31): (n.) a general agreement

consign (180): (v.) to deliver something to a person's custody; to send (something) to a person to be sold; to assign permanently

consonance (203): (n.) agreement or compatibility between opinions or actions

conspicuous (96): (adj.) standing out so as to be clearly visible

conspirator (117): (n.) a schemer

conspire (189): (v.) to secretly plan to do something harmful or illegal

consternation (182): (n.) a strong feeling of surprise or sudden disappointment that causes confusion

consummate (98): (adj.) showing a high degree of flair and skill; (v.) 1. to make a marriage or relationship complete by having sexual intercourse; to complete; 2. to complete an action or make perfect

contaminate (209): (v.) to make impure by adding a polluting substance

contemptible (38): (adj.) deserving of scorn

contentious (86): (adj.) likely to cause an argument; controversial

contiguous (188): (adj.) touching; adjacent

contingency (146): (n.) a possible event that might happen in the future; a provision for an unforeseen circumstance

conundrum (115): (n.) enigma, riddle

conventional (21): (adj.) following typical social norms/conventions

convergence (136): (n.) the act of coming together

conviction (82): (n.) 1. a formal declaration that one is guilty of a criminal offense; 2. a firmly held belief or opinion

convivial (87): (adj.) friendly, lively, or enjoyable person or environment

convoluted (51): (adj.) complicated

corridor (107): (n.) long passage in a building with doors to enter rooms

corroborate (92): (v.) to confirm or give support to (a statement, finding, or theory)

corrupt (43): (adj.) marked by immoral and dishonest behavior

cosmopolitan (91): (adj.) worldly; comfortable in many cultures

covert (110): (adj.) not openly acknowledged or displayed; secretive; stealthy

coward (189): (n.) a person who shows a shameful lack of courage

craving (212): (n.) a powerful desire for something

credulity (48): (n.) willingness or readiness to believe something is true

crude (116): (adj.) unrefined; vulgar

crux (208): (n.) the decisive or most important point at issue

cryptic (2): (adj.) mysterious, obscure

cue (207): (n.) a thing said or done that serves as a signal for action

culpable (143): (adj.) to be guilty and blameworthy for

cunning (53): (adj.) devious

curative (2): (adj.) able to remedy or heal something, typically disease

curtail (102): (v.) to reduce in quantity or impose restrictions on something

cynical (26): (adj.) holding a belief that humans are motivated only by self-interest; distrusting of human sincerity

D

daunting (58): (adj.) seeming difficult to deal with in anticipation; discouraging

dearth (36): (n.) deficiency, scarcity, lack of

debacle (175): (n.) a complete failure

debris (175): (n.) scattered fragments

debunk (63): (v.) to expose the falseness of a myth or belief

deceitful (111): (adj.) misleading, fraudulent

decipher (95): (v.) to convert something encoded into comprehensible, normal language

decisive (165): (adj.) able to make choices quickly and/or confidently

decorous (152): (adj.) keeping with good propriety and taste; polite and restrained

decorum (68): (n.) propriety in manners, etiquette

decry (7): (v.) to openly disapprove

deferential (12): (adj.) showing respect to those of authority or power or rank

deficient (215): (adj.) lacking in a specified ingredient, ability, or quality

defunct (22): (adj.) no longer in use or functional

defy (73): (v.) to openly resist or refuse to obey

dehydrated (78): (adj.) parched; losing a large amount of water

dejected (83): (adj.) sad and depressed

deleterious (188): (adj.) damaging or harmful

deliberate (31): (adj.) done with careful planning and intention

delinquent (124): (adj.) 1. showing a tendency to commit a crime, especially youth; 2. irresponsible; 3. in arrears; (n.) a youth likely to commit a crime

delude (88): (v.) to mislead someone; to fool, deceive

deluge (141): (n.) a large amount of something coming at the same time; (v.) to flood with something

delusion (175): (n.) a belief that is not true; a false idea

demeanor (93): (n.) outward behavior or bearing

demise (112): (n.) collapse, downfall

demography (4): (n.) the study of populations, especially changes in populations (birth rate, death rate, income, disease rates)

demoralize (103): (v.) to cause someone to lose hope or spirit

demure (128): (adj.) reserved, modest, and shy

denotation (144): (n.) indication of something using words, symbols; the primary meaning of a word

denounce (9): (v.) to publicly condemn, criticize

deplete (167): (v.) to use up the supply or resources of

deprecate (102): (v.) to express disapproval of

deride (7): (v.) to ridicule

derivative (186): (adj.) made up of parts from something else

desecration (122): (n.) blasphemy; violation

despair (139): (n.) hopelessness, pessimism

despondence (164): (n.) a state of low spirits due to loss of hope or courage

detached (27): (adj.) emotionally unengaged; without passion

deter (104): (v.) to discourage someone from doing something, usually by instilling fear or doubt

detonate (125): (v.) to explode; to burst

detractor (137): (n.) a person who criticizes or belittles the value of something

detritus (219): (n.) waste or debris of any kind

devoid (107): (adj.) completely lacking

devour (211): (v.) to eat or read with great intensity and in large quantity

dexterous (14): (adj.) skillful, especially with the hands

diatribe (85): (n.) a forceful and bitter attack against someone or something

didactic (32): (adj.) instructive, usually involving a moral lesson or ulterior motive

diffident (26): (adj.) shy because of a lack of self-confidence

digress (96): (v.) to depart from the main subject in speech or writing

dilate (202): (v.) to make wider or larger; to open

dilatory (19): (adj.) delaying; trying to delay

dilemma (132): (n.) a difficult situation requiring a choice between two or more equally unfavorable options

dilettante (12): (n.) an amateur

diligent (190): (adj.) painstaking; assiduous

diminutive (17): (adj.) small in stature; unusually small

diorama (168): (n.) a three-dimensional model of a scene

diplomatic (24): (adj.) having or showing the ability to deal with people in a sensitive way

disaffected (119): (adj.) dissatisfied with those in authority and unwilling to support them any longer

discern (106): (v.) to perceive or recognize something

discerning (136): (adj.) perceptive, having good judgment; able to detect great subtlety

discreet (29): (adj.) subtlety, tact, or done with such

discrete (29): (adj.) divided into separate, countable parts

disdain (41): (n.) contempt, scorn

disenchanted (164): (adj.) disappointed by someone or something previously respected or admired

disgruntled (80): (adj.) angry or dissatisfied

disillusioned (97): (adj.) disappointed when something turns out to be less than what was believed or expected

disingenuous (37): (adj.) insincere, dishonest

disjointed (146): (adj.) divided, lacking continuity or organization

dislodge (162): (v.) to knock or force out of position

dismantle (171): (v.) to take something apart

dismay (22): (n.) consternation and distress, often caused by something unexpected; (v.) to cause someone to feel consternation or distress

dismissive (204): (adj.) feeling that something is unworthy of consideration

disparage (36): (v.) to belittle, hurt the reputation of

disparity (156): (n.) a great difference between things

dispassionate (147): (adj.) uninfluenced by strong emotions

dispel (117): (v.) to make a doubt, belief, or feeling disappear

disperse (75): (v.) to spread out

disputation (139): (n.) debate or argument

disrepute (197): (n.) lack of good reputation

disseminate (34): (v.) to circulate, broadcast, spread widely

dissipate (143): (v.) to disperse; to waste away

dissolute (170): (adj.) lax in morals

distressed (204): (adj.) suffering from anxiety, sorrow, or pain

dither (123): (v.) to be indecisive

diverge (126): (v.) to separate from a path or route and go in a different direction

divert (99): (v.) 1. to cause someone or something to change from one direction or form to another; 2. to distract someone's attention from something

divisive (42): (adj.) contentious, causing disagreement

divulge (70): (v.) to disclose, to reveal

docile (27): (adj.) ready to accept instruction; submissive

doctrinaire (158): (adj.) insistent on using theory or doctrine without considering practicality

domineering (168): (adj.) overly controlling

dormant (108): (adj.) (of an animal) having physical actions suspended for a period of time; (of a volcano temporarily inactive; (of a plant) alive but not growing; (of a disease) no symptoms and uncured, but may recur

downplay (39): (v.) to make something seem less important than it actually is

dubious (31): (adj.) not easily convinced; showing distrust

dumbfounded (123): (adj.) astounded; bewildered

duplicitous (32): (adj.) double-dealing, deceptive

durable (177): (adj.) able to withstand wear, pressure or damage

dynamic (168): (adj.) always changing or active

E

ebullient (97): (adj.) cheerful and full of energy

eccentric (31): (adj.) (describing a person and his or her behavior) unconventional, bizarre

eclectic (37): (adj.) comprising of elements from diverse sources

economical (112): (adj.) 1. giving good value in return for one's money, time, or effort; 2. careful not to waste money or resources; 3. using no more of something than necessary

ecstasy (44): (n.) overpowering feeling of happiness

edify (49): (v.) to enlighten, help someone understand

effrontery (110): (n.) insolent or impertinent behavior

effusive (47): (adj.) expressing emotions or enthusiasm in an unrestrained manner

egalitarian (116): (adj.) supporting equality

egotism (42): (n.) arrogance, self-importance

elate (198): (v.) to make (someone) extremely happy

elicit (121): (v.) to evoke; to draw out

elite (46): (n.) 1. a select part of a group that is superior in ability; 2. a class of people having great societal influence because of their wealth

elongated (169): (adj.) unusually long in relation to its width

eloquent (47): (adj.) fluent and persuasive in speech or writing

elucidate (157): (v.) to clarify; to illuminate

elude (52): (v.) avoid; escape

embellish (56): (v.) to make something, a statement, or a story appear more attractive by adding extra details (often which are untrue)

emblem (197): (n.) a person or thing that represents an idea

embodiment (178): (n.) someone or something that perfectly represents a certain quality, idea, or feeling

embolden (54): (v.) to give courage or confidence to someone to do something or to behave in a certain way

emigration (220): (n.) the process of leaving one's country to settle elsewhere

eminent (59): (adj.) distinguished, well-known

empathetic (96): (adj.) the ability to understand and share the feelings of another

emphatic (65): (adj.) expressing something forcefully and clearly

empirical (57): (adj.) based on experimental trials of something rather than pure theory or logic

encumber (62): (v.) to burden with obligations

endorse (67): (v.) to give approval to

endure (52): (v.) to tolerate; to bear

engrossing (193): (adj.) absorbing all of one's attention and interest

enhance (124): (v.) to intensify, increase, or improve the extent, quality, or value thereof

enigma (36): (n.) a mystery, a puzzling situation

enmity (60): (n.) animosity, hatred

enrage (144): (v.) to make angry

entangle (64): (v.) to involve in difficulties, to ensnare

entrenched (55): (adj.) established firmly or solidly

entrepreneur (50): (n.) someone who starts and operates a business or businesses, assuming greater risk than normal in doing so

enumerate (72): (v.) to mention things one by one

envy (69): (n.) a feeling of discontent and desire caused by someone else's possessions, qualifications, or luck

ephemeral (57): (adj.) momentary, fleeting

epitomize (74): (v.) to serve as the perfect example of something

equanimity (62): (n.) calmness, emotional stability

equivocal (77): (adj.) open to multiple interpretations; ambiguous

equivocate (127): (v.) to use ambiguous language to avoid commitment or to hide the truth

eradicate (67): (v.) to eliminate completely

erratic (79): (adj.) not regular or even pattern or movement; unpredictable

erroneous (86): (adj.) wrong; incorrect

ersatz (190): (adj.) being a usually artificial and inferior substitute

erudite (51): (adj.) showing profound knowledge or learning

escalate (158): (v.) to become more serious and intense

eschew (84): (v.) to deliberately avoid using; abstain from

esoteric (72): (adj.) understood by only a few people with specialized knowledge or interest

espouse (145): (v.) to adopt and promote a cause, theory, or belief

estrange (89): (v.) to alienate; to no longer be close to someone

eulogy (94): (n.) a speech or piece of writing that praises someone highly

euphemism (45): (n.) mild expression to avoid being blunt when referring to something unpleasant

euphoria (177): (n.) intense happiness and excitement

evade (77): (v.) to avoid

evoke (56): (v.) to elicit; to consciously bring to mind

exacerbate (82): (v.) to make (usually a bad situation) worse

exacting (149): (adj.) demanding great attention to detail

exasperated (87): (adj.) to be intensely irritated; infuriated

excavate (4): (v.) to dig out

excerpt (61): (n.) quotation or passage taken from a film, writing, or broadcast; (v.) to take an extract from a text

exclude (115): (v.) to keep out, to omit

exemplar (105): (n.) a person serving as an excellent model

exemplify (9): (v.) to serve as an ideal example of something

exempt (156): (adj.) free from liability or obligation imposed on others; (n.) a person who is free of liability for something, usually paying tax; (v.) to free a person from an obligation or liability imposed on others

exhaustive (200): (adj.) complete; comprehensive; full-scale

exhort (203): (v.) to urge or encourage one to do something

exonerate (82): (v.) to free from blame or fault in wrongdoing

exotic (87): (adj.) attractive because it is foreign or not ordinary

expedient (14): (adj.) convenient or practical, though not necessarily proper or ethical

expedition (92): (n.) a journey undertaken by people for a purpose

expeditious (131): (adj.) being quick and still ensuring good result

exposé (114): (n.) a written report about the facts of something, usually something scandalous

expound (211): (v.) to present and explain an idea systematically and in detail

expropriate (125): (v.) (usually of a government) to seize and take away (usually property) from its owner

extrapolate (40): (v.) to estimate a possibility beyond the existing values/situation with the assumption that the current trend will continue

extemporize (167): (v.) to improvise; to create and perform spontaneously and without preparation

extinct (196): (adj.) no longer existing

extol (92): (v.) to praise enthusiastically

extract (191): (v.) 1. to remove or take out; 2. to obtain a substance or resource by a special method

extravagant (2): (adj.) spending money excessively

exuberant (184): (adj.) filled with energy and enthusiasm

exude (110): (v.) 1. to discharge a moisture or smell gradually; 2. to display an sentiment or quality openly and intensely

exultation (179): (n.) a feeling of triumphant happiness

F

fabricate (19): (v.) to make something up; to concoct

facetious (7): (adj.) flippant; treating serious matters jokingly

facile (119): (adj.) easy; effortless

faction (156): (n.) a small dissenting group within a larger group, especially in politics

fallacious (133): (adj.) something based on a mistaken belief

fastidious (3): (adj.) very particular about details

fatalistic (104): (adj.) belief that all events are predetermined and inevitable

fathom (35): (n.) a unit of length equal to six feet, usually to measure depth; (v.) to figure out, comprehend

feasible (188): (adj.) capable of being done, effected

feign (104): (v.) to pretend to be affected by something

felicity (183): (n.) 1. great happiness; 2. a talent for speaking or writing

fertile (24): (adj.) capable of producing things, ideas, or offspring in an abundant way

fervent (8): (adj.) energetic, passionate

fetid (128): (adj.) smelling extremely unpleasant

fetter (215): (adj.) to restrain with chains or manacles (literally or metaphorically)

figurative (162): (adj.) metaphorical, not literal

finesse (29): (n.) refined or intricate delicacy; (v.) to do something in a subtle or delicate manner

flagging (34): (v.) to decrease in intensity, weaken

flagrant (99): (adj.) blatant; obvious; deliberate

flamboyant (39): (adj.) showy and vivacious, extravagant

flippant (41): (adj.) not demonstrating a serious or respectful attitude

flora (215): (n.) the plants of a particular region, habitat, or geological period

flourish (171): (n.) 1. a bold or extravagant gesture; 2. an ornamental flowing curve in writing; (v.) to grow or develop in a healthy or vigorous way

flout (179): (v.) to openly disregard (a rule, law or convention)

foible (127): (n.) a minor weakness, defect, or eccentricity in someone's behavior

forbear (13): (v.) to refrain from doing something

foreshadow (108): (v.) to be a warning or indication of a future event

foresight (169): (n.) the ability to predict what will happen in the future

forestall (107): (v.) to prevent or obstruct by taking action in advance

forgo/forego (18): (v.) to go without; omit; decline to take

formulaic (187): (adj.) produced in accordance with a followed rule or style

formulate (137): (v.) to create methodically; articulate, express

fortify (170): (v.) to strengthen

fortitude (183): (n.) mental strength in facing adversity

fortuitous (30): (adj.) a sign of something good to come; good omen

foster (44): (adj.) concerning someone that has family ties through being raised and not through birth; (v.) 1. to encourage the growth of; 2. to bring up a child that is not one's by birth

fouled (160): (v.) made dirty, defiled, or soiled

founder (198): (n.) someone who establishes an institution or settlement; (v.) 1. to collapse or fail (of a plan or endeavor); 2. to fill with water and sink (of a ship)

fragrant (199): (adj.) aromatic; perfumed; scented

frank (66): (adj.) straightforward, direct

fraudulent (183): (adj.) cheating; dishonest

frivolous (23): (adj.) wasteful, not having serious purpose or value

frugal (182): (adj.) sparing economically

fulsome (205): (adj.) flattering to an excessive degree

futile (28): (adj.) hopeless; fruitless

G

gaffe (213): (n.) an unintentional remark or act lavishing embarrassment on its originator; a blunder

gargantuan (132): (adj.) of great quantity; huge, giant

garnish (118): (n.) a decoration or embellishment for something, often food; (v.) 1. to decorate or embellish something, often food; 2. to seize a one's salary to settle a debt or claim

garrulous (5): (adj.) overly talkative

gilded (206): (adj.) covered thinly with gold leaf or gold paint

glutton (204): (n.) a person who is usually fond of or eager for something (often food)

grandeur (131): (n.) quality of being impressive or splendid in style

grandiloquent (148): (adj.) pompous in style or manner; designed in a way to impress

grating (220): (adj.) sounding harsh and unpleasant; annoying

gratuitous (177): (adj.) not necessary or appropriate

gregarious (95): (adj.) fond of company; sociable

grotesque (217): (adj.) comically or repulsively ugly; incongruous to a shocking degree

guileless (201): (adj.) innocent and without deception

H

habituate (198): (v.) to make or become accustomed or used to something

hackneyed (33): (adj.) trite because of having been overused; dull

halting (103): (adj.) hesitant, largely due to lack of confidence

hamper (178): (v.) to slow the movement, progress, or action of someone or something

haphazard (140): (adj.) unplanned, lacking organization

harangue (201): (v.) to lecture at length in an aggressive, critical manner

harbinger (25): (n.) a sign that symbolizes or announces the approach or arrival of something

havoc (169): (n.) widespread destruction, confusion, or disorder

hedonistic (154): (adj.) seeking pleasure, especially for self-indulgence

heritage (162): (n.) 1. property that is inherited; 2. objects or traditions, values, historical buildings or countryside passed down from previous generations

holistic (159): (adj.) considering all factors, all-inclusive

hostile (98): (adj.) unfriendly; antagonistic

hovel (178): (n.) a small, squalid, and unpleasant dwelling

hover (174): (v.) to remain in one place in the air

hubris (20): (n.) excessive self-confidence or pride

humane (167): (adj.) having or showing compassion or benevolence

humble (114): (adj.) modest

hypocritical (128): (adj.) behaving in a way that indicates someone has higher moral standards than is reality

I

iconoclast (49): (n.) someone who attacks established principles, beliefs, ideas

idiosyncrasy (91): (n.) a mode of behavior peculiar to an individual

illicit (126): (adj.) illegal; prohibited

illusory (54): (adj.) not real; imagined

imbecile (220): (n.) a stupid person

immaterial (206): (adj.) unimportant under the circumstances; irrelevant

immense (153): (adj.) extremely strong, in great quantity

immerse (59): (v.) to become deeply involved in something, to be absorbed by something

imminent (205): (adj.) about to happen

immune (15): (adj.) unable to be affected by something

immutable (64): (adj.) unchangeable, inflexible

impecunious (158): (adj.) having little or no money

impediment (69): (n.) an obstruction in doing something

imperative (74): (adj.) of vital importance; crucial

imperious (12): (adj.) assuming power without justification; arrogant and domineering

impertinence (192): (n.) irrelevance, inappropriateness, or absurdity

impetuous (17): (adj.) hasty or without thought

imposter (173): (n.) a person who deceives others by pretending to be someone else

impoverish (129): (v.) to exhaust; to reduce to poverty

impressionistic (138): (adj.) based on unsystematic, subjective reactions

impromptu (203): (adj. and adv.) done without being planned, organized, or rehearsed

improvisation (improv) (113): (n.) a creation or execution of an act without preparation

impugn (79): (v.) to dispute the truth or validity of; call into question

inane (10): (adj.) silly; stupid

incarnation (176): (n.) a person who represents a quality or idea

incensed (216): (adj.) very angry; enraged

inception (122): (n.) beginning; initiation

incidental (160): (adj.) occurring as a consequence; secondary, subordinate

incision (217): (n.) a surgical cut made into the skin or flesh

incongruent (22): (adj.) not compatible; does not fit together

incredulous (96): (adj.) unwilling or unable to believe something

incumbent (194): (n.) someone currently holding office

indelible (110): (adj.) permanent

indenture (220): (n.) a formal legal agreement, contract, or document, often tying an apprentice to a master for a fixed term

indeterminate (179): (adj.) not exactly known, defined, or established

indict (5): (v.) to accuse or charge someone with a crime

indigenous (100): (adj.) originating or occurring naturally in a specific location; native

indigent (108): (adj.) poor; destitute; needy

indignant (1): (adj.) annoyed by seemingly unfair treatment

indolent (196): (adj.) lazy

induce (191): (v.) to cause someone to do something

indulge (84): (v.) allow oneself or someone to enjoy the pleasure of something

indulgent (46): (adj.) tending to be lenient and permissive to someone

ineffable (89): (adj.) too great or extreme to be verbally expressed

inept (94): (adj.) having or showing no skill; clumsy

inertia (193): (n.) 1. a tendency to do nothing or remain unchanged; resistance to change in some physical property; 2. (in physics) a property where an object remains in its existing rest state or in straight line motion unless acted upon by an external force

inevitable (36): (adj.) unavoidable

infatuated (38): (adj.) to be motivated by a short-lived but intense fascination for someone or something

infringe (77): (v.) 1. to actively break the terms of a law or agreement; 2. to at as if to limit or undermine something; encroach on

ingenious (127): (adj.) clever; brilliant

ingenuous (4): (adj.) naïve, innocent

inhabit (210): (v.) to live in or occupy a place or environment

inherent (181): (adj.) innate; native; inbred

inhibit (117): (v.) to restrict; to impede

innate (95): (adj.) inborn; natural

innocuous (9): (adj.) causing no harm

innuendo (208): (n.) a suggestive, allusive, often disparaging remark

inordinate (215): (adj.) unusually or disproportionally large; excessive

inquire (212): (v.) to ask information from someone

inscrutable (27): (adj.) impossible to understand or interpret

insidious (115): (adj.) proceeding gradually and subtly, and with harmful effects

insinuate (105): (v.) to suggest or hint at something indirectly and, perhaps, unpleasantly

insolent (14): (adj.) arrogant and rude

insolvent (90): (adj.) unable to pay debts owed

instigate (119): (v.) to influence or provoke

instill (19): (v.) to gradually establish something in a person's mind

insulate (206): (v.) to use a material to protect something from the elements or heat loss

interleave (180): (v.) to insert pages between other pages; to put something in between the layers of

interloper (24): (n.) an intruder or eavesdropper

interminable (210): (adj.) unending; unceasing

intermittent (173): (adj.) occurring at irregular intervals

intrepid (29): (adj.) fearless

intricate (51): (adj.) very complicated or detailed

intrinsic (159): (adj.) inherent, innate, essential

introspection (80): (n.) self-reflection; observing one's own mental and emotional process

intrusion (151): (n.) unwelcome entrance which disturbs; something unwelcome

intuition (190): (n.) quick and ready insight; the ability to know something without having proof

inundate (85): (v.) to overwhelm someone with things; to flood

invasive (166): (adj.) tending to spread undesirably or harmfully

invigorate (103): (v.) to give strength or energy to

invoke (56): (v.) to cite or appeal to an authority or a thing for support or action in an argument

invulnerable (101): (adj.) impossible to harm

irascible (108): (adj.) having a tendency to be easily angered

ire (111): (n.) intense anger; wrath

irksome (150): (adj.) annoying in a tiresome way

ironic (34): (adj.) happening the opposite way to what is expected

irreverent (99): (adj.) showing a lack of respect

itinerant (172): (adj.) traveling from place to place

J

jaded (137): (adj.) tired, lacking enthusiasm, or bored, usually after having too much of something

jeopardize (75): (v.) to endanger

jingoism (162): (n.) extreme patriotism

jocular (71): (adj.) joking, humorous, or playful

jubilant (192): (adj.) rejoicing; triumphant; joyous

judicious (39): (adj.) done with caution and good judgment

juxtapose (44): (v.) to place different things side-by-side, often to underscore contrast

K

kinetic (178): (adj.) of, resulting from, or pertaining to motion

knell (145): (n.) the sound of a bell, usually in reference to the dead or a funeral

L

laborious (154): (adj.) arduous, demanding great effort and time

lackadaisical (151): (adj.) lacking enthusiasm or effort

lackluster (43): (adj.) bland, lacking in liveliness

laconic (49): (adj.) using very few words, curt and concise

lament (6): (v.) to grieve

languid (54): (adj.) lazy; sluggish

laud (32): (v.) to praise highly

lavish (59): (adj.) extremely rich, luxurious, or elaborate; (v.) to bestow something in generous or extravagant quantities upon

lax (132): (adj.) slipshod, not sufficiently strict or careful

leery (200): (adj.) suspicious; wary

legitimate (182): (adj.) legal; valid; sanctioned

lethargic (64): (adj.) exhibiting a lack of energy or enthusiasm

libel (69): (n.) a published false statement attacking one's reputation; (v.) to defame someone with false statements orally or in writing

liberation (184): (n.) the act of freeing someone from slavery, imprisonment or oppression; a release

libertine (167): (adj.) characterized by a disregard for morality

lighthearted (125): (adj.) carefree; jovial

linchpin (160): (n.) a person or thing vital to a business or an organization

lingering (191): (adj.) staying beyond expected time

litigious (74): (adj.) concerning lawsuits; suitable to becoming the subject of a lawsuit

lodging (206): (n.) a place where someone lives or stays temporarily

loner (70): (n.) someone who avoids the company of others

longevity (97): (n.) concerning having a long life

loquacious (61): (adj.) talkative, wordy

lucid (37): (adj.) clear, easy to understand

lucrative (48): (adj.) very profitable, remunerative

ludicrous (65): (adj.) ridiculous, laughable

lugubrious (176): (adj.) full of sadness or sorrow

luminous (79): (adj.) full of shedding light; very bright

luxury (165): (n.) 1. a state of extravagant living; 2. an inessential desirable item that is expensive

M

machination (106): (n.) scheming; engaging in plots or intrigues

magnanimity (66): (n.) generosity, nobility

malaise (130): (n.) depression, anxiety

malice (84): (n.) ill-will; intention or desire to do evil

malign (117): (v.) to slander or defame

mandate (89): (n.) an edict, order, or commission to act

mandatory (139): (adj.) required by rule, compulsory

maneuver (153): (n.) 1. a movement or series of movements requiring care and skill; 2. a carefully planned scheme often using deception; (v.) 1. to manipulate; 2. to turn or move skillfully

manifest (171): (n.) a customs document listing the people and contents of a ship, train, or plane; (v.) 1. to show or demonstrate clearly; 2. to be evidence of, to prove; 3. (of a ghost or an illness) to appear

manipulate (71): (v.) to handle or control; to control or influence cleverly, unethically, or unjustly

manorial (144): (adj.) of or pertaining to a large country house with lands or the principal home of a landed estate (often in medieval times)

mar (90): (v.) to sully the appearance, reputation, or quality of someone or something

marshal (148): (n.) 1. an officer of the highest rank in the armed forces in certain countries; 2. a municipal officer or head of a police department; 3. an official responsible for supervising public events; (v.) to arrange or assemble in order

masterful (212): (adj.) powerful and able to control others; performed or performing extremely skillfully

maudlin (94): (adj.) self-pityingly or tearfully sentimental

maverick (76): (adj.) unorthodox; (n.) an unorthodox or independent-minded person

mawkish (211): (adj.) sentimental in a feeble or discomforting way

meager (189): (adj.) deficient in quantity or quality

meddle (183): (v.) to be involved in activities of other people, especially when they do not want your involvement

mediate (187): (v.) to intervene between people in a dispute in order to bring about a resolution or agreement

mediation (157): (n.) act of intervention to resolve conflicts

mediocre (53): (adj.) of merely moderate quality; not very good

meditation (105): (n.) 1. the process of reflection; 2. written or spoken discourse expressing one's thoughts on a subject

melancholy (41): (adj.) very sad, gloomy, sorrowful

melodic (113): (adj.) pleasant sounding; harmonious

melodramatic (141): (adj.) exaggerated and overemotional

menace (126): (n.) 1. a danger or threat; 2. a person or thing causing a danger or threat; (v.) to threaten in a hostile manner

mendacity (42): (n.) fabrication, deceitfulness

mercurial (58): (adj.) a person subject to unpredictable changes of mood or mind

methodical (118): (adj.) done systematically according to procedure; a person systematic in thought or behavior

meticulous (46): (adj.) very careful and attentive to detail, painstaking

microcosm (213): (n.) a community, situation, or place regarded as encapsulating key qualities of something larger

migrate (4): (v.) to move from one place to another

mimic (199): (v.) to imitate; to copy

minuscule/miniscule (63): (adj.) very small

minutiae (207): (n.) small, precise, or trivial details of something

miraculous (112): (adj.) being able to work wonders; inexplicable

mirth (159): (n.) amusement – often expressed by laughter

misanthrope (134): (n.) one who dislikes people in general

miscalculate (124): (v.) 1. to assess a situation wrongly; 2. to measure an amount, distance, or value wrongly

mischance (130): (n.) bad luck

mischief (166): (n.) playful misbehavior or troublemaking

miscreant (195): (n.) a person who behaves badly or in a way that breaks the law

miser (9): (n.) a frugal person who hoards money and refuses to spend

misgiving (178): (n.) a feeling of doubt or anxiety about the consequences or outcome of something

misguided (105): (adj.) exhibiting faulty reasoning

misnomer (14): (n.) using the wrong name

missive (185): (n.) a written message; letter

mitigate (19): (v.) to make seem or feel less harsh or severe

moderate (201): (adj.) 1. average in amount, intensity, or degree; 2. not politically radical; (n.) a person who does not hold radical views; (v.) 1. to make less extreme, intense or violent; 2. to preside over

mollify (24): (v.) to appease the anger or anxiety of someone

momentous (29): (adj.) of great or extreme importance; pivotal

momentum (60): (n.) the impetus or driving force behind a cause or action

monotony (76): (adj.) lack of variety and interest; repeated same routine

morass (161): (n.) 1. an area of boggy ground; 2. a complicated or confusing situation

morbid (198): (adj.) cheerless; unpleasant; morose

moribund (192): (adj.) no longer active or effective; very sick; close to death

motif (174): (n.) a theme that is repeated through a book, story, etc.; a decorative pattern

multifaceted (121): (adj.) versatile; having many aspects

multifarious (217): (adj.) many and of various different types

mundane (51): (adj.) ordinary; prosaic

munificent (81): (adj.) very generous

muster (140): (v.) to assemble a group of people; to call up (a) feeling(s), emotion(s), or response(s)

myopic (34): (adj.) nearsighted, lacking intellectual insight

mystified (204): (adj.) (for someone) to be utterly bewildered or perplexed

mythical (114): (adj.) fictitious; imaginary

N

naïve (56): (adj.) innocent; sincere

natty (215): (adj.) smart and fashionable (usually of a person or of clothing)

nebulous (47): (adj.) cloudy, hazy; ill-defined in terms of concept, idea, or shape

negligent (55): (adj.) careless; sloppy

neophyte (196): (n.) a beginner, greenhorn, tyro

nomad (50): (n.) someone who moves from place to place and has no permanent home

nonchalant (61): (adj.) not displaying interest or enthusiasm

nonplussed (190): (adj.) utterly perplexed

nostalgia (11): (n.) a longing for time past, especially childhood or home

notorious (68): (adj.) well-known or famous for having some bad quality or having done some bad deed

novel (99): (adj.) new and original; (n.) fictitious prose narrative of book length, often having somewhat realistic characters and actions

noxious (164): (adj.) harmful; poisonous; extremely unpleasant

nuance (39): (n.) a subtle difference in meaning, shade, sound, or expression; (v.) to give subtle differences in meaning, shade, sound, or expression to something

nullify (118): (v.) to revoke; to rescind

numerous (218): (adj.) many; abundant; great in number

O

obdurate (140): (adj.) stubborn, resistant to change

obfuscate (44): (v.) befuddle, make unclear

objective (73): (adj.) uninfluenced by personal opinions and feelings when representing facts; (n.) a goal or thing sought

oblivion (78): (n.) the state of being forgotten or unaware of what is happening

obscure (83): (adj.) not discovered or known about; (v.) to make unclear

obsequious (49): (adj.) obedient to a servile degree

obsolete (88): (adj.) no longer produced or used; out of date

obstinate (144): (adj.) stubbornly persistent, unwilling to yield

obstreperous (120): (adj.) noisy and hard to control

obstruction (168): (n.) a thing that impedes or prevents passage or progress

obtrusive (144): (adj.) noticeable or prominent in an unwelcome manner

obtuse (190): (adj.) stupid or unintelligent

odious (168): (adj.) extremely unpleasant

officious (102): (adj.) intrusively eager in offering advice or assistance with something

ogle (191): (v.) to stare at in a manner showing sexual desire

ominous (93): (adj.) threatening; showing that something bad may happen

onerous (45): (adj.) taxing, requiring a great amount of effort

opulence (52): (n.) great wealth or luxuriousness

oracle (171): (n.) a person with great wisdom; someone believed to communicate with a deity

organic (153): (adj.) 1. relating to living things; 2. produced without the use of chemical agents; 3. constitutional, essential as parts of a whole

ornate (57): (adj.) elegant, fancily decorated

ostensible (54): (adj.) appearing to be true, but not necessarily so

ostentatious (62): (adj.) characterized by pretentious or vulgar display, designed to impress or get attention

ostracize (130): (v.) to exclude someone from a group

outdated (133): (adj.) obsolete; no longer in trend

outmoded (59): (adj.) old-fashioned, out of date

outspoken (146): (adj.) expressing one's opinion freely and frankly

overt (133): (adj.) done or shown openly; readily apparent

P

palliate (163): (v.) to make less severe or unpleasant without removing the cause

panacea (184): (n.) a remedy for all disease; a solution for all problems

panorama (141): (n.) a wide, continuous view; an overall picture or thorough survey of something

paradox (11): (n.) two seemingly opposite but true things

paragon (64): (n.) an outstanding example, epitome

parameters (187): (n.) guidelines that control what something is or how something should be done

paramount (3): (adj.) of the greatest importance, supreme

parch (157): (v.) to dry something completely through heat

parody (67): (n.) an imitation of someone, a genre, or a style in a humorous way; (v.) to imitate someone, a genre, or style humorously

partisan (41): (adj.) supporting one side, biased

patronize (69): (v.) to act kindly while displaying a sense of superiority

paucity (74): (n.) a lack or dearth of something

pedagogy (193): (n.) the art, science, or profession of teaching

pedantic (8): (adj.) showing unnecessary knowledge or excessive concern for details

pedestrian (13): (adj.) lacking zest and enthusiasm; dull; (n.) a person walking along a road

peevish (150): (adj.) bad-tempered, tending to complain

penchant (81): (n.) strong habitual liking for something or tendency to do something

penetrate (18): (v.) to push through a barrier or boundary into something

penitent (145): (adj.) repentant, regretful

pensive (112): (adj.) engaged in or involving deep, serious thought

perennial (177): (adj.) 1. existing or continuing in the same way for a long time; 2. (of people) appearing permanently engaged in a specified way of life; 3. (of plants) living for several years

perfunctory (23): (adj.) done with minimum effort or reflection

permeate (79): (v.) to spread throughout; pervade

pernicious (151): (adj.) causing great harm, malicious

perpetual (159): (adj.) occurring repeatedly; lasting forever

perpetuate (194): (v.) 1. to make something continue indefinitely; 2. to preserve something valued from oblivion or extinction

perplexed (40): (adj.) greatly puzzled, bewildered

perseverance (199): (n.) determination; endurance

persevere (135): (v.) to persist, to refuse to stop despite obstacles

persona (214): (n.) the aspect of one's character presented to or perceived by others

perspicacious (84): (adj.) having insight into the understanding of things

pertinent (89): (adj.) relevant; germane

perturbed (121): (adj.) troubled; perplexed

pervade (207): (v.) to spread through and be perceived in all parts of a place

petulant (94): (adj.) irascible or ill-tempered like a child

philanthropic (4): (adj.) caring for humanity

piecemeal (208): (adj.) characterized by unsystematic partial measures taken over a period of time

pilfer (9): (v.) to steal

pioneer (28): (n.) 1. a person who is among the first to settle a new area; 2. a person who is among the first to research or develop a new field; (v.) to be among the first to develop or apply (a new method, technology, or activity)

pithy (125): (adj.) concise and strongly expressive

pivotal (14): (adj.) extremely decisive or important in affecting something or its outcome

placate (142): (v.) to calm, soothe, appease

placebo (213): (n.) a harmless pill prescribed for psychological benefit rather than for physiological effect

placid (33): (adj.) (of a person or animal) not easily upset or excited; calm, even-tempered

plague (146): (n.) a thing or person that causes trouble and unhappiness; (v.) to cause distress

plastic (19): (adj.) 1. easily changeable; flexible; 2. fake; superficial; (n.) a synthetic material made from a range of polymers

platitude (24): (n.) an overused remark that has lost meaning

plausible (86): (adj.) seeming reasonable, probable, or believable

pliable (152): (adj.) flexible, easily bent or molded

plight (185): (n.) a dangerous, unfortunate, or difficult situation

plunge (158): (n.) a jump or dive into water; 2. a swift and drastic fall in value or amount; (v.) 1. to move downward or drop steeply; 2. to embark on something with vigor

pluralism (151): (n.) co-existence of groups of different backgrounds within one society

poignant (29): (adj.) evoking a sense of sadness or regret

polemical (118): (adj.) concerning something contentious, critical, or disputatious in writing or in speech

posthumous (134): (adj.) happening after a person's death

postulate (176): (n.) a thing assumed to be true as the basis for reasoning; (v.) to assume the truth or basis of something for the basis of reasoning or belief

potable (126): (adj.) something safe to drink; drinkable

potentate (103): (n.) a monarch or ruler (often autocratic)

pragmatic (1): (adj.) practical; realistic

preach (115): (v.) to lecture; to deliver a sermon

precarious (181): (adj.) unstable, unsure; uncertain; dubious

precede (165): (v.) to happen or come before (in time)

precipice (135): (n.) a very tall and steep cliff (literal or figurative)

precipitous (110): (adj.) done suddenly without careful reflection

precocious (34): (adj.) mature early in mental aptitude

precursor (99): (n.) a forerunner

predation (172): (n.) the act of preying on other animals; attacking or plundering

predecessor (113): (n.) forbear, ancestor

predicament (113): (n.) difficult situation, dilemma

predilection (163): (n.) a preference or special liking for something

predispose (39): (v.) to make someone susceptible or liable to a specific attitude, action, or condition

predominant (219): (adj.) present as the main or most salient element

preponderance (143): (n.) being greater in number, importance, or quantity

prescient (98): (adj.) having or showing knowledge of events before they take place

presentiment (146): (n.) a gut feeling about the future, likely one of a foreboding nature

prestigious (153): (adj.) having great reputation

presumptive (155): (adj.) taking something to be true or adopting a particular attitude toward something

pretension (72): (n.) using affectation to try to impress others; ostentatiousness

prevalent (208): (adj.) widespread in a particular area at a particular time

primitive (35): (adj.) archaic, ancient, original and often crude

pristine (44): (adj.) pure, in the original state

probe (112): (n.) 1. a small device used for collecting information, often surgically; 2. an unmanned exploratory spacecraft; 3. an investigation of a crime; (v.) to examine thoroughly; to question

proclivity (129): (n.) tendency; inclination

procrastinate (122): (v.) to delay or put off

prodigious (49): (adj.) remarkably large in size, quantity or extent

prodigy (38): (n.) a young person with exceptional talents, a child genius

profess (216): (v.) to claim openly (and often falsely) that one possesses a certain feeling or quality

profound (54): (adj.) deep; intellectual, thoughtful

progenitor (59): (n.) a person or thing from which a person, animal, or plant originates

prognosis (209): (n.) forecasted outcome of a situation or disease

progressive (150): (adj.) advancing gradually

prohibitive (43): (adj.) 1. referring to a price or charge that is excessively high; 2. concerning a restrictive law or rule; 3. describing a condition

proliferation (107): (n.) rapid increase in numbers of something

prolific (91): (adj.) producing much or many of something

prominent (77): (adj.) 1. important or famous; 2. sticking out or projecting from something

propensity (188): (n) a strong natural tendency to do something

prophecy (148): (n.) prediction of future event

prophetic (142): (adj.) accurately predictive of the future

propitious (150): (adj.) favorable; likely to result in success

proponent (204): (n.) a person who advocates a project, cause, or theory

prosaic (1): (adj.) dull and boring

prospectus (64): (n.) document meant to advertise or describe a book, enterprise, or school to clients or investors

prosperous (186): (adj.) flourishing; successful; thriving

protégé (30): (n.) a disciple who is generally gifted

provincial (155): (adj.) narrow-minded, unsophisticated

provocative (6): (adj.) stimulating strong reactions

proximity (61): (n.) closeness in place, time, occurrence, or relation

proxy (200): (n.) the authority to represent someone else, especially in voting

prudent (48): (adj.) acting with care and showing sound judgment

prune (123): (n.) a plum preserved by drying out; (v.) to trim; to remove the superfluous elements

pseudonym (218): (n.) a fictitious name, often used by authors

pugnacious (172): (adj.) eager or quick to argue or fight

punctilious (101): (adj.) showing great attention to detail

pundit (195): (n.) an expert who usually gives speeches in public

purify (187): (v.) to make unadulterated or clear; to free from guilt or dirt

Q

quaff (120): (v.) to drink heartily

qualify (69): (v.) 1. to be entitled to a benefit by fulfilling a condition; 2. to make something less absolute; to put reservations or limits on something

quandary (61): (n.) perplexity about what to do in a tough situation; a difficult situation or dilemma

quarantine (25): (v.) to isolate or seal off

quarrel (74): (n.) a fight or argument; (v.) to fight or argue

queer (202): (adj.) strange; odd

quell (79): (v.) to put an end to something, usually by use of force; to suppress

querulous (176): (adj.) complaining in an annoyed way

quiescent (84): (adj.) period of rest, inactivity, or dormancy

quizzical (89): (adj.) showing amused puzzlement

R

rancor (181): (n.) anger or dislike for someone

ratify (209): (v.) to sign or give formal consent to a contract, treaty, or agreement to make it formally valid

rebellious (94): (adj.) showing a desire to resist authority, control, or conventions

rebut (53): (v.) to argue against; to deny

recant (5): (v.) to say one no longer holds a belief, especially a heretical one

receptacle (130): (n.) container; a place for holding or storing

recessive (140): (adj.) genetic trait that is exhibited only when inherited from both parents

reciprocity (218): (n.) the process of exchanging with others for mutual benefit

recluse (175): (n.) one who lives a solitary existence and who often avoids people

reclusive (123): (adj.) unsociable; solitary

reconcile (82): (v.) 1. to restore relations between; 2. to make things mentally consistent with each other

recourse (194): (n.) an opportunity or choice to use or do something in order to deal with a problem or situation

recriminations (211): (n.) an accusation in response to one from someone else

rectitude (10): (n.) morally correct behavior or thought; righteousness

redolent (15): (adj.) strongly suggestive of something (usually referring to sense of smell)

redundant (87): (adj.) no longer needed or useful; superfluous

refined (145): (adj.) cultivated in manner, appearance, taste; free from impurities

refract (161): (v.) to make a ray of light change direction when it enters a medium at an angle

refute (20): (v.) to disprove or show something is false

regressive (25): (adj.) becoming less advanced; returning to a former state

reinforce (30): (v.) to strengthen or supplement something

reiterate (35): (v.) to restate or redo something in order to emphasize

relegate (208): (v.) to consign to an inferior mark or position

relinquish (92): (v.) to voluntarily give up something

relish (104): (n.) 1. great enjoyment; 2. a condiment eaten together with plain food to add flavor; (v.) to enjoy greatly

reluctant (20): (adj.) showing hesitation or unwillingness

reminiscence (2): (n.) the act of recalling past events

remiss (147): (adj.) negligent, careless in one's duty

remnant (109): (n.) small remaining quantity of something

remuneration (182): (n.) compensation; pay for a service

renew (173): (v.) to make new, fresh, or strong again

renown (105): (adj.) being known or discussed by many people

reparation (127): (n.) restitution; making amends; paying money to those who have been wronged

repeal (188): (v.) to revoke or annul (a vote or congressional act)

repent (100): (v.) to express regret for one's sin or wrongdoing

replica (205): (n.) an exact model of something

replicate (11): (adj.) of the nature of a copy or repetition of a scientific trial or experiment; (n.) a close or exact copy of something; (v.) to reproduce an exact copy of something

reprehensible (40): (adj.) deserving criticism, blameworthy

reprieve (210): (n.) a cancellation or postponement of punishment; (v.) to cancel or postpone the punishment of someone

reprimand (117): (v.) to scold; to blame

reproach (182): (n.) rebuke; disapproval; discredit

repudiate (58): (v.) to reject, to repeal

reserve (129): (v.) to hold for future use

resignation (169): (n.) 1. an act of retiring or giving up a position; 2. the acceptance of something undesirable but inevitable

resigned (10): (adj.) submissive; accepting one's unpleasant reality

resilient (16): (adj.) able to recover easily after difficulty or trauma

resolute (63): (adj.) firmly resolved or determined

respite (15): (n.) a brief pause or rest

resplendent (120): (adj.) attractive because of being very colorful or splendid

resurgence (45): (n.) revival, reappearance

resuscitate (50): (v.) to revive, to regain consciousness

retaliate (55): (v.) to make an attack or assault in return for a similar attack

reticent (21): (adj.) not readily revealing thoughts, sparing of words

retract (7): (v.) to draw in; to withdraw or go back on (an undertaking or promise)

retrograde (203): (adj.) directed or moving backwards; reversed

revelation (60): (n.) surprise discovery; disclosure

reverent (66): (adj.) appreciative, respectful

revitalize (68): (v.) to imbue with new life, to rejuvenate

revive (118): (v.) to start again; to revitalize

rhetoric (21): (n.) the art or use of persuasive writing to affect an audience

righteous (161): (adj.) morally right or justifiable

rigid (163): (adj.) unable to bend or be forced out of shape

rigorous (141): (adj.) painstaking and exact; demanding, harsh

robust (26): (adj.) strong and healthy; flourishing

romanticism (207): (n.) the state or quality of expressing feelings, inspiration, and subjectivity over reason

romanticize (73): (v.) to describe idealistically and/or unrealistically

rousing (149): (adj.) inciting enthusiasm, full of energy

rudimentary (121): (adj.) basic; elementary

S

sacrilege (179): (n.) a violation or misuse of what is regarded as holy or sacred

sagacious (101): (adj.) wise; showing keen judgment and discernment

salubrious (114): (adj.) healthy; promoting good health

salutary (176): (adj.) having a good or helpful result (especially after something unpleasant has happened)

salvage (65): (v.) to recover, to reclaim

sarcastic (124): (adj.) speech using irony in order to mock or to show contempt

sardonic (78): (adj.) cynical; grimly mocking

satire (120): (n.) 1. the use of humor, ridicule, exaggeration, or irony to expose people's stupidity or shortcomings; 2. a novel, film, or play that does such; 3. a literary genre that does such

savanna (187): (n.) a grassy plain with few trees usually found in tropical or subtropical areas

scintillating (142): (adj.) shining brightly; clever and brilliant

scorn (12): (n.) the feeling or belief that something or someone is worthless or despicable; (v.) 1. to feel contempt for; 2. to reject something in a contemptuous way

scrupulous (70): (adj.) extremely attentive to details

scrutinize (75): (v.) to inspect closely or thoroughly

seclusion (80): (n.) being private and away from other people

seduce (147): (v.) to lure someone into inadvisable courses of action or beliefs

sedulous (130): (adj.) assiduous; diligent

segregation (157): (n.) separation into groups

semantic (214): (adj.) related to meaning in logic or language

sensationalism (181): (n.) the use of shocking details to cause excitement

serendipity (17): (n.) happening randomly and with a positive effect

serene (22): (adj.) calm and peaceful; soothing

serpentine (205): (adj.) winding or twisting

sever (200): (v.) 1. to divide by cutting or slicing; 2. to terminate or break off a connection or relationship

shrewd (85): (adj.) having sharp powers of judgment

simulate (213): (v.) to imitate the character or appearance of

skeptical (31): (adj.) causing doubt

slipshod (153): (adj.) done in a careless manner

slovenly (142): (adj.) ill-groomed and untidy; careless, negligent

smug (83): (adj.) excess pride in oneself or one's successes

snob (106): (n.) one who thinks his/her tastes or position is superior to those of other people

solemn (88): (adj.) formal and dignified; serious

solicitous (90): (adj.) characterized by showing interest or concern; eager or anxious to do something

solitary (119): (adj.) alone

somber (96): (adj.) gloomy; dark or dull in color or tone

somnolent (189): (adj.) likely to induce sleep

soothe (111): (v.) to relieve or comfort

sophistry (95): (n.) the use of fallacious arguments, often with the intention of deceiving

soporific (5): (adj.) inducing sleep

sovereign (93): (n.) supreme ruler or monarch

sparing (199): (adj.) economical; frugal; meager

Spartan (218): (adj.) characterized by austerity or lack of comfort or luxury

spate (154): (n.) a large number or amount of something happening in quick succession

spontaneous (71): (adj.) performed by sudden impulse without external stimulus

sporadic (106): (adj.) occurring at irregular intervals

spur (128): (v.) to incite or stimulate

squander (3): (v.) to waste (money, time, etc.)

stagnant (10): (adj.) 1. (of water) not flowing or lacking a current; 2. showing no activity, sluggish

stark (170): (adj.) severe or bare in appearance; sharply clear

steadfast (27): (adj.) committed and unswerving

stereotype (131): (n.) commonly held idea or image about a specific group of people; (v.) treat with preconceived notion

stickler (201): (n.) a person who demands a certain quality or type of behavior

stimulate (163): (v.) to make (something) more active or excited

stimulus (207): (n.) 1. a signal or event that evokes a reaction by a tissue or organ; 2. a thing that rouses activity in someone or something; 3. an exciting or interesting quality

stipulate (15): (v.) to demand or specify something, usually as part of an agreement

stoic (134): (adj.) calm, seemingly emotionless

strenuous (20): (adj.) with excessive exertion, usually excessive physical exertion

strident (25): (adj.) loud and harsh; grating

stringent (152): (adj.) rigorous, strictly controlled

stunted (180): (adj.) someone or something whose growth, development, or progress is or has been hindered

stymie (137): (v.) to hinder the progress of

subdue (8): (v.) to hold back, control

subjective (13): (adj.) biased; non-objective; throwing one's emotions into things

sublime (103): (adj.) of excellence or beauty to inspire admiration or awe

subordination (196): (n.) the act of placing in a lower rank or position

substantiate (18): (v.) to verify something

subversive (143): (adj.) attempting to undermine an established system; (n.) a revolutionist, insurgent

succinct (30): (adj.) brief and to the point

succulent (155): (adj.) juicy and tasty

suffrage (148): (n.) the right to vote

sullen (35): (adj.) gloomy, moody, brooding

summon (138): (v.) 1. to authoritatively or urgently call on someone or something to be present; 2. to call people to attend a meeting; 3. to urgently demand help; 4. to bring to the surface a quality or reaction from within oneself

supercilious (100): (adj.) behaving as if one is superior to others

superficial (86): (adj.) existing or occurring only at the surface; appearing to be true until scrutinized; not having depth of character or understanding

superfluous (36): (adj.) excessive and unnecessary

supplant (32): (v.) to supersede and replace

suppress (23): (v.) to hide or cover up something

surly (216): (adj.) bad-tempered and unfriendly

surmise (108): (v.) to guess that something is true without having proper evidence to confirm it

surmount (160): (v.) to overcome; to get over something

surpass (150): (v.) go beyond expectation

surreptitious (40): (adj.) secretive, furtive, underhanded

swarthy (138): (adj.) dark-skinned

synergy (180): (n.) increased effectiveness resulting from combined action

synopsis (134): (n.) a brief summary or outline of a text

synthesize (28): (v.) to combine something into a coherent whole

T

tacit (169): (adj.) understood or implied without being stated

tactful (45): (adj.) mild expression to avoid being blunt when referring to something unpleasant

talisman (135): (n.) an object (usually a stone, ring, or necklace) thought to possess magical powers

tangent (133): (n.) a digression from the main topic

tangential (50): (adj.) digressive, having little relevance to the issue

taunt (55): (n.) a comment made to annoy, anger, or provoke someone; (v.) to provoke or challenge with insulting remarks; to tease

taxonomy (209): (n.) branch of science dealing with the classification of organisms; the classification of something; a scheme of classification

tedious (155): (adj.) boring and tiresome due to dull repetition

teem (115): (v.) to be full or swarming with something

temperate (147): (adj.) moderate; restrained in one's behavior

tenacious (76): (adj.) keeping a firm hold of something; not relinquishing a plan of action

tenet (163): (n.) a principle or belief

tension (111): (n.) mental or emotional strain

tentative (60): (adj.) uncertain, not definite

tenuous (33): (adj.) unsubstantiated, weak and shaky; slim, fine

terminate (116): (v.) to abolish; to cease

terse (170): (adj.) brief and direct in a way that may seem unfriendly

thesis (184): (n.) a statement that someone wants to discuss or prove

thwart (191): (v.) to frustrate or baffle; to oppose

timorous (65): (adj.) physically or mentally exhausted

torpid (138): (adj.) mentally or physically inactive; sluggish

tout (186): (v.) to persuade; to promote; to talk up

tractable (70): (adj.) easily managed or controlled

transgression (136): (n.) an act that violates a rule, law, or principle; an offense

transitory (159): (adj.) fleeting, not lasting

traverse (196): (v.) to cross; to cut across

trenchant (75): (adj.) vigorous or incisive in style; having a sharp edge

trepidation (197): (n.) feeling of fear that something may happen

trivial (80): (adj.) of little value and importance

truce (131): (n.) an agreement between opponents to end their conflicts and discuss peace terms

truncate (90): (v.) to shorten by cutting off the top or end

turpitude (157): (n.) depravity; wickedness

tyranny (5): (n.) unreasonable use of authority

U

ubiquitous (81): (adj.) found or appearing everywhere

unadorned (128): (adj.) plain and simple, undecorated

unanimous (135): (adj.) two or more people in complete agreement, held by everyone involved

unbounded (209): (adj.) limitless

uncouth (210): (adj.) lacking good manners, refinement, or grace

undermine (91): (v.) to weaken or erode the foundation of something (often an intellectual argument)

underscore (10): (v.) to emphasize or underline something

unequivocal (15): (adj.) leaving no doubt; unambiguous

unerring (189): (adj.) always right or accurate

unflappable (195): (adj.) imperturbable; to be able to remain calm in a difficult situations

unforeseen (102): (adj.) unanticipated; unpredicted

unhinge (155): (v.) 1. to make someone mentally unbalanced; 2. to deprive of stability or fixity; 3. to take a door off its hinges

uniform (86): (adj.) changing in form or character; (n.) a distinctive clothing worn by members of a particular organization or profession

unimpeachable (205): (adj.) unable to be doubted or questioned; entirely trustworthy

unkempt (185): (adj.) having an untidy or disheveled appearance

unorthodox (97): (adj.) unconventional, unusual

unprecedented (20): (adj.) never seen or done before

unremitting (179): (adj.) never stopping or lessening

unsolicited (206): (adj.) not requested; done voluntarily

unstinting (25): (adj.) given without restraint; unsparing

unswerving (30) (adj.) steadfast; completely committed

unwitting (212): (adj.) a person not aware of the full facts; not done purposefully

upheaval (216): (n.) a violent or sudden disruption to something

V

vaccine (152): (n.) substance used to provide immunity against certain diseases; protective software

vacuous (35): (adj.) empty, devoid of substance

vagary (197): (n.) whim; unusual idea

vanquish (100): (v.) to defeat thoroughly

vapid (40): (adj.) dull, lifeless, uninteresting

varied (210): (adj.) showing a number of different types of elements

vast (98): (adj.) immense; of a widespread extent or quality

vehement (45): (adj.) strong, intense, forceful

veiled (171): (adj.) covered or concealed

venerate (127): (v.) to revere; to idolize

veracity (50): (n.) 1. conforming to facts, honesty; 2. habitual truthfulness

verbalize (202): (v.) to express ideas or feelings in words, often by speaking out loud

verbatim (201): (adj. and adv.) in exactly the same words as used originally

verbose (38): (adj.) lengthy, using words excessively

versatile (55): (adj.) adjustable; flexible

veteran (214): (n.) 1. a person experienced in a particular field; 2. a person who has served in the military

vex (37): (v.) to bother, frustrate, irritate

viable (124): (adj.) applicable; feasible

vibrant (194): (adj.) showing great life, activity, and energy; very bright and strong

vicarious (123): (adj.) experienced in the imagination through the actions or feelings of another individual

vignette (218): (n.) a brief, evocative account or description

vigorous (101): (adj.) strong, healthy, energetic; robust

vile (120): (adj.) evil, wicked; extremely unpleasant

vindicate (42): (v.) to clear of guilt or accusation using justification and proof

vindictive (43): (adj.) having or showing a strong desire for revenge

virtuoso (181): (n.) one who excels in something especially art, or music

visionary (107): (adj.) 1. describing a person who can imagine the future with imagination and wisdom; 2. able to see visions in a dream or as a supernatural apparition; (n.) a person who has ideas about the future or how it may appear

vital (114): (adj.) essential or crucial for sustenance

vitality (198): (n.) vigorousness; exuberance

vivid (139): (adj.) suggesting a clear and lively image; evoking strong feeling; intense in color

vocation (212): (n.) a strong feeling of suitability for a career or occupation; a person's employment or job

volatile (60): (adj.) prone to change rapidly and unpredictably (often for the worse); prone to display rapid changes of emotion

voluminous (213): (adj.) large in volume; occupying much space

voluptuous (174): (adj.) suggesting sensual pleasure by fullness and beauty of form

voracious (48): (adj.) having excessive craving and greediness for food or other things

vulgar (165): (adj.) lacking sophistication or good taste

vulnerable (47): (adj.) susceptible to emotional or physical damage

W

waft (217): (v.) to pass or cause gently to pass through the air

wane (125): (v.) to diminish or lessen

wary (106): (adj.) cautious about possible dangers of things

wax (122): (v.) to become larger

weary (65): (adj.) fearful, timid

whimsical (53): (adj.) playful; comical

wince (139): (n.) a facial or bodily response to suggest pain, distress; (v.) to recoil, draw back due to pain or fear

winnow (121): (v.) to distinguish; to sift out; to separate out

wistful (52): (adj.) showing a feeling of regretful longing

Y

yen (152): (n.) a strong yearning for something; (v.) to yearn for something

Z

zealous (166): (adj.) extremely passionate about or devoted to sometimes in a negative way